S0-BFI-039

CHAMPIONSHIP VOLLEYBALL: by the experts

CHAMPIONSHIP VOLLEYBALL: by the experts

- An extensive overview of all aspects of volleyball.
- More than 20 internationally renowned experts contributed articles.
- Includes the 1982-84 USVBA rules.

2nd Edition

Edited by Bob Bertucci

LEISURE PRESS

A publication of Leisure Press.
P.O. Box 3, West Point, N.Y. 10996

ISBN 0-88011-076-7
Library of Congress Number 82-81451

Cover photos: Mitch Williamson
Cover design: Diana J. Goodin
Text photos:
Debbie Anderson, Stacy Griffman, Dennis McGorry, Dannette Parrish,
Mitch Williamson, Mark Wolpa, and Richard Zoller.

Contents

Preface

This second edition of *Championship Volleyball: by the experts* is designed to provide the reader with an insight to the various aspects of the game of volleyball. Many of the professionals whose efforts have helped make volleyball one of the world's most exciting sports have contributed articles. This volume also includes the 1982-1984 United States Volleyball Rules which will be in effect until after the 1984 Olympic games. I hope that in its own way *Championship Volleyball: by the experts* makes the game more enjoyable for every volleyball enthusiast.

My sincere appreciation is extended to the numerous individuals - each an *expert* in her/his own area - who contributed their time and efforts to make this volume a reality. Appreciation is also extended to the United States Volleyball Association for permission to reprint the Official 1982 - 1984 United States Volleyball Rules. The Japanese Volleyball Association and The Canadian Volleyball Association are also to be commended for the contributions of members of their Associations and for their general professional support of this project. I am especially grateful to Mr. John Griffith, former publisher of the *Athletic Journal*, for permission to reprint several articles from the *Athletic Journal* in this volume. A special thanks is extended to Mr. Ralph Hippolyte, Mrs. Tina Kogut Bertucci, and Dr. James A. Peterson for their contributions to *Championship Volleyball: by the experts*.

R.A.B.

RENEGA

PART A
THE GAME

P.S.U.
Chuck's
8
NATIONAL
10

1
The Game

THE HISTORY OF VOLLEYBALL
by
Dr. William T. Odeneal
SUNY—New Paltz

The game of volleyball was first developed by William G. Morgan. Morgan was born January 24, 1870 in Lockport, New York. As a youth, he worked with his father at the Morgan Boat Yards on the bank of the Old Erie Canal. He attended Mount Herman Preparatory School, but after one year transferred to the School for Christian Workers (now Springfield College) where he received a good background in recreational skills. Morgan's education coincided with a most significant period for American physical education. This period from 1890-1900 marked the beginning of the playground movement and the inclusion of many group games. Under the influence of Dr. Luther Gulick, who believed that games should serve many participants rather than a few, Morgan developed skills for his future work.

In the original words of Morgan, the following is the story of the beginning of the game now called volleyball.[1]

> *After leaving the Springfield school in 1894, I went to Auburn, Maine as physical director of the Young Men's Christian Association, and was there for one season, then went to Holyoke, Massachusetts, in 1895. In making up my business men's class for gym work, I found I had a lot of men who wouldn't play basketball so they needed a game they could play, as I believe it was recreation more than anything else they needed, and there seemed to be nothing to just meet their need. I therefore tried to develop a game. At first we used a basketball, knocking it back and forth by hand; then we put a net between the two groups and knocked the ball over that and formulated a few rules just to make it a game. The net was raised to seven feet but*

we found the basketball too heavy and made our wrists sore, so we had Spalding Company make us a ball made of soft calfskin which didn't last long. Our staid business men used to forget themselves and jump right into the sport and enjoy it, so it filled the bill.

After we had been using the game for awhile a physical director's conference was held at the Springfield school and they asked me to bring two teams and give an exhibition before them which I did in 1896. The conference seemed to enjoy the game and asked for the rules, which I gave them merely written out in long hand.

Howard Keith,[2] author of a text, *Sports and Games,* reported that volleyball is an American adaptation of an Italian game that originated in the middle ages. From Italy the sport was introduced in 1893 to Germany where it was known as faust ball, and Morgan grafted some well thought out rules and variations for his own onto the basic essentials of the German game.

Morgan defended the originality of his ideas, saying, "I might say right here and now that I at no time had no knowledge of any game similar to volleyball to aid me, so what ever was decided upon was gotten by experience on the floor. In 1895 I took charge of the YMCA physical department at Holyoke, Massachusetts and as the work progressed the business men's classes became quite large and enthusiastic and I found the need of some form of recreation and relaxation for them. Basketball seemed suited to the younger men but there was some need of something for the older ones not quite so rough and severe.

"In looking for a suitable game, tennis occurred to me, but that required racquets, balls, nets and other equipment, so that was discarded, but the idea of using the net seemed to hold; we raised the net to about 6 feet, 6 inches from the floor, just above the average man's head. We had to have a ball and among those we tried was the bladder of a basketball, but that proved too light and slow; then we tried a basketball, which was too large and heavy. Finally we decided to ask A.G. Spalding to make us a ball which they did."[3] [sic]

The game Morgan developed in the Holyoke gymnasium was called mintonette and it was a year later in 1896 that the name was changed to volleyball. The first volleyball game, according to Morgan, was played in the old gym at the School for Christian Workers (Springfield College). He brought two teams that consisted of five players each and demonstrated the game of mintonette.[4] Dr. George Fisher, the first President of the United States Volleyball Association, afterwards stated that the origin of the game called volleyball had its christening at that demonstration.[5] According to Morgan, Frank Wood, a physician, John Lynch, Holyoke fire chief, and J. Curran, Holyoke Mayor, helped formulate the rules and develop the game. These men, with seven others, demonstrated the game called mintonette in Springfield on July 7, 1896.[6]

During the game, Alfred T. Halstead, a faculty member of the School for Christian Workers, (presently Springfield College) remarked that it looked as if the men were volleying the ball back and forth over the net and perhaps the game should be called volleyball. The suggestion was accepted by Morgan and from that day the name was changed from mintonette to volleyball.[7] It is interesting to note the similarity of the game called Minton, brought to this country in 1895 by Mr. David McConnaughly Jr. and Mr. Morgan's game of Mintonette. According to an article in the Y.M.C.A. Athletic League Handbook of 1897 the following is a description of Minton.[8] The court shall be 40 feet by 80 feet with a net 6′ to 6½′ high dividing the court. The base made of worsted thread shall be 6½″ in diameter. Teams are composed of 4 players to a side. Four innings constitute a game. The servers serve the ball with a bat (which are far cheaper than tennis racquets of equal goods) over the net. If he fails it is a fault and gets the server out; and if he is the last on his team to serve, gets his side out. The serve as well as the return must be volleyed and not to be played twice in succession, only the server may score a point for his side.[8]

The published description of the rules entitled "The Original Game of Volleyball" from the Y.M.C.A. conference was described by J.D. Cameron. "Any number of players may play the game. The play consists of keeping a ball in motion over a high net, from one side to the other, thus partaking of the character of two games, tennis and handball. The opponents then, without allowing the ball to strike the floor, return it, and it is in this way kept going back and forth until one side fails to return it or it hits the floor. This counts a 'score' for one side or a 'servers out' for the other, depending upon the side in point. The game consists of nine innings, each side serving a certain number of times, as per rules, in each inning. Should any player touch the net, it puts the ball out of play and counts against his side. Should any player catch or hold the ball for an instant, the ball is out of play and counts for the opposite side. Should the ball strike any object other than the floor and bound back into the court, it is still in play. To dribble the ball, is to carry it all the time keeping it bouncing. When dribbling the ball no player shall cross the dribbling line, this putting the ball out of play and counting against him. Any player except the captain, addressing the umpire or casting any slurring remarks at him may be disqualified.[9]

In 1897, the printed rules of volleyball appeared in the first Handbook of the Athletic League of the Young Men's Christian Association of North America. The game was thus taken by physical directors of the YMCA to countries throughout the world.

In the early years, rules and equipment were simple. Many changes were made in the weight and air pressure of the ball, and rule interpretations varied from teacher to teacher. The size of the courts depended on available space and the number of players on each team varied. Players did not rotate and there were no restrictions on touching the net, reaching over it or running under it.

Volleyball was becoming popular throughout the world. Mr. Elwood S. Brown, in the 1922 issue of the *Official Volleyball Rules,* reported volleyball as played in foreign countries. The game was introduced to the Philippines by Elwood Brown in 1910; to China by J. Howard Crocker in the North and Mr. Ned Wilbur in the South in 1910; to Japan by Mr. Franklin Brown in 1913; to Siberia and the Polish Army by an unnamed YMCA Secretary and Mr. C. Scaife in 1915; to Uruguay by Mr. Jess T. Hopkins in 1916; to Brazil by H.J. Ginis in 1919; to Latvia-Estonia by Mr. Rudy Hansenin in 1919; to Syria by Mr. Russ Lewis in 1922 and to many other European countries by YMCA physical directors who were sent over at the end of World War I to assist in the rehabilitation of the Allied Armies.

Volleyball was presented at the first annual convention of the Playground of America (now the National Recreation Association) in June 1907 in Chicago. The playground association took the game out of doors while the YMCA kept the game indoors. During the first twenty years of its existence there was no organized promotion of the game and most periodicals gave little attention to its progress.

Late in 1896, Mr. W.E. Day introduced this new sport at Dayton, Ohio. That same year he worked out some new rules. A year later he and his assistants got together to revise the rules. These new rules, after a revision based upon experience with his physical education training classes, were adopted in 1900 by the Physical Directors Society of the YMCA's. Among the major changes were to standardize the net height to 7 feet, 6 inches, eliminate the dribbling rule and to formalize 21 points a game. In 1912, the Physical Directors Society defined the regulation of the ball, the court and rotation of players. In 1916, the YMCA and the National Collegiate Athletic Association adopted and collectively published the rules. The net was raised to eight feet, game point was reduced to 15 points and the winner of the best of three games determined the winner of the match.

In the early 1920's, Mr. A. Provost Idell and his teammates helped to develop a more modern set of rules and regulations. Major changes included the adoption of the court dimensions to thirty feet by sixty feet, standardization of the composition of the ball, playing the ball above the waist only, and allowing no more than three hits to a side before the ball crosses the net.

Many changes and modifications have been made in the rules throughout the years, but the basic game has remained the same. It was not until 1976 that the United States Volleyball Association adopted International rules.

As early as 1915, the educational profession took note of the value of volleyball as a team sport, and ranked it along with baseball, basketball and football as an excellent game for the school program. The greatest drawback to the popularity of the game was the constant changing of the rules and the inconsistency of teaching methods.

The game of volleyball was most popular at the end of World War I. George J. Fisher had the job of providing athletic activity for the American Forces. He had YMCA physical directors introduce volleyball to the troops by placing nets between the barracks. When the troops witnessed the game they willingly participated. No player limit or strict rules were enforced, and mass participation resulted. Hundreds of soldiers who clearly had never played team games of any sort, who were awkward and backward, and who avoided individual performances of any kind, played volleyball with enthusiasm. The total participation from July 1, 1918 to July 1, 1919, amounted to nearly a million (985,876), and the distribution of more than 15,000 volleyballs by the YMCA alone bears out this statement.[9] After the war, returning soldiers continued to play the game. In 1929, *The Playground Magazine* reported 821 leagues with over 7000 teams throughout the country. Schools learned the value of recreation and more school and recreation leaders agreed that volleyball was one of their most popular sports.

The first scholastic volleyball program was instituted by C. Lawrence Walsh and Harry Batchelor in the Pittsburgh,Pennsylvania area in 1924.S.C. Staley at the University of Illinois organized a faculty league, taught classes in volleyball and developed the first intramural volleyball program in 1922. The first reported collegiate volleyball team was organized in 1928 when plans were being discussed for a volleyball conference in Oregon. Under the leadership of Milton Orphan, the University of Washington formed a varsity volleyball team and presented varsity awards in 1934. This team played no collegiate opponents but was a member of the Northwest Volleyball Association. In 1941, the University of Pennsylvania formed a volleyball varsity team playing a schedule of 12 matches including Temple University and Columbia University.

In 1952, the NCAA agreed to sponsor volleyball and conduct national championships if eight teams would agree to varsity status. The writer conducted a national poll, receiving fifty replies indicating interest but only six teams would definitely field varsity teams.

In 1946, schools throughout the country began to organize club teams. Among the leaders were Springfield College, under the leadership of Marshall Walters; University of California at Los Angeles, under the leadership of Harry Wilson; Earlham College, under the leadership of Merle Rousey; also, George Williams College and Stanford University. In 1949 Florida State University, under the leadership of Dr. Howard G. Danford, placed volleyball as a varsity sport and was the first college in the nation to offer scholarships for the sport and hire a full time varsity coach—William T. Odeneal. A

Midwest intercollegiate volleyball conference with seven members was formed in 1961 due primarily to the efforts of Don Shondell and Dick Nelson. Schools included: Ball State, Detroit Institute of Technology, Earlham College, George Williams, Michigan State University, Ohio State University and Wittenberg College.

The 1961 season proved to be the biggest season in intercollegiate volleyball on the West coast. There was an increase in the number of college teams competing, in the number of intercollegiate tournaments, and the amount of support given by college administrations. The man behind the California college promotion was E.B. DeGroot. In 1964 California initiated its State High School Championships and it was DeGroot again behind the promotion.

In 1955 Florida initiated a regional high school championship but after three years it was dropped. Wisconsin began high school volleyball championships about 1957 and had as many as 225 schools participating in 1958. The granddaddy of them all was the Pennsylvania State High School championships, begun in 1938, which annually held regional playoffs prior to the final state championship.

The Eastern Collegiate Volleyball League began its tournament in 1967 with West Point, SUNY New Paltz, Penn State, Cornell, Amherst, Springfield College and Westchester Community College, competing at West Point.

In 1968 the NCAA conducted a survey to find out the interest in collegiate volleyball. It showed 40 schools interested or fielding a team while thirteen schools were willing to host the National Championships. Finally in 1970 the NCAA chose a tournament committee of Norman Kunde, William T. Odeneal, Allen Scates, Don Shondell and Walter Versen to develop its first championship. UCLA won the title followed by UC at the Long Beach, UC at Santa Barbara and Ball State.

National Association of Intercollegiate Athletic schools began their championships in 1967 with Church College of Hawaii winning. Women's National Championships are promoted by the American Alliance for Health, Physical Education and Recreation.

In 1974, the National Federation of High School Athletics formed a National Volleyball Committee to promote on a national scale all state high school championships and to write their own rule book.

As stated before, the greatest influence upon the growth and improvement of the game of volleyball during the first two decades was exerted by the YMCA. This organization was responsible for its inception and promotion, not only in the United States but throughout the world. It was not until 1922 that the first National YMCA championship was played. Twenty-seven teams entered the tournament, sponsored by the Brooklyn, New York YMCA. The Pittsburgh YMCA emerged the winner.

In 1925, the Amateur Athletic Union assumed jurisdiction over the game of volleyball. In 1928 the United States Volleyball Association hereafter referred to as the USVBA was formed primarily to administer and coordinate volleyball rules on a national scale, and to create a National Open Tournament. The AAU could only interest a few teams to enter their tournaments, so in 1937 there were negotiations between the AAU and the USVBA for controlling the game. The AAU relinquished their claim and the USVBA has controlled the game nationally and internationally to this day.

The first President of the USVBA was Dr. George J. Fisher; secretary treasurer was John Brown, Jr. Up to this time (1922) the Joint Volleyball Rules Committee of the YMCA had jurisdiction over the rules and conduct of the game. Dr. Fisher asked interested organizations to affiliate with the USVBA and to serve on its Board of Directors. He was very successful and through the years the following organizations affiliated with the USVBA: U.S. Army, U.S. Navy, U.S. Air Force, U.S. Marines, Boy Scouts of America, Industrial Organizations, Playground Association of America, YMCA, National Amateur Athletic Federation (later AAU), National Collegiate Athletic Association, Alliance for the American Association for Health, Physical Education and Recreation, American Turners, National Federation of State High School Athletic Associations, American Latvian Association, National Catholic Youth Organization, Church of Jesus Christ of Latter Day Saints, National Jewish Welfare Board, and Boys Clubs of America.

The USVBA was a charter member of the International Volleyball Federation formed in 1947. They sponsored a good will team throughout Europe in 1948; in 1949 they sponsored the first National Women's Open Championships; from 1952 to 1964 conducted the National Armed Forces Championships; initiated the National Collegiate Championships in 1949 and monitored this program until 1969; sponsored a United States team to the first World Championships in 1953, sponsored a United States team to the first Pan-American Games in 1955, and sponsored a United States team to the World Olympic Games in 1964. To date the USVBA has continued to send a national representative to these competitions.

The USVBA has been a source of leadership in volleyball. It has provided an annually published rule book, a source of volunteer teachers, coaches, and officials, and a limited number of instructional films and material. Through its persistent leadership, it was instrumental in having volleyball included as an official Olympic sport. It has withstood the test of time as the leader of an amateur sport. Players must be registered as amateurs in order to play in its sanctioned tournaments. Officers and members of the Association were, until the nomination of a paid Executive Secretary in 1975, all volunteers and received no remuneration for their services. Officials who officiate at local, regional, or national tournaments receive only minor expenses for their services. Sponsoring organizations volunteer their services, equipment and facilities for the promotion of the game. Teachers of physical education and people in the field of business donate their services to the cause of fair play and good sportsmanship.

During the early years of the USVBA lack of adequate funds and dependence on unpaid volunteer leadership were two of the major features handicapping its work. Some of the most prominent features of the organization after World War II have been that volleyball was given a place in the Helms Foundation Hall of Fame; leaders of volleyball are recognized and given certificates for their services; the USVBA broke down the civil rights barrier by being one of the first organizations to go on record to state its position; an operating manual was prepared which clarifies regional responsibility of authority.

Volleyball has gained popularity both in spectator appeal and in a participant role. In 1956 the Athletic Institute reported volleyball leading other sports in number of people participating, with 60 million playing annually on an organized basis. Miss Hirr Ching Lu reported in a Doctoral study at Columbia University that more than 25 countries throughout the world ranked volleyball as their number 1 sport.

In 1956 the World Volleyball Championships in Paris drew teams from twenty-seven countries and filled the Palais des Sports on several occasions with crowds of twenty-five thousand people watching championship volleyball.

With the International Volleyball Federation holding membership of 106 countries, it is evident that the game of volleyball is here to stay—and becoming more popular every day.

In 1973 Michael O'Hara developed the first professional volleyball competition with teams from the Western United States competing. In 1977 Wilt Chamberlain, a famous professional basketball player, was elected president of an organization called the International Professional Volleyball League.

It is difficult to relate the history of a sport without listing the outstanding personalities associated with its development, especially in the United States.

Harry A. Batchelor was an outstanding coach and player who coached his team to the first five national YMCA championships and was one of the nation's active supporters of scholastic volleyball.

Robert C. Cubbon conducted the first national championship and was the first recorded volleyball public relations director.

Dr. George J. Fisher was known as the "Father of Volleyball" because he actively promoted volleyball in his capacity as leader of various organizations such as the YMCA, the Boy Scouts of America and the USVBA. He served as the first President of the USVBA.

A. Provost Idell was known as the father of competitive volleyball. He wrote many technical articles on the game and was an active member of the rules commit-

tee of the USVBA.

C.C. Robbins was an active leader and supporter of volleyball in the Chicago area for over 35 years and stimulated interest in the game for many people.

John Brown, Jr. was the first chairman of the Joint Volleyball Committee and was the first secretary-treasurer of the USVBA.

Dr. Howard G. Danford was one of the country's most ardent scholastic and collegiate supporters of the game and was responsible for initiating state tournaments in Ohio, Wisconsin, Florida and Colorado.

Robert E. Laveaga was a great teacher and ardent supporter of competitive volleyball and wrote the first text book for men in the United States.

Harold T. Friermood succeeded Brown as secretary-treasurer and succeeded Fisher as President of the USVBA. He was the guiding personality of YMCA physical education in the United States and was a key to the inclusion of volleyball in the Olympic Games. He was an impressive administrator and avid writer publishing in more than 25 national and international magazines.

Marshall L. Walters was associated with the game for more than 40 years promoting collegiate and YMCA volleyball and served the USVBA in many capacities. He is best known for his work as editor of the Official Rule Book and Guide and his promotion of the game.

Harry E. Wilson is best known for his international promotion of the game, as editor of the International Volleyball Review, *as coach of more than 15 national championship teams and the first United States Olympic Team.*

Edward B. DeGroot, Jr., known as "Colonel Volleyball," promoted volleyball in the Armed Forces throughout the world, coached and promoted collegiate volleyball and open play. A man of talent and boundless energy, Colonel DeGroot was a major force in the organization of the USVBA.

BIBLIOGRAPHY

[1]George O. Draper, "William G. Morgan—Inventor of Volleyball," *Official Volleyball Rules,* (N.Y. American Sports Publishing Company, 1970), p. 41.

[2]Harold Keith, *Sports and Games,* (N.Y. Thomas Y. Crowell Company, 1942), p. 258.

[3]William G. Morgan, "How Volleyball was Invented," *Official Volleyball Rules,* 1916-17, (N.Y. American Sports Publishing Company), p. 9.

[4]G. Draper, "Mimeo to Miss G. Carr," History of Volleyball Folder, Vault Springfield College Library, March 2, 1938, p. 1.

[5]George J. Fisher, "President's Address," *Official Rule Book,* (N.Y. A.S. Barnes and Company, 1944), p. 13.

[6]George O. Draper, "William G. Morgan—Inventor of Volleyball," *Official Volleyball Rules,* (N.Y. American Sports Publishing Company, 1940), p. 41.

[7]George J. Fisher, "Fifty Years of Volleyball," *Official Volleyball Rules,* (N.Y. American Sports Publishing Company, 1947), p. 16.

[8]Minton, YMCA Athletic League Handbook, 1897 American Sports Publishing Co., New York, p. 168.

[9]J.G. Cameron, "The Original Game of Volleyball," *Physical Education,* 5:50:51, July, 1896

[10]Elwood S. Brown, "Volleyball Around the World," *Official Volleyball Rules,* 1922, (N.Y. American Publishing Company,) p. 31.

[11]Foster Dulles, "Americans Learn to Play," (N.Y. D. Appleton-Century Company 1940), p. 348.

PART B

SKILLS, DRILLS, AND TECHNIQUES

2
Passing

OVERHAND PASS

by

Ralph Hippolyte
University of
Pennsylvania

and

Bob Bertucci
University of
Tennessee

1. Basic Technique

   a) Body Position
      - staggered stance, heel-toe relationship with feet slightly wider than shoulder width apart
      - knees slightly flexed
      - upper body forward
      - triceps parallel with floor
      - hands kept high in front of forehead

   b) Hand Position
      - palms begin facing each other, with fingers spread wide
      - as wrists are cocked back, thumbs and forefingers move closer together until they are 2″ and 4″ apart, respectively
      - all fingers should touch ball
      - lateral support and balance from ring and pinky fingers
      - progressively more contact from the middle fingers, forefingers and thumbs
      - forefinger and thumb supply power

Passing

Basic forward pass

Basic Stance

Hand & Finger Position

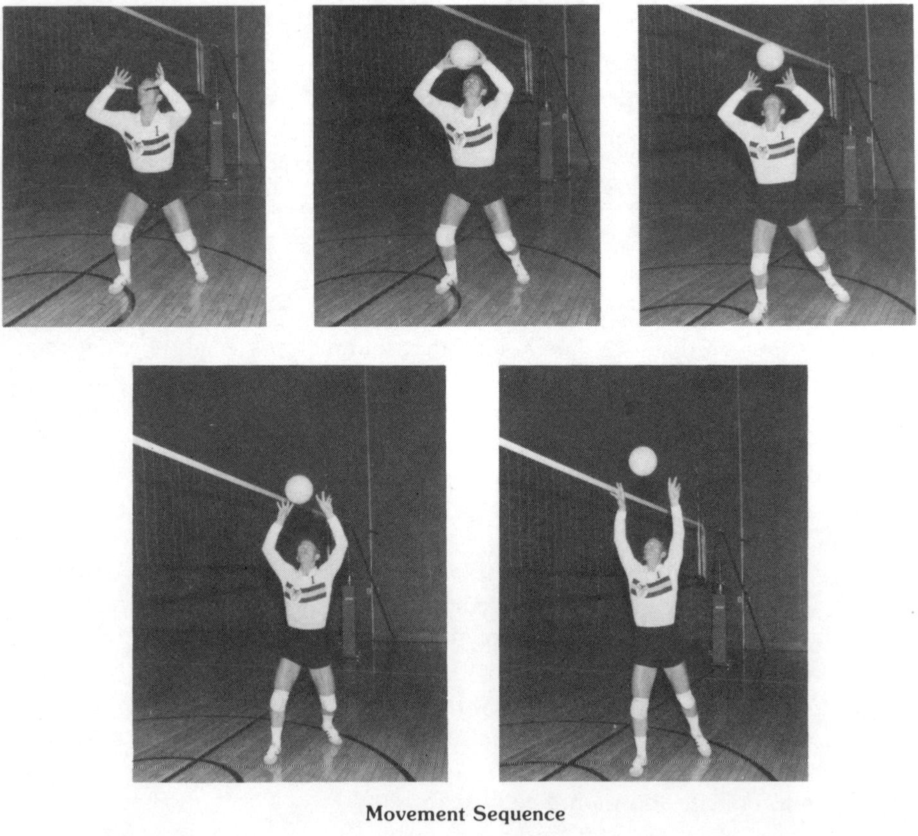

Movement Sequence

- forefinger is main directional finger
- ball is viewed through forefingers and thumbs

c) Movement
- move under the ball
- assume ready position prior to contacting ball
- from crouched position, accelerate into ball and make contact above forehead
- synchronized progressive acceleration of all joints
- transfer of weight during acceleration should be into the ball towards the target
- force of ball and structure of joints will automatically result in desired absorption
- feet, knees and hips face target
- balls above waist level should be considered for overhand pass

d) Footwork
- shuffle
- crossover and pivot
- turn, run and pivot

2. Low Ball Overhand Pass

a) Forward pass with rear ½ roll

Movement Sequence

- The player assumes a low basic position
- Hands in front of face
- Body behind and under ball
- Prior to the hands contacting the ball the knees flex, drawing the buttocks to the heels
- Rear position of the center of weight will cause a loss of balance in that direction

- The ball must be contacted prior to the buttocks touching the floor, with a quick forward thrust of the arms
- Due to the lack of leg action, the pass is exclusively controlled by the upper body
- At completion of the follow through, the buttocks make contact with the floor as the rounded back causes rocking action to further absorb the shock

b) Stride and Pivot

Movement Sequence

- The player assumes a low basic position
- A lateral stride in the direction of the ball with the striding leg flexed and the trailing leg extended
- The stride should position the body behind and under the ball
- The striding leg is flexed so the buttocks touch the heel
- Pivoting motion should turn the body toward the target
- The player plays the ball with a rapid extension of the arms, hands starting in front of the face
- Work of the arms and wrist is crucial due to the lack of leg action
- Termination of the skill can be accomplished by sitting on the buttocks, and continuing into a ½ or full shoulder roll

3. Back Set

Movement Sequence

- The basic stance and hand/finger position are the same as in the forward pass
- The main difference is in the actual execution of the set. The upper body extends slightly backward with the arms following the line
- Undue or premature arching of the back will telegraph the direction of the set to your opponents

4. Jump Set

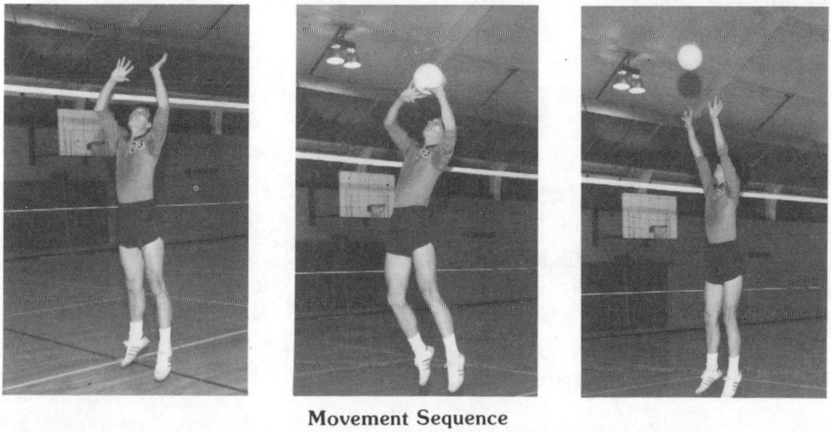

Movement Sequence

- Anticipate trajectory of the ball
- Jump as if you were spiking, but draw both hands into setting position
- Time the ball and contact it at the top of your jump
- Since you are in the air, the direction of the set should be determined by the position of your upper body, and arm and wrist action
  NOTE: The backward jump set can be executed by moving under the ball quickly and utilizing the back set technique.

5. One-handed Jump Set

Movement Sequence

- This set is an emergency technique used to save balls going over the net
- Anticipate the trajectory of the ball
- Jump as if you were spiking but reach with the hand closest to the net
- Draw your thumb and little finger closer to force the use of the finger tips
- Contact should be short and quick

A SETTER'S CHECK LIST

by

Don Shondell
Ball State University

The setters are the brains behind the offense. They must:

- ☐ be courageous in their setting but constantly have their finger on the pulse of the game.
- ☐ know the temperament of each player they set as well as his set preferences.
- ☐ keep the spikers loose by setting each of them early in the game and while doing so gain a feeling as to whom they should set later on when the chips are down.
- ☐ have an awareness of who is hitting well at any given time. Volleyball can be a game of streaks and the setter must be aware of who is hot and who is cold at any time in the match.
- ☐ be cognizant of the opponent's blocking alignment and utilize it accordingly. A short outside blocker might necessitate a high tight set to the outside spiker enabling him to hit over the blocker.
- ☐ be conscious of their own strengths and weaknesses so that in critical times in the match, they do not attempt a set that they cannot execute accurately.
- ☐ be aware of the opponents' defense.
- ☐ know how the opponents are defensing the cross. This will tell them which player will probably be open when the play is run.
- ☐ encourage their teammates to do their best, and eliminate any negative feedback.
- ☐ be willing to admit fault if a ball is blocked even though it may be the spiker's error.
- ☐ *Guard against overlap.* Move out quickly on serve reception.
- ☐ Be right up behind the receiver when the server contacts the ball.
- ☐ Move to the ball quickly so there is no question to whether they can get there. If they cannot, they should call someone else to set and prepare to cover the spiker.
- ☐ Turn slightly away from set on blind side plays so they can observe whether spiker is coming. If the blind side man does not say anything, and they cannot see him, a rule of thumb is *not* to set him. Any busted play of this nature is *their fault*.
- ☐ Be certain hand signals are seen.
- ☐ Inform a new setter coming in of the free ball play.
- ☐ Run the middle and vary your attack
- ☐ Not tip off their quick sets and try to set all their sets with the same technique.

- ☐ Remember that when the opponents are on attack, *they have a defensive responsibility first* and a setting responsibility second. If the ball is hit away from you, release to set the next ball. If you play the spike, *remind a teammate to set it*.
- ☐ Work in practice on playing the offensive and defensive positions to which you will be switching.
- ☐ On free ball plays, release as soon as they can determine the situation. Call "free" and let everyone know they are up.
- ☐ Any time they move to the front court, let the middle hitter know they are there by saying "I'm up," or "I'll set".
- ☐ Be certain their feet are set and they have perfect body balance.
- ☐ As soon as they set, move to their position and cover.
- ☐ Talk on transition plays so that no confusion results as to who is to set. The multiple offensive is dependent on setters that can make the transition from back court to front court without hesitation.

THE QUARTERBACK OF MODERN VOLLEYBALL

by

Bob Bertucci

University of Tennessee

When William G. Morgan created the game of volleyball in 1895, he envisioned a recreational activity for people of all ages. To this day, the majority of people view volleyball as a relatively noncomplex, easy-going game that anyone can play. Serious fans of modern volleyball, however, like to emphasize that volleyball has evolved into a game of power. The volleyball spiker on today's team, they quickly point out, must be as strong and agile as any hard-hitting athlete in other popular sports.

While such a conclusion is obviously valid, successful modern volleyball involves more than *power*. Volleyball is also a game of *precision*. Precision is the factor that distinguishes one powerful team from another. Thus, victory depends as much (if not more) on the play of the setters, in addition to the spikers.

The analogy may be drawn that the role of the setter is as critical to volleyball as that of the quarterback to football. Like a quarterback, the setter must possess high levels of both physical fitness and mental alertness. Throughout a match, the setter continually encounters the unexpected. Frequently, with time for no more than a brief glance at the defense, he must cope with a new and surprising turn of the game. Most of the time, he cannot afford to think through a situation; he must act instinctively. He has to handle every passed ball no matter how far he must move to reach it, how fast the ball may be traveling, how much spin the ball may have—and then turn it into an acceptable set from a tactical as well as a technical point of view. The set must have the precise trajectory, speed, height and distance from the net that the spiker expects. At the same time, the setter should be able to select the spiker best able to take advantage of any weaknesses in the opponents' defense. Moreover, he should also be able to camouflage the set, in an attempt to throw the blockers off, so that the spiker gets a clearer shot.

The setter must also sense the rhythm of the game, moving with it when it is in his favor, breaking it when it is not. If his team is sluggish, he speeds up play. If his opponents are rallying, he finds a way to slow down the game.

Only an athlete whose expertise is flawless and whose mind is composed can perform all these tasks successfully. The mechanics of setting must, therefore, have become second nature to him. Only then will the spiker be able to take advantage of the split-second opportunities that occur in modern volleyball.

In view of the setter's importance, the coach must make every effort to identify the best qualified individual to train as a setter. He considers potential for improvement as well as demonstrated ability. Among the qualities the coach should seek in a setter are quickness, coordination, agility, rapid reactions, emotional stability and mental toughness.

Having completed the first step—identifying the right athlete to train as a setter—the coach must develop an inclusive plan to ensure that the setter possesses the technical skills for his position *and* a level of physical fitness enabling him to fulfill his responsibilities. A comprehensive listing of all factors basic to an effective conditioning program for a setter is impossible here, but the program should give adequate attention to the development of cardiovascular fitness, muscular development and motor abilities. Interval sprint training promotes cardiovascular fitness; a regular program (three times per week) of high intensity weight lifting promotes muscular development. Motor abilities (e.g., agility, coordination, response time) can be improved through the use of drills involving particular motor functions.

Such drills should become an integral part of regular practice sessions. During the course of a match, a setter may run close to four miles, jump 300 times and squat a few hundred times. Physical conditioning can, thus, make the difference between winning and losing.

The best way for the prospective setter to master technique is to employ a series of fundamental exercises that lead up to actual setting drills. The coach must guide the setter carefully through even the most basic drills. It is here that good or bad habits are formed. For the benefit of the reader, the progression of drills is broken down into three stages with an explanation for each exercise.

Passing

INDIVIDUAL EXERCISES: (involves fundamental techniques)

Position	Movement	Considerations
1. Sitting	REPETITIVE PASS: continually pass the ball overhead	Check hand and finger contact; ensure proper acceleration
2. Kneeling	WALL VOLLEYBALL: pass to a spot on the wall	Correct elbow position; ball set from in front of the passer's face
3. Squatting	SQUAT AND PASS: consecutive overhand passes directly overhead, squatting between passes	Coordination of leg and arm motion (timing); footwork: passer must be directly under each ball
4. Standing	BOUNCE WALL VOLLEY: overhand pass to the spot on the wall, rebound to floor then set off bounce	Movement into position under ball; transfer of weight up and to the target
5. Standing	OVERHEAD PASS-TURN: overhand pass, then turn 90°, 180°, 360° before passing again	Adds to a player's sense of direction; footwork

PARTNER DRILLS: (develops secondary passing techniques)

Position	Movement	Considerations
1. Standing, partners facing at width of court	From basic starting position, consecutively pass to partner	Vary the distance between partners; vary height of pass
2. Standing, partners facing at length of court	Run forward to attack line, pass, back-pedal under net to other attack line, run forward; repeat	Keep eyes on the ball at all times, assume good starting position before passing; do not time the flight of the ball; beat the ball to the spot
3. One partner standing at center front, the other partner in back-court	The person in the back-court moves laterally, passing the ball to center front	Surround the ball; moving to the right, plant and spin on left foot; moving to the left, plant and spin on right foot; foot, knee and shoulder should face target
4. One partner standing at attack line, facing partner on base line	Both players move sideways in opposition; one partner sets straight, the other sets diagonally	Position yourself behind the ball; set from in front of your face
5. Standing, one partner facing the other	One partner will pass and move to another spot, the other partner must locate his partner and pass to him	Pick up both the ball and your target in your sights; face your target before passing

SETTING DRILLS: (focuses on setter training)

Position	Movement	Considerations
1. Standing position, next to net	Assume and execute overhand passing technique 10-, 20-, 30-feet apart	Vary the positioning distance of one partner, fix the other partner at spiking target area; vary height and speed of set to target area; jump-sets

2. Setter penetrates right to target area; two players positioned at spiker's target area; coach tosses ball from center court	Setter penetrates, squares off and executes a front-set or back-set	Setter must plant square to target; foot closest to net is staggered forward; vary height and speed of set. Jump-set coach vary toss (toss right, left away from net, chase etc.)
3. Setting line at left-back position, coach tosses from right-back position	Setter must move into position under the ball and set to right front	Reverse coach and setting line; run drill from right front and left front; run drill with coach in right and left front. Coach should vary height and speed of toss
4. Setter penetrates into right-front target area	Square off, back-set	Extend arms overhead with slightly backward motion (there should only be a slight arch of the back); keep eyes on the ball; jump back-set. Another variation: execute the side-set
5. Positioned at attack line	Move beneath a blocked, dinked or wristed ball and set	Body must be beneath the ball; make sure setter is passing the ball from in front of his face

Execution of these exercises and drills exposes the prospective setter to gamelike situations. Coaches and players should remember, however, that these drills are only a few examples. Other effective exercises await your imagination.

The technical development of a setter, however, must include more than merely setting the ball. A good setter learns the subtleties that are so critical, and there are few shortcuts to acquiring them. Of course, experience is the best teacher, but many elements can be worked on in practice.

One of the most important additional skills is the development of peripheral vision. A good setter will be able to see the movement of blockers even as he keeps his eye on the ball. He makes his set selection depending on the block formation. He can develop this ability through careful practice.

The setter must also work on disguising his set so that blockers can't "read" the direction of the intended set. The setter must approach all sets the same way and not commit himself until the last second. In practice, the coach can throw balls up to the setter and call out, at the last moment, either a back-, front-, or play-set. The setter can later add faking, prior to the set, to further confound the block. Remember that all these advanced techniques require proper execution of setting fundamentals.

The setter should be the coach's primary representative during an actual game, for it is the setter who touches the ball every play and determines where each set goes. The coach must share his insights with the setter—which spiker to set in tight spots, what play-sets are working best, who the weaker blockers are on the opposition, how to react to changes in offense or defense. Both before the game and then throughout the match the coach must communicate closely with his setter.

A smoothly run offense is a thing of beauty, and it is the setter who must conduct it. Every beautiful spike is the result of a beautiful set. Remember, the setter is the key.

THE UNDERHAND PASS

by

Ralph Hippolyte and **Bob Bertucci**

University of Pennsylvania

University of Tennessee

Basic Stance

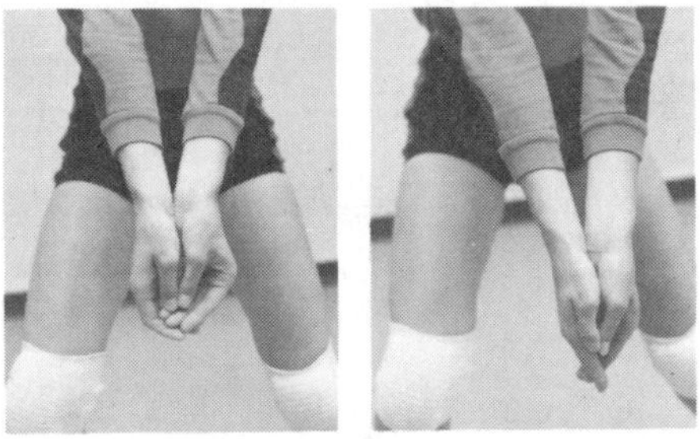

Hand & Arm Position

Basic Forward Pass

Movement Sequence

a) Body Position
- staggered stance, heel-toe relationship
- feet spread shoulder width apart

- knees flexed approximately 110°
- back fairly erect
- arms outstretched with elbows locked and rotated toward each other
- place back of one hand into palm of the other and fold thumbs down evenly
- wrists cocked down
- arms parallel to thighs
- balanced position, with weight on balls of feet

b) Contact
- contact ball in front of body and between knees
- ball contacts 2-6″ above the wrists on fleshy part of forearm
- maintain eye contact with ball throughout execution of pass
- step to target and extend arms for a slow ball
- slightly retract or relax arms for a fast ball

c) Movement
- sight ball in midline of body
- step into ball with arms extended
- step with foot closest to target
- step toward target making sure knees, hips, shoulders are in direction you want ball to go

2. Lateral Underhand Pass

a) stride and pass

Movement Sequence

- The player strides laterally towards the ball
- The striding leg is flexed with the trailing leg straight
- Attempt to line-up the ball inside of your striding leg
- Follow through towards target

  NOTE: Arm movement is directly related to the speed of the ball.

b) Side Pass

Movement Sequence

- Whenever you cannot get your body in front of the ball, execute the side pass
- Rotate your upper body towards incoming ball
- Lower inside shoulder to create a platform behind the incoming ball, following the direction of your target
- Follow through towards the target

IMPORTANT POINTS ABOUT SERVICE RECEPTION

by
Yoshiaki Kazio
Japanese National Coaching Staff

Service Reception

A. What is it?

1. The service reception is the defensive skill of receiving a serve from the opposition.
2. The service reception should be placed in a position from which the setter can set or spike.

B. Reminders

1. A misplayed service reception enables the opposition to score a point.
2. Make contact with the ball close to your body, with your waist low to the floor. Make sure that your body is in line with the ball and the setter, especially for a floater service which will change its course of flight as it passes over the net.
3. It is important to bump (pass) the ball into a position where the setter has the maximum number of options.
4. Adopt a position on the court relative to your teammates and assume the responsibility of receiving all balls served into that area. For example, back court players should receive those balls that are served above a front court player's shoulders or chest.
5. This skill decides whether or not you win. Namely it is one of the techniques to be stressed in practice.

C. Points

1. Lower your wrist, step in the direction to which you intend to return the ball to the setter.
2. A served ball will travel at a speed less than a hard driven spike but will often change its course as it comes to you, thus keep watching the ball through its flight with full attention. Make contact with the ball close to your waist.
3. During these motions be physically and mentally relaxed.
   a) Move quickly under the ball
   b) Carefully watch the ball
   c) Bend your knees
   d) lower your waist and make contact with the ball about 2 to 5 inches above your wrists.

4. Back row players should receive approximately 70% of all balls.
5. Back row players cover front row receivers.
6. Front row players shouldn't receive balls above waist level.
7. Open up to the player receiving the ball.

3
Attack

THE SERVE — AN ATTACK WEAPON
by
Scott Mose'

One of the most off-quoted cliches through the years is: "Hard serves—roundhouse or tennis variety (sometimes called hotdogs)—are okay against poor teams, but a good team will bring it up everytime—especially West Coast teams in the Nationals."

The fact that stands out most vividly is that the most effective point-makers on East Coast teams playing in the Nationals through the years were roundhouse or tennis type serves. Heinz Schall, Andrea Volkoff of West Side, Stanley Zmiudens, when he played for Des Moines and Newark, and, of course, the late Gabriel Budishin . . . These players scored strings of points against "good" teams in National play. Not only did they score clean aces, but they would force opponents into easily determined setting situations and thereby enable their own block to form effectively. The success of these players in National play was due in part to the fact that many teams play an entire season and never even see a "hotdog". And it takes a bit of adjusting to receive it properly.

Flo Hyman of So. Bay Spoilers, Winners Women's Open National U.S.V.B.A. Championship 1933, again demonstrated this when she employed a hard overhand spin serve against the Adidas Team and scored many points.

Flo is also a member of our National Team, and in a match against the C.V.B.A.W. National Team, experienced the same result.

I can't help but speculate about the outcome, of an entire team mastering both a drive and floater serves and using them like a baseball pitcher uses his repertoire in setting up the opposing batter.

This is not intended to mean that float servers fail to get their share of tournament points. It is only that in the past 2 decades I can count on one hand the number of float servers who could break up a game with just their serve. Taking into consideration that many hundreds of players exclusively use the float serve, this is a small percentage indeed.

On the other hand, there have been relatively few practitioners of the roundhouse or hard tennis serve, and yet in compiling a list of 10 outstanding servers, I would have to list five of them users of roundhouse or tennis serve. In the brief space available, I'll attempt to touch on a few of the approaches to the serve.

Most films of International and Olympic play indicate that players boast a variety of serves they can call upon: Floaters, tennis, roundhouse, and even a peculiar float serve that appears to originate from a roundhouse motion that the Japanese teams use. International players, employing different types of serves for different situations, seem to have mastered at least two individual serves. They serve to various court positions, not just to gain an ace, but as the first step in their defensive play.

The serving philosophy seems to be to attack—to gain an advantage for your team's block by having the opponents bump to an area from which the setter has only one choice, or better still, have the set originate from the backcourt so your team can anticipate and set up a solid block.

Most volleyballers appear to "play it safe" by eliminating serves down the line, or very short, or very deep, not to mention power serves. Result: The target receiving area is eight feet in from either side line, ten feet in from the backline and ten feet from the net. The typical serve is a high arching float or a dead ball. The principle is to play it safe and allow the block and defense to score.

What is the merit of just putting a ball into play consistently, and having your opponents make a routine bump-set spike play, as against a hard serve that is not as safe, but is capable of intimidating the receiving team, and does not lend itself to routine plays? With today's bump as the primary receiving technique, I believe the bump has cut down the attacking effectiveness of a team that just employs the float type serve, especially if that team ignores the extreme outer boundaries of its opponent's court.

There are instances where a hard serve can be the team's primary attacking element. An opponent who uses a multiple offense system will at times bring up a backcourt court setter from court position # 1. A hard roundhouse serve down the right side to fourth position # 5, could prove effective. First, the serve is in the air a shorter time, allowing the setter less time to reach his position at the net before the bump. Second, the receivers find it more difficult to bump this serve to a pre-determined position. It will most likely be bumped up in the same direction from whence it came, thereby forcing the setter to run the entire width of the court to reach the pass. Setting over his head to position # 2's spiker is difficult, as is the probability of a low over-the-head set to the center hitter (position # 3).

Conclusion: This serve almost assures that the right side hitter will receive the set. The block has time to form accordingly. Should the receiving team step up a foot or two to compensate for the drop of a spinning drive serve, the server could switch to the float and serve a tough floater into the corners.

While I am not advocating the mass conversion of float type servers to the ranks of roundhouse and tennis types, I do feel that those players who are both young and flexible enough should experiment with different serves. Those of us who are too set in our ways have many aids and strategies available to improve our serve, thereby taking them out of the defensive area and into an attacking one.

SERVING

by

Ralph Hippolyte
University of
Pennsylvania

and

Bob Bertucci
University of
Tennessee

1. Underhand Serve

Movement Sequence

a) Starting Position
- staggered stance, feet approximately shoulder width apart
- right handed—left foot forward, weight on right foot
- left handed—right foot forward, weight on left foot
- forward foot pointing in direction serve is intended
- knees flexed to insure stability
- body should be facing court with a slight angle based on individual preference
- stand between 2-10′ from baseline

b) Toss/Weight Transfer
- from starting position initiate toss
- tossing arm should be extended with ball resting in palm of hand
- serving hand should be placed directly behind the ball
- initial movement starts with slight flex of rear knee
- at same time, tossing arm is raised at shoulder joint
- toss should be low with no movement of tossing wrist
- toss should be straight up and in front of striking hand
- transfer of weight occurs during tossing phase

c) Arm Action/Contact
- while ball is being tossed, serving arm is drawn back in a pendulum motion
- when tossed ball reaches peak, weight is transferred and forward armswing is initiated
- contact with heel of hand, palm of hand or fist, with best results attained by small, hard surface area
- contact ball at midline or slightly below with arm at full extension
- limit follow through with serving arm
- wrist held perfectly rigid to prevent spin on ball
- eye contact maintained throughout serve

2. Overhand Spin Serve

a) Starting Position
- stand facing the net, feet staggered and shoulder width apart
- left foot forward for right handed servers
- ball is held in tossing hand and supported by serving hand

b) Toss/Weight Transfer
- toss ball approximately 3′ above head and in front of serving shoulder
- transfer weight from rear to front leg

c) Arm Action/Contact
- using a throwing motion, swing arm in an up and over fashion
- contact the ball with the palm of the hand, wrapping the fingers around the ball

- use quick movement of wrist to impart topspin
- one can put different spins on the ball by varying the hand position on contact
- follow through with serving arm to the center of the body
- movement is a transfer of weight from back to front
- keep all movements in a straight plane—avoid lateral movement

Movement Sequence

3. Roundhouse Serve

Movement Sequence

a) Starting position
- feet shoulder width apart with left foot closest to baseline (right handers)
- shoulders are perpendicular to the net
- the body is leaning forward with ball being held at waist height by the tossing hand and supported by the serving hand

b) Toss/Weight Transfer
- the toss is approximately 3-4′ overhead
- weight should be transferred to the right leg
- move the left hand down while quickly shifting the weight to the left leg
- simultaneously, the right arm travels up and over the top of the ball

c) Contact
- contact the ball with a straight arm above your service shoulder
- the contact point is on the heel of the hand
- the remainder of the hand and fingers cover the ball
- a quick wrist movement is critical to impart topspin
- after follow through the body should be turned facing the net

4. Japanese Floater Serve

Movement Sequence

a) Starting Position
- parallel stance with the feet at a slight angle to the baseline
- knees flexed
- back rounded
- tossing arm supporting the ball outside the service shoulder
- serving hand placed on top of ball

b) Toss/Weight Transfer
- from the starting position the weight should be transferred to the rear foot
- serving arm is drawn down and back
- tossing arm is lowered preparing to toss

c) Arm Action/Contact
- the weight is again transferred forward
- toss is made outside serving shoulder
- hip rotates towards net
- serving arm moves forward leading with the shoulder
- contact is made at the midline of the body
- heel of the hand contacts the center of the ball
- wrist is kept stiff
- no follow through

THE OVERHAND SERVE - "FLOATER"

by
Bob Bertucci
University of Tennessee

Introduction

The floater serve is the most widely used serve in today's competition. It has been recorded that 90 to 95 percent of all serves at national competition are overhand floaters. This serve, when properly executed, is most effective because of its unpredictable path to receivers.

To achieve the floating action, the ball must be contacted with a small surface area and momentary contact. There should be no follow-through and wrist must be held rigid not to impact any spin. This will eliminate the stabilizing action of the spin. Without the spin the ball is free to be acted upon by any other existing influences—for example, the air current present at playing area, or imbalances in the ball caused by the compression of the ball on contact with the hand. Another contributing imbalance is the area of the ball where the valve stem is located. Because of the added weight to this area of the ball, there is a tendency for the ball to move in the direction the valve is pointing.

Important points which should be mentioned are that the toss of the ball must not have any spin; or the location of the valve on contact will change. This may cause an unexpected flight in your serve. Therefore if all previous principles are adhered to, the following action will result:

- valve facing right will have tendency to break in a floating fashion to the right.
- valve facing left will break to the left.
- valve facing the center of the serving target will break from side to side.
- valve facing up will tend to keep the ball suspended longer with floating action. This will facilitate the long serve if desired.
- valve facing down or toward the floor will give the ball a flight culminating in a quick dropping action. This will facilitate the short serve.

Serving Strategy and Psychology

1. Always know where you are going to serve prior to the start of the serving motion.
2. If a team has an especially weak player or pass receiver, serve to that player.
3. If a team has a weak area, serve the area. Usual weak areas are deep corners, side lines and short middle.
4. Serve the "seams." This simply means serving the ball between two receivers. If one receiver is weaker, have the valve facing in that direction.
5. Serve away from a team's strong spiker. This way there will be greater difficulty in passing him the ball.
6. If a receiver mishandles the first serve, continue serving to him.
7. Serve to a substitute who has just entered the game. This player will be cold and possibly a weaker player.
8. Against a multiple offense, occasionally attempt to serve into the path of the setter coming up from the back court.
9. Alternate serving pattern. Serve a few serves shoulder high to front row players. If adjustment is made and receiving formation is moved back serve a few short.
10. Make sure your first serve is a 100% serve but not just a serve that simply goes over the net. Through practice you should develop a serve which has 100% accuracy but is still an offensive threat.
11. If a point is scored because of your serve, your second serve should be a 90% serve.
12. The third serve, if two points have been scored, should be no less than 80%. You want to make it a different serve because of placement not necessarily because of speed of the ball.
13. The fourth and succeeding serves, if you gain the opportunity to serve

a fourth time, you have gained a great psychological advantage. Don't take a chance now! Let the opposing team make mistakes. Begin using your 100% serve.

14. At 12 pts in the game it is important that no player misses a serve.
15. The serve is an offensive weapon! Use it as one, but your first priorities are to serve the ball over the net and in bounds.

The Don'ts of Serving

Never miss a serve

1. After a time out
2. After a substitution
3. If your teammate who served before you missed a serve
4. At game point
5. After your opponents have won a few points

Components of Floater Serve

1. Body Position:
   a) Stand between 2'-10' feet from baseline. A control server will stand closer opposed to a power server.
   b) Player's body should be facing the playing court. The angle at which a player stands is based on individual preference.
   c) Foot placement should be shoulder distance apart to ensure comfort and balance. The forward foot or the foot that will be supporting the player's weight at the end of the serve, should be pointing directly to where the ball is to be served.
   d) Knees should be slightly flexed to insure comfort and balance.

Starting Position

2. Toss and Weight Transfer:

The Toss

a) While in ready position your weight should be centered on the right rear foot (right handed server)
b) From the ready position the toss will be initiated. The tossing arm should be extended out with ball resting in palm of hand. Your serving hand should be placed on top of the ball facing down. This will help to control the ball.
c) Now the player is ready to begin serving motion. The initial movement is started with a slight flex of the rear knee. At the same time the tossing arm is being raised up. The serving hand stays in contact with the ball as long as possible.
d) The toss is continued by the extension of the knee and further upward movement of the arm.
e) There should be no movement in the tossing wrist. This will impart some spin and inconsistency in the toss. The ball should leave the palm of the hand due to upward movement of arm and knee extension. Inconsistency in toss will cause inaccuracy because each time you serve you will be contacting the ball differently. Also if spin is imparted the placement of the valve will be of no benefit.
f) The height of the toss should not exceed 18″ from the tossing hand. The higher the toss the greater the chance of error.
g) The ball should be tossed straight up in front of serving shoulder.
h) When the toss reaches its highest point, the weight is transferred from the right foot to the left foot or rear foot to front foot.

3. Arm Action:

Arm Swing

a) While the ball is being tossed the server's arm motion is external rotation with retraction of the shoulder. This will form a 90° angle out of the serving arm. The retraction of the shoulder will cause a slight twist in the trunk. These motions are similar to throwing a baseball.
b) When the ball reaches its highest point, the weight is being transferred from back foot to front foot. While weight is being transferred forward the forward arm swing is also initiated. The forward arm action consists of internal rotation, shoulder protraction and elbow extension.

c) The only difference from the arm action in the floater serve and throwing a baseball is that there is no follow through with the serve. When the player's hand makes contact with the ball, the arm is stopped. This should result in a quick momentary point of contact resembling a jabbing action.

4. Hand Action and Contact:

After Contacting the Ball

a) The best contacting surface of the hand is the heel of the hand. This provides a small hard surface area.
b) The wrist should be held perfectly rigid in hyperextension. This will prevent the impartment of spin.
c) Contact will be made with hand at midline of or slightly below middle of ball, with arm in full extension.
d) The player's eyes should be focused on the ball before, during, and after contact.

SPIKING

by
Ralph Hippolyte and Bob Bertucci
University of Pennsylvania
University of Tennessee

SPIKE APPROACH

1. Ready Position
    - allows immediate movement
    - legs bent
    - upper body relaxed, shoulders forward
    - in position to see everything that's happening
    - weight is evenly distributed until movement begins
    - distance of approach is approximately 2.5-4 m., depending on size of player
2. Steps
    a) Preparatory Step
        - taken prior to actual approach

Movement Sequence

- # of steps taken based on individual preference
- simply initiates movement
- no more than one step recommended
- many players exclude this step

b) Directional Step
- first primary step of approach
- recommend beginners start with this step
- taken with left leg (for right handers)
- brings spiker closer and in direction of ball
- taken carefully watching the ball's speed and trajectory
- arms begin to move backward
- center of weight is gradually lowered
- this gradual lowering used to help time the set

c) Approach Step
- much longer, quicker and deeper than directional step
- prepares the body for making jump
- arms are back and up as much as possible
- land with the heel of the right foot first, in direction of intended spike, almost perpendicular to the net
- left foot swings in front of right, almost parallel to net
- center of weight is low and behind you on landing
- most of the body weight is on the right leg
- swing arms down next to body
- the length of the step is directly related to the speed of the approach.

3. Jump
- initiated with heel-toe rock
- start arm swing upward as legs begin to push upward
- ankles, legs, hips and trunk extended in proper sequence
- action is explosive
- jump should be vertical

Note: Horizontal flying can be extremely effective for advanced spikers but detrimental to the beginner.

BASIC SPIKE

1. Spiking Action
- when arms reach top of upward arc, spiking arm moves into a cocked position
- maintain spiking elbow higher than shoulder
- upper body rotates away from net
- back is arched and legs drawn back for balance
- the non-hitting arm sights the ball while the body stays suspended in the air
- the spike is initiated by dropping the non-hitting arm and raising the hitting shoulder
- arm swing consists of an up and over movement of the shoulder, elbow and hand
- simultaneously, the legs and upper body snap forward
- contact should be made with an extended arm in front of the hitting shoulder
- the distance of the ball in front of the hitting arm is related to the length of the spiker's arm

2. Hand Contact
- contact is made with the heel of the hand
- contact should be made on the upper half of the ball
- the wrist snaps forward with the palm and fingers covering the ball

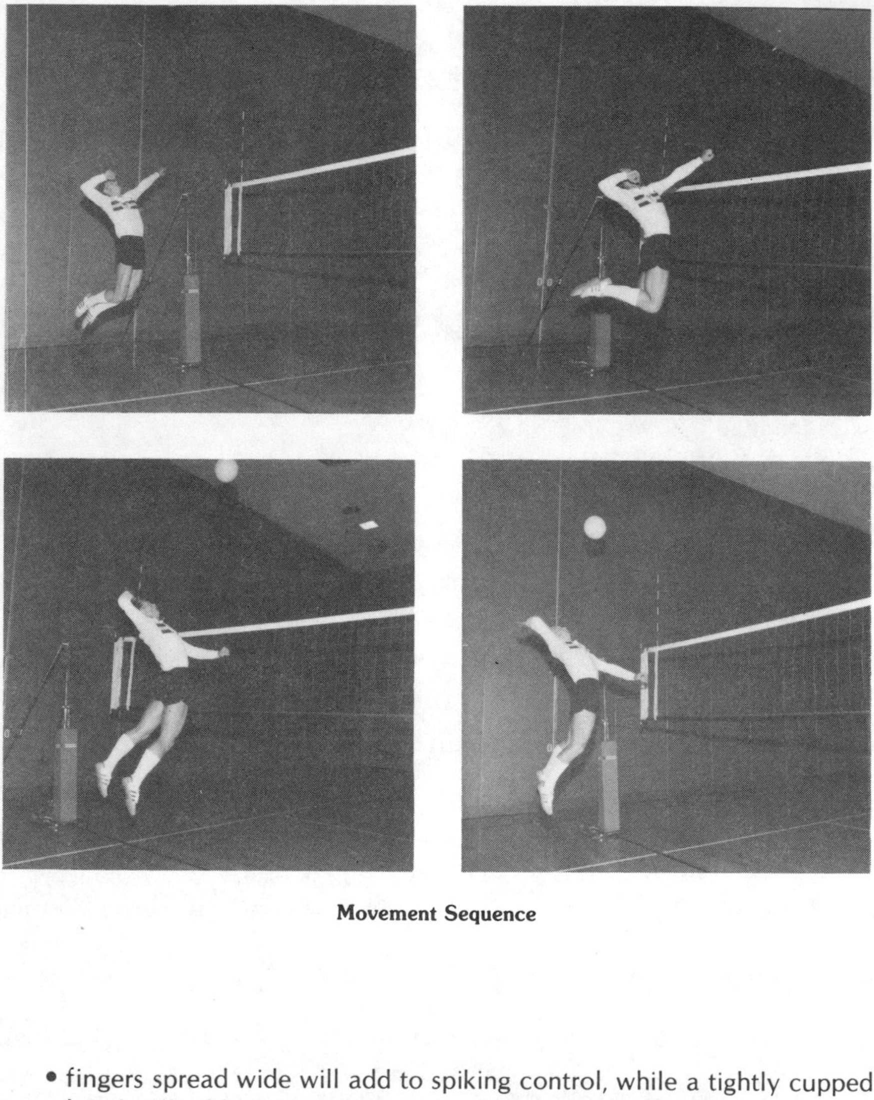

Movement Sequence

- fingers spread wide will add to spiking control, while a tightly cupped hand will add power
- contact ball as high as possible & about 1-1.5′ in front of your body
- after contact, arm swing should follow through to the midline of the body

3. Landing
   - landing should be at almost the same place as ascent began
   - land on the toes of both feet
   - flex knees to absorb impact

BACK-COURT SPIKE

Movement Sequence

- similar to basic spike
- spiker must take off behind the 3m line
- Jump will be vertical but may also have a horizontal fly depending on whether the setter sets the ball in front of the 3m line
- contact the ball further in front of the body than normal
- arm swing modified to hit long, not sharp

HIGH-HIT SPIKE

Movement Sequence

- the approach and all its components are the same as previously explained
- the basic spike is slightly different since the objective of the spike is not power, but control
- back arch is not as much a factor
- arm swing is identical up to point of contact
- contact is made almost directly overhead with total extension
- at contact the arm swing stops—no follow through
- hand contact and wrist snap are critical for direction and speed of spike
- this spike is very effective against a small blocker

CROSS BODY SPIKE

Movement Sequence

- the approach and all its components are the same as previously explained
- basic spike is different since the objective of this spike is deception, based on the position the body is facing
- the upper body is rotated away from the net
- the spiker allows the ball to fly to his non-hitting shoulder
- without turning the upper body, the spiker swings across his body
- contact is made slightly in front of the non-hitting shoulder
- follow through across the body

- landing is the same as the basic spike
- this shot is an advanced technique and is not recommended for beginners

Note: A basic line spike would require the spiker to turn his body toward the line and execute the basic spiking action, contact and follow through.

CUT SHOT SPIKE

Movement Sequence

- the approach and all its components are the same as previously explained
- the basic spike is different since the objective is also deception, again based on the direction the body is facing
- the upper body is facing the net with hitting arm cocked
- the spiker allows the ball to fly almost to his hitting shoulder
- without turning the upper body the spiker swings away from his body in a crosscourt direction
- contact is made in front of the hitting shoulder on the inside top of the ball
- follow through is away and down to the side of the body
- this shot is an advanced technique not recommended for beginners

Note: A basic crosscourt spike would require the spiker to turn his body in a crosscourt direction and execute a basic spiking action, contact and follow through.

ROUNDHOUSE SPIKE

- the approach is the same as previously explained
- spiking action is considerably different in this hit
- when arm reaches top of upward arc, spiking arm moves down in a circular motion
- upper body rotates away from net
- hitting arm begins its upward circular motion

- non-hitting arm sights the ball directly overhead
- the attacking motion will be initiated by the non-hitting arm dropping as the hitting arm begins the forward path of the circular motion
- simultaneously, the legs and upper body snap forward
- contact should be made with an extended arm and with the heel of the hand
- after contact, the follow through should face the spiker toward the net

1 2 3 4 5

Movement Sequence (1-5)

DINK SHOT

- the spiking action is identical to that of a basic spike
- the difference is the speed of the spiking action and the hand contact
- the objective of this shot is also deception based on the speed of the arm swing and the method of contact
- just prior to contacting the ball the arm swing is slowed down almost to a stop
- the fingers of the hitting hand spread and move forward slightly to form a cup

- fingertips contact the ball
- wrist must be kept stiff
- the change-up in speed and placement of the ball can make this shot extremely effective

SPIKING CHECKLIST

by
Ralph Hippolyte
University of Pennsylvania

Approach and Timing

- ☐ Be aware of the angle of the set, trajectory and speed of the ball.
- ☐ Quick set timing—spiker jumps as the ball is coming into the setter's hands.
- ☐ Semi-quick set timing—start your jump as the ball is leaving the setter's hands
- ☐ High ball set timing—do not commit yourself until the ball reaches its apex.
- ☐ Deepness of your knee bend will correct some mistiming of the ball

General

- ☐ Watch the block and defensive movement of the opponents as you are leaving the ground.
- ☐ Vary the direction and speed of your spikes.
- ☐ Make the block work for you; wipe off the block and vary your spiking swing and timing.
- ☐ Be able to hit anywhere on the opponent's court without mistakes.
- ☐ In a split second be able to hit a hole created in your opponent's defensive system.
- ☐ Raise your hitting shoulder for added height.
- ☐ The aim of a great spiker is to be powerful, smart and effective.

OUTRIGGER
2

4
Counter-Attack

THE MOST DEVASTATING WEAPON IN VOLLEYBALL

by

Ted Dulany

With the emphasis in volleyball moving toward the specialization of personnel and developed skills, we find one area neglected. Blocking continues to develop as purely an art form. The individual skills of setting, spiking, receiving and serving have been studied and outlined, but there have been no programs for the development of the most intimidating weapon a team possesses. In all cases, good blocking will upgrade the general receiving defense of a team, while above average blocking will frustrate and destroy the morale of all but the most experienced teams.

The intent of this article is not to instantly make great blockers out of all volleyball players, but hopefully to prepare a player to understand the basic fundamentals of blocking, and through practice to develop an improved individual and team blocking.

Historically, many "good" blockers have been tall people with above average reflexes who through sheer strength have performed adequately at the net. We admit that a 6′11″ person with a 40″ vertical jump would have a certain advantage over a 5′6″ person with a 20″ jump, but our contention is that even that 5′6″ person can develop into an effective blocker.

The first section will concentrate on positioning, watching the ball and observing the position of the opposing spiker, and special recommendations for middle and outside blockers.

I. A. Positioning:

"If you're not where the ball is, you can't block it." An over-simplification, maybe, but being out of position by inches will allow the opposing spiker to beat your block and possibly your secondary.

1. Positioning previous to play:

   It is of prime importance to find a starting point previous to the beginning of each play. Get familiar with placing your feet on a spot, preferably as close as possible to the center line. The reasons for establishing a starting position close to the center line are the following:

   a. The closer you are to the net prior to the block, the closer you will tend to be when you jump. This in effect will prevent balls from being driven down between the blocker and the net. Standing 4′ or more from the net often results in a player being late or flying into the air to reach his blocking position.

   b. The closer the blocker gets to the net, the more the opposing hitter will concentrate on the blocker instead of hitting. This is the ultimate result desired.

2. When considering a close starting position, negative thoughts might arise about the following:

   a. Foot Faults: If the jump is vertical, the descent will be vertical. Remember, touching the line is not a foot fault.

   b. Lower height of the block; true, with no approach, there probably will be a loss of two to three inches, but this will be compensated for by the closeness of the block to the net. This closeness produces a greater protective angle and therefore greater effective penetration.

   c. Movement: there will be no detraction from your blocking effectiveness since side movement and pivoting will be the same under any circumstance.

   Freeballs: Many players are continually waiting for a freeball. You may observe them standing 3′-4′ from the net, preparing for the big wind-up and jump to propel the ball 3,000 miles per hour straight down. Admittedly, this is impressive, but while waiting for this one over-set or bump per tournament, they have sacrificed solid positioning for the majority of plays in which they are involved.

B. Watch the Ball

Whether the preferred terminology would be total concentration, court awareness, or good anticipation, the blocker must always know where the ball is, and decide upon the probability of where the set is going. For example, if the pass to the setter is perfect, the setter has the option of setting any hitter. At this point the blocker can expect any type of set with the high probability of defending without the aid of another blocker. On the other hand, a bad reception will probably lead to a defensive high set with the high possibility of a two or three man block.

C. Watch the Man: Midline of body to hitting shoulder.

After we have observed path of the ball toward the spiker and determined approximately where the ball will land, we now turn our total attention to the hitter.

Previous to the set, the blocker should note the spikers (whether the position is off center, off the court, etc.). The position should indicate what type of set the spiker is expecting and the angle of preference.

When total concentration has returned to the spiker, watch the eyes and spiking arm. The direction of the arm and elbow turn will outline the general angle of the spike.

Observing the opposing team during warm up periods will generally point out the spiker's type of approach, preferred set height and angle preference. Another important statistic would be to note how and where the spiker hits on crucial points. There may be a time in the future where a block at this point of the game will demoralize him totally.

Always follow the ball. If the block is successful, follow through to add direction into the opposing court; if the ball is deflected or passes the block, turn in the direction of the ball and expect to react quickly in case of a low trajectory dig.

D. Responsibilities:

The first objective of the block is to prevent the spiker from hitting his preferred angle, usually into the middle of the court. With a high set, the blocker positioning the block most likely can expect additional support. Cover the middle of the court with your inside hand and allow the other blocker to close and block the remainder of the preferred angle.

When faced with a low set, it is advisable to expect a "one on one" block; therefore, protect the middle with the outside hand.

The hand positioning is in a direct line intercepting the flight of the ball between the spiker's arm, through the ball, to the middle of the court.

E. Middle Blockers:

The personnel used for middle blocking should be quick of hand and eye and possess a good vertical jump. It is also an added plus to have this person be aggressive in nature.

After the middle blocker has made visual contact with the opposing middle spiker for positioning, the concentration should shift to the setter with special emphasis on hand positioning. In most instances a setter with low hand positioning will set a low set to the outside. A dropped shoulder toward the net will probably signify a short set to the

middle, while a strong follow through with the legs will mean a high set.

Keys for mid-blocker: (1) Watch setter's body. Usually a setter telegraphs a back set by squirming his body well under the ball. A normal pass from the setter as he faces the spiker usually comes from a point off that setter's forehead. (2) Poor bumps usually result in high outside sets.

The middle blocker's first responsibility is to protect the middle of the court from the quick middle hit, then for closing to help the outside blocker on higher sets. The middle blocker should be the first person to see the play develop. It is the responsibility of this blocker to react decisively upon the set, and attempt to close on the outside blockers. On every hit the middle blocker must jump, even if a huge hole is left. At least with this hole the defense can form and fill in around the block.

F. Outside Blocker:

This person is responsible for controlling the high power attack. A strong blocking position must be obtained to allow the center blocker to close. It is of utmost importance not to reach after the ball once you have committed your defense. At this point it will be the responsibility of the middle blocker to close and for the defense to fill the gaps. The blocker will not always take the correct position, but if it is consistent in movement and vertical ascent, the defense can fill in adequately. Generally, an outside blocker concedes part of the sideline, with his outside hand on the ball. The outside blocker must be within 3′ of the sideline. If he stands further in the opposing setter will be able to beat him with a shoot set to the sideline.

If the block is inconsistent, the whole defense will crumble.

Remember:
1. Initiate position
2. Observe the opposing spiker
3. Watch the ball
4. Intercept the path of the hitter's hand
5. Follow the ball

II. THE BLOCK

The second section will concentrate on the movement to the correct blocking position and the sequence of the vertical ascent and interception.

A. Movement

Lateral movement along the net should be quick and precise. The move should be either a side step or cross over technique ending approximately the same distance from the net as the starting position. During this movement, hand position should be approximately shoulder height with the legs in a slight crouch position.

- Side Step

Movement is a straddle hop laterally along the net minimizing all forward movement.

I maintain that a player, with one short step, can reach sufficient height to block effectively and minimize mistakes in timing and positioning.

The movement is initiated with the foot on the side the blocker wishes to travel. When the blocker arrives in the desired position, there should only be vertical movement, with the hands being lifted from the sides.

It is not necessary, but I feel the person positioning the block should initiate the jump. The jump should be timed as to have the block intercept the ball just prior to it passing over the net. This timing will take practice to perfect. A general rule of thumb (except on short or very close sets) is to initiate the jump just after the spiker has left the floor.

- Cross-over.

Another method of movement would be "cross-over" which is performed running parallel to the net. This is helpful for blockers who feel the need for greater height or extension. With this movement it is difficult to coordinate the closing of the outside and middle blockers. This technique is used by many international players but is difficult for beginners.

The move is initiated with a ninety degree turn alongside the net. The first step is made with the trailing foot and positioning is estimated by approximating distances between blockers. To initiate ascent, the last step by the foot closest to the net is extended which leads to a ½ squat upon the closing of the outside leg. At this point the blocker should be parallel to the net with both hands below knee level. The ascent is a continuation of motion with a rotation toward the net while extending both arms. A rotating motion is continued through the ascent until the block is finished. The descent must be made with total body control not to cause any net faults.

B. Interception—Surround the Ball

Now that we have the blocker in the air in the proper position, we come to the interception. At this point the blocker should be watching the spiker's shoulders, head and arm for the direction he is attempting to hit. The interception is accomplished by lowering the head and shoulders in a "pike" position as to deflect the ball downward into the opposing court. The coordination of the hand flip and body pike should be in direct proportion to the force of the spike. A slow spike should trigger a slow pike while a hard spike should cause a quick pike and snap of the wrists downward. Fingers should be spread. Thumbs almost touch. Look at ball through thumbs and forefingers, wrists, cocked. Hands should remind you of "elephant ears" always spread. One blocker should cover approximately 18-20′ from pinky to pinky.

The hands should be spread in accordance to the angle of interception. If the hitter is directly in front of the blocker and attempting to hit in that direction, the hands should be fairly close together, approximately a foot, with spread fingers. As the angle increases, the hands and arms should be spread to increase the area of coverage.

Position hands above and over net in line with the opponent's strongest and most direct spiking angle.

We have covered the basic fundamentals of blocking. With concentrated practice and reflex drills a team can expect to control the net and therein control the game.

ADDITIONAL COMMENT:

If blockers have a tendency to reach to the outside and/or not turn the ball into the opposing court, it may be beneficial to practice the positioning of the outside foot 5 to 6 inches in front of the inside foot previous to the jump. This positioning will have a tendency to force the blocker slightly off angle which will automatically turn the blocker toward the opposing court.

III. TRAINING RECOMMENDATIONS:

Blocking is a developed skill which demands a great amount of endurance and body coordination. Strengthening specific parts of the body is recommended to enable a blocker to perform adequately during a long tournament. Refer to the chapter on physical training.

IV. TEAM DEFENSE

The coordination of the block into the team defense is by far the most important concept for the defensive coach. Team defense and area dig concepts all revolve around the positioning of the block and the anticipation of an effective block protecting a specific portion of the playing surface. The defensive coach must mandate consistency of the block and coordinated movement and penetration in order to develop a functional defensive program. The block does not have to be towering or flashy to be effective. What is needed is consistency to enable the defense to revolve and maneuver into an acceptable alignment behind the block. A good block stops the opponent from hitting the heart of the court, forces the opponent's spiker to hit extreme angles, thereby taking the "steam" off his hit.

The block should be coordinated to control the power of the opposing team. By power, I refer to both the power angle of the individual spiker, and the opposing team's offensive strategy. The coordination should be accomplished by observing the opposing team prior to the game and making statistical notations. Through this method, the preferences of the setters and spikers, as to the height of the set, general approach, power, and angle can be noted. Observations during game sequences, especially during crucial plays should be noted. For example, on crucial plays: (1) does the setter use only certain personnel? (2) will the set be high or low? What angle does the hitter prefer in this situation? Will the setter attack the middle or just use it as a fake?

After statistics have been taken in these situations, a pattern may develop which will allow the preparation of defensive alignments to nullify this play and possibly remove the safety valve the opposing team depends on.

Serving:

Serving is an important weapon which is often neglected in the utilization of the block. If at any time there are no players on the other side with weak receiving technique, attack the corners (all four) to cause an awkward bump and eliminate certain sets. If a setter shows a preference in setting a certain individual, serve to an area which will force the setter to attempt a low percentage set or set into a prepared block.

Prepared Block

Reviewing our previous concept of preparing a consistent block to protect a specific area of the court, this block can be:

a. Inside protective: The block preparing to channel the attack down the outside lines and protect against the middle attack.
b. Outside protective: This method will align the block almost on the outside line to force the attack inside and cross court.
c. Split: This would be a combination of the above methods which

would attempt to force the spikers to channel their hits between two blockers to a position defended by a waiting defensive player.

d. Combination: Any and all the above mentioned methods to confuse and or force the opposing team to change its preferred strategy. Again we state the most important factor of the block is to be consistent and be sure all personnel on the floor are aware of what the block is attempting.

Personnel

The deployment of personnel and the team defense will depend greatly on the type of offense your particular team is using. Whether the offense is one of the popular penetration offenses, 5-1 or 6-0, or one of the more controlled offenses, 4-2 or 3-3, which depend a great deal on the high outside attack, will almost force your team into certain defenses to protect specific personnel. With the penetration offenses, it is of great importance to protect the setter coming from the back court and allow him to control the offense during a rally. When playing a 5-1 offense, the coach will usually have the setter block either the middle, or right side to enable the setting of the ball during a rally. In general, coaches should try and arrange formations which will allow the quicker, more aggressive players to block the middle, and the setters and power hitters to block the outside.

Rule Changes:

With the new rule changes adopted by the U.S.V.B.A. we find the block taking on slightly different tactics. The inward movement of the antenna has virtually moved the deep line corner from the spiker given an outside set. The block should therefore concentrate more on the inside protection than previously.

The Interception by the Block Not Counting as One of the 3 Allowable Contacts.

This rule can be of great advantage to a mobile team. Now it is advantageous to touch the ball whenever possible. Whenever the block has a chance it should deflect the ball upward as to allow a play to develop. At this point I feel it is important to distinguish that fine line between extending and wild reaching. If a blocker is capable of maintaining proper body positioning and still be within reaching distance of the ball, by all means go for the ball, but if that touch means leaning, or flying, the chances of deflecting the ball within the playable area are very small.

Objectives:

The objective of the block is to prevent the opposing team from putting the ball down on your court, not to "roof" the ball everytime it is spiked. Confidence in the block has to be instilled to a point where the defense knows it can prevent the opposing team from hitting the floor with the ball.

BLOCKING: WITH BLOCKERS OF DIFFERENT HEIGHTS

by
Mario Treibitch
Rutgers University

On many competitive teams there is an obvious difference in height between the prime spiker and the setter. For both coaches and players this is becoming a serious problem. How will players communicate to achieve maximum precision for a double block between two players of different heights? Take as an example a team who has a setter 5′5″ tall who blocks right front position, and a middle blocker 6′ tall. In the following pictures you will see the ideal situation which should occur in a two man block involving these players.

1

2

3

In picture #1, a spiker is preparing to attack from the left front against the middle blocker and setter. The blockers observe the trajectory of the set and prepare to block.

When a block is going to be made by two players of different heights, the timing of the jump is different. The smaller blocker must jump earlier than the taller one. This is because of the extra vertical height the smaller blocker must cover. The difference in timing assures that both blockers' hands will reach the same height together.

(A point of clarification must be made concerning height. The height we are finally concerned with is the player's block reach, which is the jump plus the reach when the arms are totally extended. This height is usually directly related to the standing height of a person. The shorter the player, the lower the block reach.

This is why in picture #1, the smaller blocker is squatted deeper and prepared to jump. The taller blocker is not in any rush. She does not need a maximum jump, for she is simply concerned with setting a good, even block.

The second picture shows that the taller girl, because of her height advantage, does not have to squat deeply to reach the same level as the smaller girl. Also, since she has a shorter distance to cover, she does not have to jump with the smaller blocker.

The block is now above the net, with the hands of both blockers at the same height. Because the hands are even, it will be difficult for a ball to go through the block. The taller player is the more important player in this block, for she must adapt her height to the smaller player's to allow them to block in unison.

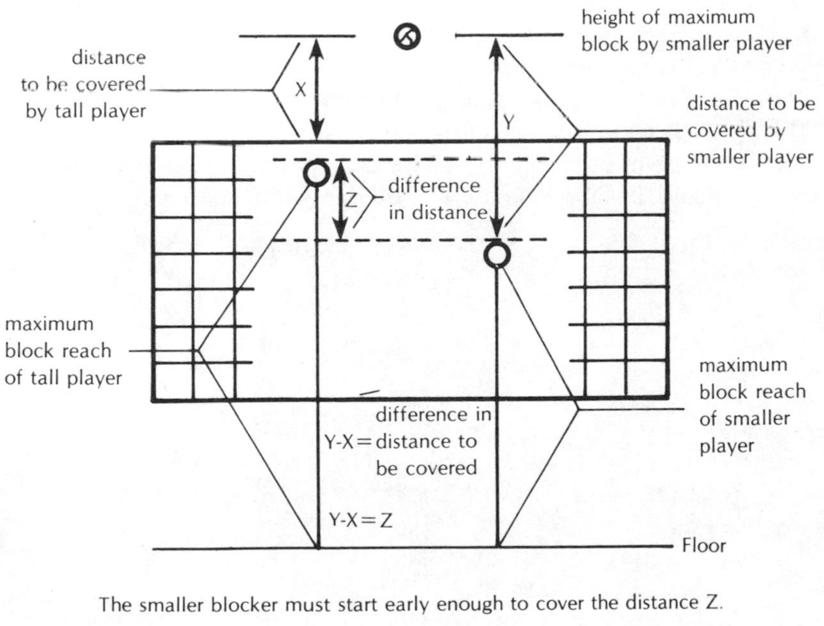

The smaller blocker must start early enough to cover the distance Z.

ILLUSTRATION #1

The spiker observes that the central area of the court is well defended, but that there is a free angle of attack on the line. This has been left open by the blockers, who are effectively covering the main area of the court. They have forced the spiker to find this shot and use it. Because of the even "area block" the direction of attack would be no surprise for a defensive secondary.

The backcourt defense is now able to predetermine the spiker's possibilities and cover them accordingly. This well formed block, channeled the ball to a specific area of the court.

DIGGING

by

Ralph Hippolyte
University of Pennsylvania

Unlike spiking, digging is not enhanced by glory or heroism. Volleyball players are recognized more often for their net play rather than their back court play. Only diving saves receive the admiration that a hard-driven spike does. Nevertheless, the quality of the defensive dig largely determines the possibilities of counter-attack. A good dig off of a powerful spike is often a psychological blow to the opposition. In top competition, the team with superior digging technique will beat an otherwise equal opponent.

Knowledge of the proper stance is essential to good defensive execution. In the basic position, the athlete's center of weight is extended forward, almost to the point of losing one's balance forward. To assume this stance, the feet should be approximately shoulder-width apart with the weight

Basic Stance

Knee Drop
(Lateral Movement)

Forward Collapse

equally distributed on the inside balls of the feet, while the outside edge of the foot is slightly off the floor. This position can only be accomplished by forcing one's knees inward as far as possible. This position facilitates good lateral movement by simply dropping the knee opposite the direction you desire to move. The foot closest to the sideline is slightly ahead. The knees should be bent at an angle slightly greater than ninety degrees, thus projecting the knees over the toes. This knee forward position facilitates quick forward movement. The back should be fairly erect with the elbows close to the hips.

A good defensive player will vary his defensive stance in anticipation of a particular play. If expecting a fast or sharp spike, the defensive digger lowers his center of weight and widens his stance. If a less difficult spike is expected, the digger assumes a running stance, ready to cover a greater area of the court.

The stance of the player behind the block, who covers roll shots and dinks, differs from that of the actual digger. This player is less able to predict the direction of the ball and must therefore be in a position best enabling him to move quickly. Movement is the element most crucial to this position, thus the player must maintain a running stance on the court.

The arms should be fully extended only when a hard, direct spike is anticipated. A higher defensive position should involve the arms still bent with the elbows close to the hips. If the arms are kept at the sides, a player can react equally well to a ball driven to his left or his right. A player is in a better position to dive for a ball when his arms remain close to his sides; he can use them to gain speed and direct himself toward the ball.

It is imperative to use both arms whenever possible in digging. The arms must be brought quickly together to form a flat, horizontal surface. The horizontal position is necessary in order to keep the ball on the digger's side of the court. At the very moment of impact, the arms must remain motionless, then to absorb the impact, the arms must spring back from the ball, while the body moves closer. The harder the spike, the more the digger must absorb the impact of the ball. It is imperative to contact the ball with a smoothly accelerating motion; a convulsive motion toward the ball will only result in loss of control. Immediately after digging the ball, the player's concern is getting back into the flow of the game.

A one-handed dig should be used only when there is no other practical alternative. Balls that are to the side or far in front of the digger may of necessity be reached with one arm. A one-handed dig may be used when doing a dive or a lateral roll. The ball in these instances should be contacted in the middle of the fall.

Dives and rolls are generally unnecessary when the spike is correctly anticipated. But there are situations that are difficult to foresee. Balls deflected by the blockers, dinks, and net balls represent some of these situations.

One should maintain a stance of moderate depth and be ready to move in any direction to adjust to these and other unpredictable occurrences.

If the player is able to reach the ball quickly enough, he should receive it in an upright position. If he is late in getting to the ball, he should take a long, deep step, a lunge. A lunge to either side should follow through into a lateral roll, or dive to that side. A lunge straight forward should progress into a slide or collapse.

No matter how polished a player's physical technique, effective defensive play requires a strong mental element as well. Anticipation and judgment are qualities a defensive player must possess. He must be constantly aware of various determining factors:

1) The blocking formations of the player's own team.
2) His own physical and technical limitations and those of his teammates and the other players on the courts.
3) The defensive stance and positioning of his teammates.
4) The type of set used by the opponent.
5) Finally, assessing the qualities of the opposing spiker.

The position of the block with regard to the ball and to the spiker must also be examined by the defensive players. Primary diggers must play around the block. They should position themselves in areas of the court left open by the block. If the digger's vision of the spiker is obscured by the blocker, then the digger should expect the blockers to handle any balls hit in his area. Therefore, he may move in for dinks and tips or he should move to receive a sharper hit where his vision of the ball is not impaired.

A player must recognize and adjust for his own physical characteristics. A taller player, for instance, may position himself closer to the net than a shorter player, because the trajectory of a ball coming over his head will go out of bounds. A ball coming over the head of a shorter player in the same position might still remain inbounds. The player should stand so that his weaker side is lower than his stronger side; generally a right-handed player should lower his left side slightly more. A player moves better towards his stronger side, so a right-handed player should position himself more towards his left.

A good team defense is the fruit of a collective organization. The individuals must form a unit that performs with a certain kind of rhythm. If one player shifts to the left to receive a ball, the entire team should flow with him. If a player is out of position, the team should automatically move to fill any gaps left in the defense. And finally, if a ball is mis-hit by a player, the other players must conform to the new situation and mend the error.

The defensive player must make certain decisions with regard to the opponent's set. A set close to the net suggests a sharp spike; thus the players should move forward, staying low and directing their weight towards the spiker's arm. A set coming diagonally from the back court will probably result in a crosscourt spike. If the set is a deep one, the defensive players should expect a deep spike; thus, the players should position themselves further from the net and should maintain a higher stance, a running stance.

The defensive player should develop the ability to predict or read the opposing spiker's action. The spiker's position in relation to the ball, the direction or angle of his approach, his shoulder rotation, and his wrist action determine the spike. The defensive player should learn to integrate mentally all of these factors and to react accordingly. He must also evaluate the opposing spiker as an individual; every player prefers certain shots.

The above article, while touching on many key points, serves merely as an introduction to volleyball defense. In short, volleyball defense comprises a complex series of skills, both mental and physical.

EMERGENCY TECHNIQUES

by

Ralph Hippolyte and Bob Bertucci
University of Pennsylvania — University of Tennessee

1. DIVING

a) Dive and Catch

Movement Sequence

- The player assumes a low ready position
- Movement is initiated by stepping toward the ball
- The player transfers his weight to the ball of his forward foot
- The player reaches out at the same time he is kicking his trailing leg up
- While contacting the ball, utilizing the underhand pass technique, the forward foot maintains contact with the floor
- After contacting the ball, the lead leg must be kicked upward to prepare the player's landing
- The player's body is completely extended with all his body weight behind his outstretched arms
- The player, upon hand contact with the floor, eases his body weight forward and down
- The back must be arched, legs flexed, and the chin kept up
- The above position centers the player's weight near the mid-section of his body
- Using a push-up type movement, the player eases his chest down for short and safe landing

b) Dive and Slide

Movement Sequence

- The dive and slide is usually employed when retrieving a ball which is a great distance away
- Mechanics are basically the same as described in the dive and catch
- This technique more often utilizes a one-handed save because of the additional reach needed
- At the moment the player's chest makes contact with the floor, he not only continues to lower his body, but he also pulls his body through his hands in an attempt to slide
- The ball is contacted with the back of the outstretched hand
- This technique also assures one hand in almost immediate contact with the floor

c) Dive and Turn

Movement Sequence

- The dive and turn is usually employed when retrieving balls to the side or behind the defensive player
- Mechanics are basically the same as described in the dive and catch
- This technique more often utilizes a one-handed reverse spiking technique
- The player must pivot and step in the direction of the ball
- Prior to the player's total weight being transferred onto the lead foot, he must initiate his turn back toward the target while going for the ball. By rotating about the ball of the foot, the turn can be accomplished.
- While the lead foot is still in contact with the floor, the pass should be made with the follow through being in the direction of the target

2. ROLLING (JAPANESE STYLE)

a. The Reaction

Movement Sequence

b. The Roll

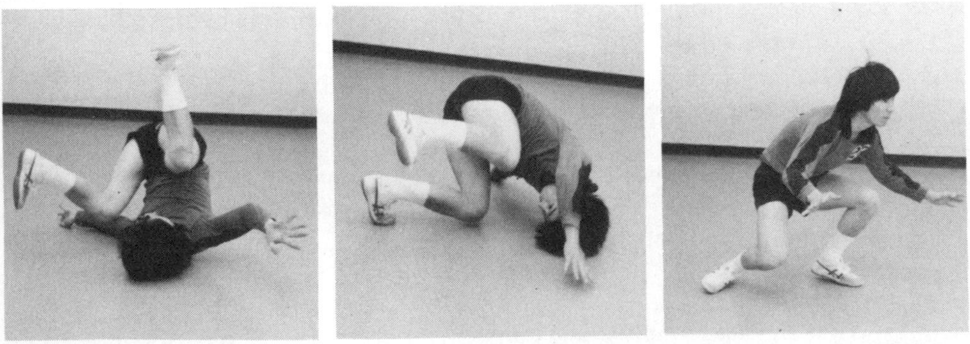

Movement Sequence

- Move quickly in the direction of the ball with striding step long and low.
- The striding leg is flexed with the trailing leg straight.
- While stretching for the ball gradually lower the center of gravity, until the body weight is completely over the flexed leg.
- Contact the ball with an outstretched arm using the hand, wrist of forearm.
- Pivoting on the ball of the striding foot, the player turns toward the target.
- After contact, the player continues pushing off lead leg and slides on the side of the striking arm.
- Tuck head to the shoulder of the striking arm.
- Simultaneously, kick both legs up and over the shoulder of the non-striking arm.

5
Drills

PROGRESSIONS FOR VOLLEYBALL DRILLS

by
Mick Haley
Kellogg Community College

I. Overhand Pass

A. Assume the correct hand position (window pane).

B. Place ball in hands and pass to floor.

C. Toss low to self and pass head high to partner; partner catches using overhand pass technique.
Partner checks technique prior to tossing to self and passing to partner. (partner at least 15 feet away)

D. Emphasizing full body follow-through, partners pass and catch checking each position upon completion of the pass. The ball should be passed high with a trajectory that will allow the ball to drop straight down on the partner's head.

E. Toss to self and pass ball high with same trajectory. Partner should allow ball to bounce in front and play it off bounce by passing high back to partner.

F. Sit and set drill — Have partners sit 8-12 feet apart and set ball back and forth. Emphasis on wrists and arms.

G. Partners 15 feet apart — Set ball low back and forth. Keep hands and arms up.

H. Partners 10 feet apart set ball high back and forth.

I. Set to self; set to partner.

J. Set to partners left and then to right. Alternate and get foot patterns correct.
K. Set in front of partner; partner moves in, plays ball, and backs up 3 strides.
L. Set to self, set to partner, run around partner. Partner does the same.
M. Set to self, ¼ turn, set to self, ¼ turn, set overhead.
N. Name game: ½ pivot, find ball, get positioned and make perfect pass.
O. Jump setting with partner. 10-20 consecutive.
P. Triangle setting; reverse on whistle.
Q. Set to self, touch floor with both hands, set to partner.
R. Set to self, make full pivot, set to partner.
S. Set to self, roll, set to partner off bounce.
T. Set to self, set to partner, turn and dive.
U. Set to partner or self depending upon hand signal.
V. Set with partner using 2 balls.
W. Set triangle using 2 balls.

II. Forearm Pass

A. Passing action (arms only).
B. Passing a held ball.
C. Passing a dropped ball.
D. Pass to partner off a bounced ball.
E. Pass to partner off a tossed ball.
F. Pass back and forth.
G. Pass ball tossed to either side (footwork)
H. Up and back movement — Ball tossed by partner.
I. Crossover step playing balls shoulder height, overhead or to the side.
J. Passing tossed balls into a basket or to target.
K. Pass, ¼ turn, pass, ¼ turn, and pass overhead.
L. Two tossers, 1 passer: Passer moves laterally passing balls back to the target in which they were tossed, working on foot patterning and arm swing.
M. All drills used in overhand passing may be used in one way or another.
N. Coach controlled drills:
   1. Coach serves from 15 feet. Passers cover whole court. When she gets five good passes next person is in.
   2. Coach tosses and points to target. Passer gets into position and attempts to pass.

O. Emergency passing: Coaches throw balls anywhere. Partners chase it down and communicate who will contact it first and who will cover up.
P. Three players, two balls: Tosser overhand throws over net, passer plays ball to catcher at net: Continuous 50 attempts.

III. Spike Reception

A. Ready position.
B. Throw at ankles — Partner passes and checks body position.
C. Partner spikes ball from standing position — Partner passes and spiker catches ball. (on bad spike or pass both people chase ball.)
D. Pepper — One spiking, one passing. 50 then switch.
E. Wall drill — Passer plays 10 feet away from wall. Thrower stands behind passer and throws ball against wall; passer attempts to react.
F. Introduce stride, stretch, and roll techniques.
G. Master technique to verbal or visual directions going forward with the left and right arms.
H. Play tipped balls from partner. (Overhand) Work on form and technique.
I. Practice front layout or collapse technique with either left or right leg forward.
J. Have partner spike from floor to a target on the floor in front of partner. Partner will attempt to pass ball using layout technique. Alternate forward leg.
K. Coach stands on table and hits ball to player who uses layout technique. Coach tips ball periodically so that a dive and roll may be used also.

IV. Dive and Slide

A. Slide from knees.
B. Slide from a front leaning position.
C. Dive from one foot track position.
D. Dive with partner assistance on back leg.
E. Play ball from stationary position on floor and dive.
F. Dive and slide for distance from low kneeling position.
G. Play tossed ball from low kneeling position and slide.

V. The Attack

A. Simulate arm action (Bow technique).

B. Spike a held ball.
C. Spike a tossed ball to the floor.
D. Present spiker's jump (Heel - toe).
E. Rocking jump — No approach.
F. Step close and jump.
G. Four step approach — Repeat 10-20 times daily.
H. Approach and throw tennis ball.
I. Approach and hit a stationary ball being held by a partner on a table.
J. Approach and catch a tossed ball.
K. Spike a tossed ball.
L. Spike a set ball.
M. Spike a tossed ball 10 consecutive times recovering each time.
N. Spike a tossed ball from left, center, and then right side of court.
O. Spike a set ball at targets on the court.
P. Repeat with two blockers.
Q. Partner stands on the other side of net 20 feet away. Spiker attempts to approach and jump into the air for a set ball looking for a signal from the partner. Upon seeing the signal, the spiker will spike or tip depending upon the signal.

VI. Blocking

A. Simulated upper body action, partner using arm touch.
B. Jump and pike with shoulders, not hips.
C. Jump and penetrate net.
D. Jump and penetrate net, lock elbows, and throw ball to the floor with wrists only.
E. Partner on each side of net. One jumps and attempts to throw ball over and down, other partner penetrates for a block. Alternate.
F. At net, partner spikes ball into block.
G. Coach on table spikes ball straight ahead, blocker practices attack block.
H. Coach on table spikes against two blockers who attempt to area block.
I. Mock blocking using 2-1, 3-1, 3-2 crossover footwork.
J. Coach on table attempts to close and complete the block. (Reverse — outside blocker to middle)
K. Three tables, three blockers: Coach calls a series of combinations. The hitters on the tables spike in staggered rhythm. Blockers attempt to react.

L. Blocking tag — one against one.
M. Blocker spikes a tossed ball over net.
N. Blocker attempts line blocking and then turns and dives for tossed ball.

VII. Serving

A. Throw basketball - Alternate arms to 60 feet.
B. Serve line from 20 feet. Work on form and technique.
C. Work up to serving 60 feet.
D. Work on serving accurately to areas 1, 6, and 5.
E. Change trajectories to areas 1, 6, and 5.
F. Serve to areas 2, 3, and 4 without changing technique.
G. Serve at different formations (2 and 3 persons) on both sides of courts
H. Serve at whole team trying to find weaknesses.
I. Serving games:
   1. 3 point game.
   2. Serving at passer in area. Count number of times he can't pass ball to area out of 20 or 50.
   3. Target serving.

DRILL IDEAS

by

Ralph Hippolyte
University of Pennsylvania

and

Bob Bertucci
University of Tennessee

The following drills have been developed to assist the coach in designing his practice sessions. These drills should be used to stimulate one's own imagination. The drills have been divided into two basic sections: Section 1—simple drills; Section II—consists of drills designed to train multiple aspects. As you will see these drills will emphasize different training variables. Before we actually look at the drills I would like to spend some time explaining what a drill consists of, how to make a drill and the method of running a drill.

The Four Training Variables

1. Intensity - time interval between exercises
2. Quantity - Total # of contacts
3. Quality - degree of perfection
4. Movement - static/dynamic

How to Make a Drill

The aforementioned training variables are a crucial part of every drill. Before a coach can implement a drill he must:

1. establish a purpose
2. review training variables
3. select variables to emphasize
4. design drill structure to accomplish desired result.
5. execute the drill as planned.

Method of Running a Drill

There are two basic methods to running a drill:

1. Coach oriented - the coach is the center of action. He can control the training variable directly. The non-active players should constantly shag balls to increase the efficiency and maintain flow in the drill.
2. Player oriented - the players perform the drill by themselves. The coach's primary duty is to supervise all players.

Drill Outline

The following is an outline of drills designed to assist the coach:

Section I *Simple Drills*

1) Passing
   a) overhand and underhand pass (Fig. 1-4)
   b) setting (Fig. 5-9)
   c) service reception (Fig. 10-17)
2) Attack
   a) serving (Fig. 18-19)
   b) spiking (Fig 20-21)
3) Counter-Attack
   a) blocking (Fig. 22-23)
   b) digging (Fig. 24-25)

Section II *Combination Drills*

1) Ball Control
   (Fig. 26-30)
2) Net Oriented
   (Fig. 31-35)

Code

Path of Player

Path of Ball

Spiked Ball

Player

Player's New Position

Player With Ball

Setter

Coach

Player Jumping

Player on the Floor

Table

Chair

Ball Cart

Below is the numbering system for the volleyball court.

During a drill if reference is made to a court position it will correspond to the diagram below.

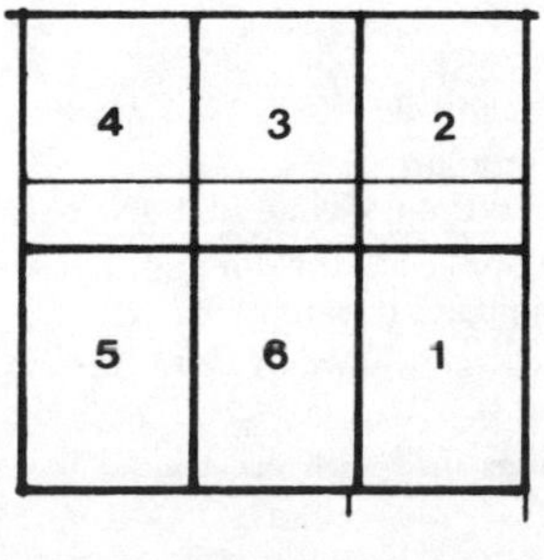

Illustration #1

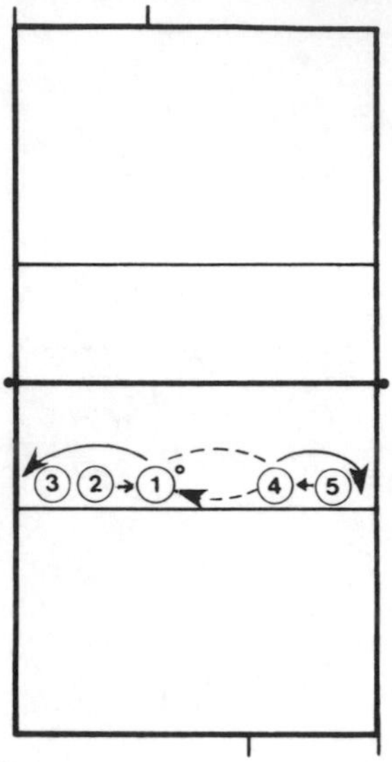

Figure #1

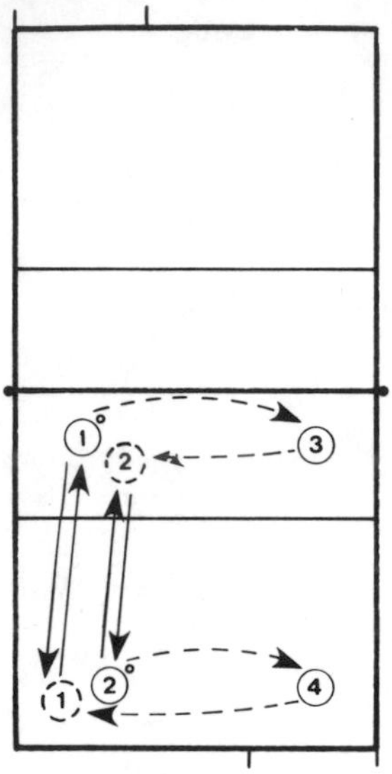

Figure #2

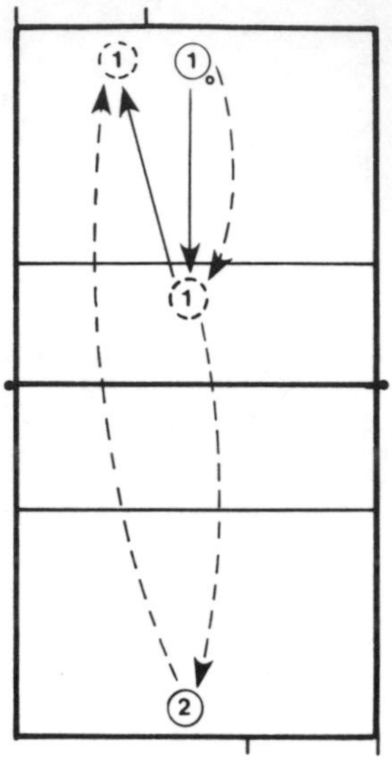

Figure #3

FIGURE #1

Purpose: Develop passing technique

Explanation: Player #1 starts the drill by passing to #4

Player #1 moves to the end of the same line

Player #4 passes back to player #2 who has moved into player #1's original position

*This is a continuous line drill. A variation would be to have player pass and go to end of opposite line.

FIGURE #2

Purpose: Ball control, ability to pass after movement conditioning

Explanation: Players #1 and #2 both have balls and they simultaneously pass to players #3 and #4

Immediately after passing they switch positions

Player #3 will return pass to player #2

Player #4 will return pass to player #1

Players #1 and #2 will again pass to players #4 and #3, respectively, then switch

FIGURE #3

Purpose: Develop passing control

Develop setting strength

Explanation: Player #1 starts on the baseline and self-passes to the 3m line

Player #1 quickly moves to the 3m line, passes over the net to player #2 who is standing on opposite baseline

Player #1 immediately returns to the baseline and waits for #2's full-court pass

Player #1 continues drill with no stop

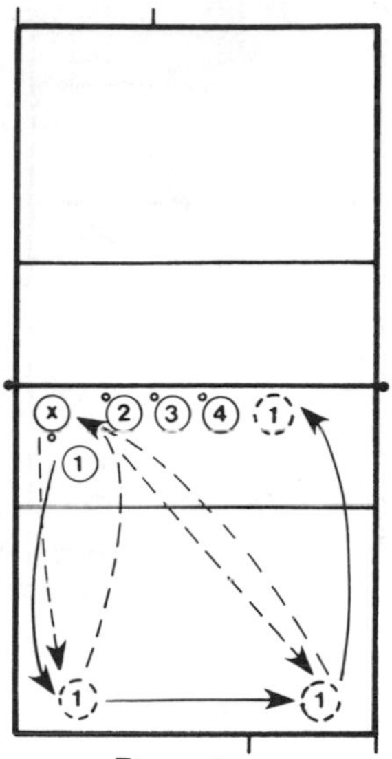

Figure #4

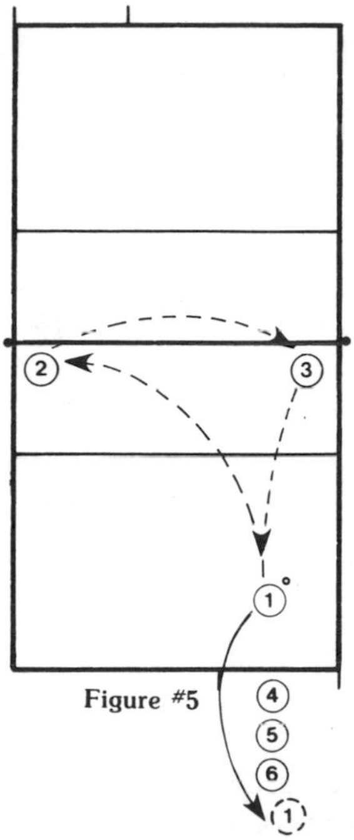

Figure #5

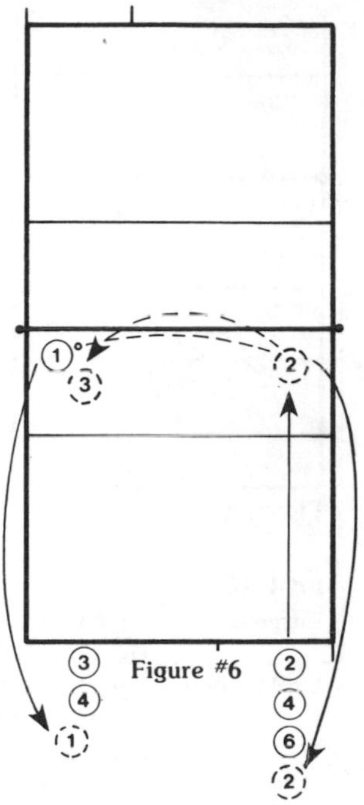

Figure #6

FIGURE #4

Purpose: Develop ability to play a ball using a dive

Explanation: Coach tosses the ball to court position #5

Player #1 must run and dive playing the ball back to the coach

Coach immediately tosses the ball to position #1

Player #1 must again run and dive repeating the pass to the coach

FIGURE #5

Purpose: Develop the backcourt set

Ability to set along the net

Explanation: Player #1 starts the drill by setting the ball to #2 and returns to end of line

Player #2 sets along the net to player #3

Player #3 overhand passes the ball to court positions #1 or #6

Player #4 moves for ball, faces player #2 and sets

FIGURE #6

Purpose: Develop movement combined with setting

Improve ability to set along the net

Accuracy in setting, the pass should be made with intentions of setting up an attack

Explanation: Player #1 starts the drill by setting the ball to court position #2 then returns to end of line

Player #2 moves as soon as player #1 begins to pass

Player #2 executes a set to position #4 then returns to end of line

Player #3 moves as soon as player #2 begins to set

*This drill is continuous and can be done with players switching lines.

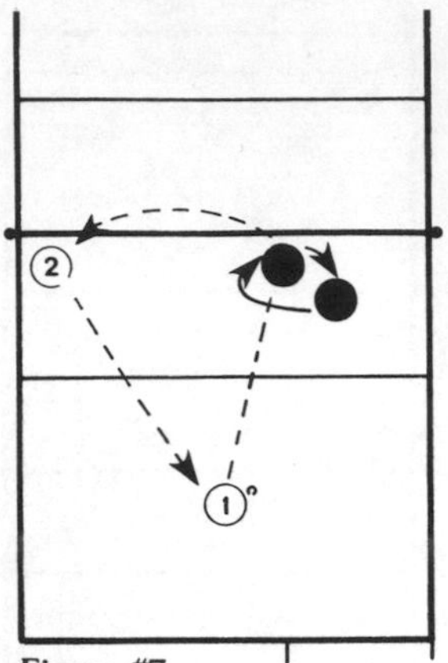

Figure #7

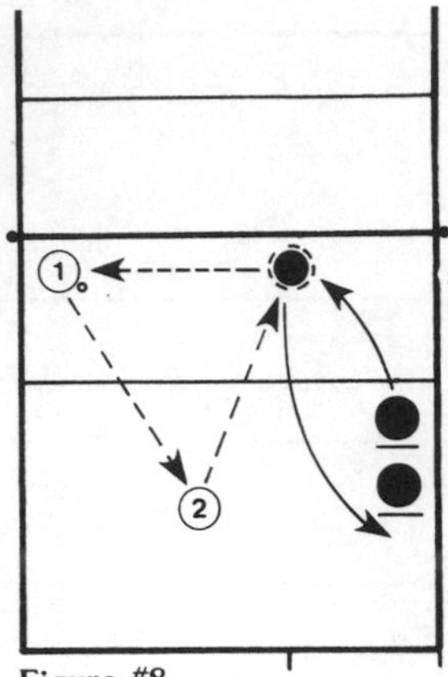

Figure #8

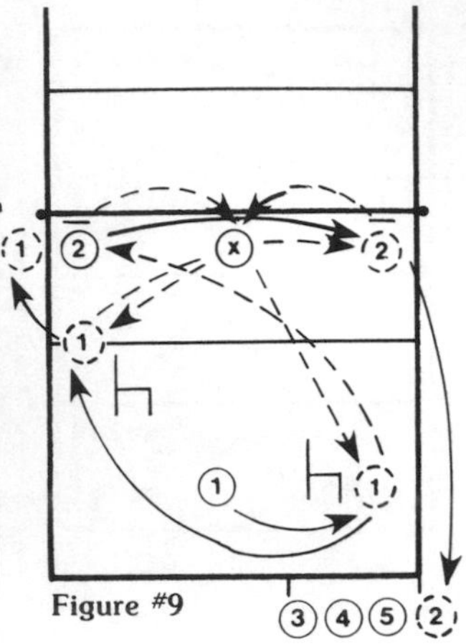

Figure #9

FIGURE #7

Purpose: Teach setter how to change direction and deliver an accurate set
Develop a fake technique in setting

Explanation: Player #1 starts the drill by passing the ball in front of the setter
Setter will step forward and pivot as if he wanted to set position #2
Setter will execute a back set to player #2
Player #2 passes to player #1 and repeat

FIGURE #8

Purpose: Speed and agility training for setter
Setting accuracy after movement

Explanation: Player #1 starts drill as soon as he passes to player #2, the setter gets up off the floor and moves to position
Player #2 passes the ball to setting position
The setter must execute an accurate set to player #1 then returns to original position
When player #1 touches the ball, setter #2 gets up and penetrates—sets

FIGURE #9

Purpose: Develop backcourt setting
Develop jumpsetting at the net

Explanation: Coach sets the ball to court position #1
Player #1 moves from position #6, must run around a chair and set to player #2 in position #4
Coach sets the ball to position #4
Player #1 runs around the chair and sets to player #2 who has moved to position #2
Player #2 again jump sets to the coach while player #1 has assumed player #2's starting position at position #4
Player #2 moves to the end of the backcourt setting line
Player #3 has already moved into player #1's starting position and the drill is repeated

*This drill can become a non-stop drill depending on skill level.

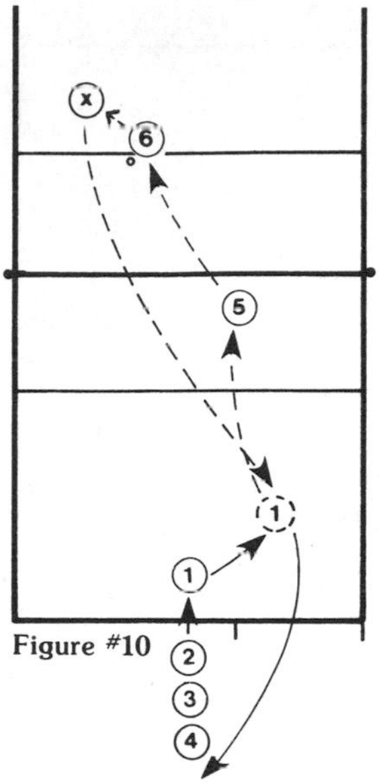

Figure #10

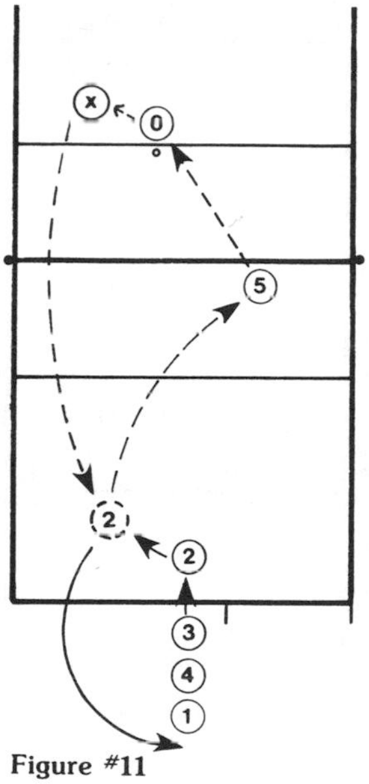

Figure #11

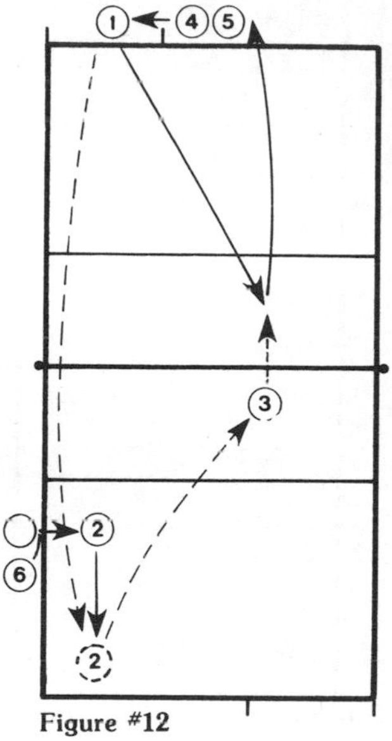

Figure #12

FIGURE #10

Purpose: Lateral movement in service reception
Accuracy of service reception after movement

Explanation: Coach serves ball to court position #1
Player #6 immediately hands the coach another ball
Player #1 must move from court position #6 to court position #1 and receives service

FIGURE #11

Player #1 passes to player #5
Player #5 rolls the ball to player #6 while player #2 moves into position
Coach serves to position #5
Player #2 moves to position #5 and receives service
Player #2 returns to the end of the line while player #3 moves into position
Repeat drill

FIGURE #12

Purpose: Service accuracy
Ability to judge trajectory of service
Improve backward movement combined with accurate service reception

Explanation: Player #1 serves to court position #5
Player #2 moves as soon as judgment of service trajectory can be made
Player #2 quickly back peddles and executes accurate service reception pass to player #3
Player #1 retrieves his own ball and returns to end of service line
Players #2 and #6 assume #1's and #2's starting positions

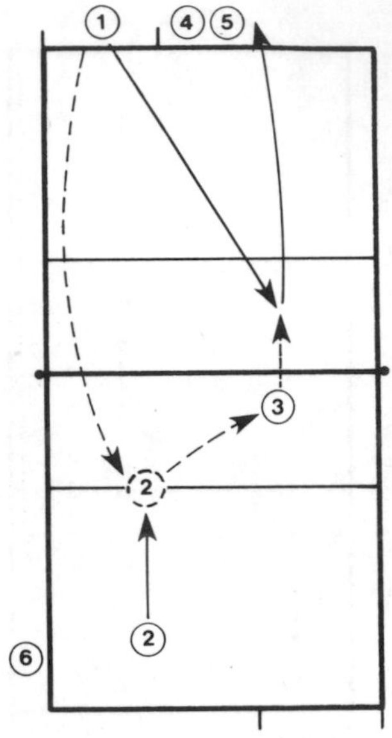

Figure #13

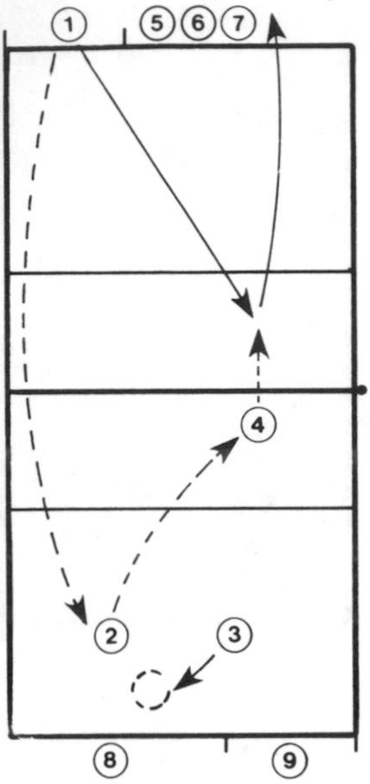

Figure #14

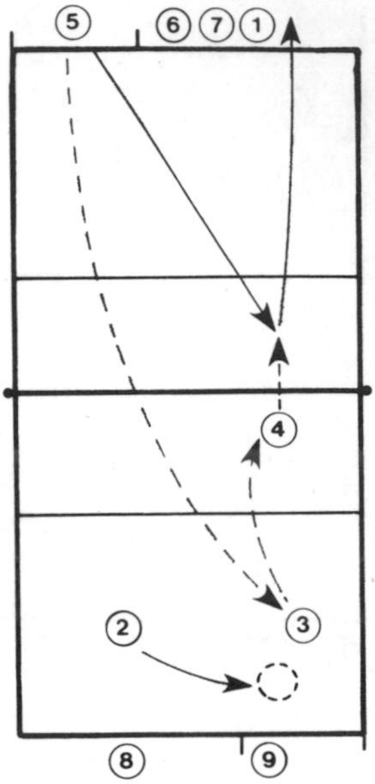

Figure #15

FIGURE #13

Player #1 serves to position #4

Player #2 starts in as soon as the service trajectory can be judged

Player #2 moves forward and executes an accurate service reception pass to player #3

Player #1 retrieves his own ball and returns to end of service line

Players #4 and #6 assume #1's and #2's starting positions

***Both these drills should be run to the right side of the receiving court (positions #1 and #2)**

FIGURE #14

Purpose: Service reception teamwork between the two back receivers

One receiver will pass the ball while the other backs him up, calls ball in or out

Service accuracy

Explanation: Player #1 serves to court position #5

Player #2 receives service while player #3 moves to assist

Player #2 passes to player #4

Player #1 retrieves his own ball

FIGURE #15

Then player #5 moves into the service corner and serves to position #1

Player #3 receives service while player #2 moves to assist

Player #3 passes to player #4

Player #5 retrieves his own ball and returns to end of serving line

Repeat drill with players #8 and #9

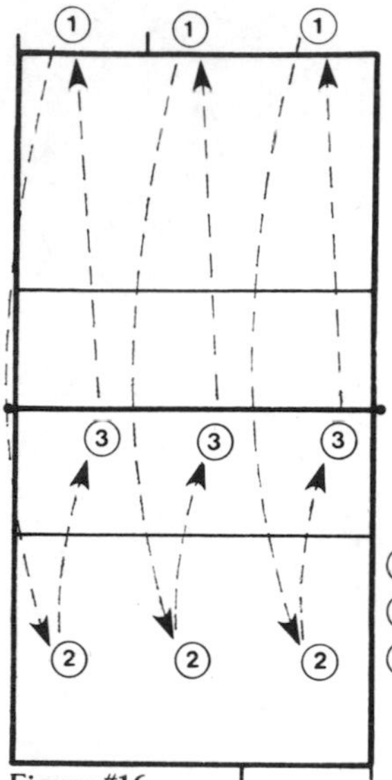

Figure #16

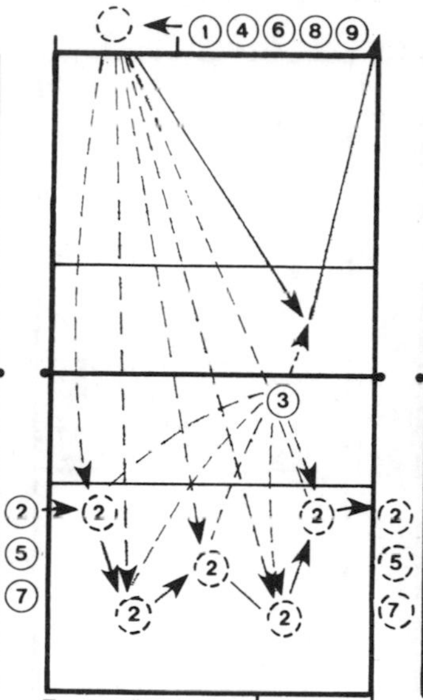

Figure #17

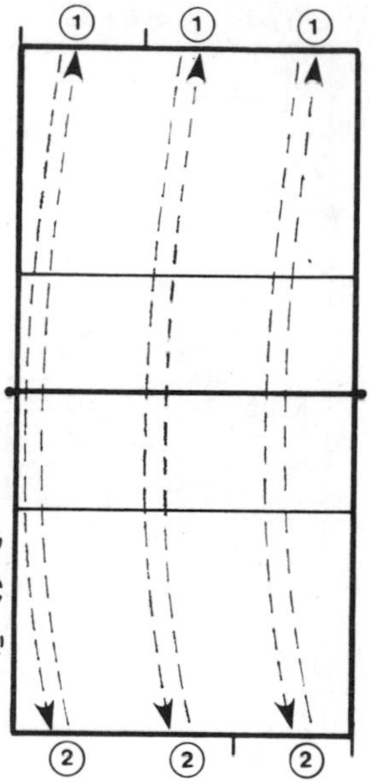

Figure #18

FIGURE #16

Purpose: Service accuracy
Correct positioning of receiver for reception
Service reception accuracy

Explanation: Player #1 serves to player #2
Player #2 passes to player #3
Player #3 catches the ball and quickly rolls it back to player #1

FIGURE #17

Purpose: Service accuracy
Develop ability to receive from all positions
Service reception accuracy

Explanation: Player #1 moves into service corner and serves to court position #4
Player #2 receives service and passes to #3 and moves to left back reception position
Player #1 retrieves the ball from player #3 while player #4 serves to player #5
The drill continues until player #2 receives in all 5 receiving positions and players #1, 4, 6, 8 & 9 all served one ball
Repeat drill with player #5...

FIGURE #18

Purpose: Improve service technique
Develop service accuracy

Explanation: Player #1 serves straight ahead toward player #2
Player #2 retrieves ball and immediately returns service to player #1

*A variation to this drill is to tie a rope approx. 2' above the net and have players serve between the net and rope.

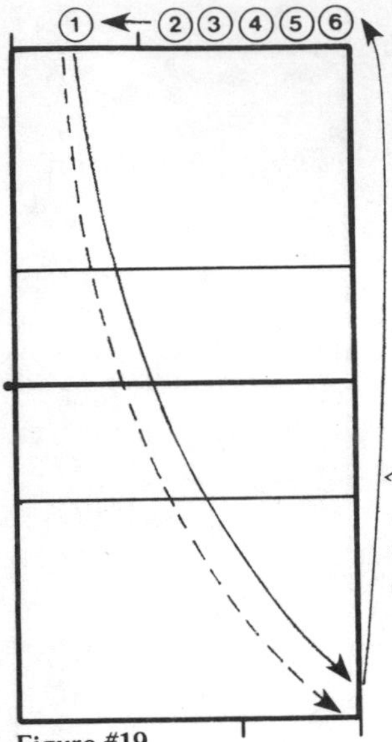

Figure #19

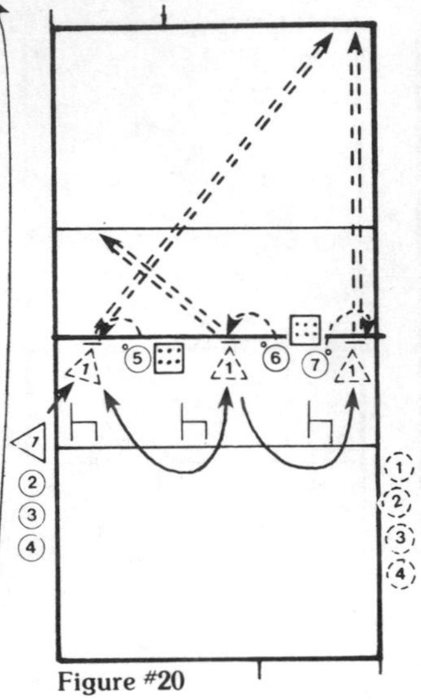

Figure #20

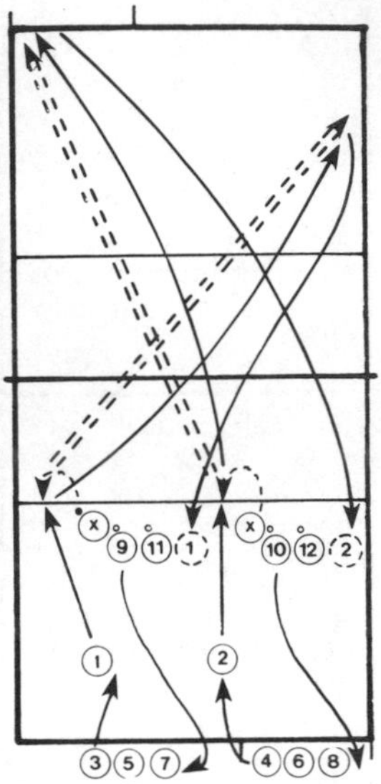

Figure #21

FIGURE #19

Purpose: Tactical and precision service

Explanation: Player #1 serves to court position #1 then retrieves ball and returns to end of line

Player #2 moves into service corner as soon as player #1 completes service

Player #2 immediately serves to position #1 and retrieves ball

*This service drill should be used to all 6 court positions.

FIGURE #20

Purpose: Spiking efficiency under pressure

Conditioning

Explanation: Player #5 tosses a ball for player #1

Player #1 spikes and immediately runs around the center chair to attack at court position #3

Player #6 tosses the ball as soon as player #1 reaches the center chair

Player #1 completes spike in position #3 then proceeds around the chair to position #2 as player #7 tosses the ball

Player #1 completes the 3rd spike and waits till the last player completes the drill then repeats the drill from right to left

FIGURE #21

Purpose: Develop the ability to spike from behind the 3m line

Explanation: Coach tosses the ball about 8' from the net

Player #1 starts from the service reception position in court position #5

Player #1 approaches and jumps behind the 3m line, flys forward and spikes to position #5 on the opposite court

Player #1 retrieves the ball and assumes position at the end of the feeding line

After he hands the coach the ball he returns to the spiking line

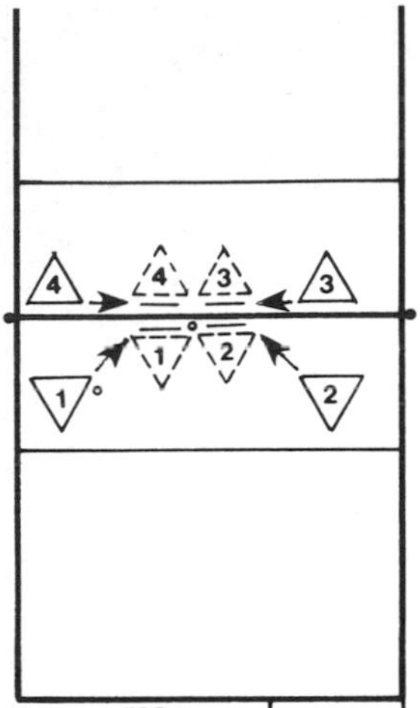
Figure #22

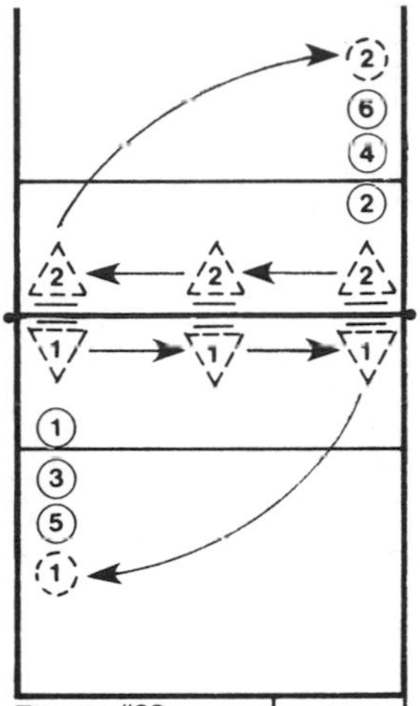
Figure #23

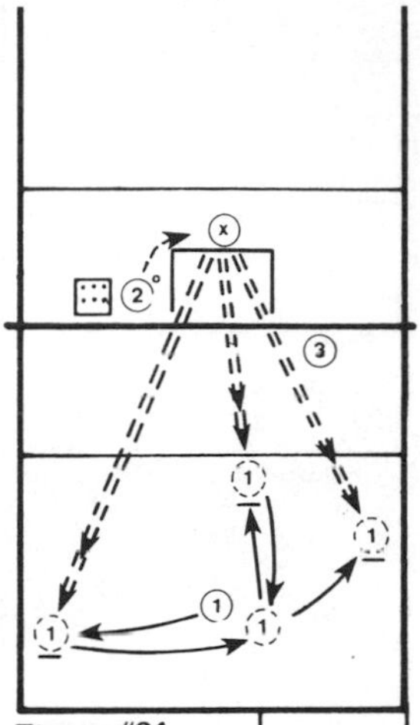
Figure #24

FIGURE #22

Purpose: Teach teamwork in blocking

Explanation: Player #1 holds ball in his right hand

Player #1 moves toward net, players #2, 3 & 4 also move toward net simultaneously

Players #1, 2, 3 and 4 jump and form block around player #1's ball at the same time

After landing they return to starting position and repeat

FIGURE #23

Purpose: Teach blocking footwork and form

Explanation: Player #1 moves forward maximum jumps and blocks

Player #2 also moves forward and blocks in court position #4

Players #1 & 2 meet at position #3 and block against each other

Player #3 approaches to block against player #2 at #3 position while player #1 will block against player #4 at player #4's court position #4

After completing 3 blocks the player returns to the end of original line and drill continues

FIGURE #24

Purpose: Court mobility

Backcourt defensive techniques (dive & roll)

Explanation: Coach stands on a platform with one player handing him balls

Player #1 starts in court position #6 and on coach's signal moves to position #5

Coach control spikes to position #5, player #1 must pass ball to player #3 using any possible technique

Player #1 immediately returns to starting position, coach control spikes to position #3, player #1 receives ball and passes to player #3 and again returns to starting position

Coach control spikes a 3rd time to position #1, player #1 moves from starting position and must pass to player #3, then player #1 stays on right side of the court until all players are done and then drill is repeated from right to left

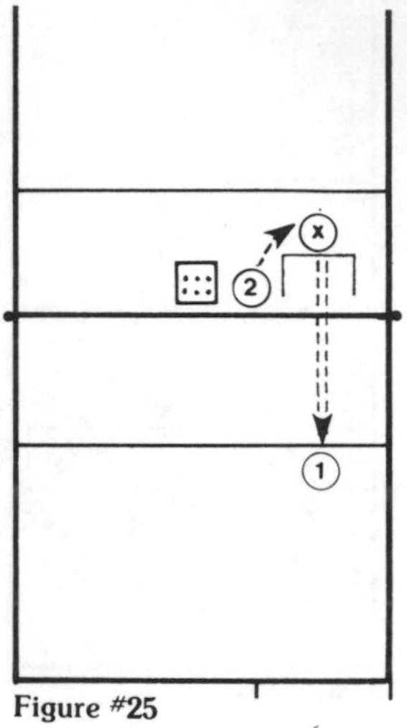

Figure #25

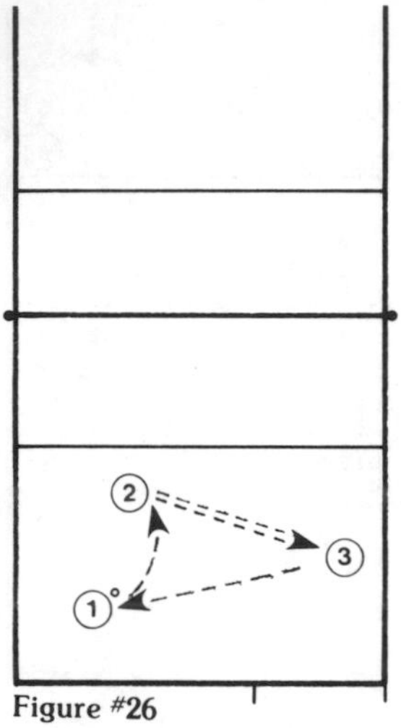

Figure #26

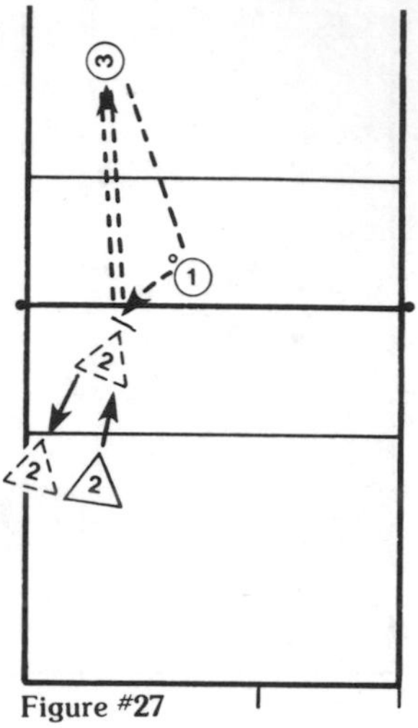

Figure #27

FIGURE #25

Purpose: Develop player reaction time
Develop courage in receiving hard spike

Explanation: Coach stands on a platform with one player handing him balls
Coach spikes hard to player #1
Player #1 must attempt to dig every ball
Player #2 feeds the coach balls as fast as possible
Player #1 digs 20 balls then is relieved

FIGURE #26

Purpose: Ball control
Variation of pepper drill which combines 3 basic skills
Conditioning

Explanation: Player #1 starts the drill by setting to player #2
Player #2 spikes to player #3
Player #3 digs the ball to player #1
Player #1 continues drill by setting to #2

FIGURE #27

Purpose: Ball control
Pepper drill variation
Skill development
Conditioning

Explanation: Player #1 sets the ball over the net to player #2
Player #2 approaches and spikes to player #3
Player #3 digs ball back to player #1
Player #1 continues the drill by setting player #2 who approaches and spikes to #3

*The speed of the spike should be geared to the skill level of players.

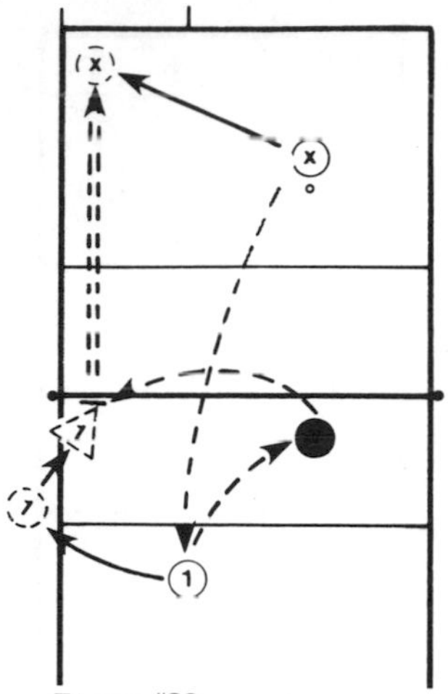
Figure #28

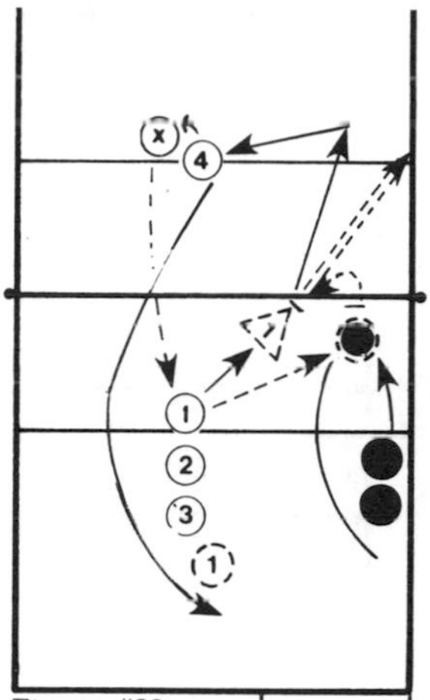
Figure #29

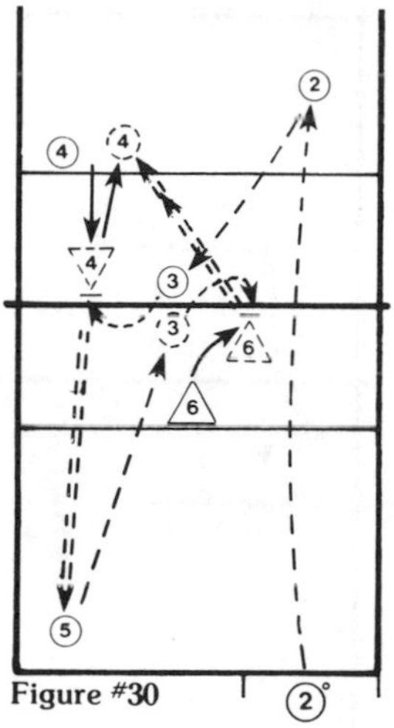
Figure #30

FIGURE #28

Purpose: Develop spiking precision

Explanation: Coach tosses a ball to player #1

Player #1 passes the ball to the setter who sets the ball high outside

Player #1 approaches to spike

Coach moves from his original position to another area of the court

Player #1 must find his target (coach) and spike in his direction

FIGURE #29

Purpose: Freeball passing

Quick attack after passing

Jump setting quick attack

Explanation: Coach tosses a freeball to player #1

Player #1 passes to the setter who has penetrated from the right side of the court

Setter jump-sets a quick to player #1 and returns to setting line

Player #1 retrieves ball, hands it to player #4 who feeds the coach

Player #1 returns to end of line

FIGURE #30

Purpose: Ball control

Skill execution of all basic skills

Explanation: Player #1 serves to player #2 who service receives to player #3

Player #3 sets to player #4 who spikes to player #5

Player #5 is digging line and passes spiked ball to player #3 who has moved under the net

Player #3 sets to player #6 who controls spikes to player #4

*This drill can end with player #4's dig or can be continued between players #3, 4, 5 & 6.
**This drill should be to the skill level of the players—e.g., player #4's spike may also be a controlled spike.

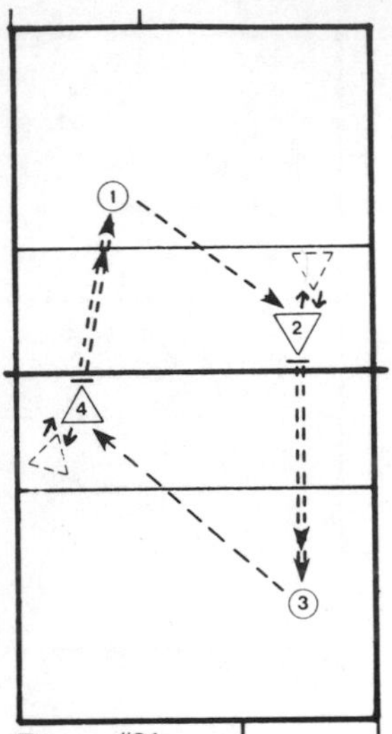

Figure #31

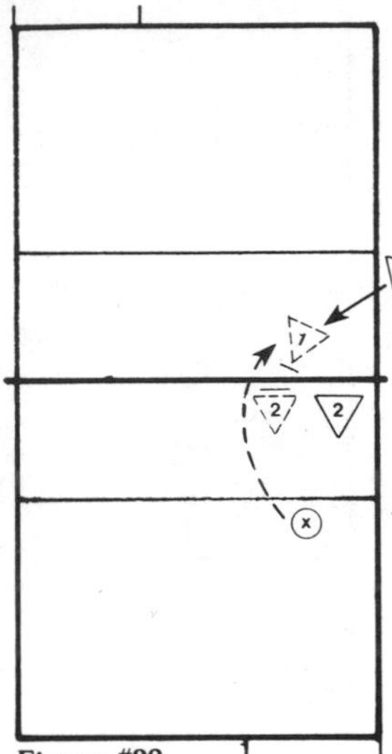

Figure #32

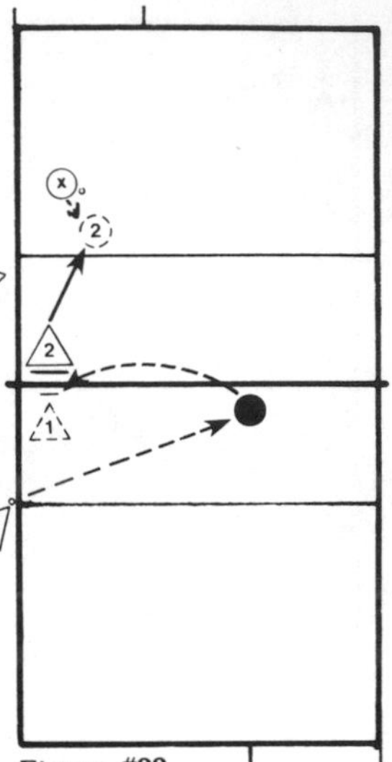

Figure #33

FIGURE #31

Purpose: Spiking control
Digging control

Explanation: Player #1 starts the drill by setting to court position #4

Player #2 moves off the net as soon as player #1 sets the ball and spikes to player #3

Player #3 dig passes to player #4 who has moved off the net to spike

Player #4 spikes to player #1 who continues drill by dig passing again to player #2

FIGURE #32

Purpose: Develop blocking in a 1 on 1 situation
Improve spiking against a block

Explanation: Coach standing behind #2 tosses a high pass above the net inside the 3m line

Player #1 approaches and attacks the ball

Player #2 attempts to block

*Use this drill in all 3 positions at the net.

FIGURE #33

Purpose: Spiking against block
Blocking 1 on 1
Movement from net after blocking to recover ball

Explanation: Player #1 tosses the ball to the setter who sets to court position #4

Player #1 approaches and spikes against player #2

Player #2, immediately after landing from block, must turn and pass the ball the coach tosses

Repeat drill

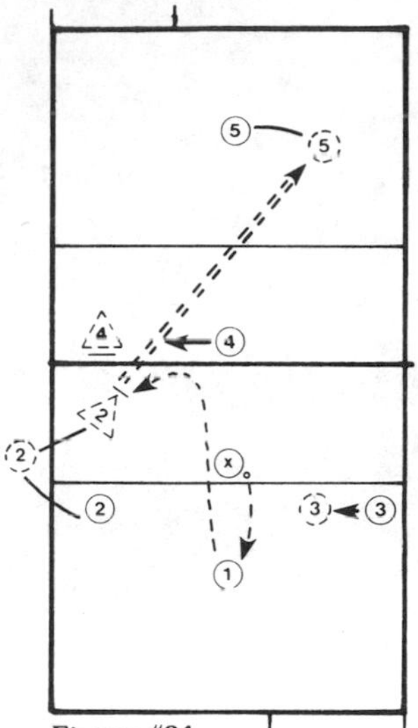
Figure #34

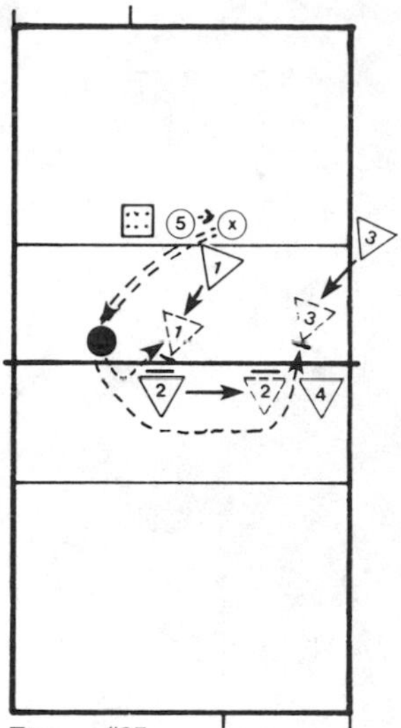
Figure #35

FIGURE #34

Purpose: Teach quick anticipation of a blocker and digger against a backcourt set

Explanation: Coach tosses the ball to player #1

Player #1 sets to either court position #2 or #4

Player #2 in this illustration is receiving the set so he moves into position to spike

Player #4 anticipates the set by player #1 to player #2 and moves to block

Player #4's assignment is to area block the line

Player #5 also anticipates the set and moves to cover cross-court spike by player #2

Player #5 bases his position in relation of the spiker to the block

After the dig, player #5 recovers to starting position and player #4 also returns to the starting position

Coach repeats the drill

FIGURE #35

Purpose: Develop middle blocker's ability to block short ball and still get outside to block

Teamwork on blocking of outside position

Setting short middle and high outside

Improve spiking against block

Explanation: Coach tosses a ball to the setter who sets quick to player #1 while player #2 blocks

Player #5 has already handed the coach another ball which he quickly tosses to the setter

The setter sets high outside while player #3 attacks

Player #2 now must move to the outside to help player #4 defend against the high outside attack

This completes one full sequence but it must be repeated a number of times

*A variation to this drill is to use the back set or combine all 3 options.

California
12
13
Cal

6
Offense

OFFENSIVE SYSTEMS

by
Mick Haley
Kellogg Community College

Court Positions—The court is usually divided into six zones *(Fig. #1).*

The Players' Positions—The six starting players must assume a rotational order which is similar to the court positions. The player rotation when the serve is won is always clockwise.

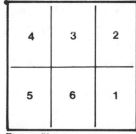

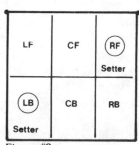

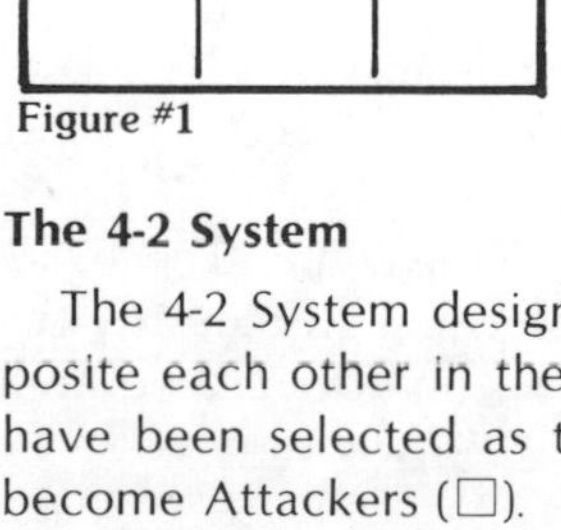

Figure #1

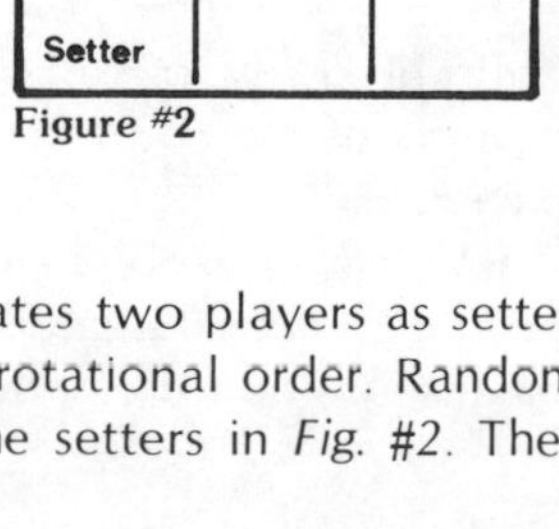

Figure #2

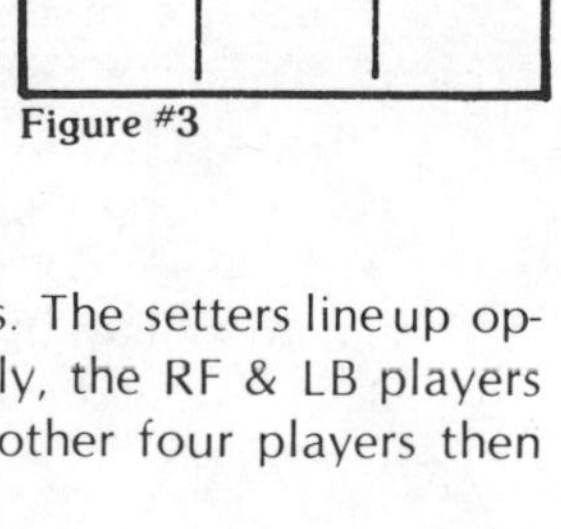

Figure #3

The 4-2 System

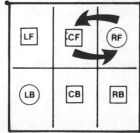

The 4-2 System designates two players as setters. The setters line up opposite each other in the rotational order. Randomly, the RF & LB players have been selected as the setters in *Fig. #2*. The other four players then become Attackers (□).

System #1—4 Attacker—2 Setter Offense

In this system the front row setter always moves to the center of the court within 10 feet of the net as the ball is served. The attackers position themselves on the outside boundaries of the court. Some advantages of this system include:

A. The attacker has more area diagonally to hit the ball into (42′ across court) *(Fig. #4).*

B. The attacker may intentionally spike the ball off the opposing blocker's hands so that it lands out of bounds *(Fig. #5).*

C. There is much less total team movement in this system therefore eliminating many errors and allowing teams whose players possess only adequate movement fundamentals to still be efficient and consistent. (**NOTE**: *BL stands for blockers — - - - - - indicates attackers' approach position.)*

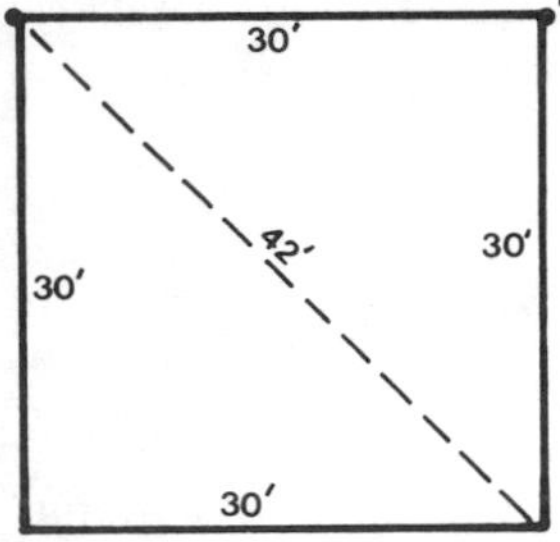

Figure #4

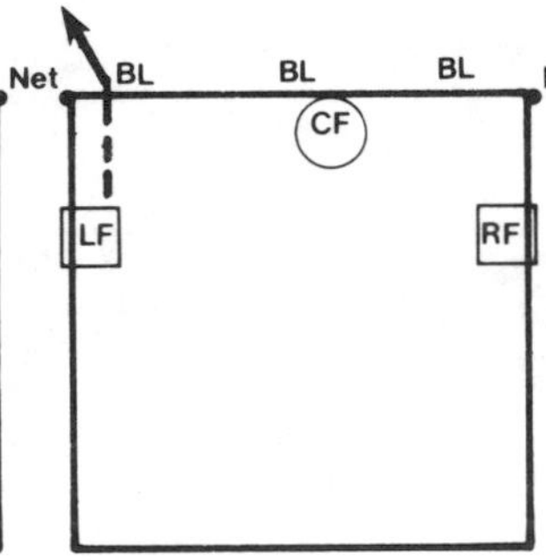

Figure #5

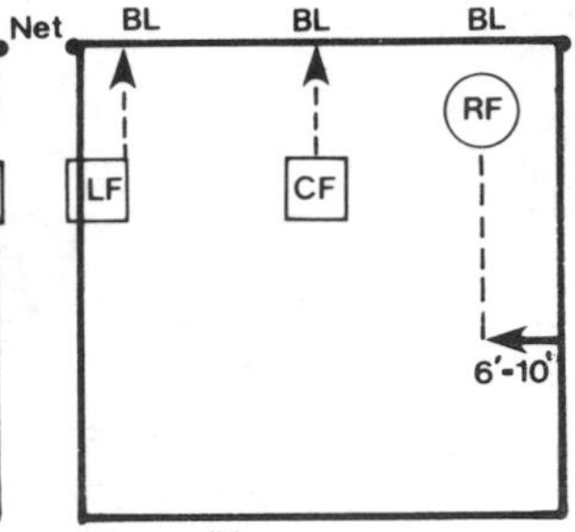

Figure #6

System #2— The International 4 Attacker—2 Setter Offense

In this system the front row setter attempts to position himself approximately 6′ to 10′ from the right side boundary line and within 10′ of the net. Both front row attackers will position themselves to the left of the setter, one in the middle of the court and one on the left boundary line *(Fig. #6).* Several advantages of this system include:

A. By having one attacker in the middle, more pressure is placed on the opposing center blocker. He must now guard against the center attack first, prior to moving to block the outside left attacker.

B. Attacking from the center of the court can be very effective against certain opposing players.

C. Some teams don't want their setters blocking in the center. The 4-2 international system can eliminate repeated blocking switches by the attackers and setter and position the setter in one designated area repeatedly.

The 4-2 System line-up at serve reception.

Players may not overlap positions until the server contacts the ball. Adjustment must then be made in the basic player position. The following diagrams illustrate the basic positions assumed by each player following the serve. *Fig. #7* shows the basic adjustments from the original positions in *Fig. #2* while *Figs. #8* & *#9* illustrate appropriate adjustments after the first and second rotations.

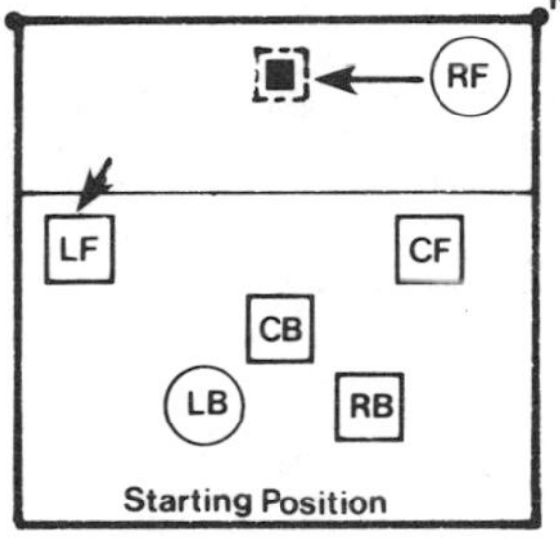

Figure #7

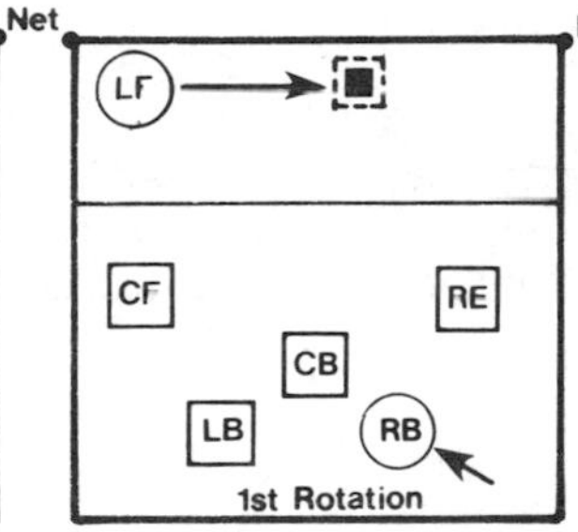

Figure #8

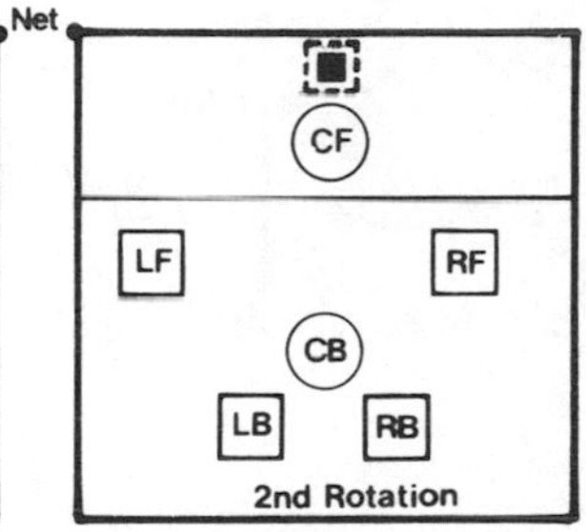

Figure #9

NOTE: *indicates approximate spot setter will move to.*

In each of the first two diagrams above, the front row setter moves to the center of the court as soon as the ball is contacted by the opposing server. In *Fig. #9*, the setter's natural position is in the middle and therefore no switching is required.

The International 4-2 System at serve reception.

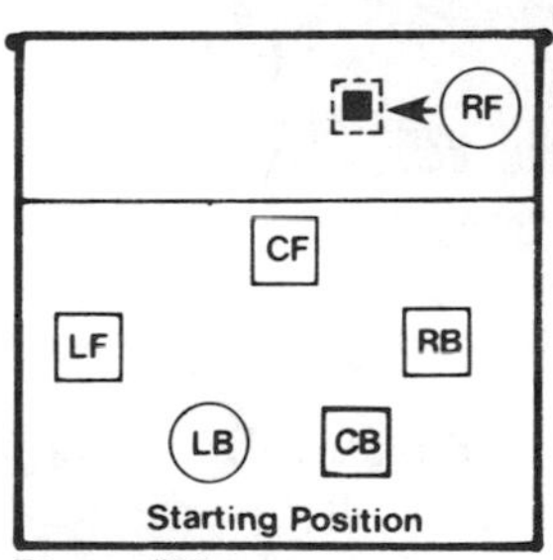

Figure #10

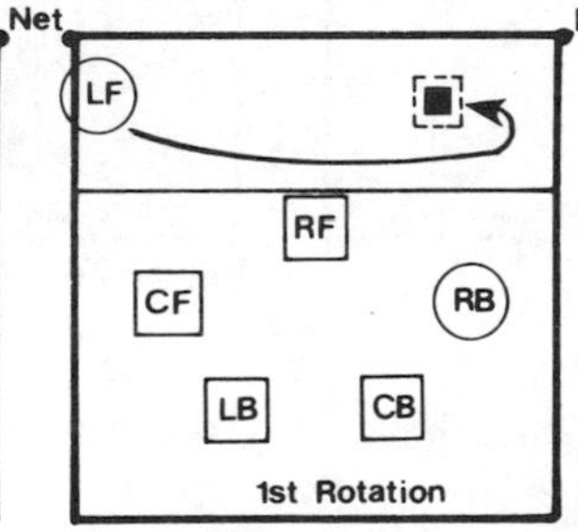

Figure #11

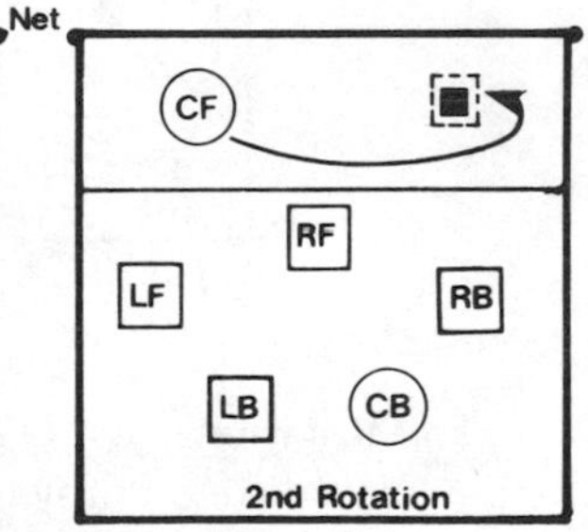

Figure #12

NOTE: *indicates the position on the court that the setter will move to in anticipation of the pass.*

In each diagram the setter positions himself about 10 feet from the right side line immediately following contact by the opposing server. The attackers will then be spiking in only the left and center portions of the court at the net.

THE STANDARD 6-2 MULTIPLE OFFENSE SYSTEM

From a Basic 5-Man Serve Reception Formation.

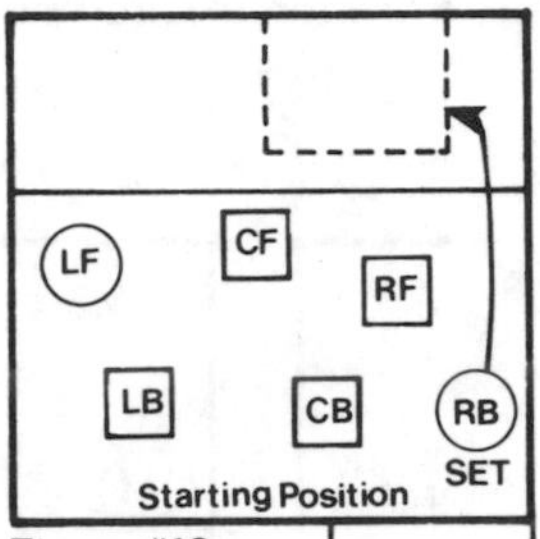

Figure #13

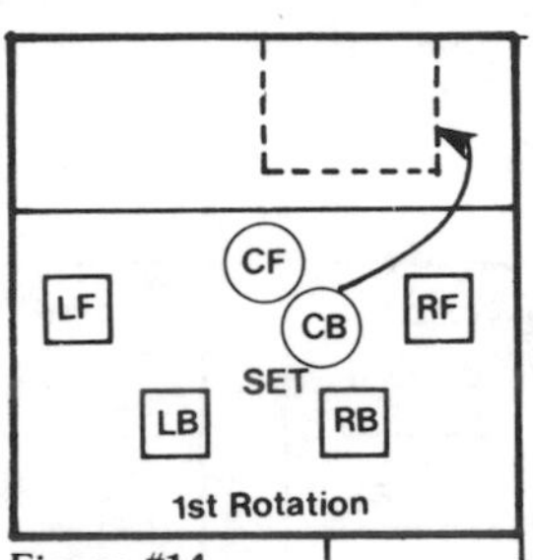

Figure #14

In *Figs. #13 and #14* it is relatively easy for the back row setter to slip to the front row and into position prior to the ball passing over the net. In each case, the setter may not overlap prior to the serve being contacted. If the pass is good, this system will allow the team to have three (3) spikers available to attack from three (3) different areas. This will make blocking much more difficult for the other team.

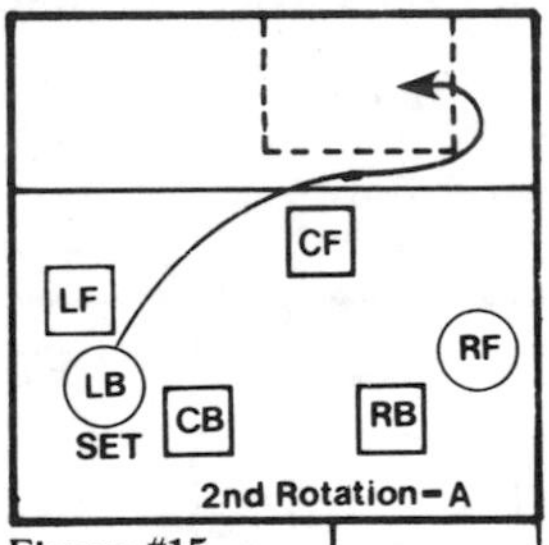

Figure #15

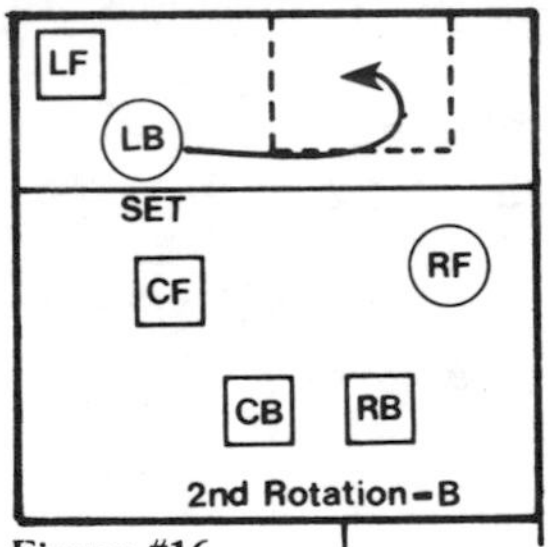

Figure #16

2nd Rotation—A *(Fig. 15)*—In this rotation the setter in the left back position has a difficult move in front of the Center Front and Center Back partially blocking their view as the serve is in the air. This move should be made quickly with the setter being in position prior to the ball being passed by a teammate.

2nd Rotation—B *(Fig. #16)*—2nd rotation from a 4-man reception pattern is common for teams with less mobile setters but good passers.

NOTE: *LB may not overlap vertically with LF or horizontally with CB until the serve is contacted.*

THE STANDARD 5-1 MULTIPLE OFFENSE SYSTEM

From a Basic 4-Man Serve Reception Formation.

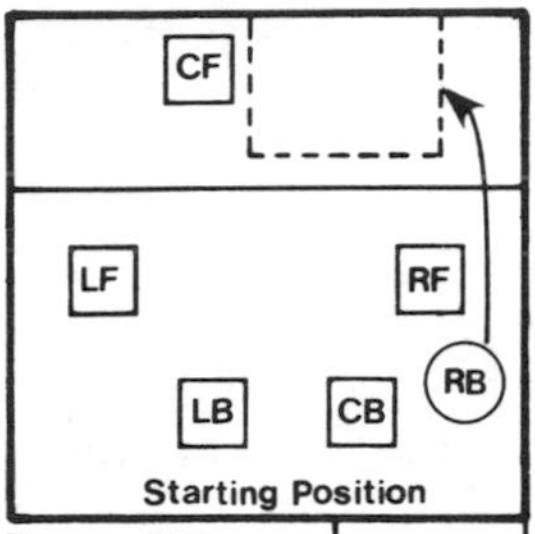

Figure #17

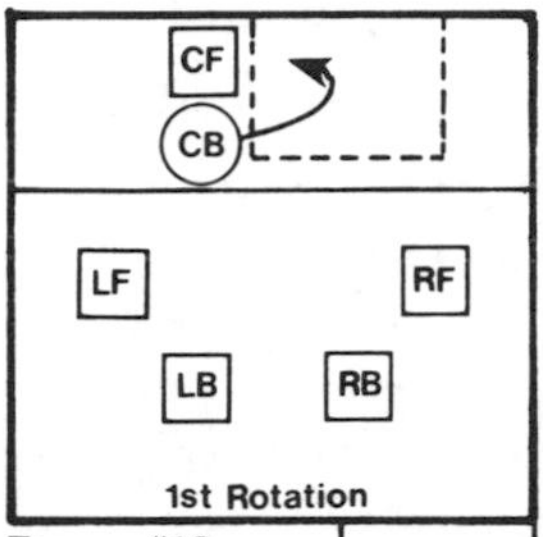

Figure #18

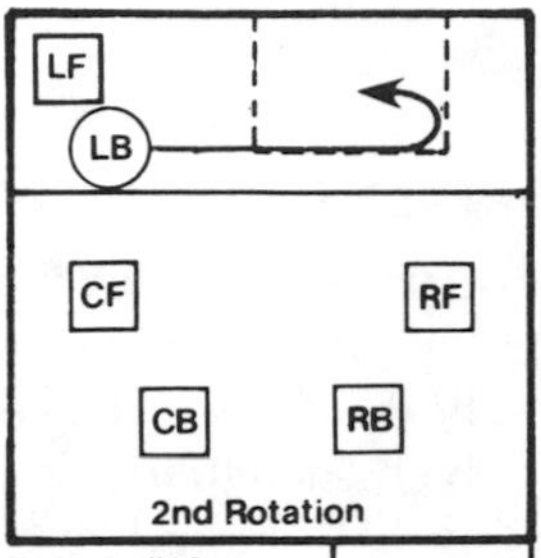

Figure #19

In *Fig. 17* & *18* we observe the same situation as described in *Fig. 13* & *14*.
2nd Rotation—*(Fig. 19)* is the same as *Fig. #16*.

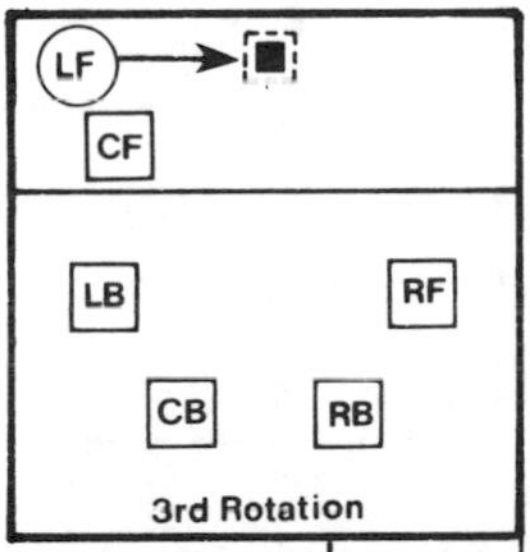

Figure #20

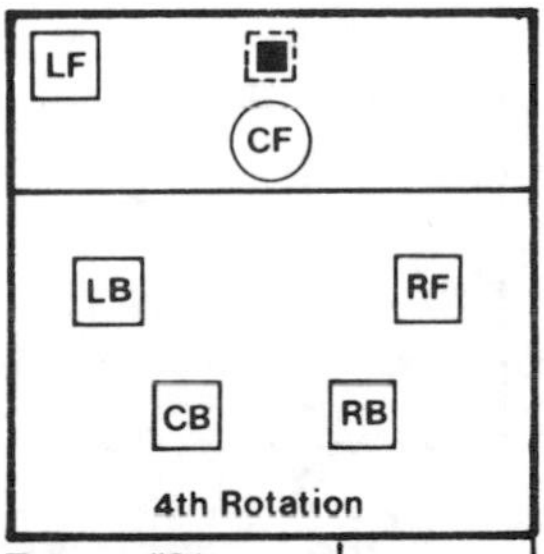

Figure #21

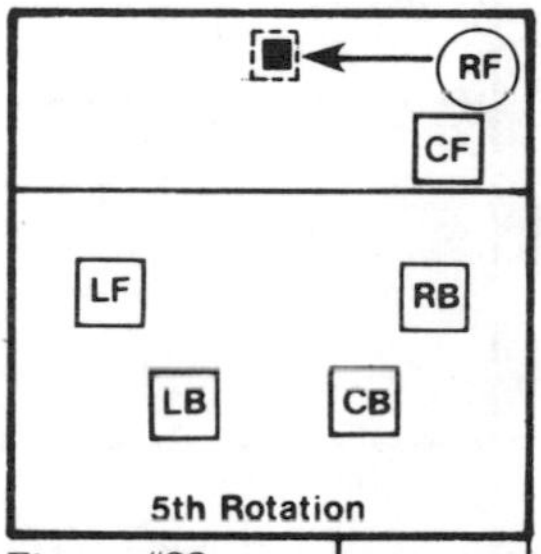

Figure #22

3rd Rotation—*(Fig. 20)* is the same as *Fig. #8* except using a 4-man reception pattern.

4th & 5th Rotations—*(Fig. #21* and *#22)* are the same as *Fig. #9* and *#7* with the exception of the 4-man reception pattern.

The 5-1 system designates one player as the setter. The other five players then become attackers. This system combines both the 6-2 Offense and the 4-2 Offense. When the setter is in the backcourt *(Figs. 17, 18* and *19) he is running a 6-2 Offense system as shown in Figs. 13, 14* and *15)*, with the only difference being a 4-man service reception pattern.

*Note: Both service reception formations can be used in either offensive system. For illustration purposes we diagrammed the 6-2 system using a 5-man receive and the 5-1 system using a 4-man receive. When the setter has rotated to the front court *(Figs. 20, 21* and *22)* he is running a 4-2 offensive system as shown in *Figs. 8, 9,* and *7*, again with the only difference being a 4-man service reception pattern.

TEAM OFFENSE AND ATTACK TACTICS

by
Vic Lindal
British Columbia Volleyball Association

FAST SET OFFENSIVE SYSTEMS AND TACTICS

I Fast 4-2 principles and tactics

The key is to create deception with only two hitters. This can be achieved best if the setter uses the jump set option. All passes to the setter should be high enough to allow him to spike or set. The two spikers can vary their attack positions in order to create deception. The ultimate in this system is to have only the front row player be the setter.

A) These diagrams show the basic medium length sets.

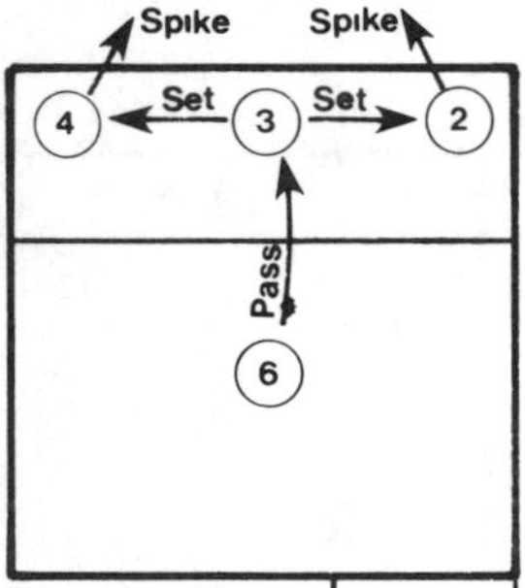

Diagram #1

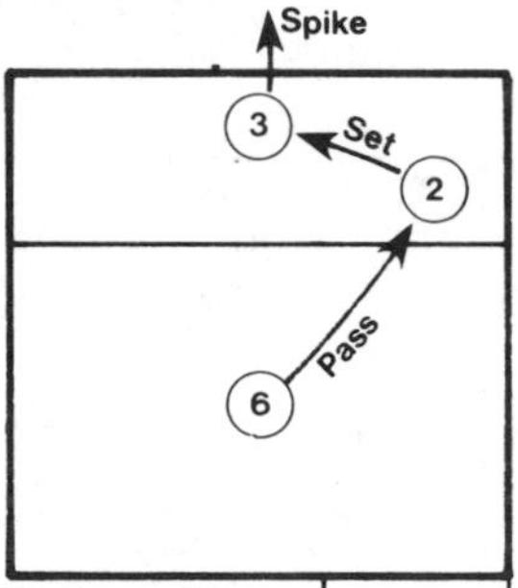

Diagram #2

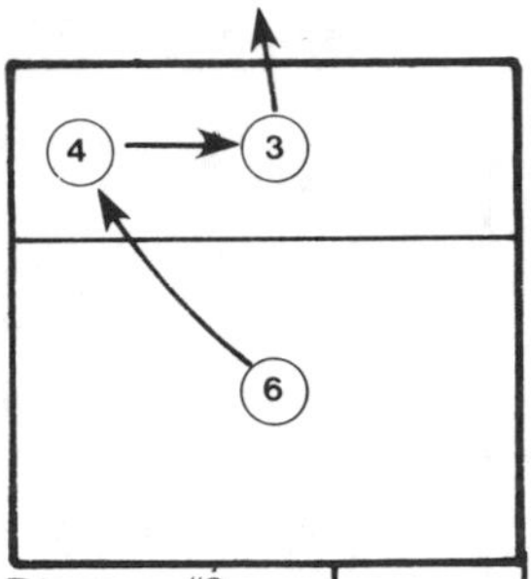

Diagram #3

B) The next phase is to add the longer cross court sets to the above progressions.

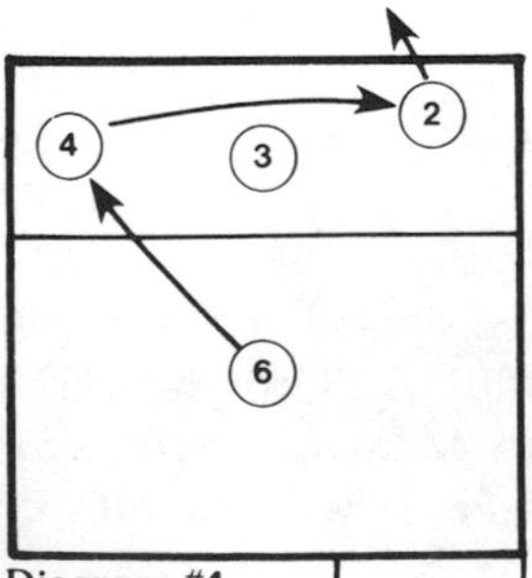

Diagram #4

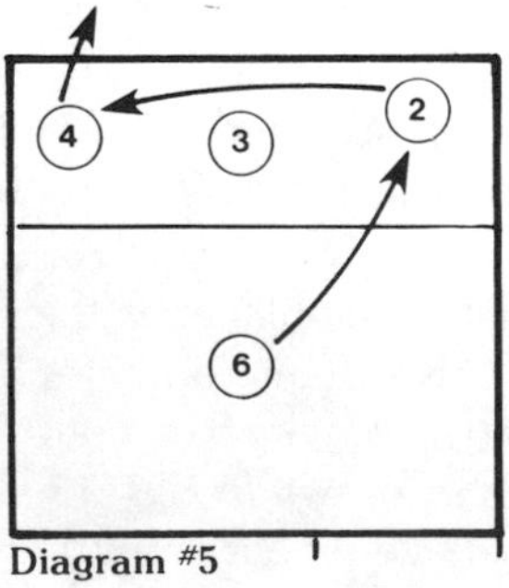

Diagram #5

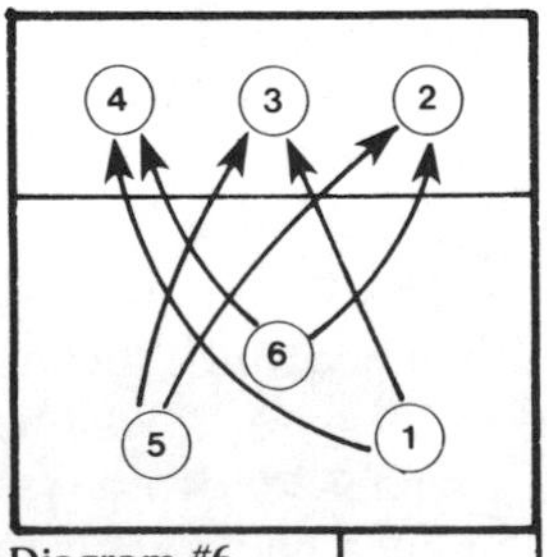

Diagram #6

From the above stages we can move to interesting combinations. First we can look at the first pass option. The above diagrams show the possible flights of the first ball when played by the back row.

C) Special options on a 4-2 system

Option #1

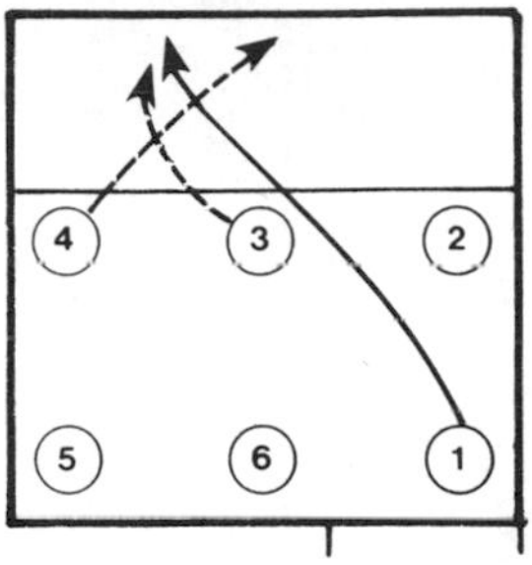

In this option number 4 approaches for a spike and does a fake spike with an overhead jump set to #3 who has moved behind.

Diagram #7

Option #2

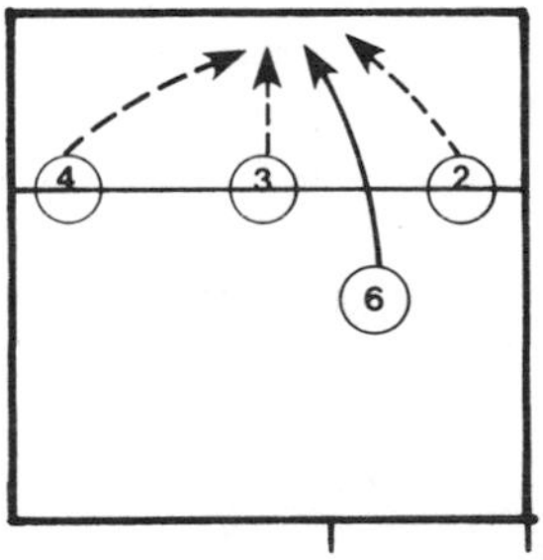

#6 passes the ball directly to #3 who approaches for a spike. #4 and #2 follow closely to #3 in anticipation of a quick set to either of them. #3 has the option of spiking the first ball or using a short set to either #4 or #2. The 4-2 system can be combined with all other systems to give new approaches to the game.

Diagram #8

II "Fast" Multiple Offense

This system can only be used effectively if a good pass is made to the setter. It has been found that shoot sets can be made to the corners even when the pass is well off the net. The next thing of interest is that to run fast shoot sets is not really very difficult if the setter will place the ball in the same place everytime.

Because the attack system uses a fast set as part of the attack it becomes very important for setters to learn how to have the set die at the right time. That is to say, the ball should end its flight at the side line or just past. Many setters have what is referred to as live shoots (they sail past our spiker).

For the fast attack system to have maximum effect players should specialize in certain positions. Some players should learn quick hits and some should learn the necessary shots from the left and right front positions.

Coaches will need to determine who calls the play. Some teams have the spikers call; others leave it in the hands of the setter and still others have the coach direct it. When the setter calls the plays, all players go and he decides who will get it based on the circumstances. Some teams will use this but allow the spiker to call off the play. In the coach directed situation all service reception and "attack" ball plays are determined ahead of time. The team usually sticks with the set reception plays and changes the attack ball plays to fit the needs of the game.

A key factor in running fast attacks is to stay with the game plan and only move when you have firmly established the first play.

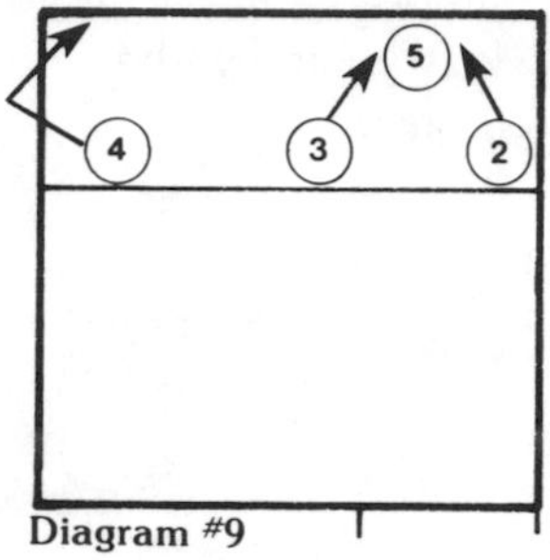

Diagram #9

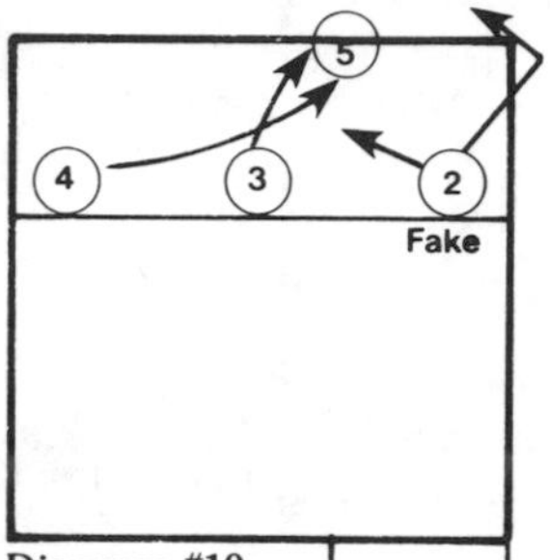

Diagram #10

Use the above basic play (diagram 9) for a good portion of the game to set the opponents up for this play. (diagram 10). Now #4 comes in to hit a tandem after #3. The tandem will only be effective if the "51" or quick hit by #3 has already been established. Note that #2 can approach at the line for a "72" or overhead shoot set after faking to the left. #2's play is again predicated on establishing a good quick hit directly behind the setter shown in the first diagram. Most teams only need a small number of options to be effective, but for general information we can diagram other variations.

Interesting 6-2 options using all players for spiking.

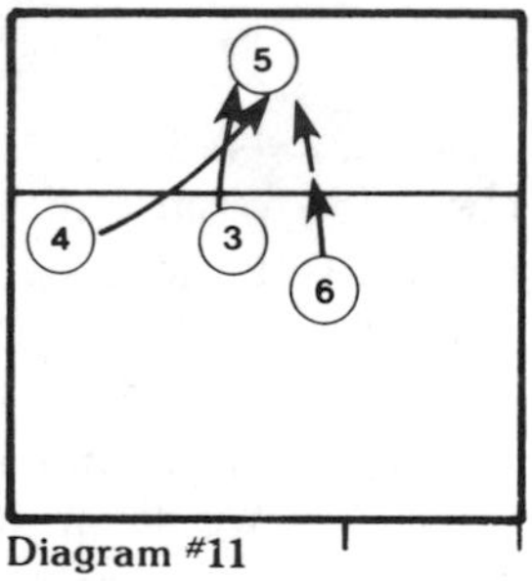

Diagram #11

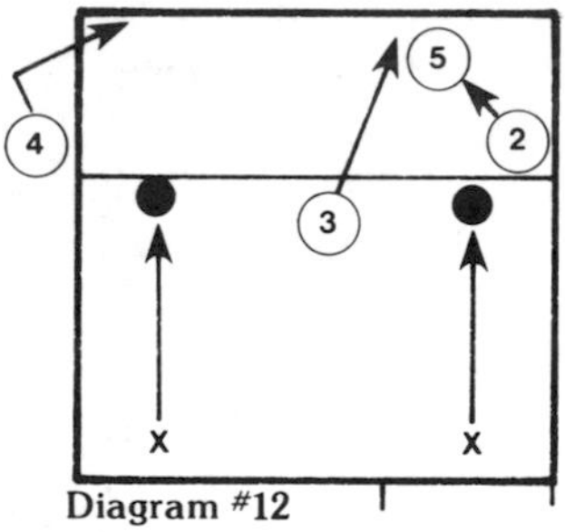

Diagram #12

Diagram 11 illustrates a double tandem with #6 taking off from the 3 meter line. In diagram 12 all front row players attack in a normal fashion with set going to the left back player who leaves from the 3 meter line.

Diagrams 9 & 10 show an attack system that was based on lateral play at the net. In Diagrams 11 & 12 we have combined this with the use of back row hitters. This vertical play adds a new dimension to attack systems. All attack systems are an attempt to beat the defense in the following ways: (1) by increasing the number of players at the net, (2) by making the attack so fast that the opposition doesn't have time to form the block, (3) by fake action spikes so that the opposition cannot form the block, (4) by attacking the full length of the net, and (5) by introducing back row attackers.

DISGUISING THE SETTER IN A 5-1 OFFENSIVE SYSTEM

by
Lorne Sawula
University of British Columbia

The 5-1 offensive system employs one setter and five attackers. The one setter must set every play into attack. When in the back row no difficulty results, there will always be three attackers in the front court. This part of the offense is similar to the 6-2. However, once the setter moves into the front court, or the No. 4 position, he must continue to set. The advantage here is that you will be able to use his strong setting. Because he is usually involved in setting only two attackers are left. At this point, the opposition, if alert, can more easily key on two attackers, rather than the normal three.

Normally the rotations for a 5-1 offense are as follows:

Back Court

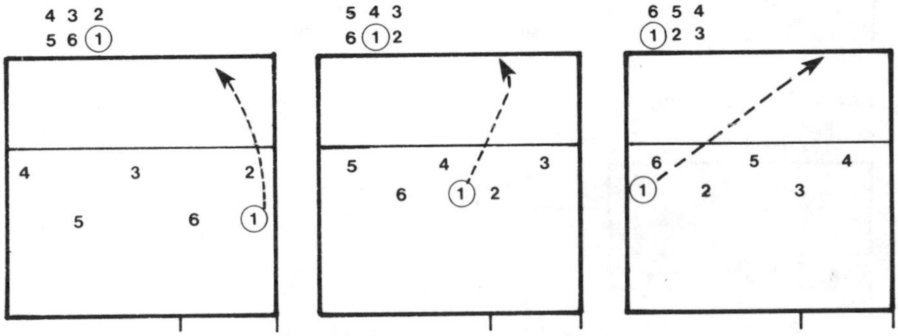

Front Court

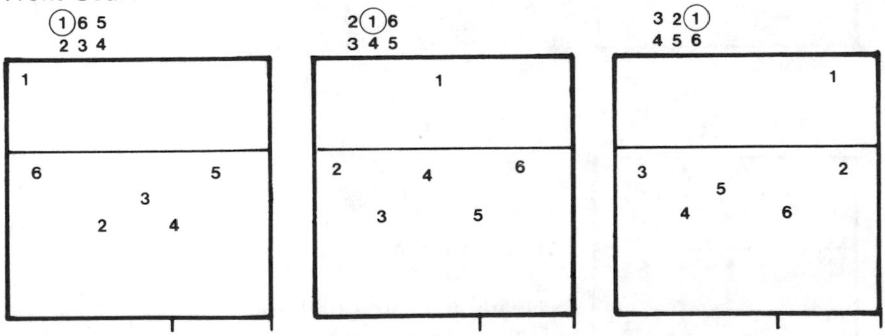

In the front court the setter can play either of the three blocking positions. Since most attack zones are to the right half of center, it is highly probable that the setter will play R F or the No. 2 position. In the front court diagrams, no effort was made to make the opposition think they may have to defend against three attackers. Except for rare cases when the setter, No. 1, attacks, only two attackers are available. This should make it easier for your opposition to block you.

Since the game of volleyball is very fast, an effort should be made to try to take advantage of this trait. By disguising the front court setter in a 5-1 system, one may be able to make the opposition block three hitters anyhow. This can be done in many ways; some I will now show.

I. SETTER IN THE NO. 4 POSITION

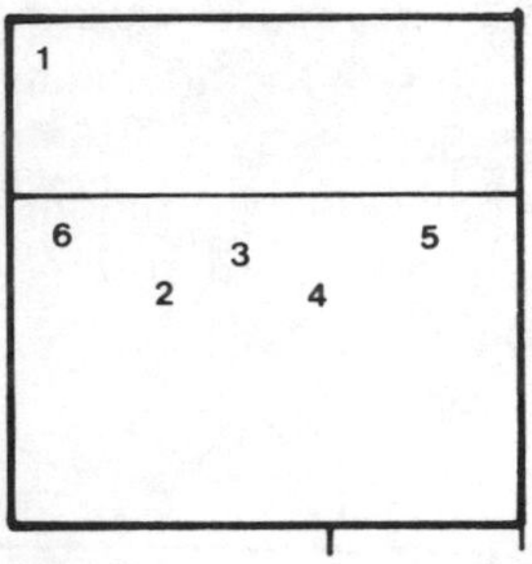

* Normal 4-2

* No. 1 is the setter

* Try to make the line-up look the same when the setter is in No. 5 position or No. 4 position.

EXAMPLE A:

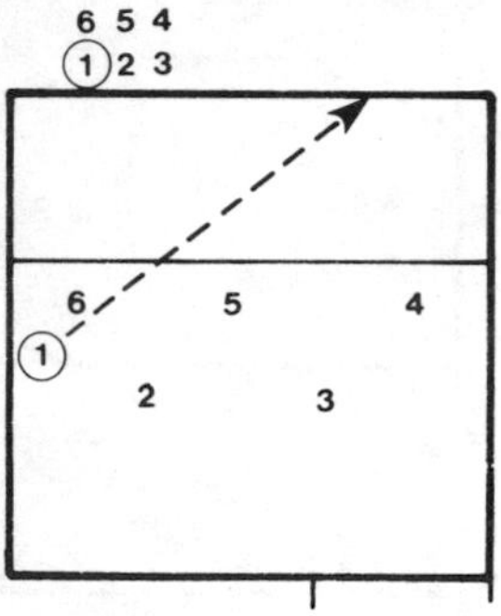

* Line-up when setter is in the No. 5 position

* No. 1 can either cross in front of 6 or behind 6.

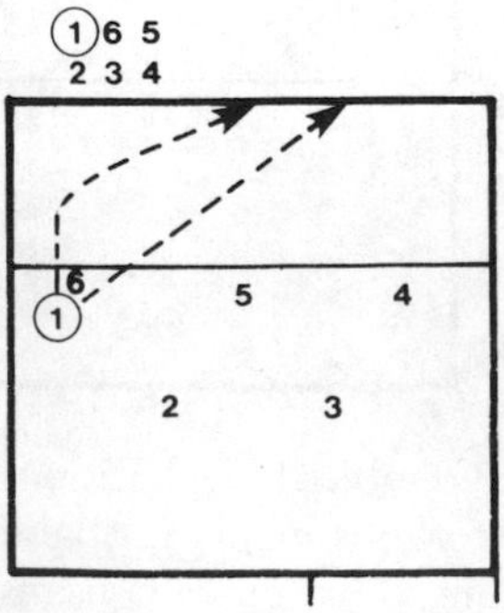

* Line-up when setter is in the No. 4 position.

* Nearly the same pattern as above but No. 4 has to be careful not to overlap with No. 5.

These two patterns in example 'A' are good if No. 6 is a power hitter. He will be able to hit twice on the left side without switching. Notice that the setter in the second diagram looks like a backcourt penetrator. No. 1 must take care to have No. 6 to his right. In order to get into the attack zone No. 1 may move up to the line. Then when the ball is contacted for service, No. 1 may move directly across the net. This forward movement is legal as long as No. 1 doesn't cross No. 6's path. Also it can prove distracting for the server.

The No. 4 player may be used to fake an attack or attack taking off from behind the 3 meter line. This also is a very interesting use of a back court player.

EXAMPLE B:

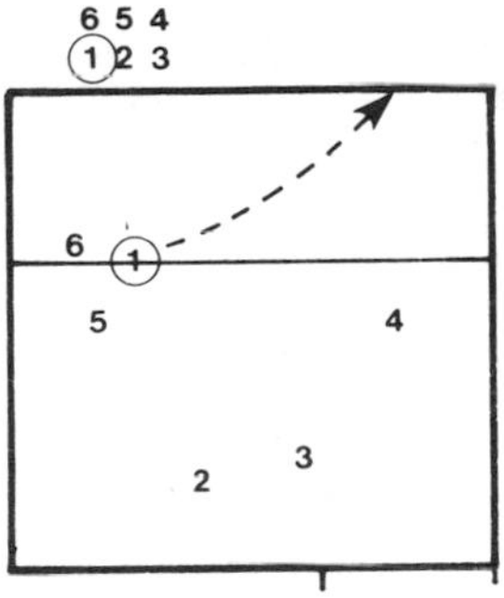

* Line-up when setter is in the No. 5 position

* No. 1 has to be concerned with No. 2 in regards to the overlap rule. No. 6, 5 and 4 are legal front court attackers.

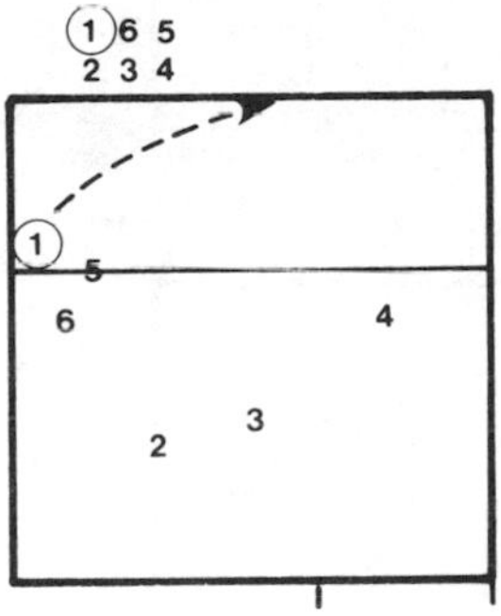

* Line-up when the setter is in the No. 4 position

* Nearly the same pattern as above. No. 1, 5 and 6 must be careful with overlap, as shown No. 4. This is a "stack".

Probably when the setter is in the No. 4 position it would be better to have No. 6 be the power hitter and attack from the outside, but he also could be the center hitter. No. 5 would spike and block from the center position. To keep the opposition honest, No. 4 can either fake the attack or spike from behind the three meter line.

EXAMPLE C: Disguise your penetration. This alignment only allows two attackers and can cause difficulties if the ball is served at No. 1.

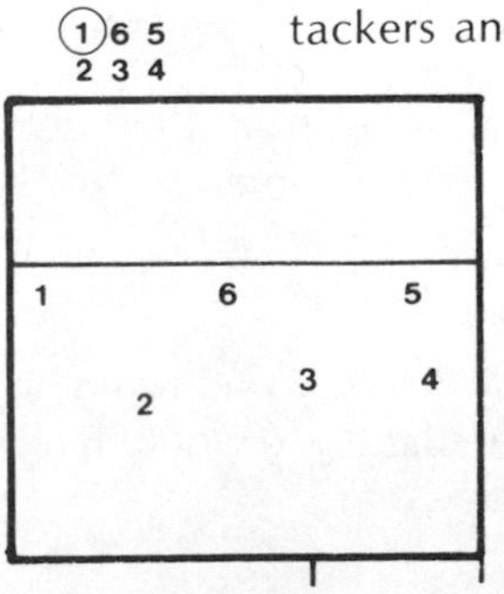

* No. 1 is the setter.
* No. 4 gives the appearance of penetration, either inside or outside.
* No. 1 stays until service made, then step up the bump is to the middle area.

II. SETTER IN THE NO. 3 POSITION

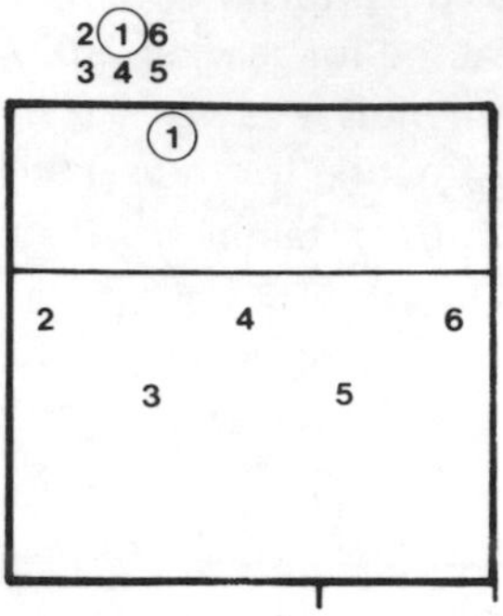

* Normal 4-2

* No. 1 is the setter.

* Try to make the line-up look the same when the setter is in the No. 3 position or the No. 6 position.

EXAMPLE A:

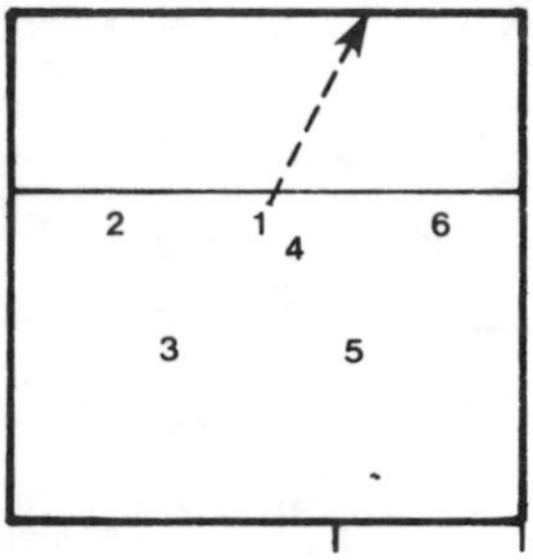

* Normal Penetration from Back Court

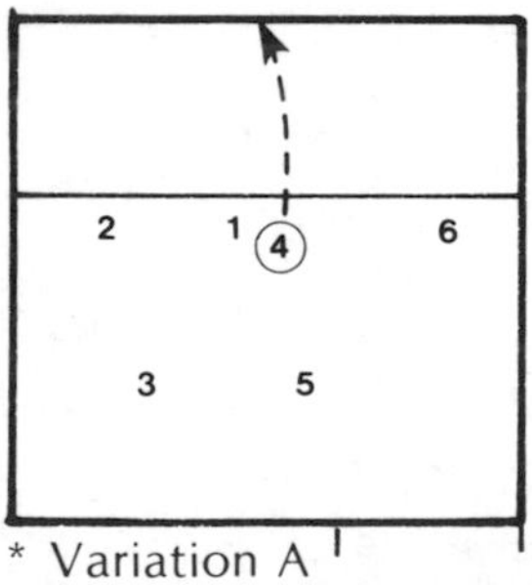

* Variation A

* As service No. 1 leaves his position it is covered by No. 4. No. 4 can be used in a fake attack if needed.

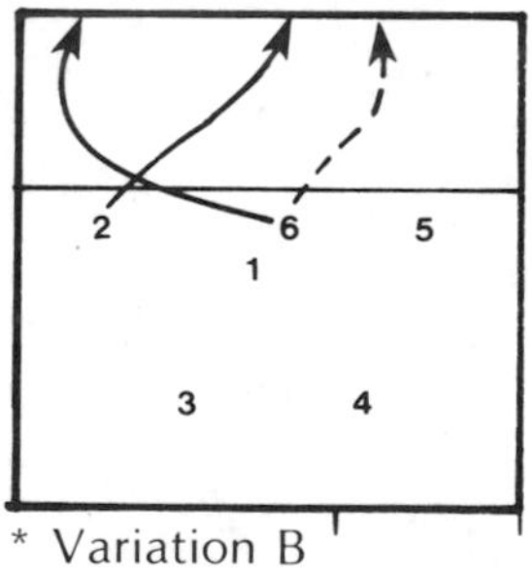

* Variation B

* No. 1 can enter from left to No. 6 if ball is served to No. 6's right or
* No. 1 can enter from the right of No. 6 if ball is served to No. 6's left.

Normally if No. 6 is a power hitter he could cross with No. 2 and again hit the power side. This would be the third time in a row that No. 6 would have hit the power side (See I—Example B). No. 1 as the setter can move ahead before service provided he does not overlap with No. 6. At the moment the service is contacted he can dash into his attack zone. No. 5 has to be alert for overlap with No. 6. No. 5 can also be a back court attacker, if needed or wanted.

III. SETTER IN THE NO. 2 POSITION

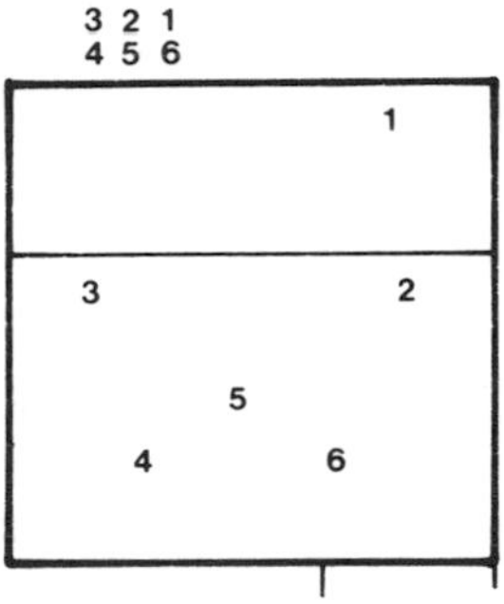

* Normal 4-2

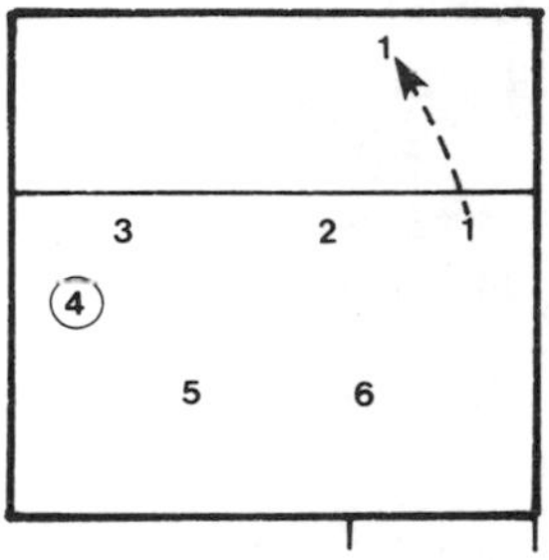

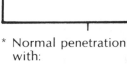

* Normal penetration with:

a) using a setter out of the No. 5 position

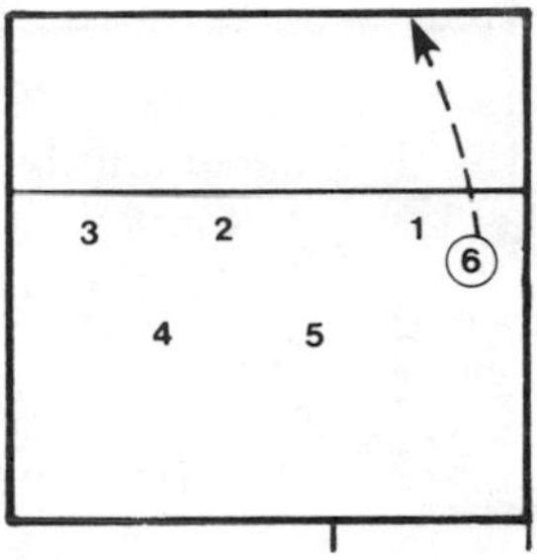

b) using a technique player

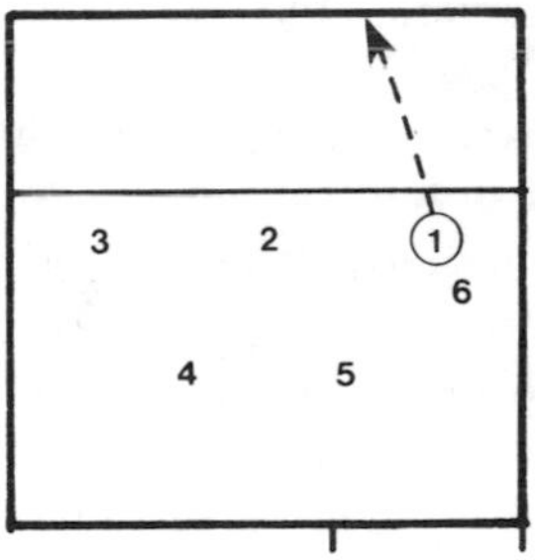

* Disguise A:

* No. 6 pretends to penetrate but No. 1 does the setting. Only two attacks unless No. 6 hits from back row.

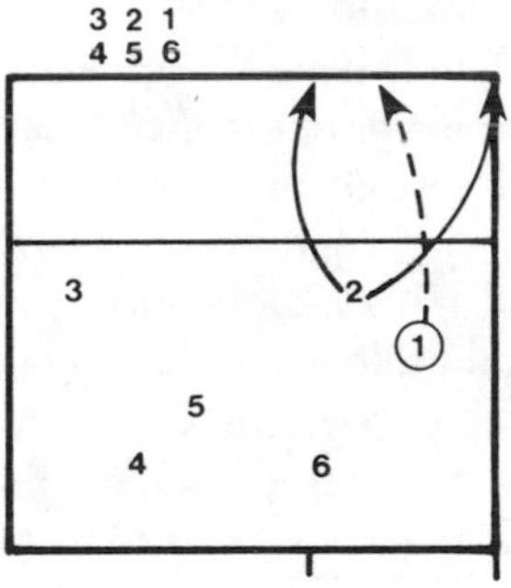

* Disguise B:

* No. 1 gives the appearance of being a back row penetrating setter.

* No. 2 can attack inside or outside.

* No. 5 can be used as a fake if No. 2 attacks outside. No. 1 can move ahead of the contact of the ball.

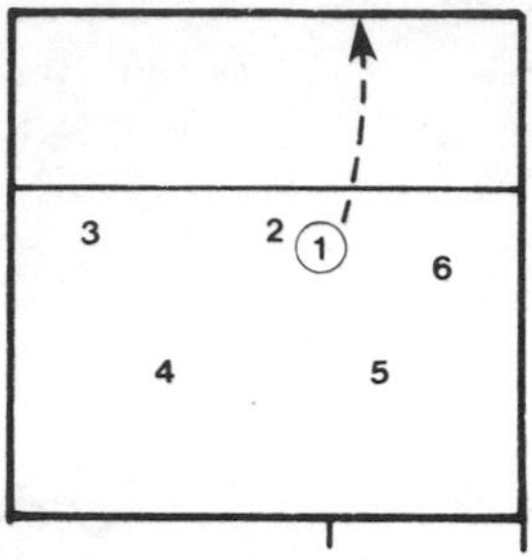

* Disguise C:

* Danger is No. 6 and No. 1 on the overlap. This gives the appearance of penetration from the center. If
* No. 2 is a middle hitter, this is good because he is right in position
* No. 6 can hit from back line or fake an attack.

(IV) General Rules:

(i) Normally there are only two attackers during 3 rotations of the 5-1. In this situation it is better to have a fast attack or at least a semi-fast attack with variation.

(ii) Setter must be trained to attack. It would be ideal if the setter was a left-handed person. Then attacks could be made from a jump set which would be an essential part of every play for the setter. If the setter was not left-handed then he must know:

a) how to tip well off a jump set—Korean tip

b) learn to use his left hand

c) learn to hit with his right hand by turning his body at the last possible moment

d) use the jump set, vary often and two hand pass the ball quickly over the net into a weak position

e) set out of the center position and back set balls to the No. 4 position. Then he could, off a jump set, spike balls with his right hand. This is your most important player—he must be an exceptional athlete and be trained well.

(iii) Backcourt players may be used to disguise attacks. However, they must remember, as must the setter, that they are a backcourt player and cannot spike. After the fake, they must return to their defensive position.

(iv) Backcourt players can hit high balls by taking off behind the three meter line. Hitter must learn to broad jump.

(v) Service reception and offensive patterns should be similar during all rotations. When a setter is in the front row it should look like he is in the back row and vice versa. This will help to confuse your opponents and make them wonder if you are penetrating.

Conclusion

These examples were given to provide an avenue for the team that was forced into playing with only one good setter. The 5-1 offense formation can be extremely advantageous. It is not necessary to use two setters all the time. One setter with his specific traits of setting, will make it easier for the hitters to key upon. Also, one setter may cut down on the team's setting errors if he handles most of the setting situation balls.

The purpose of disguising the 5-1 is to take advantage of each rotation. If the formations look the same most teams will not even realize that you are only attacking with two players. Therefore, they will not be able to key. Ideally, with a left-handed setter, who can attack, and with faster or varied offensive plays for your two hitters, the 5-1 can devastate teams This is especially true when a better hitter and blocker is next to the setter. The ideal line-up would be:

Center Blocker	Best Power Hitter	Setter
Extra Hitter	Power Hitter	Center Blocker

BALL STATE'S "CROSS" AND ATTACK COMBINATIONS

by

Don Shondell

The basic play in our offense is the fast, tight cross. This play causes the middle blocker to "low block" the middle hitter in order to assist on the "cross man". This makes it easier for the middle hitter to function effectively. Running two players into a close area with different hitting angles forces the back court players to adjust quickly to two positions—a very difficult task.

Most teams have great difficulty in defensing the "cross". If the blockers switch, the first man through should be open on a cut back shot. If the middle blocker blocks twice, and the set to the cross man is quick and low, the middle blocker should be late and the cross man should have two shots available.

The play is FAST and simple and if both spikers' approaches are short and quick, this should be a very effective and consistent play.

The "cross" should be coupled with a low outside lob shot to keep the outside blocker from "cheating in" to assist blocking the "cross man".

To keep the offhand blocker "honest" a "backdoor" or "double quick" should be run anywhere from one-sixth (1/6) to one-fifth (1/5) of the time. This play is designated "Q", and starts by faking the cross route and very quickly moving behind for a set approx. 2′ behind the setter and 2′ high.

Another backdoor play is designated as "S". This is a low lob back set near the right sideline. The closer the setter is to the sideline, the lower the set. The shot on this play, if run correctly, will probably be down the line as the fake leads the blocker to anticipate a cross, thereby moving on court and giving the spiker a one-step advantage on the blocker if the ball is hit down the the line.

In addition to the tight cross (B), the double quick (Q) and the off hand lob (S) we have two other variations of the tight cross. The wide cross (A) is used as a variation to make it difficult for the middle blocker to double block the play and to catch any "on hand" blocker that may be lazy or asleep.

The tandem (C) is designed to catch the middle blocker after he has gone up on the middle hitter, and is back on the floor, or has blocked and is moving out to block the expected cross. The ball is set 3′ to 4′ back from the net and is usually hit toward the back one-third of the court. It is only effective if the off hand hitter is tall and can hit a deep set well. Below are the various routes for each of the plays.

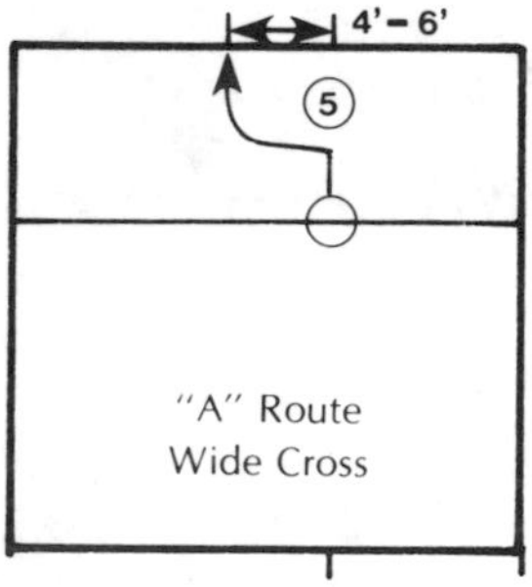

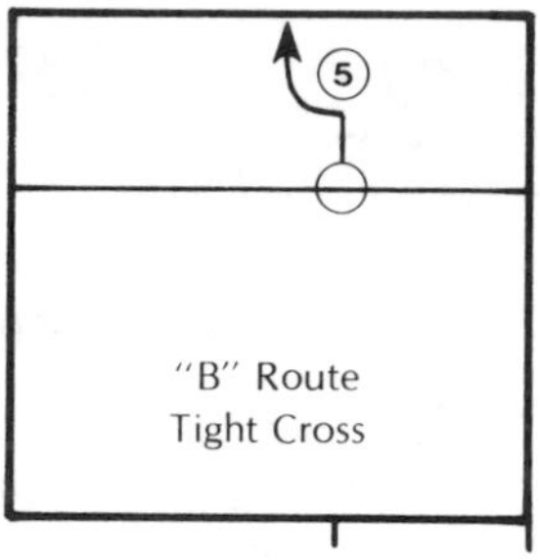

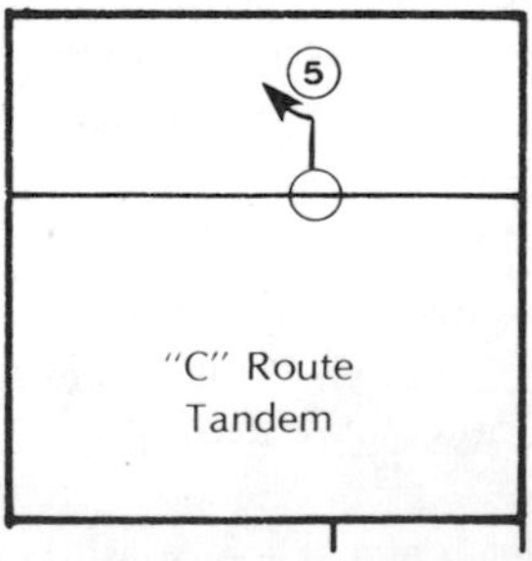

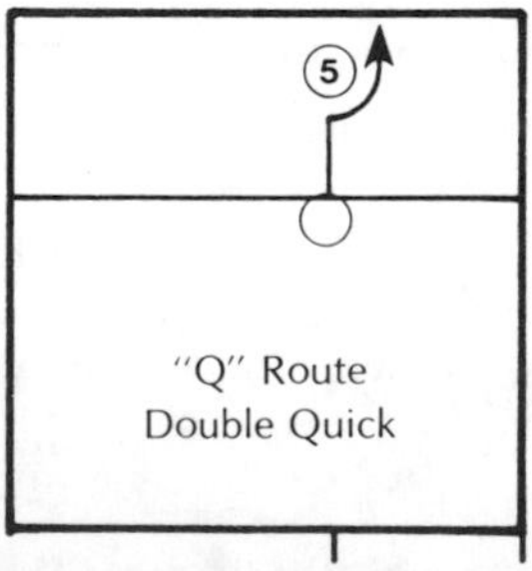

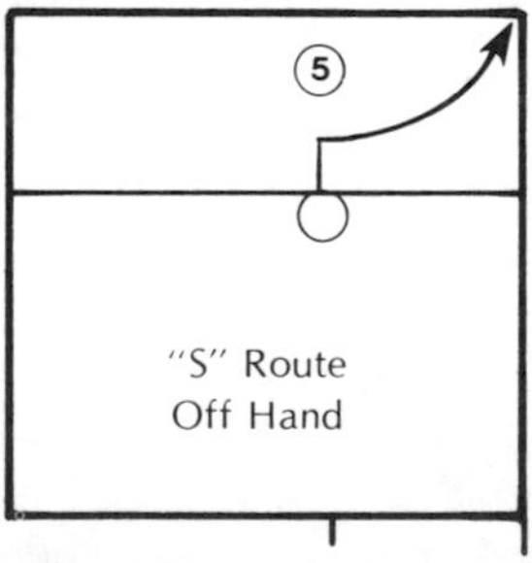

On each of these routes, you may have no blockers, one blocker, two blockers or three blockers working against you. The single blocker may be to your right or to your left. Your job is to position yourself to hit the correct shot. Always plant with the left foot ahead of the right facing the right rear corner of the court. This gives you a power shot to the right of the block or a body turn out back shot to the left of the block. If two blockers are in position against you, a well directed dink should score.

THE "DOUBLE PUMP"

by
Ralph Hippolyte
University of Pennsylvania

One can still remember how the Japanese startled their opponents and the world by using a lot of sharp combinations. This started a new trend and set the standard for the future development of volleyball. It's been a few years and now every top team in the world is trying to outsmart their opponents by using all kinds of movements and combinations along the net. In order to win the World Championship a team must either have exceptional individual players or must add new technical and tactical elements to their existing game. This article explores a method of creating more options for the spikers when running a combination play.

The method we will explore is called the "double pump." This play is used to isolate one spiker against one blocker. This fake puts additional mental and physical pressure on the blockers. The success of this play depends on the ideal cooperation between the setter and the spikers. The speed, height, trajectory and position of the set in relation to the spiker and net must be accurate. The double pump must be casted and practiced long hours before it will be totally effective.

Most plays in the past were executed by two or more players until Jungo Morita, a Japanese player, introduced the one man combination in the mid 60's. The double pump, internationally known as the "Morita variation," is performed in the following fashion: the spiker drives toward the setter using the timing of a quick set, initiates a jump to force the blocker up, recovers, and quickly jumps to hit a semi-quick set 3 feet above the net while the blocker is descending.

Another example of this type of combination is as follows: The spiker in the 3 position drives for a quick set about 6 feet away from the setter, initiates a jump, recovers, and takes a step toward the setter to hit a semi-quick set about the setter's head. In this type of combination one player does 2 distinct moves. The first movement (fake) draws the blocker to jump. The second step moves the player to a position where there is no block. A similar play involving 2 players may also be a very interesting combination.

Some advice for players running this type of play is listed below:

1. The approach toward the setter must be quick and decisive, to confuse or freeze the opposing blocker
2. You must have total confidence in your setter. Once the play is called, even if the receive is not perfect, you must go all out and assume the

set will be there.

3. You must establish the quick set prior to running the fake

4. Short players with a big jump should avoid running this play against much taller opponents, due to the time differential between the two players

5. The fake must be executed slightly before the ball reaches the setter's hands

In closing, to efficiently run any combination, your receiving must be flawless, your spikers quick and versatile, and your setter a virtuoso.

RUNNING THE "X"
by
Doug Beal
Head Coach, USA Men's National Team

The offensive system of play in modern volleyball centers around a team's ability to execute certain crossing patterns with their front row attackers. Almost without exception every team runs a *combination play* we will call the "Right X". This type of offense was popularized by the Japanese in the late 1960's and refined by the Polish men in the mid-1970's. What began as 2 hitters merely running to specific areas along the net to receive a certain set, has progressed to a highly organized inter-relationship between 3 players (a setter and two hitters).

The combination nature of an offense frequently is used to characterize a team and can serve to define a team's strengths and weaknesses. Teams which run numerous offensive combinations involving many crossing patterns are probably telling you they have no confidence in their hitters' abilities to score on high-wide sets and must attempt to fool the blockers to side-out. Teams which run fewer or more simple combination plays may have larger, slower hitters or less agile setters and must rely on a wide, slow offense to score and their hitters' abilities to defeat a well formed block and prepared defense.

Japan's initial development of this style of offense was in reaction to their belief in their hitters' inability to defeat the opponent's blockers and back-court defense through traditional channels. More recently the trend toward all teams running these crossing plays is a reaction to the vast improvement in blocking skills as a point producing weapon and the interest in gaining an advantage for the offense against a confused defense.

It is well to remember the following points as you read this discussion of the "X". (Relative to men's volleyball.)

(1) Japan ran the most sophisticated and complex offense in the world from 1964 to 1970; but didn't win a major international championship until 1972 (Munich Olympics) when they dramatically improved their skill in attacking high-wide sets.

(2) The East Germans won the 1970 World championships running almost no combinations and close to a 4-2 style offense; setting the ball extremely high.

(3) Poland won the 1974 World Championship and 1976 Olympics with only one real *combination play* in their offensive repertoire.

(4) The best team in the world today (the USSR) runs fewer combinations and crossing plays than any other top team.

Personnel Required:

The "X" play requires 2 hitters with very different roles yet somewhat similar skills for the successful execution of the play. The middle hitter ordinarily attacks from the #3 position and hits a fast set in a position immediately in front of the setter.

There are at least 2 methods of hitting this quick set (called "1" or "A"); fast or slow. If it is attacked as a "fast 1", the hitter will be in the air *before the setter releases the ball.* The set can also be hit as a "slow 1", when the hitter is on his last step and *about to take off as the setter is releasing the ball.* In either case the play can be effective. The USA men's team favors a "fast 1" hit with an almost vertical style jump by the attacker. The real key is the hitter's upper body movement and especially his arm swing. The middle hitter must jump in as erect (straight up and down) a posture as possible with his arm cocked (elbow back) ready to hit the ball as quickly as he can. The middle hitter may attack the ball as soon as it clears the net, or delay and cut the ball left or right to avoid the block. However, if the hitter broad jumps dramatically or has a slow, long arm swing and exaggerated upper body torque, he will limit his range on hitting the "1" set, and limit the play's effectiveness.

The other hitter is called the "play set" hitter. His role is to wait until the ball reaches the setter and the "quick hitter" has jumped, and then he must make a very fast approach from the #2 zone past the setter and "quick-hitter" and attack the ball in an area somewhat off the left shoulder of the first hitter and 3-5′ above the net. This set has commonly been called a "2" set, however, we prefer to call this set the "x" set on the USA team.

The X-set can be hit with several different approaches: (see diagram below).

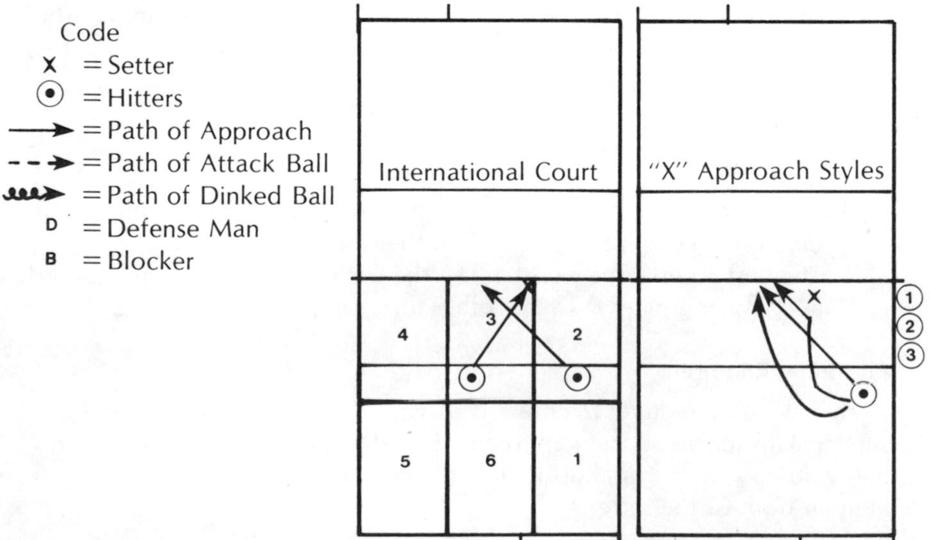

Diagram A   Diagram B

Basically I have outlined 3 approach styles to be used on the X-set. Style #1 involves the hitter moving into a position behind the setter and perpendicular to the net as the ball is passed to the setter. The hitter then runs directly at the setter and breaks to the left just as the setter releases the ball. This style can be very effective for a hitter who uses a "hop" or "pre-jump" style of spiking approach; however, the hitter almost comes to a complete stop before "flaring" out to hit the "X" and this makes last second adjustments difficult to make. This style also can decrease the zone the hitter can effectively run the play from.

Style #2 is an arc approach or curve, and is very popular in running this play. The hitter merely curves around the quick-hitter and receives the set at the end of his arc. This style does allow for a fast, adjustable approach by the hitter and can be done quite effectively. The problems here are twofold:

(1) The hitter frequently must leave too soon for maximum deception as this approach style is too long;

(2) The final part of the approach is almost run straight at the net, limiting lateral range and the ability to compensate for setting errors.

The 3rd approach is obviously the one I favor. It is a straight line approach run at an angle to the net starting where the hitter receives serve or can quickly adjust to as the ball is passed. We use this on the National team for several reasons:

(1) We favor a 4 step, step-close style approach that allows for maximum speed and range. This can best be done is a straight line.

(2) We encourage our players to hit this set *with* a broad jump at the end of their approach. This allows them the greatest area along the net to execute the play from and puts the least pressure on the setter to pin point the set.

(3) We want the X-set delivered deeper off the net than the quick middle set and therefore the angle approach can *more* easily allow our hitters to avoid netting and still retain their range to hit the ball back to the right corner.

[For a Righty] This approach starts with the right foot and the 2nd step is with the left, made almost perpendicular with the setter and the net. Then a large step with the right and the last step is with the left before jumping. This is a normal approach which most simulates running. The approach should accelerate to the point of takeoff and each step should be longer.

Objectives of the X Play:

Basically the play is designed to free up the right front hitter by running his blocker into the middle blocker. [Very much like a screen play in basketball.] The middle blocker should be committed to stopping the quick hitter.

If everything goes perfectly the play-set hitter will have a completely

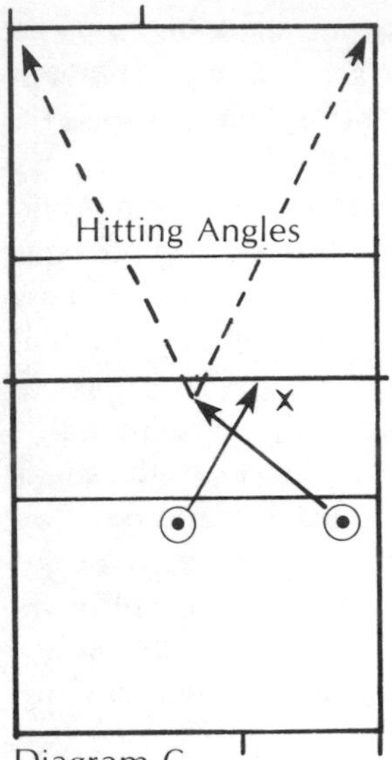

Diagram C

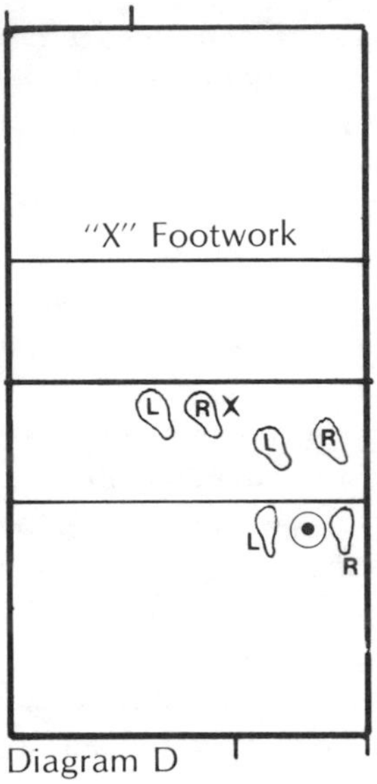

Diagram D

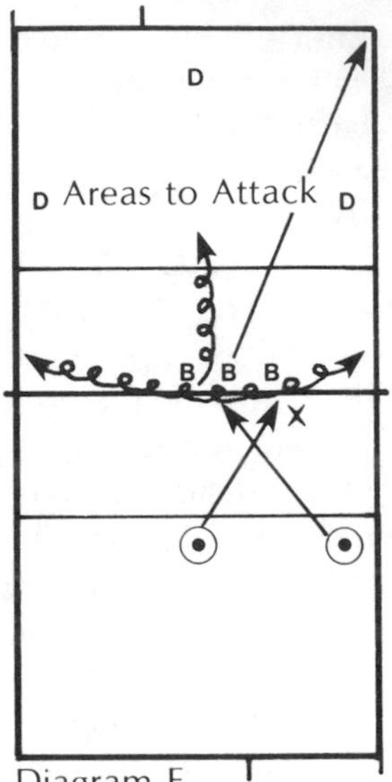

Diagram E

open net to hit over from mid-court someplace, as his blocker cannot get around the immobilized center blocker who just landed after jumping with the middle hitter.

If the defense is blocking man to man, this strategy usually works rather well, as the center blocker must respect your quick hitter who has jumped before the ball is set and the defense's right blocker cannot react quickly enough to move to the center to block.

If the defense guesses correctly and the blockers don't jump with the 1st hitter there may be 2 or even all 3 blockers in front of your X-hitter. This is also fine as the play produces a nice secondary effect of freezing the defensive back row men.

Both short sides are normally available for a soft dink over the end blockers, and even the middle is free over the center blocker. The defenders have dug in to be ready for the quick middle hit and will have a difficult time adjusting to a short dink to an unprotected area.

Because many teams practice defending the "X" they can be ready for these dinks, in which case a hard-deep shot against the grain of the defense, i.e. back to the hitter's right, is most effective. The entire play flows to the defenders' right and this hit goes to their left, usually leaving them going the other direction.

A final objective of the play is to make the defense so conscious of the X-hitter that they forget the first man through and you can easily score on the quick set. We encourage our setters to go to the middle hitter whenever he detects the blockers overplaying the "X" by shifting or he can hear them call out the play verbally. If the blockers are concentrating on the play-set hitter, the quick hitter will usually be open

Timing

The play is designed to be run rapidly, with as little time as possible between the potential "1" set attack and potential "X" set attack. The quick hit from the middle should be contacted as rapidly as possible so the center blocker knows that he must jump or he can't successfully block the ball. Certainly the higher it is contacted, the better; but the key is to hit the set quickly. The slower the "1" set, the more likely the center blocker won't commit himself until the ball is set and the more likely he can be in a good position to block the entire play with help from his outside blocker.

If the center blocker commits completely to the 1st hitter, the X-hitter's job is relatively easy and timing is less critical. Normally he must assume he should hit the ball just after the quick hitter lands on the ground from jumping. Certainly the timing varies with the distance the 2 hitters are apart. We try to give the setter the option of running the "X" in a zone approximately 1-1½ meters wide. The closer the X-hitter to the quick-hitter the faster is the play.

Since the setter must run the offense and determine who to set, we also want him to be responsible for the position of the play. If our hitters use the proper angled approach and broad jump they should be able to hit the "X" very wide or very tight; depending on the setter's judgment as to the placement around the center blocker.

Practice Techniques

(1) Learn to hit the various sets by themselves: A good method of practicing hitting the quick "1" is for the coach or setter to stand at the net and hold the ball for the hitter. The hitter approaches, jumps and then the setter pushes the ball up for the hitter. The coach should have his arm extended with the ball held near the top of the net. It is merely pushed up after the hitter jumps.

(2) The middle hitter must learn the correct timing and key to being on time by practicing hitting 1's from all types of passes to the setter; high, low, left and right of the target area. This is done by hitting the middle set from a serve receive drill where the passes may not be perfect.

KEY: The middle hitter's approach should *not* be perpendicular to the net; rather he should watch the ball over his right shoulder as it is passed and approach at about a 45° angle to the net to hit the "1" set.

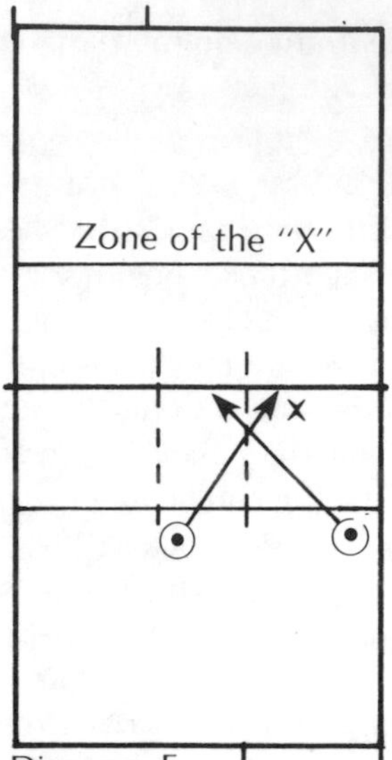

Diagram F

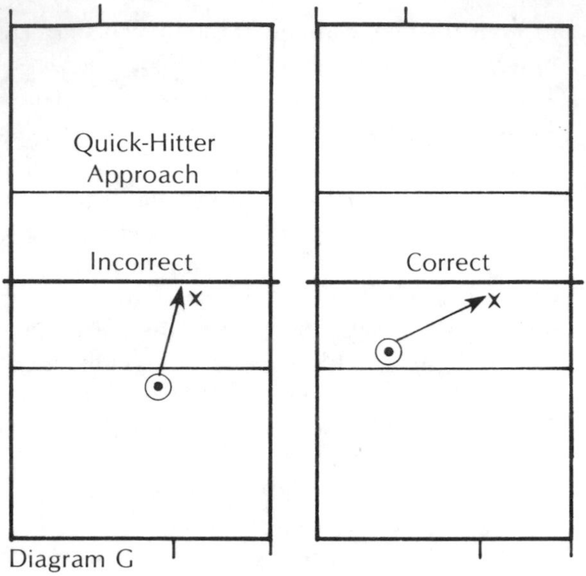

Diagram G

This allows a good vision of the incoming pass, and better adjustment possibilities for stray passes. To achieve this approach the middle hitter drops off to the left side of the center if he doesn't receive the ball, and he may even be in front of the 3 meter attack line to start his approach.

(3) The play-set hitter must work on the timing from thrown balls to the setter. Again the key is adjusting to the variable passes so that he is in the same relative position when the ball is released by the setter. (Approximately 5′ from the net and behind the setter.)

(4) After the sets are learned by themselves the hitters and setter must learn the timing of the play in combination. A good way to start is with the setter holding the ball and the hitters approaching and receiving a *thrown* set.

(5) Next the hitters will run the play from a tossed pass by the coach to the setter.

(6) Finally the hitters must learn to run the play from a served ball or free-ball and against the block.

Tips for Success:

(1) Practice your foot work until it becomes 2nd nature, this is especially a key for the play-set hitter.

(2) The middle hitter must convince the blockers that he is getting the set; to do this he must jump early and he must be very vocal; i.e., call for the ball from the setter.

(3) The setter must remember to set the "X" deeper off the net, to adjust for the broad jumping "X" hitter.
(4) The setter can control the speed and tempo of the play by releasing the ball at a high or low point. He can compensate for a middle hitter who is early by jump setting or releasing the ball quickly; and for a hitter who is late by crouching low to allow more time, or by jumping to set and releasing the ball on his descent.
(5) Good communication is critical if the play is to be effective. The setter and hitters must know each other very well and adjust quickly to the pass. If this play is executed as designed the hitter should never have more than one blocker to defeat.

3
22

7
Spiker Coverage

SPIKER COVERAGE

by
Tina Kogut
University of Tennessee

Spiker coverage is an integral part of a team's attack involving all of its players. A team which possesses good spiker coverage has the ability to keep the ball in play despite the strength of the opposing block. All players must cover the spiker with the intent to play any balls blocked and rebounded into the spiker's court.

There are many combinations which can be used based on the needs of your team or the strength of the opponents. In this article we will only address the two most common types of spiker coverage—the 3-2 and the 2-3. A 3-2 alignment should be utilized when playing an opponent with a strong block. It is also the suggested coverage if your team is composed of small attackers. The 2-3 system should be employed when playing a team with a weak block or a team which uses deep blocking tactics.

In women's high school volleyball the 2-3 coverage will generally prove to be more effective. This is true because of the lack of a strong offensive block, and the tendency for high school teams to quickly send a dug ball over the net, deep into your court.

The keys to successful coverage are 1) follow the ball toward the attacker 2) flow in that direction in 2 waves 3) stay low to the ground 4) fill the holes (spaces between the players of the first wave).

In the following two diagrams, let's assume that the receiving team passed the ball to the #3 position or the center front. This is the target area in the

4-2 offense. The setter (player #3) is in proper position to set, and the spiker is taking a normal approach.

3-2 Spiker Coverage

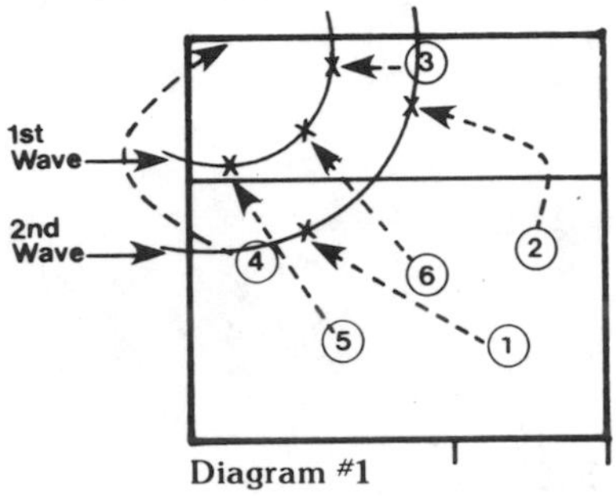

Diagram #1

a. Player #1. This is the "swing" player who moves to her left and near the center of the court, fifteen feet from the end line. She has responsibility for a left portion of the back court and must be ready to react quickly to move for the ball. Generally the ball that comes into her area will not be hard-driven. This player is part of the second wave coverage and fills the hole between players #5 and #6.

b. Player #2. This is the "unused" attack player. Her first consideration is to attack the set if and when it is set to her. At the instant that the ball is set to the other attacker, she must turn inward (towards her left) and fill the hole between players #6 and #3. Her position is seven feet from the net and ten feet from the right sideline. Her assignment is any ball that rebounds off the block deep right into the second wave of coverage area.

c. Player #3. The setter has a major responsibility in covering the attacker. This responsibility is often neglected, as setters tend to watch their set. After setting the ball, the setter should follow her set. Her position as the ball is being struck by the attacker is three feet from the net and five feet to the right of the attacker. When the setter is back setting over her head to the other attacker, this makes coverage even more difficult. The correct move is to step directly backward along the net, with the foot closest to the net and pivot 180 degrees. This move must be quick, and gives her a superior angle to approach the point of coverage and responsibility. Specific responsibility is to receive or save balls rebounding sharply from the block to the inside of the court.

d. Player #4. This is the attack player.

e. Player #5. The outside player in the first wave of coverage. Her move is predicated by the attacker's approach, speed, and angle. Her position is directly in back of and to the inside of the attacker. (Exception: when the attacker is drawn inside on a set, the #5 player should cover to the outside of the attacker. However, at no time should she be closer than three feet from the sideline.) Her specific responsibility is to receive or save balls rebounding sharply from the block in back of the attacker.

f. Player #6. This is the middle player in the cup of the 1st wave of coverage. Her lateral position is predicated by the #3 and #5 players. She should station herself equidistant between these two players. She should not get closer than seven feet from the net. Her responsibility is for balls rebounding from the block into her area.

To cover the right side attack the coverage is simply reversed.

2-3 Spiker Coverage

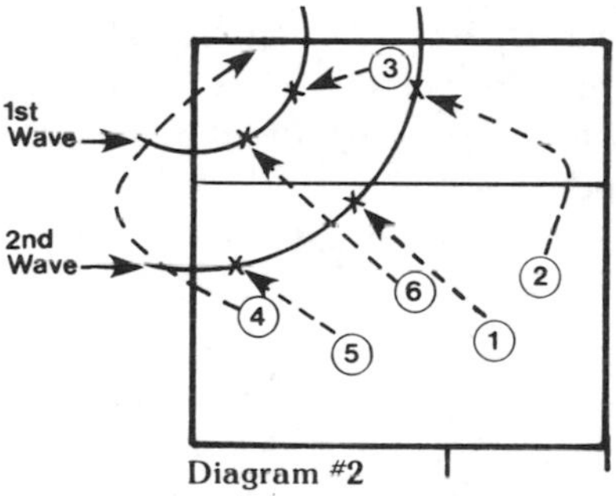

Diagram #2

a. Player #1. The player is the center player of the second wave of coverage. She fills the hole between players #6 and #3. Her responsibility is balls blocked deep into the heart of the court.

b. Player #2. The difference in this coverage for player #2 is that she positions herself about three feet from the net and ten feet from the sideline. She should be filling the hole between player #3 and the net. Her area of responsibility is balls blocked deep along the net and approximately ten feet away from the net.

c. Player #3. The specific responsibilities are the same, as previously mentioned, the difference is in her positioning. Since there are only 2 players covering the 1st wave coverage responsibilities, it is necessary for player #3 to position herself equidistant between the net and player #6. She should not be closer than five feet from the net.

d. Player #4. This is the attacker.

e. Player #5. She is the outside player of the 2nd wave of coverage, and therefore has the responsibility of balls blocked deep down the sideline. She positions herself in the hole between player #6 and the left sideline, approximately fifteen feet off the net.

f. Player #6. She is the outside player in the first wave of coverage. She positions herself equidistant between player #3 and the left sideline. However she should not get any closer than five feet from the sideline. Her responsibility is to receive or save balls rebounding sharply from the block.

In the next two diagrams, let's assume that the receiving team passed the ball to the target area for the 6-2 offense (between position #2 and #3), and the spiker is taking a normal approach.

3-2 Spiker Coverage (6-2 Offense)

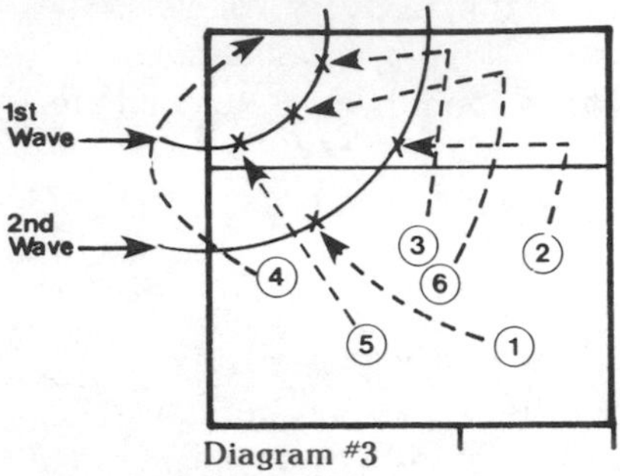

Diagram #3

a. Player #1. The same as in the coverage from a 4-2 offense. (Diag. 1, a)

b. Player #2. The same as in the coverage from a 4-2 offense. (Diag. 1, b)

c. Player #3. This is the quick attack player in the middle. In the 6-2 offense with all 3 front row players hitting, player #3 usually is hitting a quick set in the middle. Therefore she is always committed to jumping. But immediately after she lands she moves along the net and covers three feet from the net and five feet to the right of the attacker. Specific responsibility is the same as player #3 in Diag. 1, to receive or save balls rebounding sharply from the block.

d. Player #4. This is the attack player.

e. Player #5. Moves the same as in the coverage from a 4-2 offense (Diag. 1, e)

f. Player #6. This player is the backcourt setter. Her first consideration is to penetrate to the target area and deliver an accurate pass. After the set is made she immediately moves to cover the same position and responsibilities as player #6 in the coverage from the 4-2 offense. (Diag. 1, f)

2-3 Spiker Coverage (6-2 Offense)

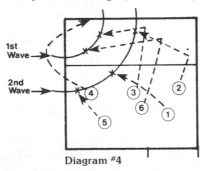

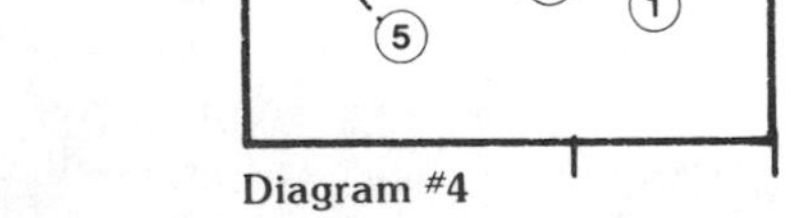

Diagram #4

a. Player #1. The same as in the coverage from a 4-2 offense. (Diag. 2, a)

b. Player #2. The same as in the coverage from a 4-2 offense. (Diag. 2, b)

c. Player #3. This is the quick middle attack player. Since she is always committed to jump, immediately after she lands she must move to cover the position and responsibilities the same as player #3 in the coverage from a 4-2 offense. (Diag. 2, c)

d. Player #4. This is the attack player.

e. Player #5. Moves the same as in the coverage from a 4-2 offense. (Diag. 2, e)

f. Player #6. This player is the backcourt setter. Her first consideration is to penetrate to the target area and deliver an accurate pass. After the set is made she immediately moves to cover the same position and responsibilities as player #6 in the coverage from the 4-2 offense. (Diag. 2, f)

The 3-2 and 2-3 presented here are the most basic spiker coverage formations. Adaptations can be made in these patterns to fit the needs and desires of individual coaches. A team that runs very fast offense may not be able to get the designated players to the first wave of coverage because of the quickness of the set. This team must adjust its spiker coverage to conform to its attack.

If a team has specialized defensive responsibilities, players can move to the spiker coverage positions which most easily allow them to return to their defensive areas. Referring back to Diag. 4 #1, who is receiving in the right back position, always plays left back on defense. Spiker coverage directly from serve reception would take this player to the middle position in the second wave of coverage. Once the attacking player gets the ball past the block, #1 must switch to her left back defensive area.

If #1, directly from service reception, assumes the spiker coverage position close to the sideline in the second wave, she is already in her defensive area. This helps to assure that the defense will be set up for a quick counter attack by your opponents.

Positioning and areas of responsibility for two types of spiker coverage have been thoroughly covered here. These formations can easily be taught to any team. However, one must not lose sight of the main objective—to keep a blocked ball from hitting the floor on your side of the net. Players must be drilled until they are conditioned to flow in the direction of the ball, fill in the holes, stay low, and react to rebounding balls. The team that can do this will prolong the volley for at least one more attack—maybe the one that will win the match.

8

Defense

DEFENSIVE SYSTEMS

by
Mick Haley
Kellogg Community College

There are two basic defensive patterns used in the USA today. Each has many variations or options similar to other sport defenses. These two systems are easily recognizable because one places a player from the back row approximately 10 feet behind the block (man-up defense) while the other leaves the center of the defensive court open by starting with 4 defensive spike receivers or diggers (man-back defense).

Figure #1

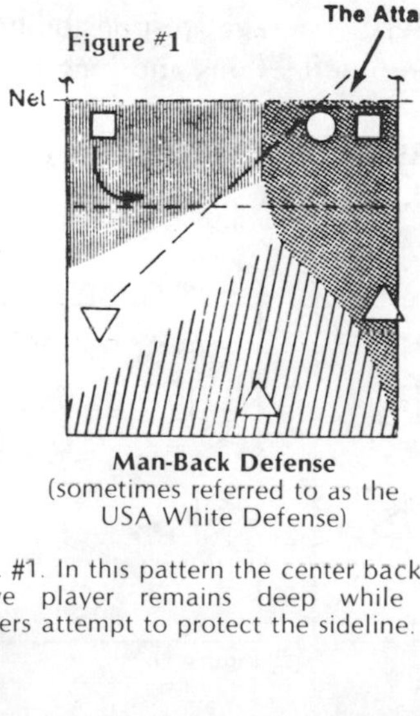

Man-Back Defense
(sometimes referred to as the USA White Defense)

Fig. #1. In this pattern the center back defensive player remains deep while the blockers attempt to protect the sideline.

Figure #2

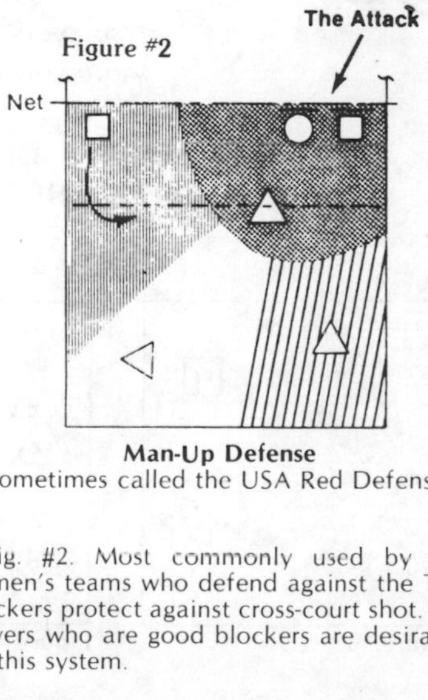

Man-Up Defense
(sometimes called the USA Red Defense)

Fig. #2. Most commonly used by the women's teams who defend against the TIP. Blockers protect against cross-court shot. Big players who are good blockers are desirable for this system.

Starting Positions

In both defensive systems the starting positions are relatively the same. Some types of offenses force changes in these starting positions (i.e. a team that attacks from the center quickly will cause the starting positions for the back row diggers to move closer to the net.) If the attacking team does not attack from the middle, the players return to the positions shown in *fig. #3* prior to making their final adjustment.

The team defense in each case may be discussed in three levels.

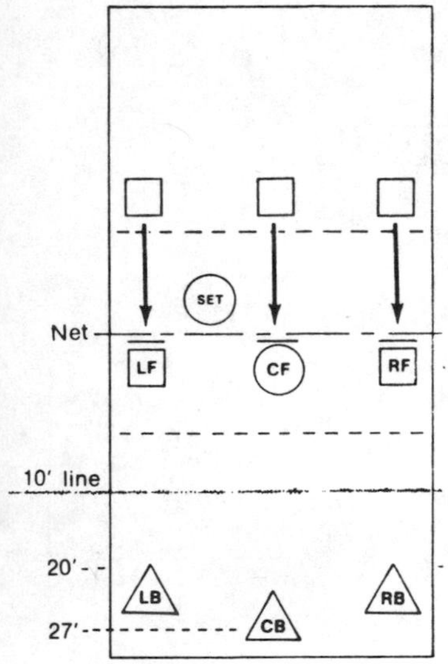

Figure #3

Level One — The first line of defense

The first line of defense starts with the blockers at the net. In most cases it is desirable to have two blockers up to defend against each attack.

Level Two — The second line of defense

This line of defense includes the front row player who is not blocking and the opposite back row player in the man back defense. In the man-up defense, the front row non-blocker and the person playing the up position on the 10′ front line form the second line defense.

Level Three — The last line of defense

The last line of defense consists of the remaining two deep defenders. They have a little more time to react, but have less margin for error. These two players have deep coverage responsibility for power attacks, deep deflections and long tips.

THE THREE LINES OF DEFENSE ARE ILLUSTRATED BELOW FOR THE MAN-BACK DEFENSE

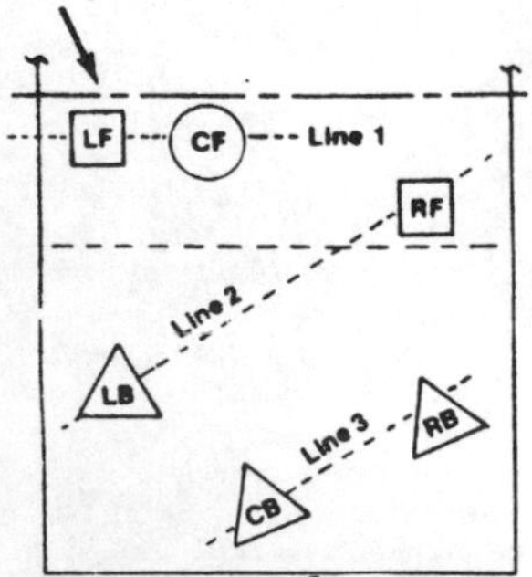

Figure #4

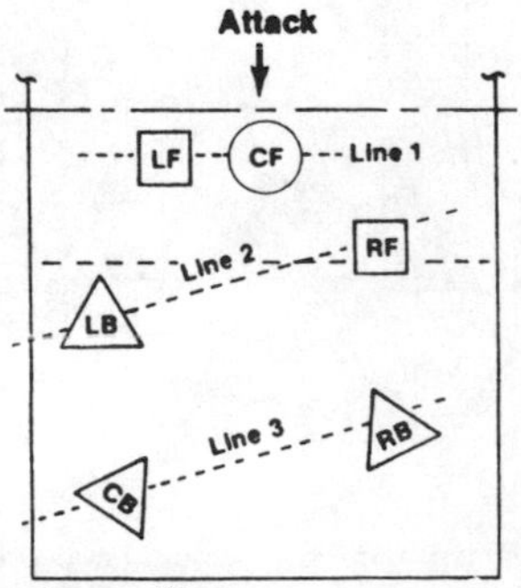

Figure #5

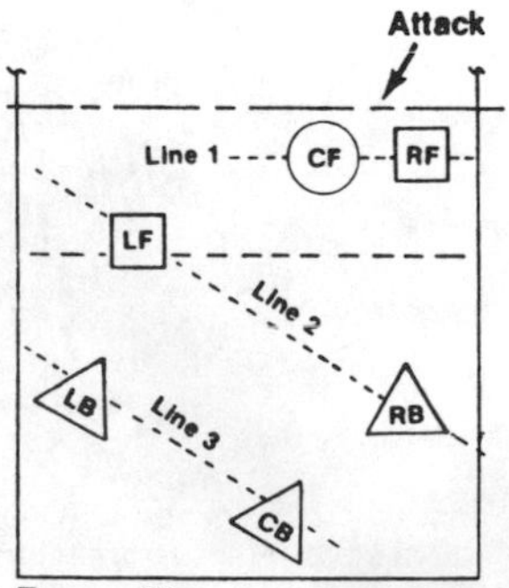

Figure #6

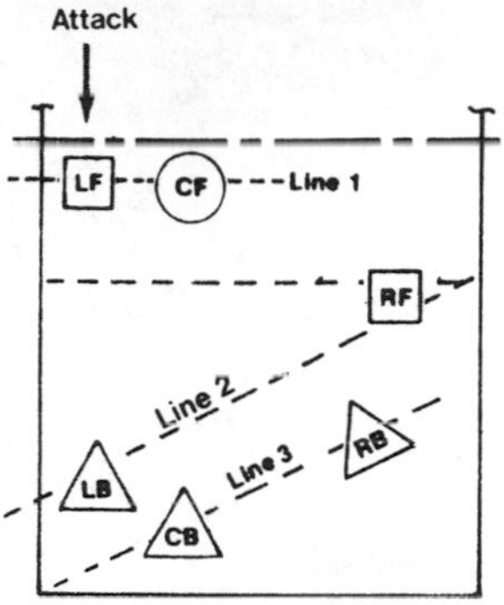

Figure #7

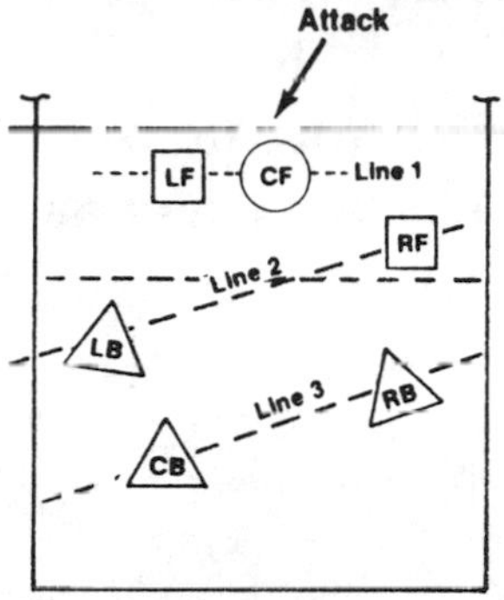

Figure #8

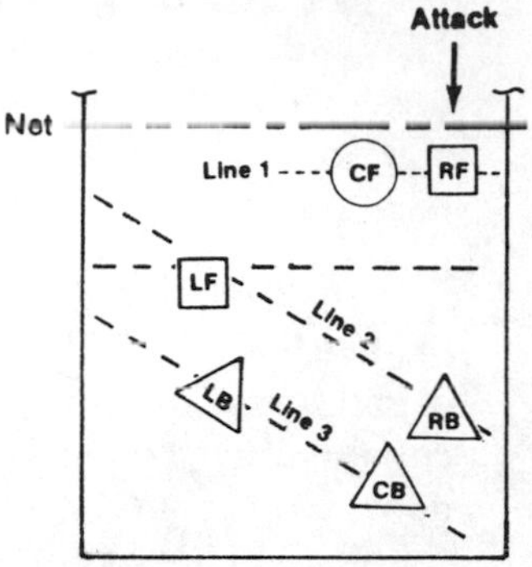

Figure #9

THE THREE LINES OF DEFENSE FOR THE MAN-UP DEFENSE

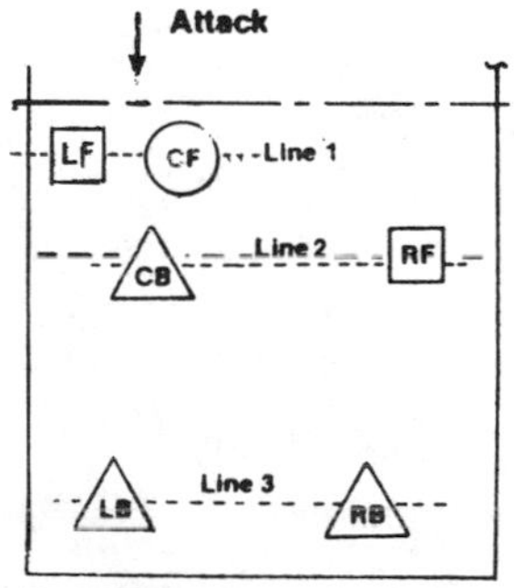

Figure #10

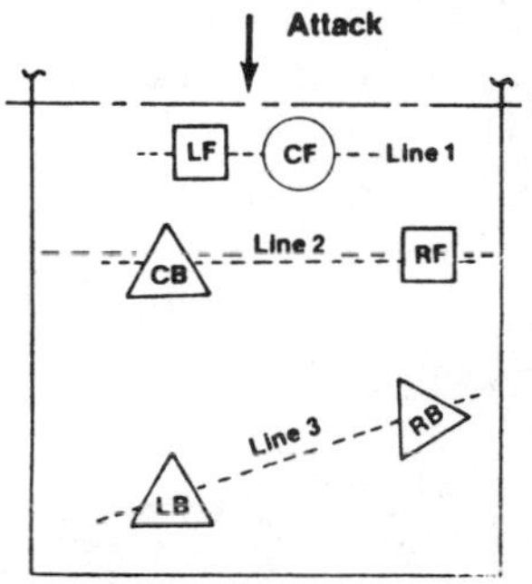

Figure #11

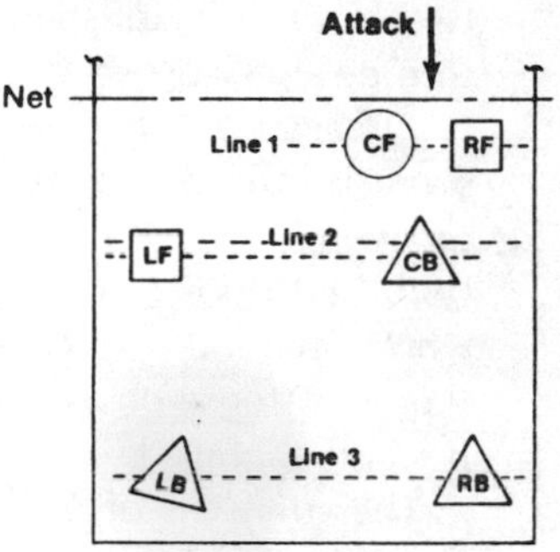

Figure #12

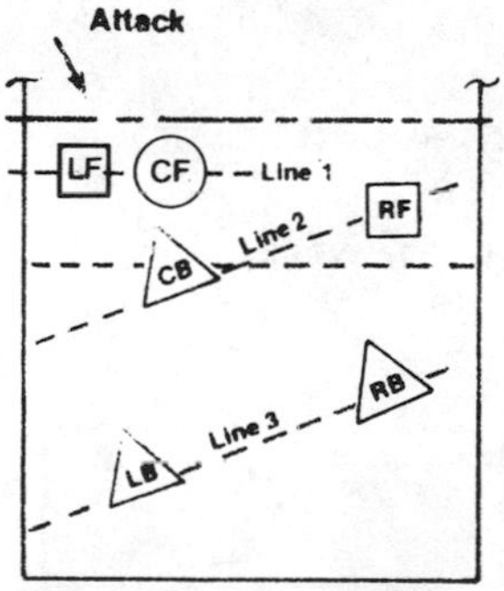

Figure #13

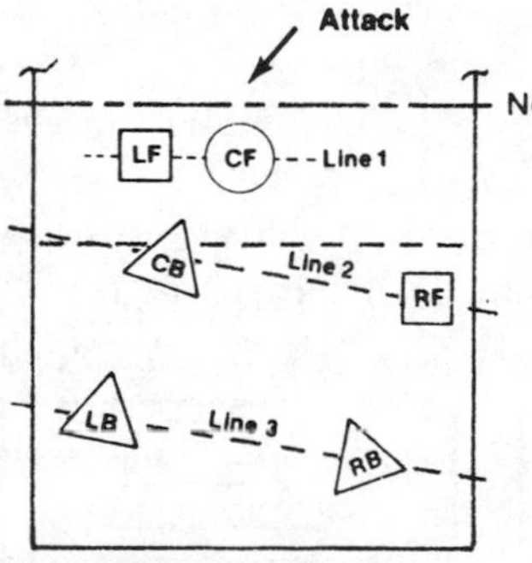

Figure #14

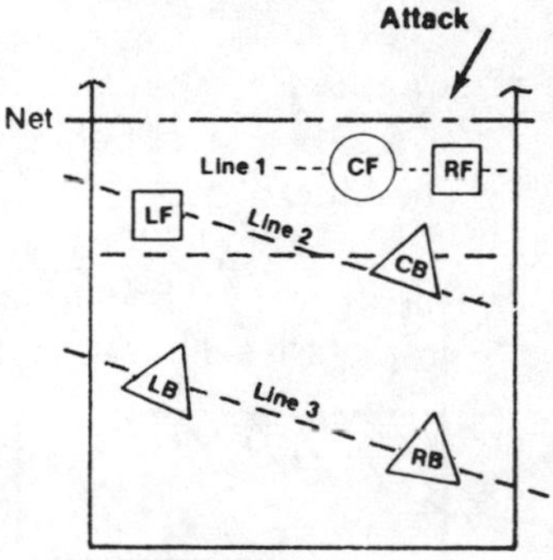

Figure #15

Please note that the player in the up position does not have to be the center back. Some teams put their weakest defensive player here, while others like to have their backrow setter in this position.

THE 2-1-3 AND THE 2-4 DEFENSE

by
Jerre McManama
Ball State University

In the United States there are predominantly two defenses used in competitive volleyball. They have varying names such as man-up and man-back or red and white. In this article, we will attempt to describe the style of defense after the placement of the players on the court similar to what is done in other sports.

The exact starting positions and final fielding positions of the players in these defenses vary according to the level of play and the spiking abilities of each opponent. The philosophies and positions discussed in this article are based upon observations of men's intercollegiate volleyball over a period of twelve years. With slight modifications the ideas presented can be adapted to men's or women's competition at every level of play.

Diagram 1 shows the basic starting positions immediately following the serve by the defensive team. From these positions the players can easily move into the 2-1-3 or 2-4 defense. The choice of defense that is used should be based upon a variety of factors. There is no one defensive formation which guarantees success. Factors such as individual defensive abilities and type of offense of a coach's own team, and the offensive abilities of the opponents dictate the choice of defense.

The strengths of the 2-1-3 defense are as follows:

- A weak defensive player can be hidden by moving him to the position behind the block.
- A back row setter can be moved behind the block providing a good transition to the three-hitter offense.
- The player behind the block can best cover soft shots over or around the block.
- A tall block can prevent the hitter from spiking to the weak area near the middle of the baseline (Diagram 1). Diagram 1 also shows the weak areas in the 2-1-3 defense.

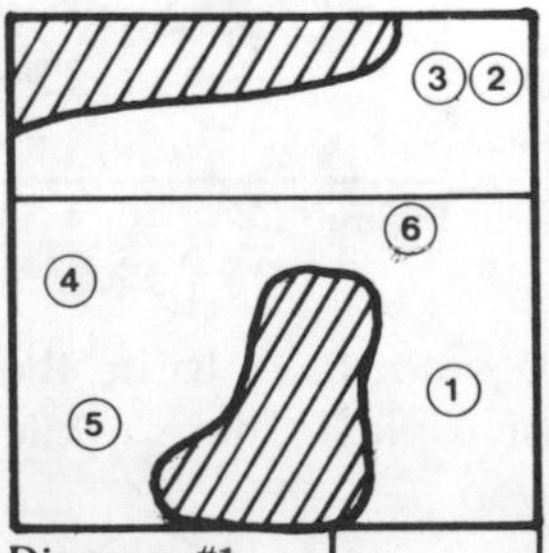

Diagram #1

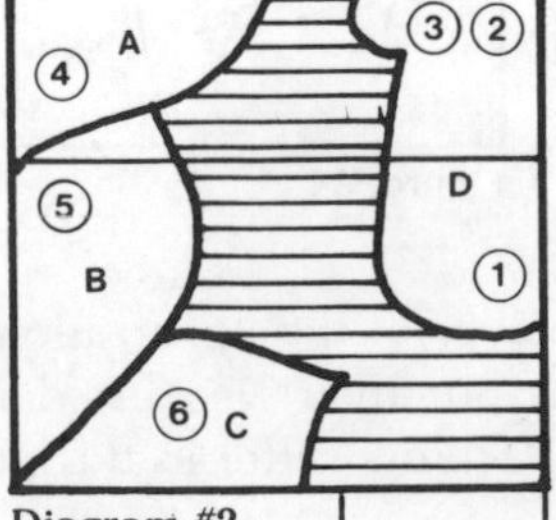

Diagram #2

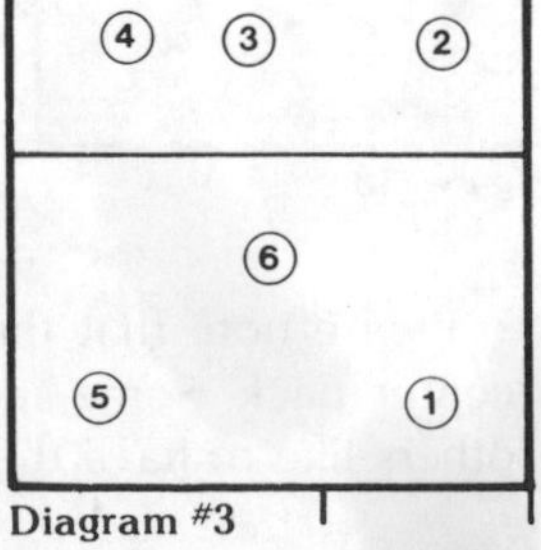

Diagram #3

• A block with no holes in it (both blockers' hands together) can also protect the weak middle area when blocking shorter hitters.

The following are the strengths of the 2-4 defense.

• The cross-court diagonal shot most often used by hitters is covered by three fielders.

• The power shot inside the block is covered by two fielders.

• A hole between the blockers, which often happens in the case of inexperienced players, is more adequately covered.

• The weaknesses of the 2-4 defense as shown in Diagram 2 relate primarily to off-speed or soft shots into the weak areas.

The 2-1-3 and 2-4 defenses are based on three factors—reading, positioning, and executing—in that order. If any one of the three is missing or forgotten, defense will suffer. Defense starts as soon as the ball crosses the net into the opponent's court and actually ends with a skillful and deliberately planned attack by the team on defense. If there is not a skillful and deliberately planned transition from defense to offense, a team is still on the defensive even though it has the ball. Defense and the transition to offense are the keys to success. The reading is mental, the positioning is physical, and the execution is skill.

Reading

This mental process must be in operation by the players at all times. It is an individual mental skill which, when every player performs successfully, blends into a team skill. The success of defense starts with the blockers and their ability to read and perform.

Blocking Rules and Starting Positions. These are the three basic concepts from which the defense operates.

• No hole in the block—each blocker operates independently as though he were blocking alone; however, when both players read and execute properly, their hand movement with the ball will close any possible holes in the block.

• Take away the power alley shot, give the spiker the line shot (straight ahead), and make certain that the power alley (cross-court) angle is adequately covered. This means that the outside blocker's hands must set the block with the middle blocker covering the inside angle. The outside blocker should have his outside hand on the ball as it touches him and be definitely turning the ball in toward the center of the court. Continue this coverage until the spiker proves that he has a good consistent line shot.

• Assign responsibilities—the outside blocker sets the block (position where he thinks the ball will cross the net). Any ball hit between the blockers is the responsibility of the outside man because he must close the block. Any ball hit past the middle blocker's inside hand is the responsibility of the middle blocker because he must not allow the inside shot.

• Starting positions—the blocker's positioning varies according to the opponents and their offense. Diagram 1 and Diagram 3 show the positioning of blockers Nos. 2, 3 and 4. The basic starting positions are:

Blocker 4—Start two yards from the sideline, anticipate a weak-side spike, and help the middle blocker (No. 3) on middle hits of the multiple offense.

Blocker 3—The starting position depends upon the opponent's offense. When blocking the multiple offense position approximately 10 to 12 feet from the left sideline, vary the positioning depending upon the opponent's setter and the first pass. When blocking the 4-2 offense position near the center of the court (15 to 17 feet), expect a strong-side hit by the opposition.

Blocker 2—Start one yard from the right sideline and anticipate a strong-side spike by the opposition. Assist in blocking a high set in the middle.

Blocker's Reading Thoughts

a) The blockers must concentrate and be able to predict very early where the ball is going to be set.

• If the first pass is bad, the ball will usually be set to the strong side. Disregard the center hit.

• If the ball is passed to the right side of the center of the court, it will probably be set to the left side hitter and vice versa.

• On a good first pass try to read the setter's hand positioning in order to beat the hitters. Be ready for the center hit.

• On a good first pass the center blocker must keep in mind that the good center hitter is not going to hit straight ahead so he should be ready to adjust his hands with the hit. The weak-side blocker should try to assist the center blocker.

• Be aggressive and take pride in blocking 1-on-1 with a hitter.

• The block is not responsible for blocking every hit, but it is responsible for making the spiker use a less advantageous shot and one which is predictable.

b) The blockers must be aware of the position or relationship of the ball with the net and then block accordingly.

• If the ball is close to the net the blocker should be across the net and above the ball at contact on every hit. The spiker has only the cut shot (extreme angle along the net). To combat this, block him to the inside. In the case of the wipe off, which is the terminology for a shot spiked off the hands, the blocker should pull his hands down or turn them in towards the court. The other possibility for the spiker is the soft shot and this is not the blocker's responsibility.

• If the ball is away from the net, delay the jump to allow it enough time to reach the net, and take away the power alley angle. A deep set will rarely be hit down the line.

- If the ball is set too wide (two feet or more out-of-bounds) and away from the net, both blockers should stay down, not block, and allow the fielders to dig the ball. The spiker has no chance of putting the ball down, and attempting to block most often results in errors by either the blockers or the other defensive players.
- If the ball is too far from the net, and the spiker is not going to attack, the free ball position should be assumed.
- If the ball is set too far inside and the spiker has to run to get there, block inside because it is the only power shot he has.

c) The blockers should know or read every hitter. They block against the same man throughout every game and face the same players in every tournament. What are the hitter's favorite shots? Does he hit the same way most of the time? Is he short? Can he hit a long shot? Does he use the hands of the block? Does he have a variety of shots? Can he *dink* and where? Does he blow when blocked? Does he watch the block for holes?

d) Blockers should form a sequential pattern for each attack by the opponents.

- Where is the first pass and who are the probable hitters? Eliminate certain possibilities.
- Watch the setter's hands for quicker recognition of the direction of the set.
- Watch the ball leave the setter's hands to locate where it is going to land in relationship to the net—outside or inside, high or low, close or away.
- Immediately concentrate on the hitter—his approach angle, his take-off, his shoulder and arm action in the air.
- Make blocking adjustments to compensate for the spiker's actions.
- Land ready to make the next play (recovery play or position for possible attack).

Reading By Non-Blockers

The fielders (players Nos. 1, 4, 5, and 6 in Diagrams Nos. 1 and 2) must be aware of the same factors presented in the previous explanation because it tells them whether to expect a dink, a power alley shot, a deep hit, no block, a free ball, a line shot, etc.

Positioning For 2-1-3

If the players have read properly, they should be in position to make a good defensive recovery which assists in a skillful transition to offense. If they have not read properly or are not in good defensive position, they are almost certain to lose the ball or give it back to the opponents without making an offensive attack. Positioning refers to being in a predictable spot on

1

2

3

4

5

6

the court and closely relates to reading.

I. Defensing the Outside Spike is shown in Series A, Illustrations 1, 2, 3, 4, 5, and 6 and Diagram 1.

a) Player No. 4's responsibilities and positioning are shown in Diagram 1.

- He should expect the power alley shot inside the blocker's hands and the dink inside the block.
- Analyze when the ball will not be set to the left side and move rapidly to a position near the 10-foot line (10 to 12 feet). The movement should be toward the ball at the moment of contact by the spiker. Any ball that comes chest high is out-of-bounds unless the player is too close to the middle of the court, therefore, out of position.
- He should attempt to play every ball in front of his body with a forearm pass.

• Defense is dependent upon player No. 4's ability to play the power alley shot.

b) Diagram 1 shows player No. 6's responsibilities and positioning.

• When the ball crosses to the opponent's side, player No. 6 should move to the middle of the court and just behind the 10-foot line. Then he should move laterally to cover behind the block as the ball is set and remain near the 10-foot line. Line up the ball between the blockers.

• Cover all dinks.

• He should attempt to play all balls off the block using an overhand pass to player No. 4 to spike. When using the forearm pass, play the ball high so another player can set it and the spikers can position for an attack.

• Play balls hit between the blockers which are usually head or chest high.

• Player No. 6 should move into the setter's position to run the multiple offense after determining that the ball is going to be played by a teammate.

c) Player No. 5's responsibilities and positioning are shown in Diagram 1.

• His movement should be primarily lateral (side-to-side). Cover approximately one-half the baseline, one-half the sideline, the cross-court corner, and any area forward.

• He should start approximately two yards from the baseline and two yards from the left sideline.

• Cover any hole in the block.

• He should play deep diagonal rolls, balls hit over the block, and any ball played off the top of the block.

• Move down the sideline to play a possible power alley shot if the middle blocker is not able to assist the outside blocker.

• Player No. 5 should not creep into the court, but wait to see where the ball is set (second contact), make a slow adjustment of position and a quick controlled movement toward the ball when it is spiked (third contact). Attempt to play a hard spiked ball with the forearms while keeping the body in a low position. If the ball is contacted first by another player (other than the block), usually No. 5 should attempt to set the ball for spiker, No. 2.

• Attempt to play the soft roll in the middle of the court.

• He should return to the original starting position near the sideline and baseline every time the ball goes into the opponent's court so a deep hit ball can be played with forward movement.

d) Diagram 1 shows player No. 1's responsibilities and positioning.

• He should play the hard line shot which few spikers possess. Move to approximately 17 feet from the net.

• Move laterally on the baseline covering approximately one-half the baseline.

• He should start on the sideline and two yards from the baseline.

• Player No. 1 should play the deep dink or roll and the ball played off the top of the block to area D.

- He should not creep into the court but wait to see where the ball is set. Make a slow adjustment of position and a quick controlled movement toward the ball as it is spiked. Attempt to play a ball that is spiked down the line with the forearms. If the ball is first contacted by another player (other than the block) usually attempt to set the ball for spiker No. 4.
- Attempt to play the soft roll in the middle of the court.
- He should return to the original starting position near the sideline and baseline every time the ball goes into the opponent's court so a deep hit ball can be played with forward movement.

e. Responsibilities for the weak area are shown in Diagram 1. Players Nos. 1, 4,and 5, should have the movement toward these areas if all have read properly.

II. Defensing the middle spike. There are three situations which occur when blocking the middle spiker—the one-man, two-man, and three-man blocks.

a) One-man block and coverage is shown in Diagram 4.

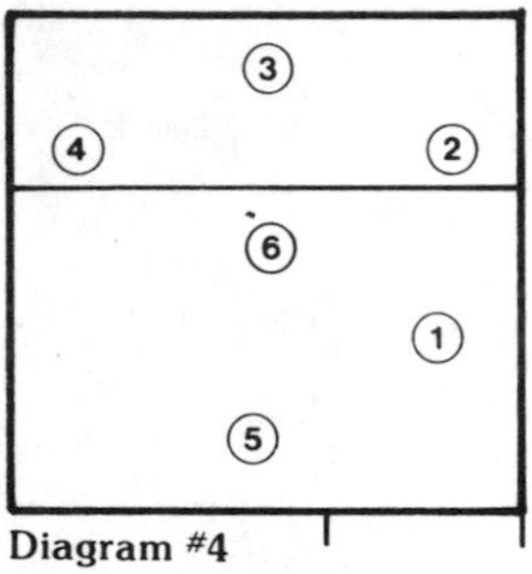

Diagram #4

The middle blocker, No. 3, is the only player who is able to block the quick (1 foot high) hit. He should key on the position of the setter and the possibility of a quick hit. This position will vary along the net (10 to 15 feet from the left sideline). If the setter is away from the net more than three feet the block position will then be more dependent upon the position of the spiker instead of setting the ball directly above and in front of the setter's position. The blocker should block with his hands spread and then close them in the direction in which the ball is hit. It should be a roof block due to the ball being close to the net.

- Blockers Nos. 2 and 4 drop away from the net to the vicinity of the 10-foot line and the sidelines to protect against the hard spike. They should also be ready for the dink along the net or to the side of the court.
- Player No. 6, the setter, should position himself directly behind the middle blocker (No. 3) in the middle section of the court and play all dinks over the block.
- Player No. 1 is responsible for the cutback sideline shot around the block.
- Player No. 5 should move to the middle back position to play the ball hit deep off the block and defend the entire back one-third of the court.

b) Two-man block and coverage is shown in Diagram 5.

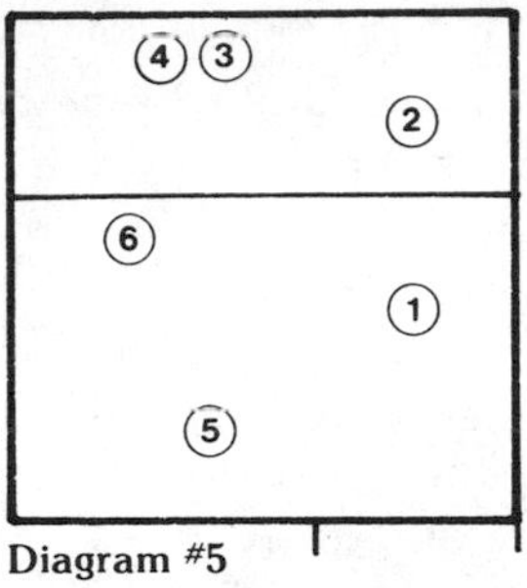

Diagram #5

On a ball set two feet or higher near the middle and to the left of center court, both blockers No. 3 and No. 4 should block. Their inside hands should be on the ball taking away as much of the court as possible.

- Blocker No. 2 drops off the net near the 10-foot line and is ready for cut back and dinks near the net.
- Player No. 6 (setter or up man) moves to the left of the block and is ready for soft shots behind and to the left of the block.
- Player No. 5 moves more to the middle of the court. He defends the back one-third and is ready for lateral movement in both directions plus forward movement for any shots through the block or deflecting deep off the block.
- Player No. 1 moves down the sideline to approximately 15 feet. He has lateral and forward movement from this position playing the cross-court hit.

c) Three-man block and coverage is shown in Diagram 6.

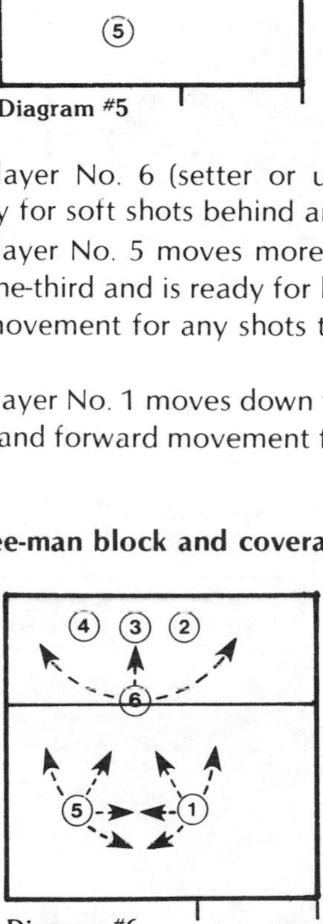

Diagram #6

All three blockers should attempt to block any high set in the middle with the middle blocker lining up on the ball and the outside blockers taking away any cut back.

1. Player No. 6 covers all dinks and positions near the 10-foot line.
2. Players Nos. 1 and 5 pinch toward the middle of the court and cover the back two-thirds of the court.

III. Free ball positioning for the 2-1-3.

A free ball results when the opponents cannot use a power attack on offense.

Free ball positioning when running the multiple offense with the setter in the man-up position is shown in Diagram #7.

a. Players Nos. 3 and 5 should position in the center one-third of the court to make the first pass with an overhand pass if possible. Then player No. 3 approaches to spike.

b. Players Nos. 2 and 4 should position to cover the right and left sideline. After the pass is made they will quickly move into position to spike.

c. Player No. 6, the setter who is playing behind the block, releases to be in position to set.

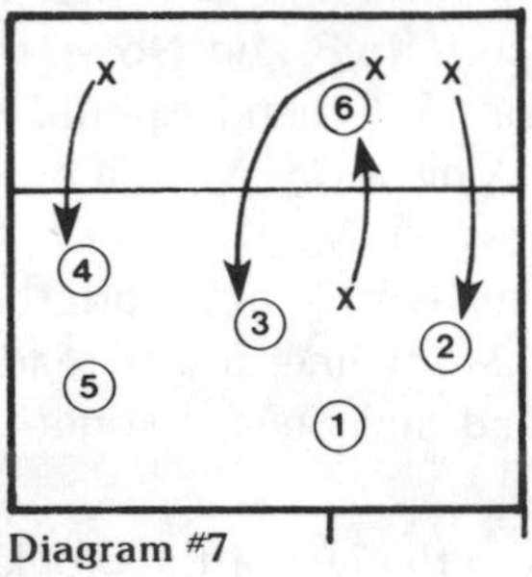

Diagram #7

In Diag. #8 an alternate method of covering a free-ball is shown. In Diag. #8 player #3 stays down near the net. He attempts to stay out of the play watching for any ball contacting the net and dropping into the middle of the court. Then he prepares to approach for the middle spike. If the middle blocker is not a good fielder, he should use this positioning. This formation does not afford as good a coverage as shown in Diagram #7.

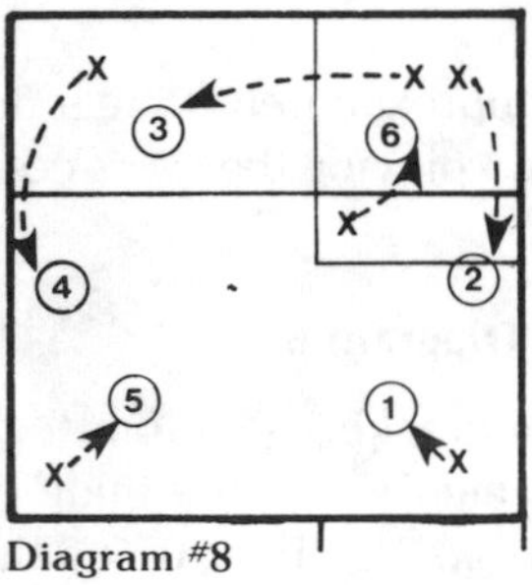

Diagram #8

a. Players Nos. 1, 2, 4 and 5 should move to form a four player defensive cup as the ball is contacted by the spiker.

b. Player No. 3 should move at the net preparing to approach for a spike and not field the ball. Players Nos. 2 and 4 should position to spike after the ball is fielded.

Positioning 2-4

I. *Defensing the outside spike* is shown in Series B Illustrations 1, 2, 3, 4, 5, and 6 and Diagram 2.

a) Player No. 4's responsibilities and position are shown in Diagram 2 (Zone A).

- Position 8 to 10 feet off the net and near the sideline.
- He should expect the extreme inside power shot which only high level players use.
- His movement should be toward the ball at the moment of contact by the attacker.
- After eliminating the power shot by reading, expect either the dink (soft shot) inside the block along the net or the deflection of the ball off the block. Do not move laterally in front of player No. 5.
- Be in position to attack if he does not play the ball.

1

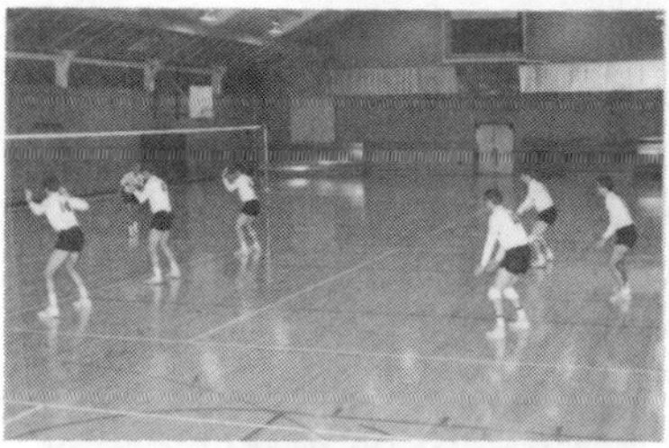
2

3

4

5

6

b) Diagram 2 (Zone B) shows player No. 5's responsibilities and positioning.

- Defense is dependent upon his ability to play the power alley shot.
- He moves down the sideline until he lines up diagonally seeing the ball just inside the middle blocker's hand (Series B Illustrations 2, 3, 4, 5, and 6).
- His movement is from the sideline toward the ball at the moment of contact.
- Proper positioning results in his always playing the ball with a forearm pass in front of him.

c) Player No. 6's responsibilities and positioning are shown in Diagram 2 (Zone C).

- When the ball is set to his right, he slides laterally to his left aligning with the ball and the space between the two blockers (Series B Illustrations 2 and 3).

● He moves toward the ball into the court if there is a hole in the block to defend the power attack.

● If no hole exists he stays near the baseline in the left one-third of the court attempting to play any ball hit off the blockers' hands to the back court. He defends the back one-third of the court.

● He is responsible for shots over the block deep to the back court with the corner behind the block difficult to protect.

● He must be mobile with good lateral movement.

d) Player No. 1's responsibilities and positioning are as shown in Diagram 2 (Zone D).

● He protects against the power line shot, if the block is too far inside, positioning about 18 feet from the net.

● If the line shot is not possible he moves to about midcourt on the sideline expecting a dink or a shot off the blockers' hands.

● The weak area near the middle of the court can be defended by player No. 1 if he reads properly and is certain there will not be a line shot.

● When using the multiple offense, this is the conventional position for placing the setter. After making certain that he will not play the ball, he moves to the front court to set the ball on the second contact.

Defensing the middle attack (one-man block) is shown in Diagram 9.

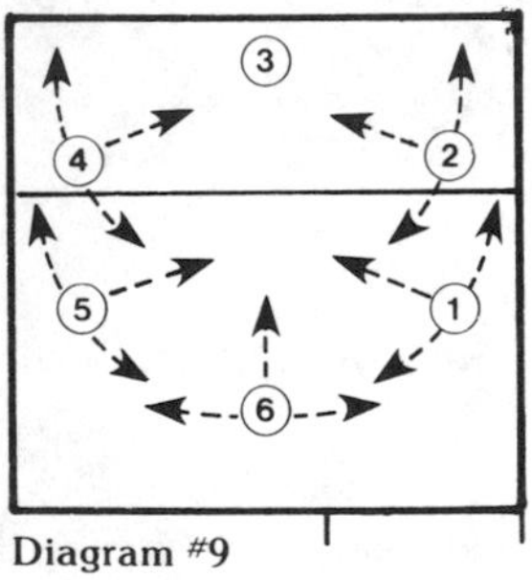

Diagram #9

a) Blockers Nos. 4 and 2 drop off the net 10 feet expecting the extreme power angle shot or the dink.

b) Players Nos.1 and 5 move down the sideline to approximately 15 feet expecting the power angle shot.

c) Player No. 6's position varies dependent upon the blocker or the spiker.

● If the spiker hits long or if the block is good, he stays near the baseline.

● If the spiker can execute the good middle hit or the block is not up in time, he moves to the middle of the court in a straight line with players Nos. 1 and 5.

d) Player No. 3 attempts to block the ball or at least take out a portion of the court with his hands and make the spiker hit around the block. Player No. 6 must be aware of the area covered by the block and swing in the opposite direction.

Defensing the middle attack (two-man block) is shown in Diagram 10.

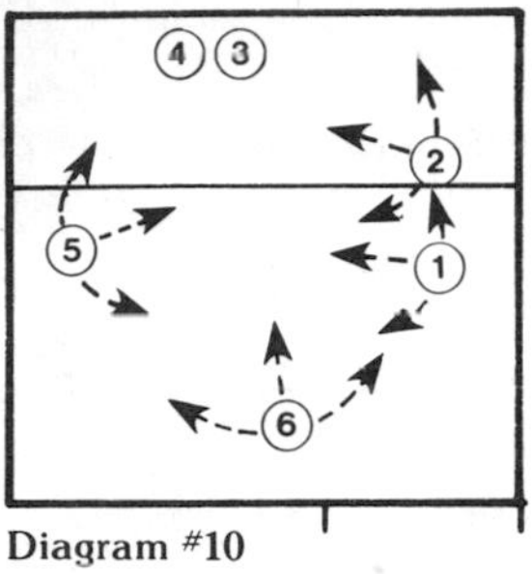

Diagram #10

On a high set to the middle, the defensive team should attempt to place at least two blockers on the spiker.

a) Blockers Nos. 4 and 3 form a two-man block attempting to block the ball or take out a great portion of the court with a tight block. Their positioning on the spiker will vary depending upon the spiker's ability to hit certain shots or the weaknesses in their own defensive fielders.

b) Player No. 1 who is the back row setter in the multiple offense protects the cut-back power alley shot. He plays defense first and releases quickly after seeing that he will not field the ball so that he may move to the setting position near the net.

c) Player No. 6 stays deep on the back line protecting the back one-third of the court watching for balls deflecting off the block or ones hit over the block. He moves toward the ball and to a position about 18 feet from the net if there is a hole in the block.

d) Player No. 5 moves toward the net along the sideline until he sees the ball outside the end blocker's hands. He expects the power angle shot or the dink.

e) Blocker No. 2 drops off the net to about the 10-foot line expecting the cut-back power shot or the dink.

Defensing the middle attack (three-man block) is shown in Diagram 11.

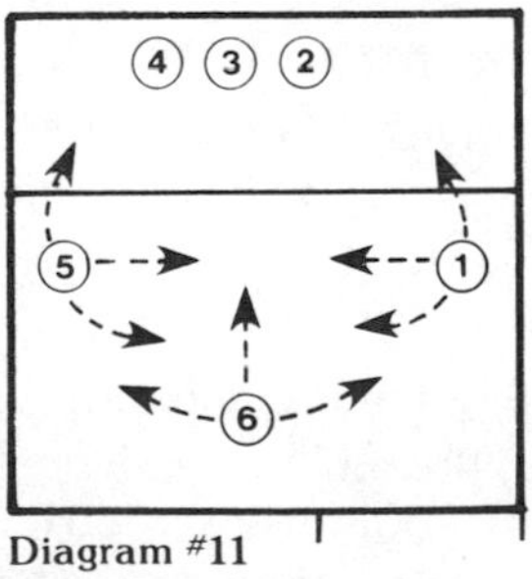

Diagram #11

The high middle set offers the opportunity for the defense to block with three men.

a) Blockers Nos. 2, 3, and 4, form a tight block attempting to block the ball.

b) Players Nos. 1 and 5 move down the sideline toward the net to about 12 feet expecting the dink since the block should cancel out any power angle spikes.

c) Player No. 6 stays near the baseline waiting for deflections off the top of the blockers' hands. He defends the back one-half of the court. If he sees a hole in the block, he moves toward the ball to about 18 feet from the net.

II. *Free ball positioning* is shown in Diagram 9. A free ball results when the opponents cannot use a power attack on offense. Diagram 10 show similar action with only the middle blocker, player No. 3, assuming different positions and responsibilities.

a) Player No. 1 who is the back court setter releases his sideline position and moves to the net to set immediately upon determining that the opponents cannot attack the ball. He watches for any ball deflecting off the net.

b) Player No. 6 moves laterally to his right from his middle back position to protect the right corner.

c) Player No. 5 moves from his starting position toward the middle of the court and becomes a prime fielder since many free balls are played to the middle of the court in the back one-third.

d) Player No. 4 drops off the net about 10 to 12 feet and is the prime fielder for the diagonal cross-court hit.

e) Player No. 2 drops off the net 12 to 14 feet watching for the soft shot and preparing for his spiking approach.

f) Player No 3's position and responsibilities are entirely different in the two Diagrams.

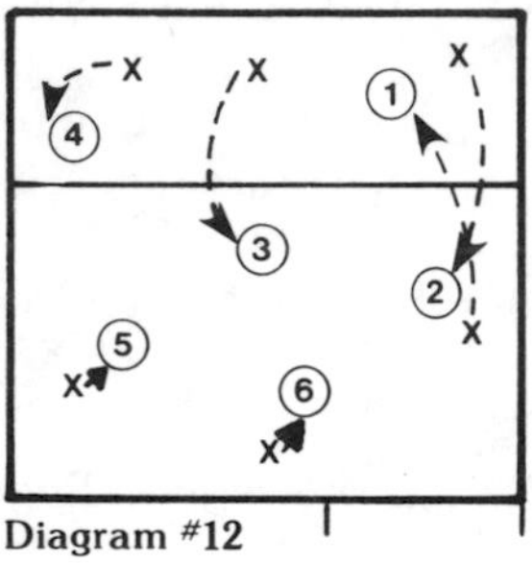

Diagram #12

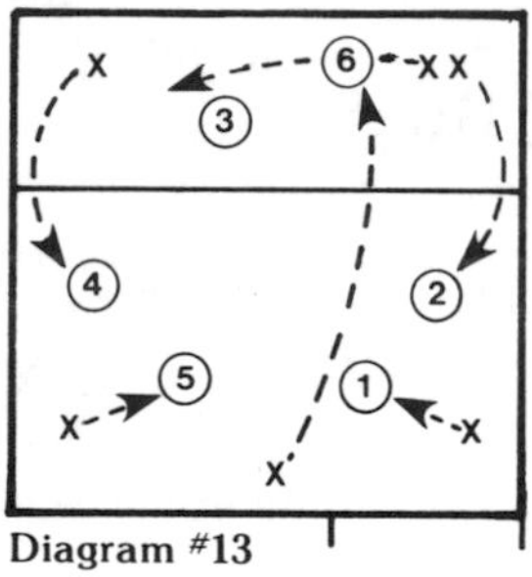

Diagram #13

Diagram 12—player No 3 moves to a prime fielding position in the middle of the court. If the player is a good defensive player, this positioning provides better court coverage and places him in better position to approach for the middle hit.

Diagram 13—player No. 3 stays down near the net. He attempts to stay out of the play watching for any ball contacting the net and dropping into the middle of the court. Then he prepares to approach for the middle spike. If the middle blocker is not a good fielder, he should use this positioning.

a) Players Nos. 1,2,4 and 5 should move to form a four player defensive cup as the ball is contacted by the spiker.

b) Player No. 3 should move along the net preparing to spike.

c) Player No. 6 the setter releases from position #6 to the right front and prepares to set.

d) Players Nos. 2 and 4 should position to spike after the ball is fielded.

If a player has read and positioned properly, the only thing left is to make the skilled play or execute. A player must develop fundamental defensive skills such as the forearm pass, stride-and-flex, dive and catch, dive and slide, one-arm dig, and back-of-the-hand shot. Consistent execution of these skills greatly enhances a player's ability to play good defense.

Desire is most important for developing a volleyball player's defensive abilities. He must have a desire to read, position, and execute, but even more important is the desire never to let the ball contact the floor without touching it first. Anything less than this attitude will not develop good defense. Players cannot use excuses. The same attitude must prevail whenever they are playing or practicing. When practicing never give up on a ball that appears to be out of reach.

DEEP HOLLOW DEFENSE

by

Yoshiaki Kazio
Japanese National Coaching Staff

I. Two Blocking Techniques and Deep Defense Positioning

1. Allow a team 3 contacts after a touch on the block.
2. Move antennas 20 cm. inside previous location on the tape.

These were major rule changes in 1977, which were soon used in every domestic game in Japan. The 1977 Japan league, which is the strongest and most prominent in Japanese Volleyball Association's competition, adopted these new rules. Each team in the league has experienced these changes and worked hard on the adjustment.

This article will discuss some results of changes, how the new techniques were applied, what kinds of tactics were successful, etc. The topics here will be based on various discussions I had with players and coaches as well as what I saw and felt in that league.

First, consider what types of offensive techniques were more successful. Then we will proceed to the discussion of blocking and defensive techniques.

1. High Outside Spike with Maximum Reach
   A hard hitting spiker like Mr. Tanaka of Japan Steel Co. showed better spiking statistics. Therefore, it is apparently better to have spikers who can execute a spike from high reach with tremendous power.
2. Irregular Type of Spike
   If a spiked ball travels in an irregular course, such as curving or floating, the defenders often have a difficult time controlling it.

3. Smart Dink
   In the league, a dink which went over the blockers into the middle was very effective because defenders stayed deep near the endline and left the middle of the court open.
4. Wipe Off
   Most spikers, especially shorter ones, expressed difficulty beating the block because of rule change 2. Thus they had to drive the ball off the blocker's hand very hard using this technique more often.
5. More intricate and precise fast offense than before.

These lists were common observations made by many coaches during the league. It should be noted that (1) was the most effective means of gaining points and side-outs. A power hitter with a high reach had great advantages under the new rule.

Next are the kinds of blocking and defensive alignments that were considered difficult to attack by spikers.

1. Blocker with high percentage of successful blocks.
2. Blocker who can soft block a ball and enable his team to run their offense from the dig.
3. Defensive player who can make a dig from deflected balls. For example, middle back players who stayed deep and played balls hit deep off the block; or, line diggers who waited outside the line for balls wiped off the block out of bounds. Then, the team can convert a hard spike into a free ball.
4. Good defensive movement against dinks and soft hits.
5. High reaching blocks with good timing.

These points mentioned above are not really new but have become more important under the new rules. As a result the attack relies more on cross court hits rather than simple down the line spiking due to the change in antenna position.

Blocking and defensive techniques have also been changed as a result of the new rules. When blocking over the net was illegal, the block was considered a passive technique. The legalization of blocking over the net turned this technique into a very aggressive, offensive one. In a similar sense, new rules have caused certain modifications to the blocking concept. For example, soft blocking is more suitable than the aggressive type when the blocker cannot reach high enough to kill. Soft blocking makes a free ball out of hard hit by eliminating the error of lowering the blocker's height against a high reaching spiker. The blocker must understand that the worst block is one in which the jump is too early or the hands are too far from the net. It is also better to delay so that the hands will deflect the ball upward. Therefore, it is usually better that the blocker jump even if he thinks he is late. On a tight set, the aggressive block is still more effective.

Are there any changes in defensive formation? The answer is yes. During the Japan league many teams changed their formation into a deep, hollow shape, in which the front defenders stayed wider and the back court defenders stayed very deep. These changes allow front players to prepare for wipe offs, and allow back court players to play deflected balls. Of course, this defense leaves a big hole in the middle of the court.

II. Illustration of Blocking and Receiving Formation

(1) Relation between blockers and defenders against strong side attack

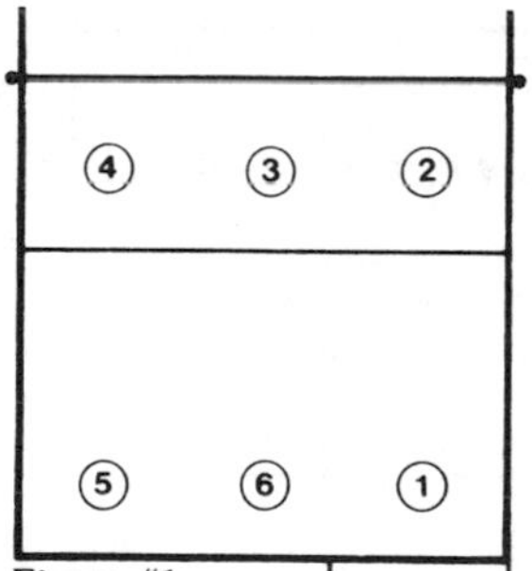

Figure #1

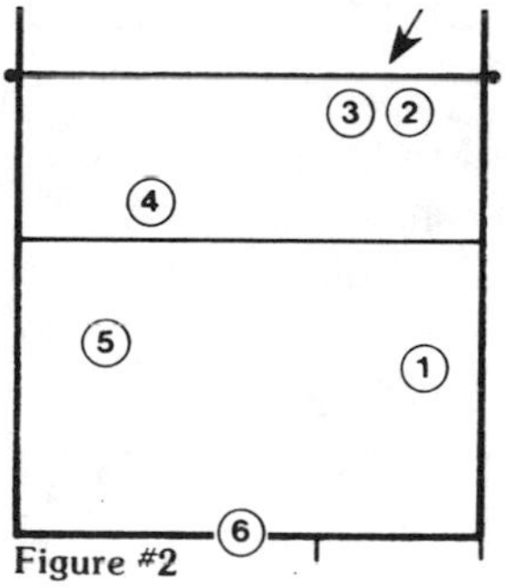

Figure #2

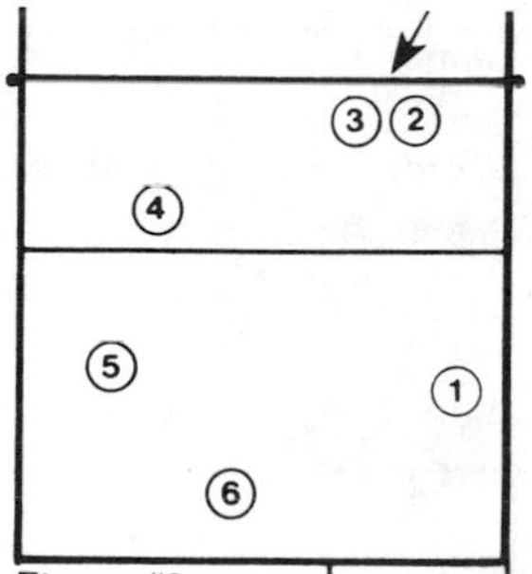

Figure #3

Fig. 1 shows starting positions of a team. As shown in Fig. 2, #6 is positioned on the end line in order to play all balls hit long off the block. The dink has to be covered by #1. This formation was the most frequently used in the last Japan league compeition. Fig. 2 should be compared with Fig. 3, which was commonly used in previous competitions.

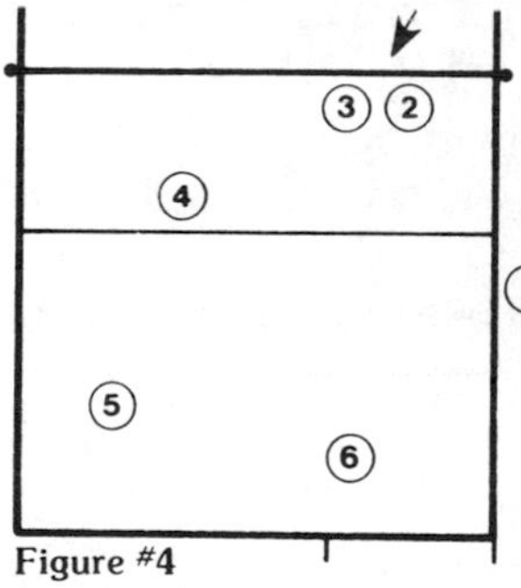

Figure #4

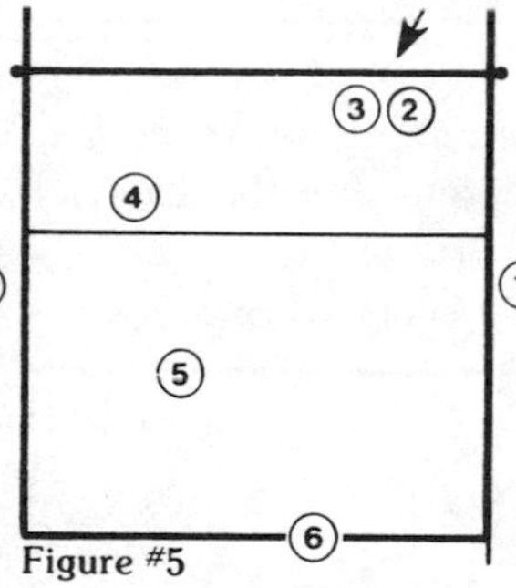

Figure #5

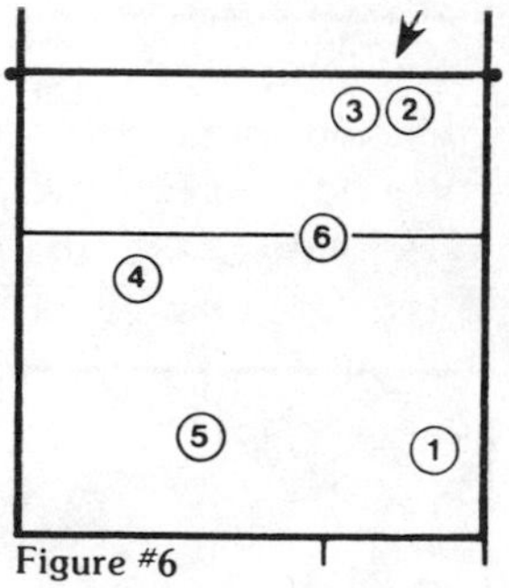

Figure #6

Fig. 4; #1 has moved quickly off the court to play the hit, because the spiker would not try to wipe off if he stayed out of the court. #1 will cover the down the line kind, while #4 will be in charge of the cross court dink. It is obvious that the deep spike is hard to defend in this formation.

Fig. 5; #1 stays off the court and #6 waits on the endline in order to play the deep shot. Here the dink defense will be weaker.

Fig. 6; illustrates a "man up" defense, in which #6 plays up for the dink. #1 and #5 stay deep. The defense for the sharp crosscourt spike and dink is weak in this alignment due to #6's position. The left deep area is also hard to cover.

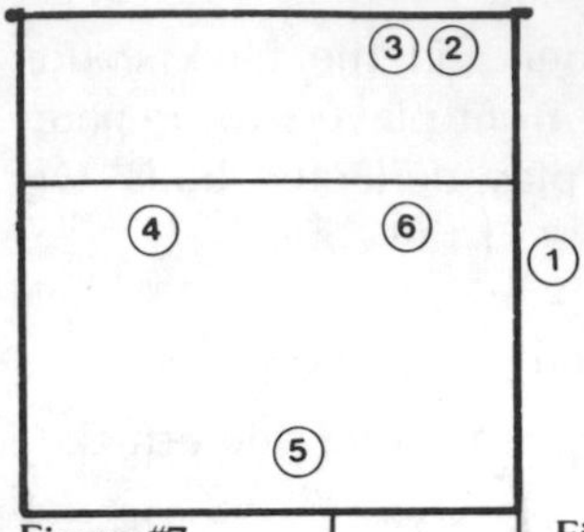

Figure #7

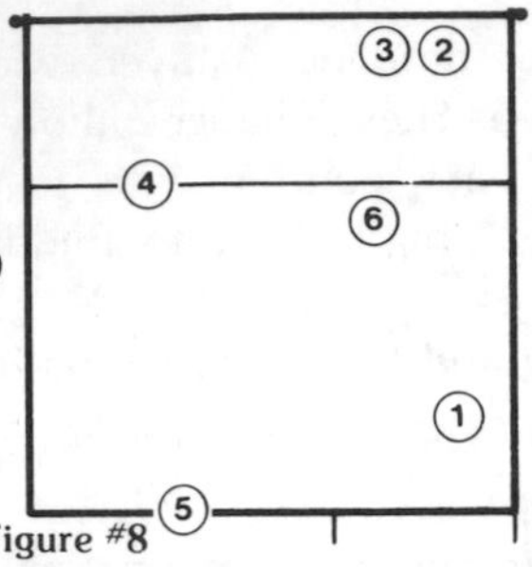

Figure #8

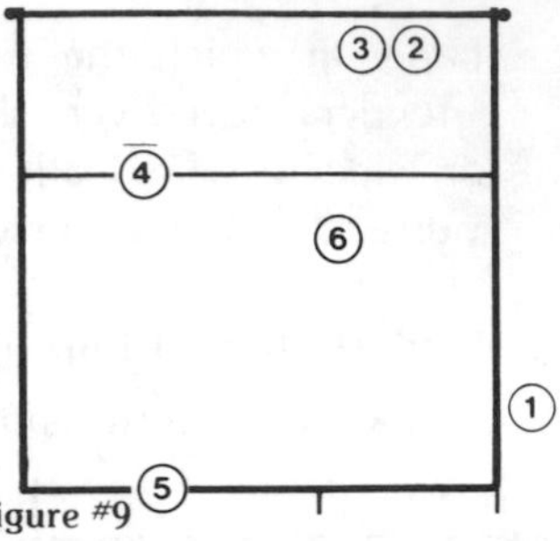

Figure #9

Fig. 7; #1 plays for wipe off by moving off the court as soon as the hit is made. #6 takes dinks. Weak in left back area.

Fig. 8; #6 plays dink and #5 plays on the endline shifted away from net.

Fig. 9; #1 plays for the wipe off, #6 plays for the dink (but slightly deeper than in 8), #5 plays on the endline.

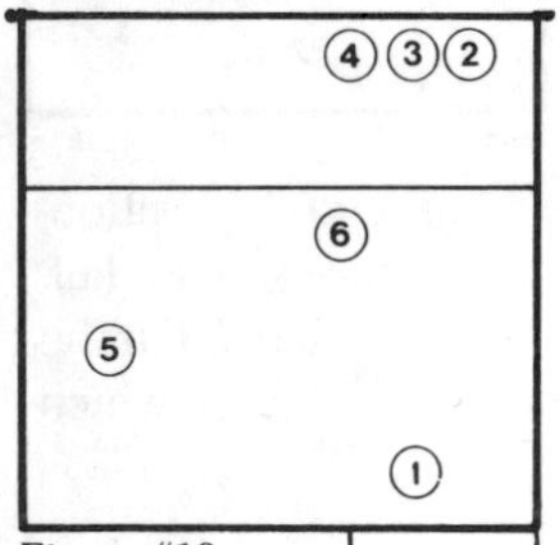

Figure #10

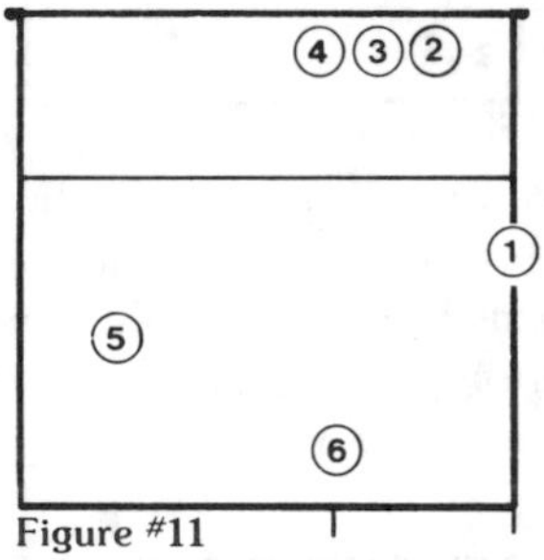

Figure #11

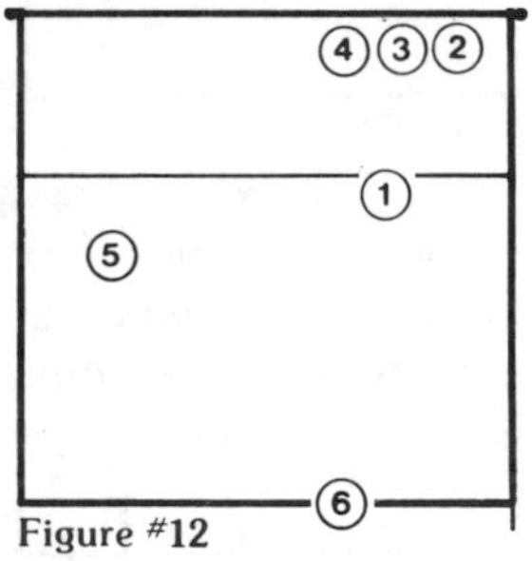

Figure #12

Fig. 10; 3 man block with #6 man up. The block must be very good.

Fig. 11; 3 man block. #1 covers for the wipe off as well as the dink. Tough to defend against crosscourt dink.

Fig 12; 3 man block. #1 covers all dinks, while #6 plays on the endline.

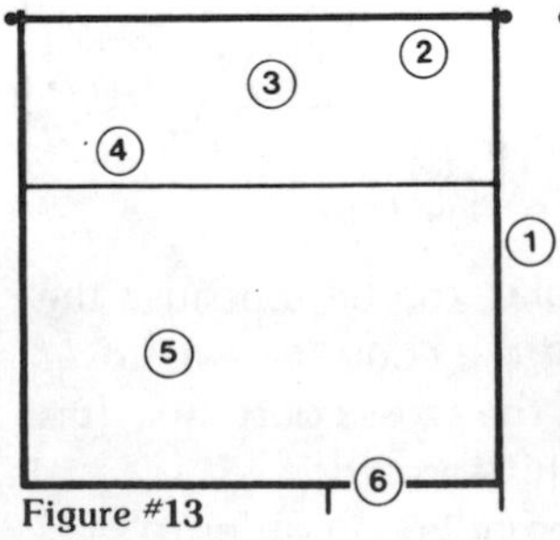

Figure #13

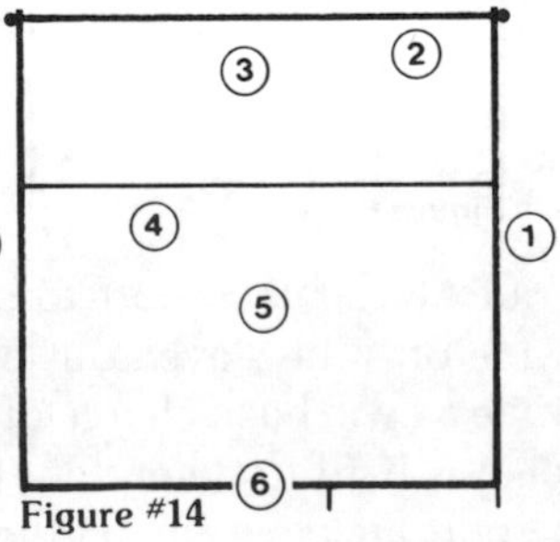

Figure #14

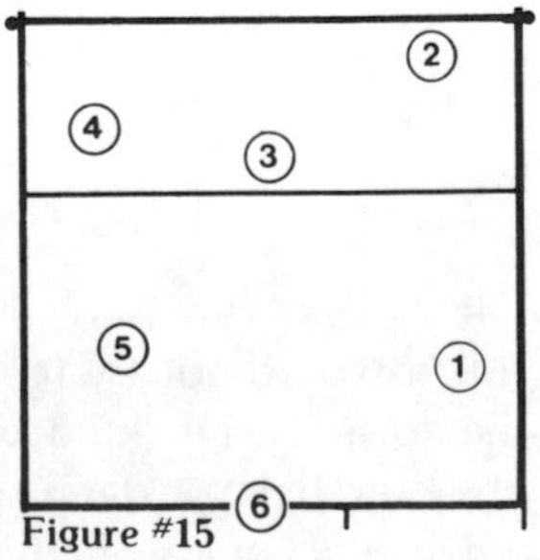

Figure #15

Fig. 13; #1 covers the wipe off and the down the line dink. #3 plays the crosscourt dink, #6 plays the endline. This formation is weak against the crosscourt spike.

Fig. 14; #5 is in the middle for the dink. This formation dangerous for a long, line hit.

Fig. 15; #3 is off the net, while #6 has endline hits.

(2) Relation between blocks and defenders against right side attack.

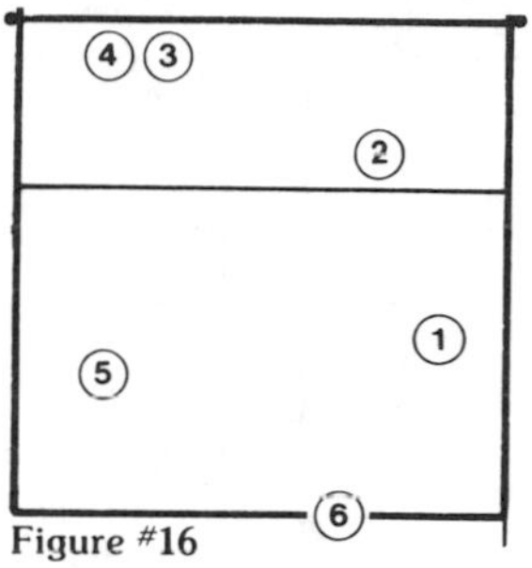

Figure #16

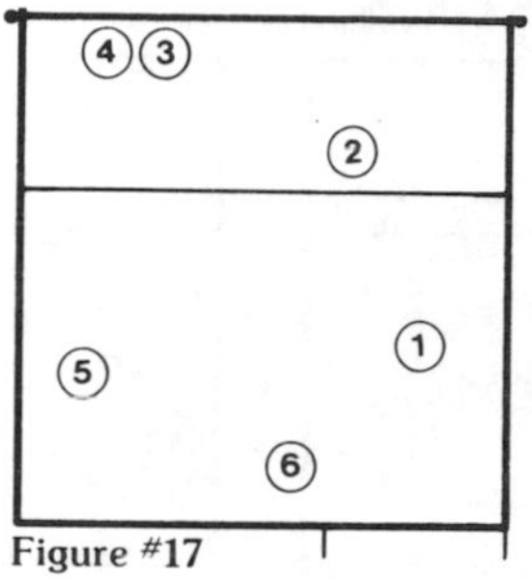

Figure #17

Fig. 16 is the most commonly used formation after the rule change. On the other hand, Fig. 17 used to be very popular prior to the rule change. Notice how the two can be modified more.

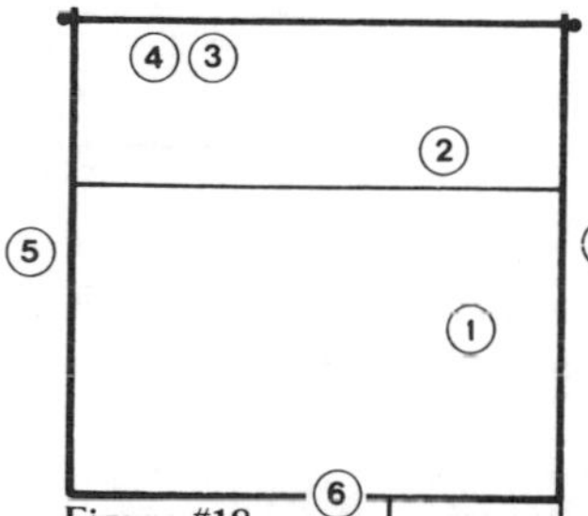

Figure #18

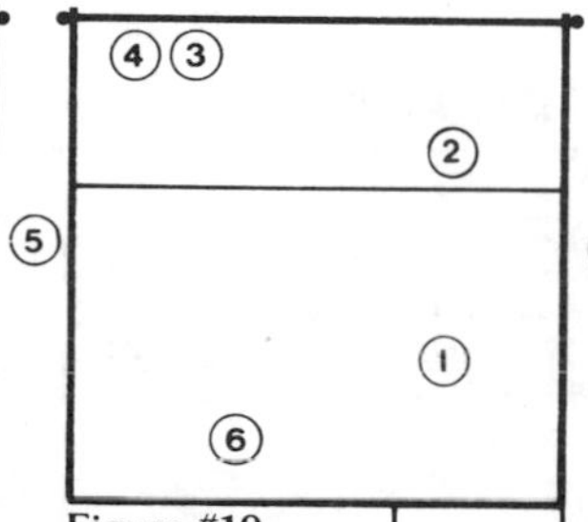

Figure #19

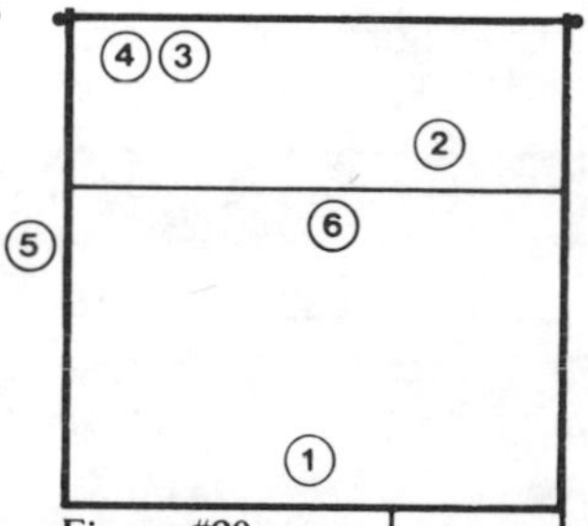

Figure #20

Fig. 18 shows that #6 stays very deep for deflected balls, but this formation is weak for the middle dink.

Fig. 19; In this alignment it is hard to defend against the deflected ball deep. #5 moves off the court with the hit and also covers the straight dink. #2 takes the crosscourt dink.

Fig. 20; #5 stays off the court for the wipe off. #6 covers the dink. Weak for back left and right.

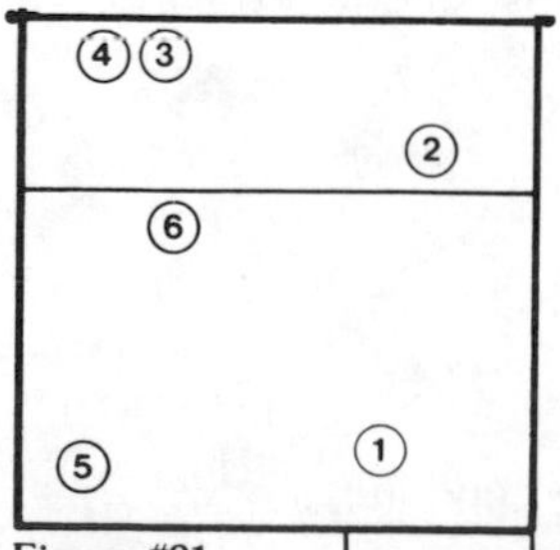

Figure #21

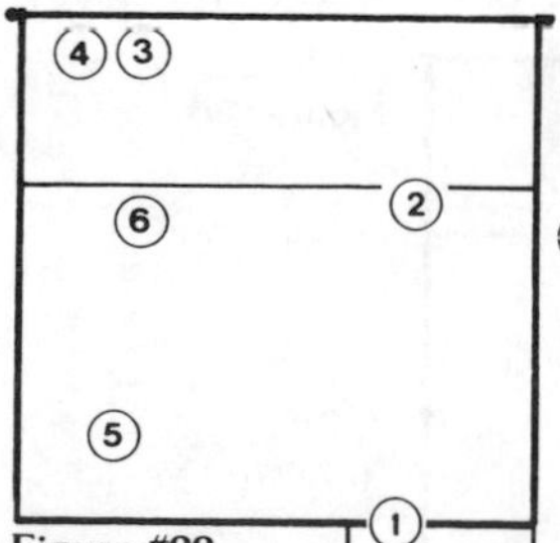

Figure #22

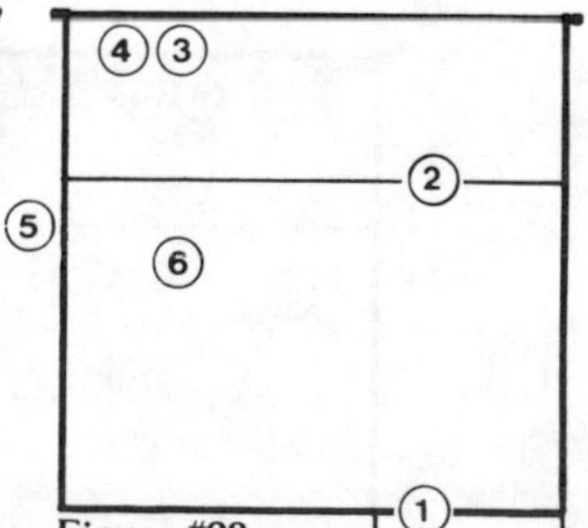

Figure #23

Fig. 21; #6 covers and #5 stays deep down the line.

Fig. 22; #6 covers all the dinks and #1 stays deep on the endline.

Fig. 23; #6 covers all the dinks but is slightly deeper than in Fig. 22. #5 stays outside of the court, while #1 plays on the endline, vulnerable against deep down the line spike.

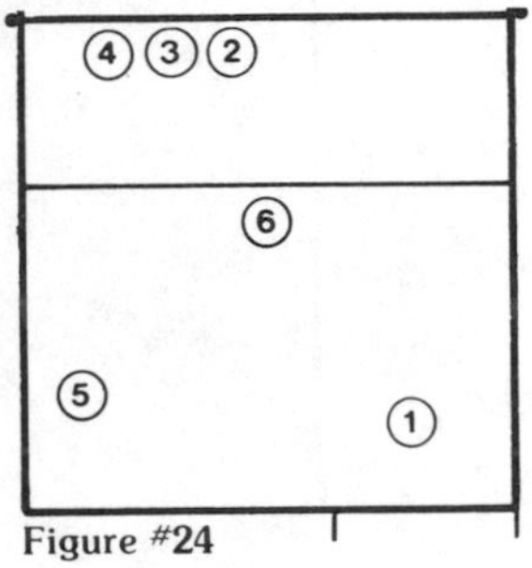

Figure #24

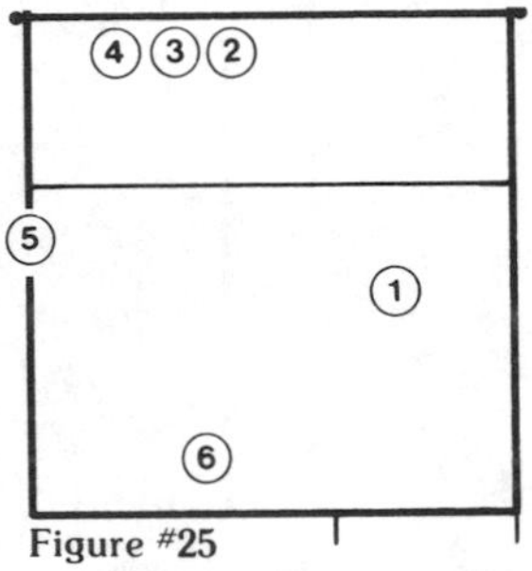

Figure #25

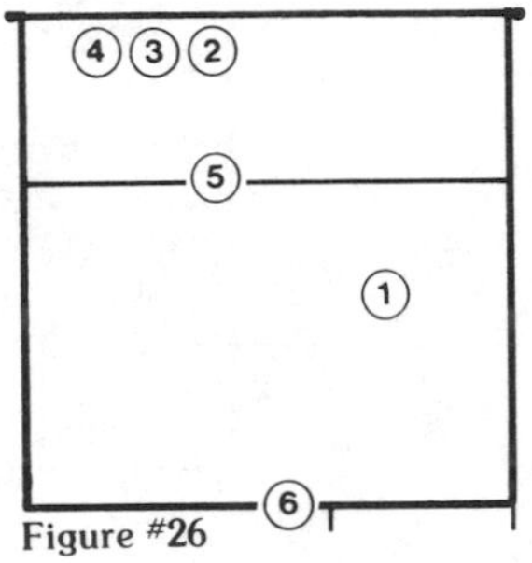

Figure #26

Fig. 24; 3 man block system. #6 covers all dinks. Hard to cover the sharp crosscourt dink. Must have an excellent block.

Fig. 25; 3 man block with #5 covering the wipe off and dink. Weak for crosscourt dink.

Fig. 26; #5 covers dink and #6 for the endline spike.

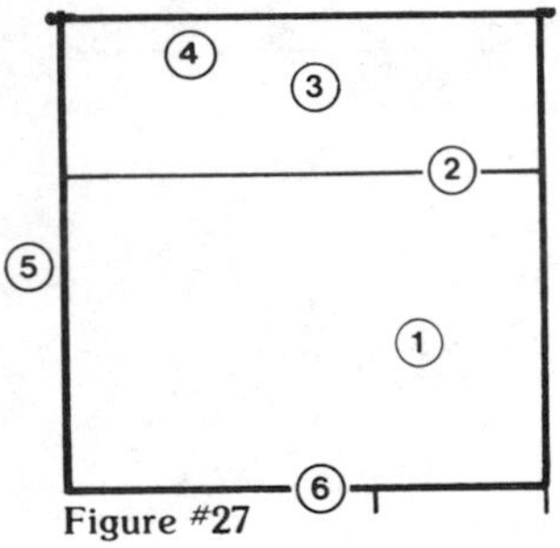

Figure #27

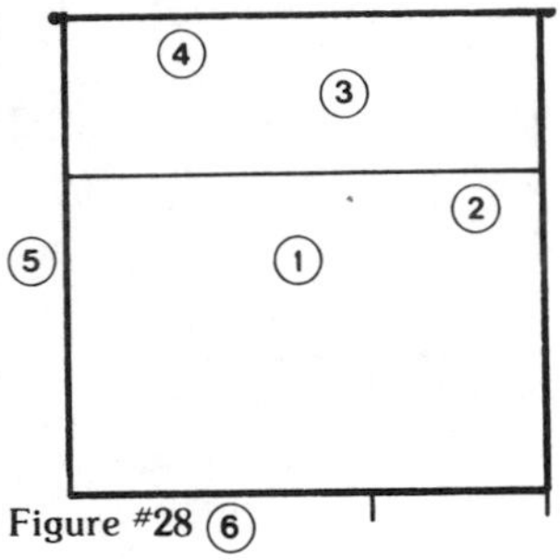

Figure #28

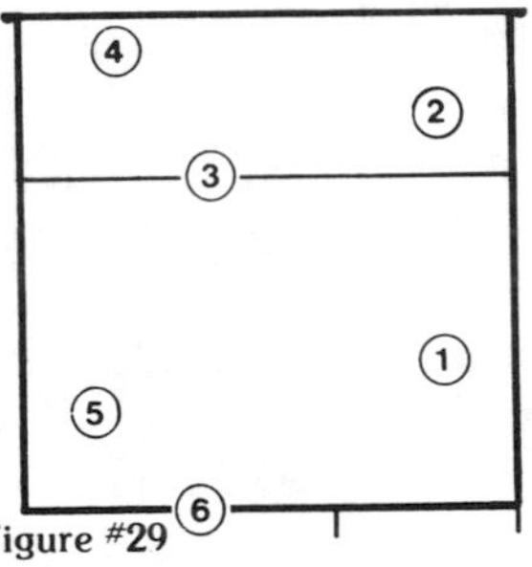

Figure #29

Fig. 27; #5 plays for wipe off as well as down the line dink. #3 covers crosscourt dink and #6 has endline. Tough to defend the middle of the court.

Fig. 28; #1 covers dink. Weak for back left.

Fig. 29; #3 is off the net (around 3M line), #6 is on the endline.

(3) Relation between blockers and defenders against middle attack.

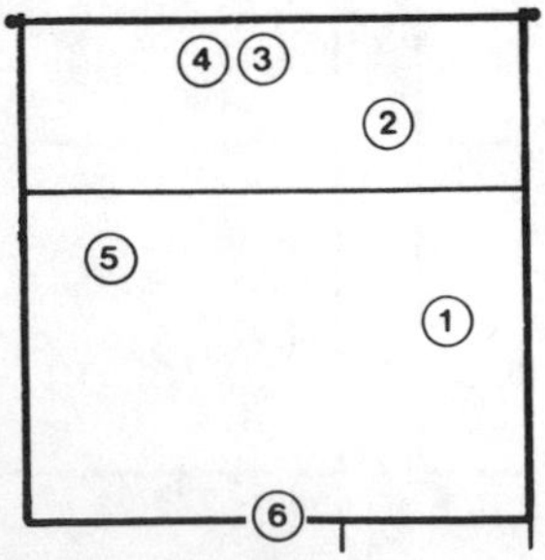

Figure #30

Fig. 30; #6 is on the endline.

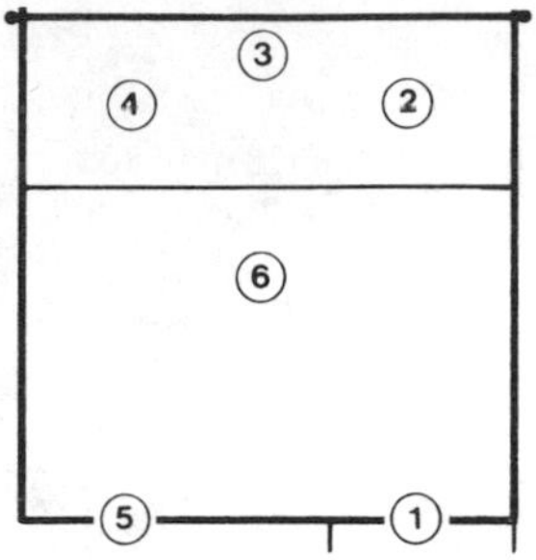

Figure #31

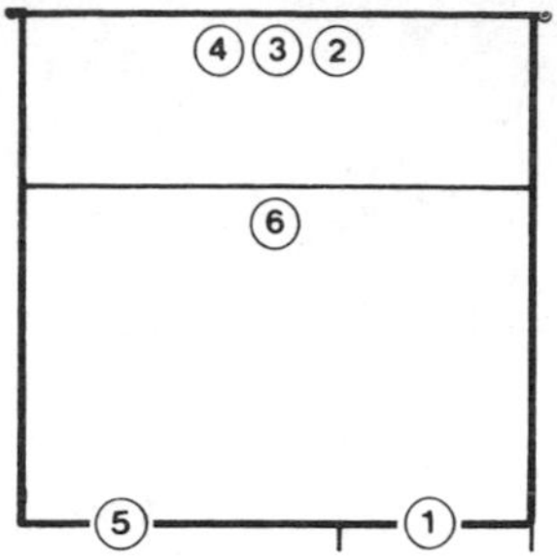

Figure #32

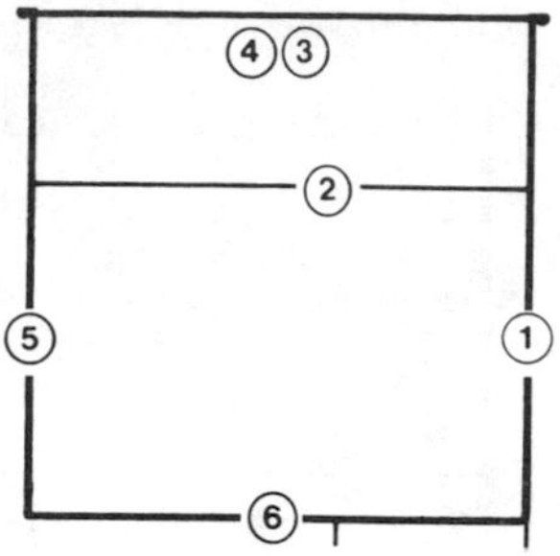

Figure #33

Fig. 31; #6 covers all dinks, while #1 and #5 stay on the line.
Fig. 32; 3 man block with #6 covering all dinks. Weak against shots to the left close to the net.
Fig. 33; #2 covers all dinks.

These are the various types of formations using the illustrative examples. However, when we apply these formations, we must be aware of the basic blocking techniques, as well as the spatial limit of the spikes. These are discussed below.

(1) Blocking Techniques

Figure #34

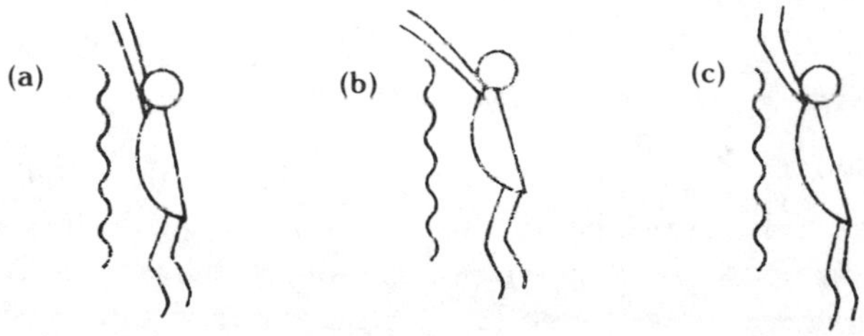

Fig. 34 illustrates 3 different techniques used in blocking.

a) Used before the Tokyo Olympics, when over the net was illegal.
b) The only technique used before the rule changed.
c) The new technique that can be used with a). This enables defenders to play a hard hit and make it a free ball. Thus, it is called a soft block.

It is important under the new rule to master both b) and c), and to be able to execute the suitable one for every blocking situation.

(2) Spatial Limitation for Spiking

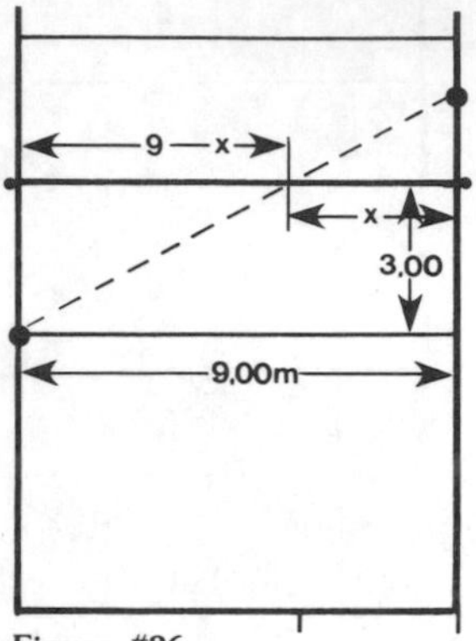

Figure #36

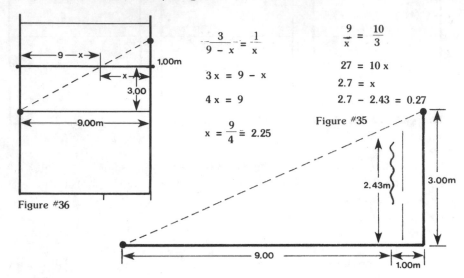

$$\frac{3}{9-x} = \frac{1}{x}$$

$$3x = 9 - x$$

$$4x = 9$$

$$x = \frac{9}{4} = 2.25$$

$$\frac{9}{x} = \frac{10}{3}$$

$$27 = 10x$$

$$2.7 = x$$

$$2.7 - 2.43 = 0.27$$

Figure #35

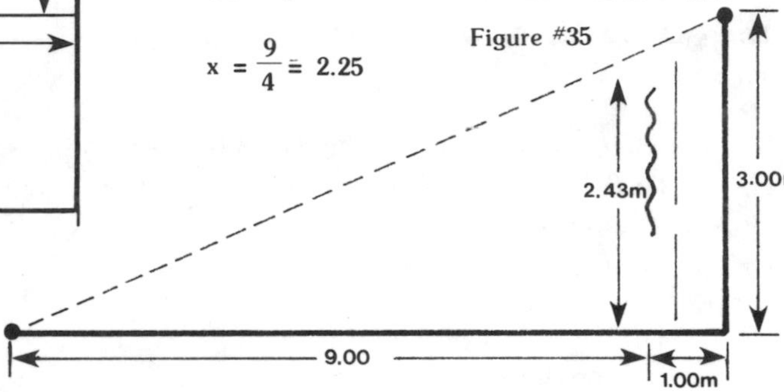

Figures 35 and 36 show the angle and course of a spike coming to the defenders.

If a spike comes from 3m off the ground and 1m off the net and lands on the endline (a bâll travelling along the sideline), the hit will clear the net by 0.27m. according to the calculations as seen in the formula. This is shown in Fig. 35.

Fig. 36 illustrates a situation in which a spike comes from the point (B), 1 m off the net and lands on the 3m line in the crosscourt at the point (A), it should cross the net 2.25m. inside of the antenna. (see formula with Fig. 36).

Using the concepts described in Figs. 34,35 and 36, we should consider the relationship between blocking and defense. Then, the best defensive formation can be chosen from the examples discussed in this article.

However, most examples listed here are assumed to have good blocking and defensive players with equal abilities. Also, in the actual game situation, one must consider the opponent's offensive system. Thus it is obvious that defensive formation should be different case by case and time by time. Of course, there is no one formation which can be applied to all situations. Therefore, most of the teams in the Japan league can execute several different formations. However, generally speaking, any team should master the two blocking techniques (the penetrating and/or soft blocking) as well as the deep hollow defense formation with quick coverage against dink and wipe off shots.

To conclude this discussion, I would like to emphasize the importance of mastering basic techniques. Before these formation techniques can be attempted, one must excell in the fundamentals.

CASE STUDY OF SOME DEFENSIVE FORMATIONS

by

Chon Il Park

Trainer of the USA-East

Acknowledgments:

The author acknowledges the assistance of Mr. Ralph Hippolyte and Mr. Scott Mosé, fruitful discussions with Mr. Yoshiaki Kazio.

Experience is one of the most important ingredients to winning. However, experience takes time. How can a coach begin to train his team and cut down the length of time required to gain experience? One possibility is my theory of a "Case Study of Defense and Offense". The definition of case study is what possible action can occur on each contact of the ball. Each case study has various channels, that is, avenues or courses that each contact of the ball may take. For example, the channels in beginner level play are very limited. The channels in advanced level are very diverse.

The intention of this paper is to list possible channels of attack by the opponents. Players can learn these channels by the drills which a coach designs accordingly.

Classification of Cases

(1) Defense against a hard spike—
When the set comes with a regular trajectory, the pass is close enough to the net and into the setter's hands. The spiker can hit with regular approach and motion which enables him to reach maximum jump.

(2) Down Ball Defense—
When the set is not accurate, too far, too low, behind the spikers, the ball can not be hit down, sharp and hard.

(3) Defense against tight balls—

(4) Change of Pace Defense—
  a) Against Dinks
  b) Power Dinks (Placement Shots)
  c) Against a wipe off
  d) Against setter's toss over and second hit

(5) Defense against a back court spike

This list describes the possible channels during a game when defenders are under the opponents' attack. When you are on defense, you must remember these channels and anticipate the opponent's next move. Then, if your team anticipates the next play that the opponents may take, your defensive system must be flexible and adjust to situations (1) to (5). You must be familiar with the channels and practice a different system for each situation.

Study of Cases

(1) Defense against a hard spike—

CASE-A. From the No. 4 position

1-A) Regular arc set:

Diagrams in (a) section illustrate the setter's position, approach of the spiker, range and direction of the spike and the expected position of the defensive player. Diagrams in (b) show the setter's position, path and angle of the set in relation to the net, and arc of the set.

As in Figure 1-a., the direction of the spiker's approach is the direction of his strong hit. The middle blocker will cover this angle and the other blocker prepares for the line spike when the spiker changes the direction by using his arm, wrist and shoulder. If the set has a slight angle to the net (see Figure 1-b.), then hit will be sharper.

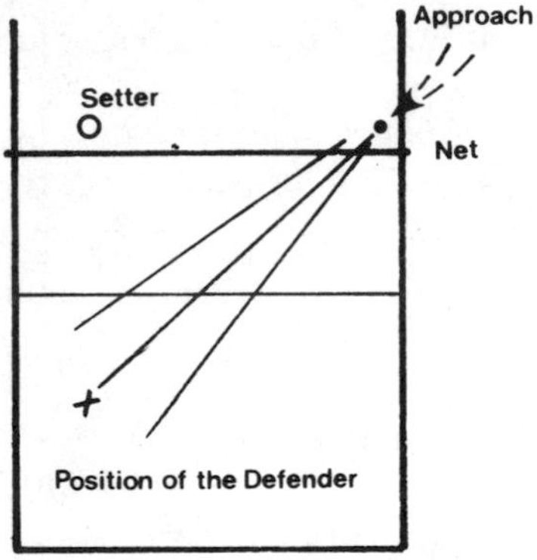

Figure 1-a.

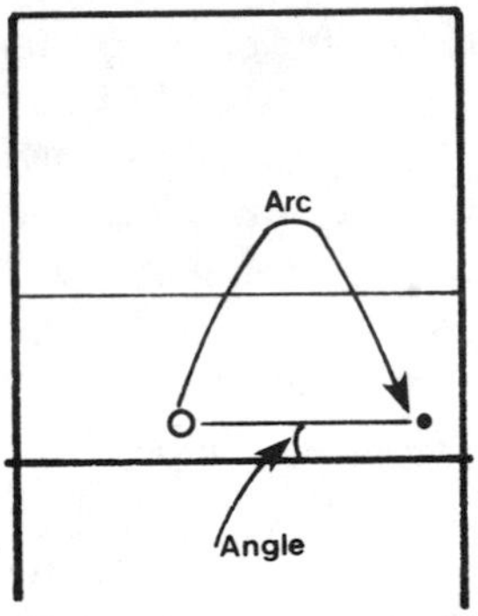

Figure 1-b.

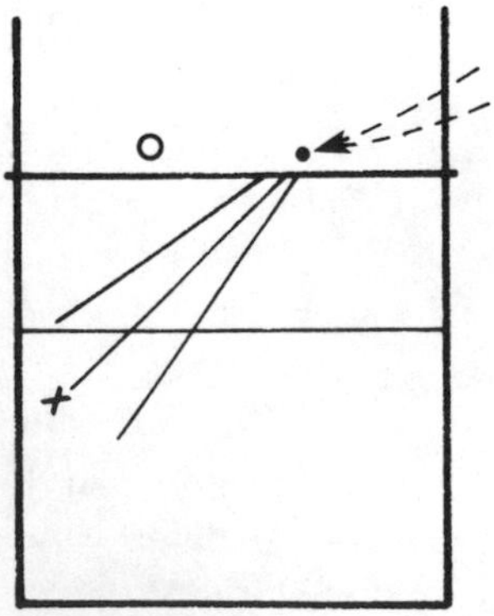
Figure 2-a.

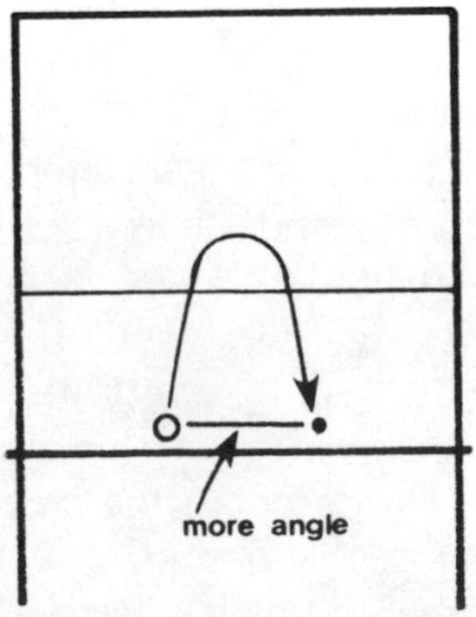

Figure 2-b.

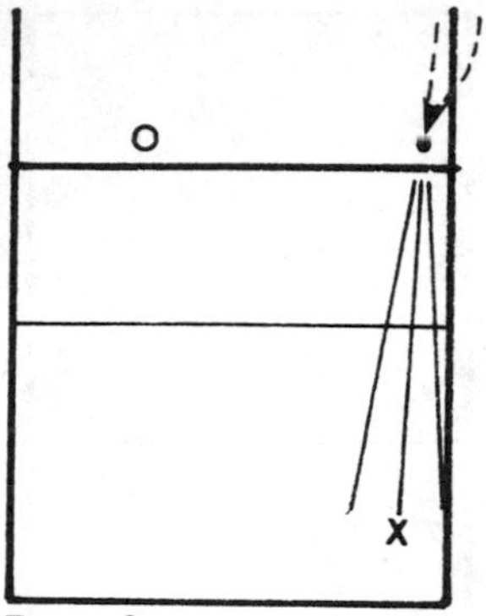

Figure 3-a.

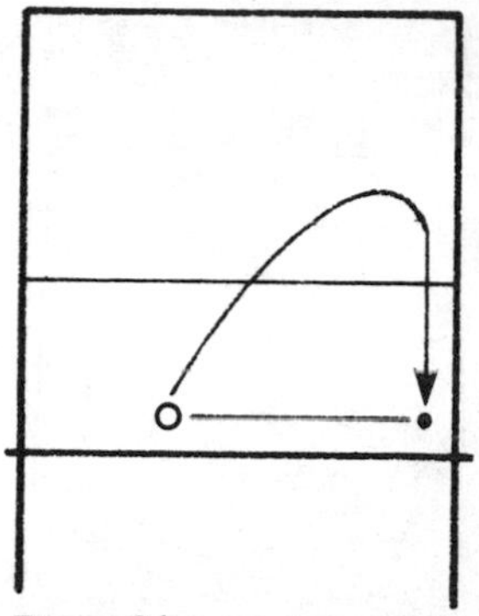

Figure 3-b.

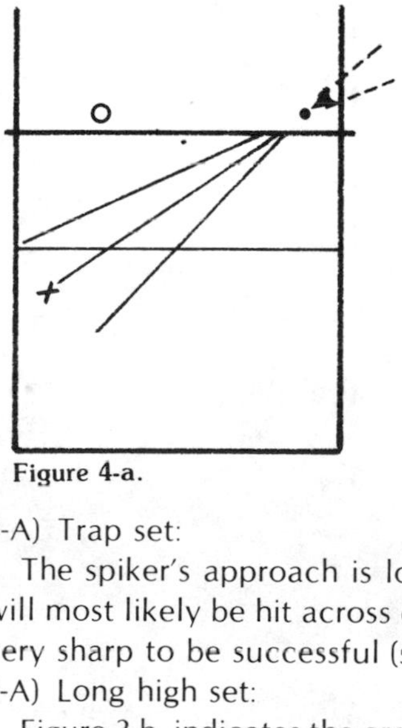

Figure 4-a.

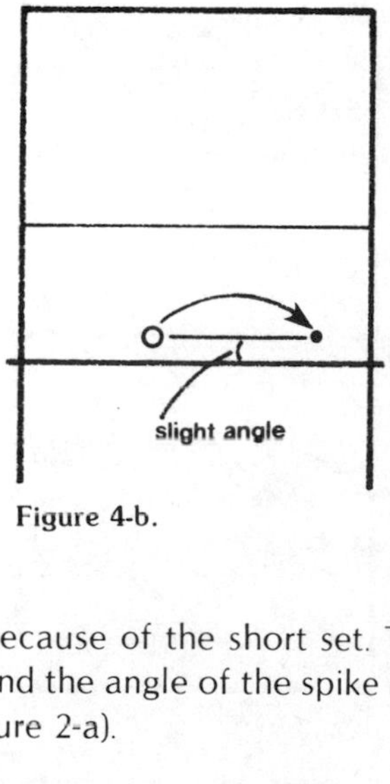

Figure 4-b.

2-A) Trap set:

The spiker's approach is longer because of the short set. The ball will most likely be hit across court and the angle of the spike must be very sharp to be successful (see Figure 2-a).

3-A) Long high set:

Figure 3-b. indicates the arc of the ball that the setter sends with top spin. Also, it shows that the ball travels parallel to the net. The approach may vary. However, this particular set is effective when hitting down the line. (See Figure 3-a.)

4-A) Semishoot and shoot:

Figure 4-a and 4-b.; A ball travels to the net with a single angle and the setter uses back spin. Anticipate a cross court spike. On the other hand, if the ball travels with topspin parallel to the net, anticipate a down the line spike. (See Figure 5-a and b.)

6-A) Back court set:

Figure 6-a and b show the spike from a set coming from the

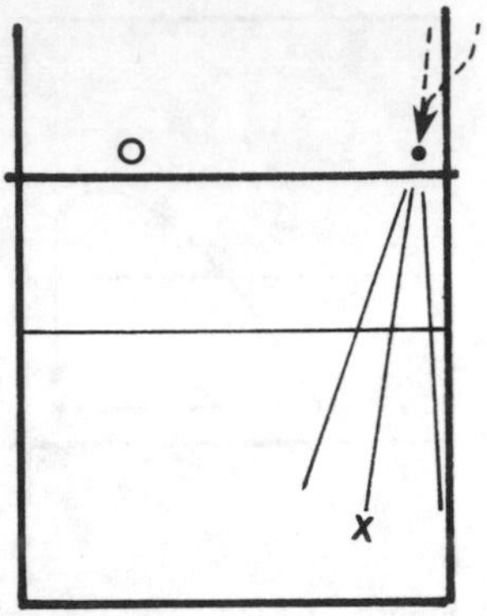

Figure 5-a.

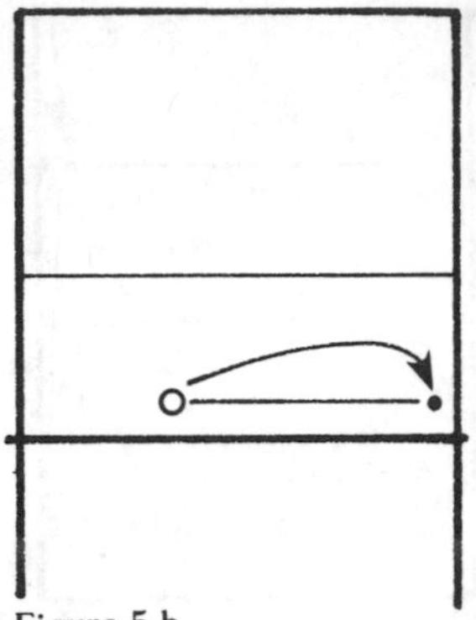

Figure 5-b.

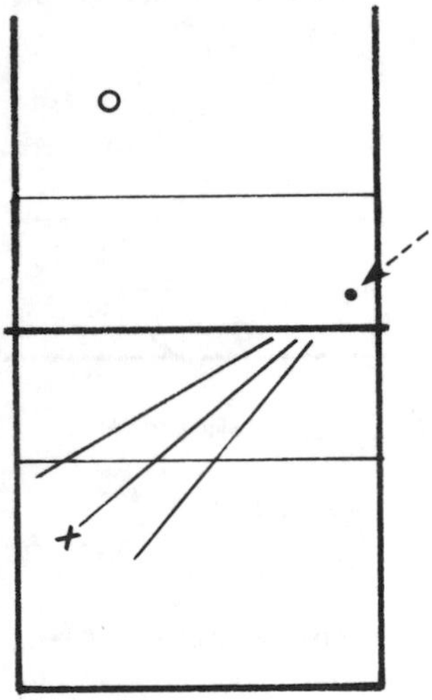

Figure 6-a.

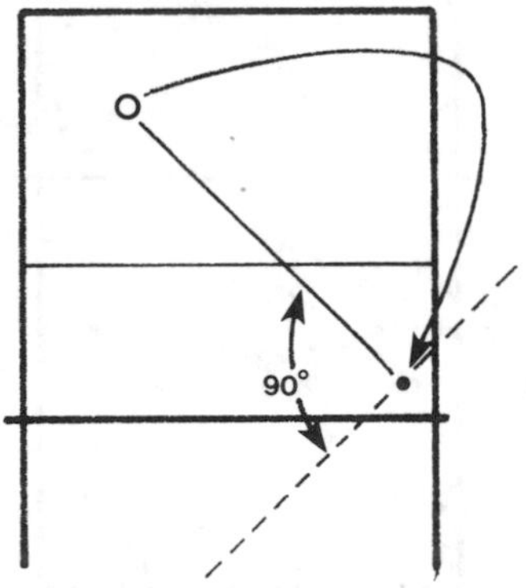

Figure 6-b.

backcourt. Notice the angle between the setter and spiker is 90 degrees. The relative position of the player setting and the spiker allows you to anticipate the direction of the spike.

CASE-B. From the No. 3 position

Figures 7,8 and 9 show the direction of the approach, the direction and range of the spike, and relative position of the defender. The spiker's hit from the middle (including A and B quick) is very predictable. It is the direction of their approach and where they are facing at the moment of the spike, unless they quickly change their shoulder, arm, and wrist action while in the air. However, they will lose some strength and power. Thus, the block takes away the spiker's most powerful shot, and defenders move to play in the direction of weaker shot.

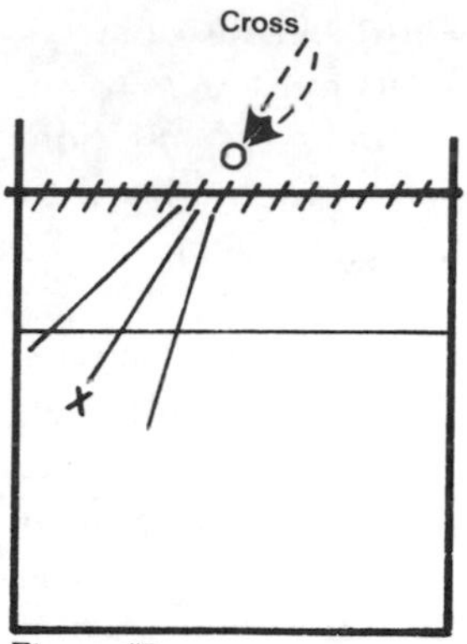

Figure #7

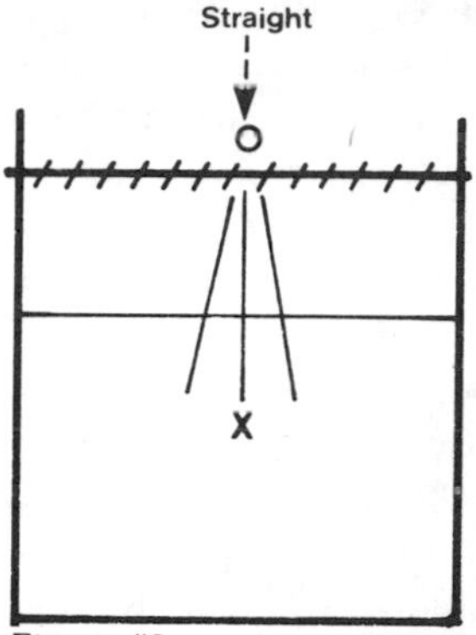

Figure #8

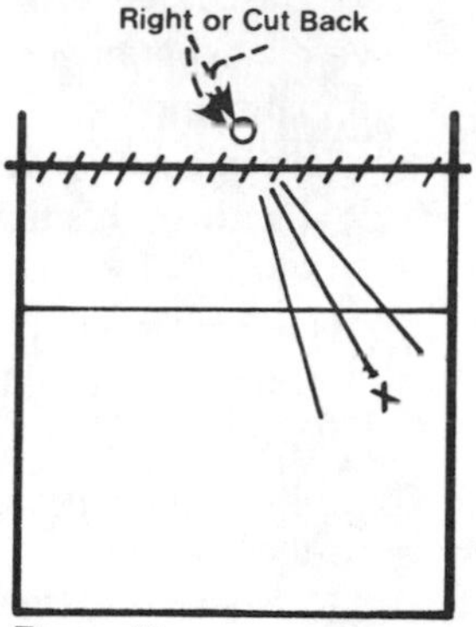

Figure #9

CASE-C. From the No. 2 position

The spikers from the No. 2 position, the right side of the opponent's offense, are a mirror image of the spikers from the left side(No. 4 position). Note: Very few women can spike down the line sharp from the right side (if right handed) because they lack shoulder strength.

(2) Down Ball Defense—

When the set is not accurate, it is a broken play, the ball is too far, too low, or behind the spiker. If this occurs the spiker can not reach his maximum potential power and the ball can not be hit down sharp and hard.

CASE-A.

When the third ball is far from the net and slightly behind the spiker, the defenders can expect a long or a roll shot. The backcourt players move back to take a long shot while the players defending close to the net cover the roll shot. The blocking of such a shot may not be effective.

CASE-B.

When the set is close to the net, or the set is too far from the net. The spiker is off balance; and a one man block is used. Front players, prepare for the dink or roll shots and backcourt players keep their position. Note: It is up to defenders to call the down ball defense formation instead of the hard spiking formation as in section (1). The judgment of this type depends largely upon the relative strength between the offense and defense. However, it is always true that the defenders should call it as early as possible and the transformation from the (1) situation must be smooth. It would be better to designate the player (a captain or/and setter) in charge of such a call.

(3) Defense against tight balls—

The defense against tight balls is sometimes a neglected art. Coaches tend to leave that aspect of the training to experience. However, many coaches have experienced bitterness of a game lost because players were inexperienced in this situation. Therefore, players must learn to anticipate and react to various tight ball situations (balls arc, position, height in relation to the tape) and also they have to understand how to deal with such situations according to the block they are facing.

CASE-A.

Against a ball whose descending arc will bring it to the net on your opponents' side (See Figure 10). If it is away from the potential attackers, the defensive blockers should not attempt a penetrating block, because it is illegal to touch such a ball before the opponent does.

Therefore, the blockers wait for a ball until the opponent touches it or let it drop to the opponent's court.

CASE-B.

Against a ball whose descending arc will bring a portion of the ball on your side of the net.

B-1) If the descending trajectory is more vertical, using only a quick wrist snap, spike the ball straight down within the 10 foot line.

B-2) If the descending trajectory is horizontal (See Figure 11), and the blocker tries to hit as in B-1), the chance of hitting the ball into the net is greater; if the ball flies into the defender's hand with high speed, he tends to hit it out of bounds. Therefore, the defender should quickly change the direction of the ball using a slashing action from left to right, or right to left. The ball should fall within the 10 foot line to avoid incoming defense.

Note: If such opportunity occurs while the opponents are not in blocking positions (such as an over pass on the service reception), the ball should be hit downward as quickly as possible. However, if it happens while the opponents are in blocking position or within blocking range, such as volleying sequence, then the ball must be slashed away from the incoming blocker's hands.

CASE-C.

Against a ball whose descending arc will bring it clearly on your side of the net.

C-1) As shown in Figure 12, whether vertical or slightly horizontal, the ball must be attacked. Of course, great attention should be paid to the opponents' block. The other front court defenders should let the defender attacking such a ball know whether or not the blockers are coming.

C-2) Figure 13 illustrates a ball with ascending trajectory while crossing the net. It is difficult to spike without commiting a net foul. One should try to block it or pass it.

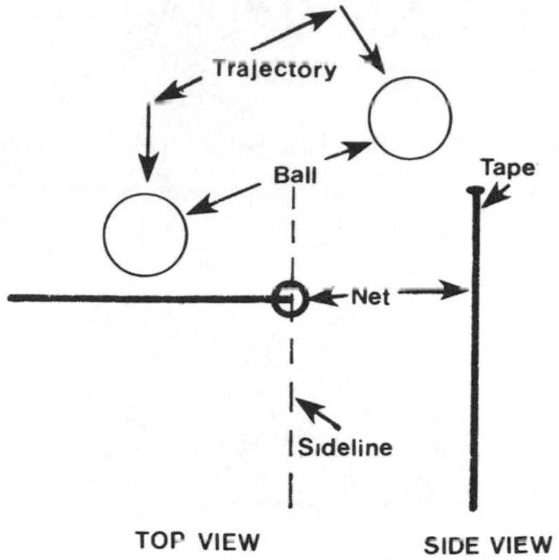

Figure #10

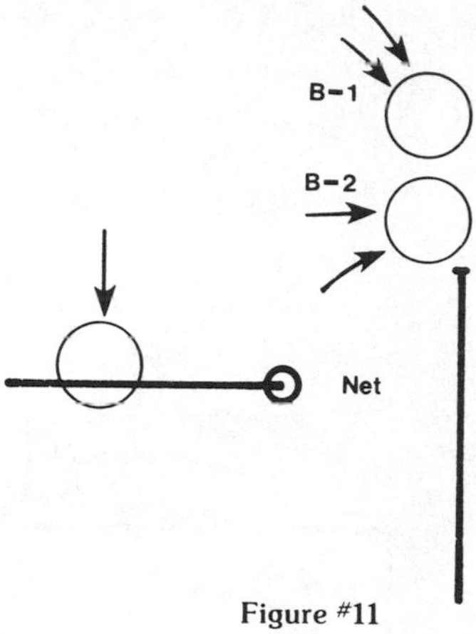

Figure #11

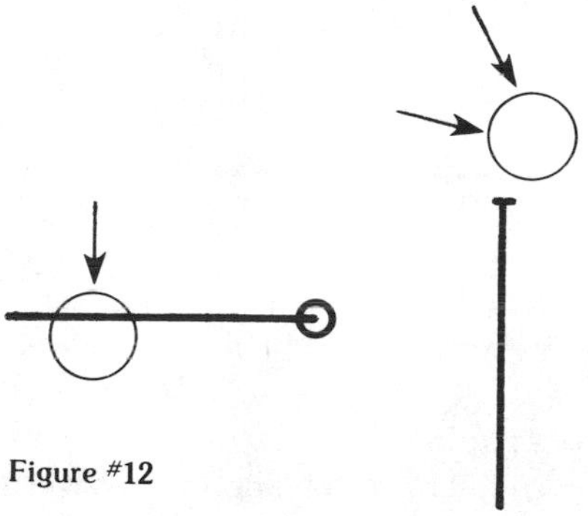

Figure #12

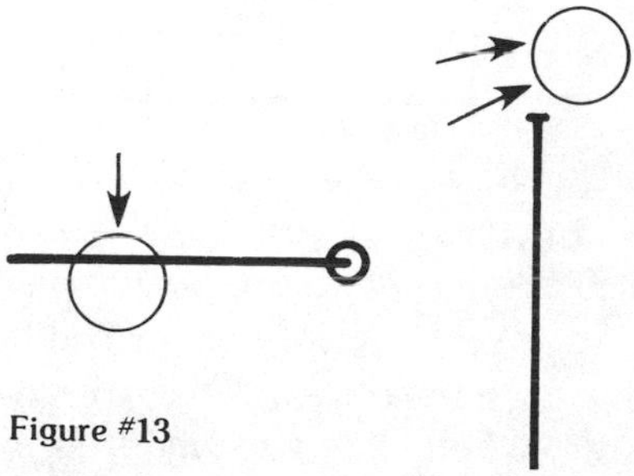

Figure #13

Note: The slashing actions tend to cause a net foul, or tend to cause one to hit a ball into the net. If the blocker in the other court is in position, the blockout or a wipe off should be attempted. Sometimes, it is better to set the ball to the spiker or to the setter, and initiate your next offense. That way you may draw the opponents' net foul.

(4) Change of Pace Defense

CASE-A. Against a dink

The defensive formation against situations (1) and (2) must allow players to cover the dink.

Note: The player must move quickly under the ball, and bump or set it high so that a better transition from the defense to offense will be possible.

CASE-B. Against a power dink, long or short

The ball is pushed by the spiker and travels faster than a regular dink. The ball is usually placed behind or between the defenders.

Therefore, the defenders often have to employ emergency techniques such as dive, roll and collapse.

CASE-C. Against a wipe off

As soon as the defender(s) (usually down the line) realizes that the block protects his area of coverage, he must anticipate the wipe off shot and move outside the court (See Figure 14). It is recommended that the blocker call the wipe off.

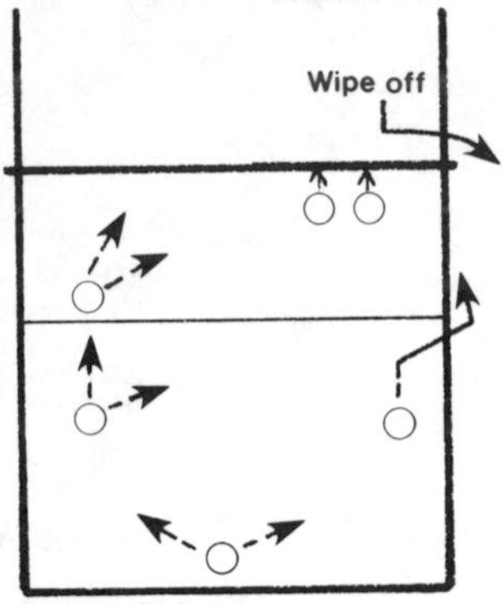

Figure #14

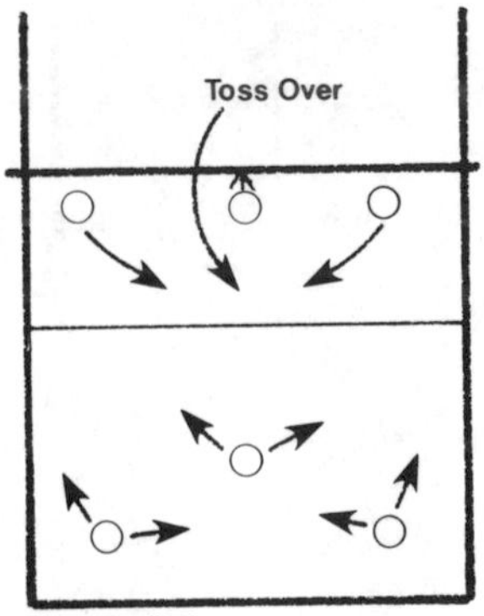

Figure #15

CASE-D. Against setter's toss

As the setter jumps, one blocker must jump with him if he is a front court player. Watch whether he will spike it. If he does not, but he still tries to toss it over, the two front court players move quickly away from the net, while the back court players move slightly forward because this kind of toss is seldom very long (See Figure 15).

(5) Defense against a back court spike

There is increasing interest in the back court spike in the last few years of international competitions. However, very few spikers can hit a ball sharp within the 10 foot line. Also, it is extremely difficult for regular spikers to change direction of a hit with their arm and/or wrist motion. Thus, the direction of the hit can be read by looking at their approach and body motion. The defenders in that direction stay deep while the front court players cover the ball deflected by the block or the tape. The regular dink is easy to cover in this case.

Summary of Spike Defense

1. Determine who is going to spike

This is easy when the service reception goes wrong and the set is coming from the opponents right corner. The only possible attack that they can use is from the No. 4 position.

2. Anticipate the probable direction and range of the spike. Move to an adjusted position quickly.

3. Determine whether the ball will be hit hard, dinked, a down ball or a free ball. If you read a hard hit, look at the spiker and try to anticipate the direction and range of the spike before the spiker hits.

- Approach Course
- Body Movement

  Shoulder Wrist
  Arm Eyes

4. Face the incoming ball as the ball leaves the spiker's hands.

5. Judge from the angle and spin of the hit whether it is in or out.

6. Reach it and try to direct the ball to the setter.

7. If you are late such that the opponent is hitting directly over the net, play as from point No. 4.

RSITY
RENEGADES
6
5

9
Transition

THE "TSUNAGI" TRANSFORMATION CONCEPT
by
Yoshiaki Kazio
Japanese National Coaching Staff

The rule change of 1976, not counting the touch off the block, has had some interesting effects on the game. One effect has been that teams now have the tendency to use a deflection block much more frequently. With the use of the deflection block the dug ball (first ball off block) can be passed overhand. This increased accuracy of this first pass and also the fact that two more contacts are allowed after it, opens up many possibilities. In the 1977 Japanese League games, fewer fast offenses were used contrary to my expectations. However, depending upon how and where the first ball goes after the block, offensive patterns will vary. It will differ depending upon whether you have one or two setters, as well as their positions.

We will now discuss how to use the second ball. In other words, how the setter or any other player for that matter, can run his team by changing the tempo and or direction of his team's attack after a dug ball. This transfer from defense to offense by way of the second ball is known as the "tsunagi" transformation concept.

There are many interesting offensive patterns if all six players are acquainted with the "tsunagi" concept.

For example;

1. Send the first ball to a spiker rather than directly to the setter.
2. Instead of having the setter in the number two position, the setter stays on the left side or center of the court. Even if the setter stays on the right, use more weak side hitting.

3. Transfer the defense so that the spikers will have the opportunity to attack the second ball. This is to change the rhythm of the offense so that you can disturb the opposition's defensive tempo. This technique was commonly used in the nine player system as was the jap set and the shoot. Also the first or second ball can be "passed," "attacked" or "dumped" in an attempt to disturb the defense's tempo.

4. Since the zone between the antennas is now smaller, you should transfer the ball in such a way as to use as much of this zone as possible, such as, having the left cannon get the second ball and faking a spike and setting a shoot cross court to the right side cannon.

There are many offensive variations that can be used as have been examined above. Overall, the fundamentals must be mastered before they can be executed. Another important requirement is that the defensive players must know how and where to play the first ball so that the best transfer to an offensive play can be accomplished.

We will now discuss some of the examples. These are just my imaginative examples, some may not be practical!

Illustrative Examples of "tsunagi" transformation

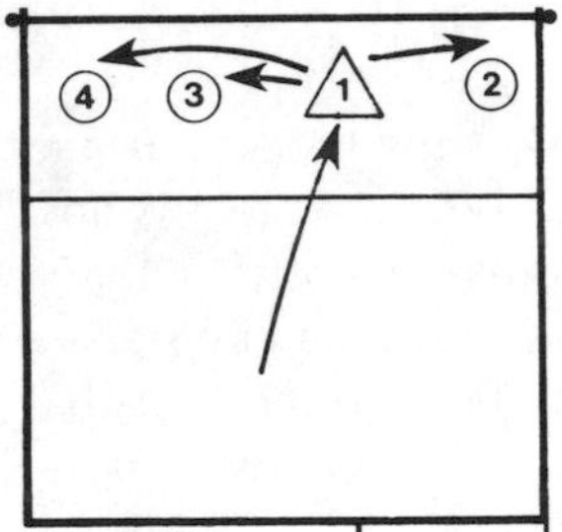

Figure #1

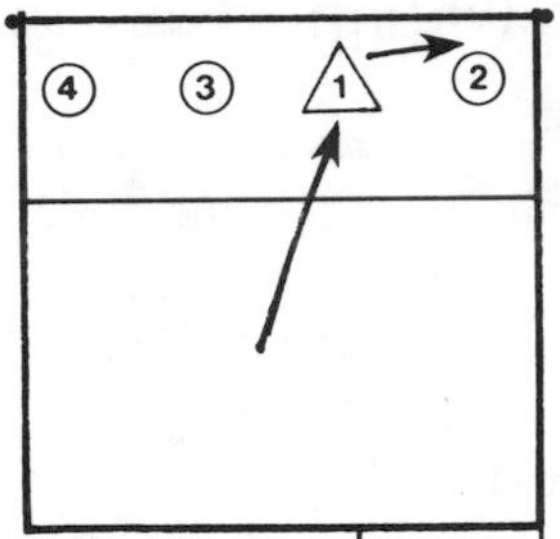

Figure #2

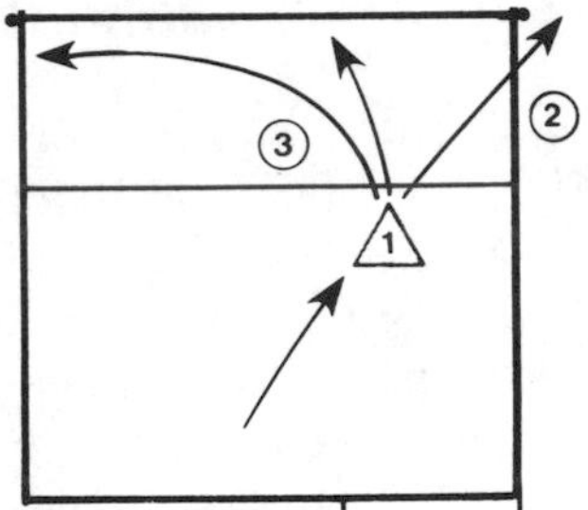

Figure #3

Figure 1, all digs go to setter 1, spikers 2, 3, and 4 get the sets. This is very conventional.

Figure 2, similar to figure 1 but use weaker side offense more. This should disturb the opponents' tempo.

Figure 3, setter sets first ball to the spikers, this is commonly used.

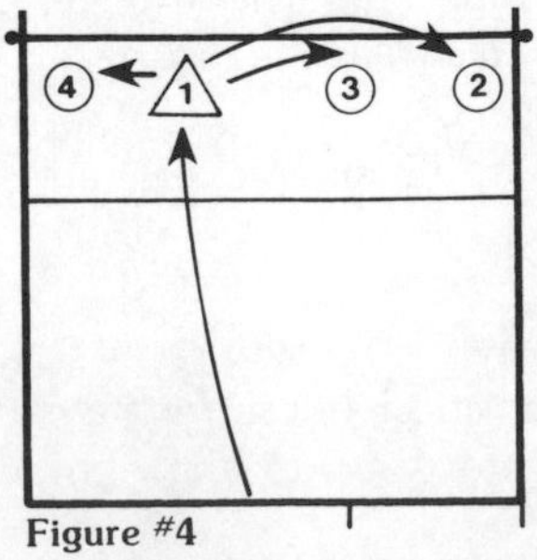

Figure #4

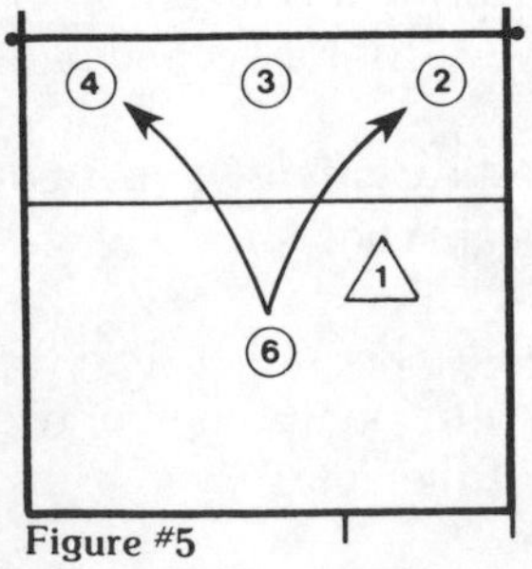

Figure #5

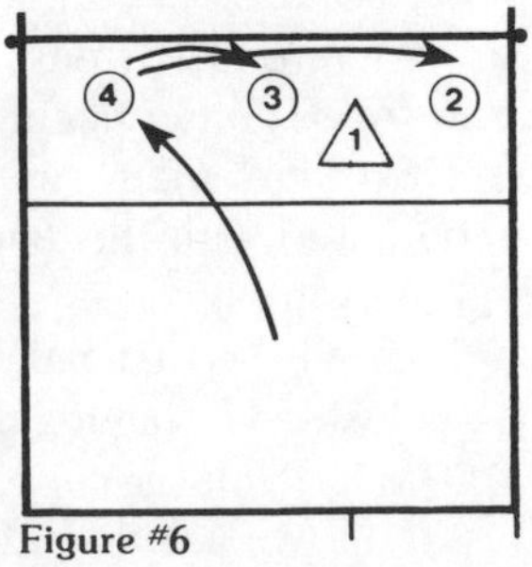

Figure #6

Figure 4, 1 stays at left front, this formation has not been used often, it could be interesting.

Figure 5, 6 sets the first ball to 4 or 2.

Figure 6, instead of getting the first ball to 1, send the ball to 4 who sets to 3 or 2. This can be very deceptive because #4 also has option to spike.

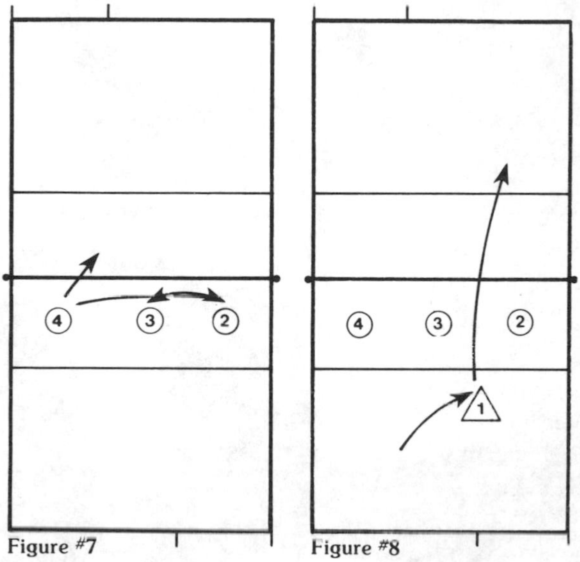

Figure #7 Figure #8

Figure 7, 4 gets the first ball and gives it to 2 where 2 sets back to 3 or 4. This will shake up the blockers.

Figure 8, 1 uses "pass attack" to open spot.

Above we have discussed how to handle the first and second ball. The im portance of fundamental techniques (pass and set) can not be overemphasized. Mastering these techniques will make the "tsunagi" transformation smoother and more precise.

Mr. Yoshiaki Kazio is the Chief of Development and Techniques for the Japanese Volleyball Association. He was trainer for the Mexico, Munich, and Montreal Olympics. He is recognized as an influential person in Japanese Volleyball.

Coors
USVBA
USVBA

PART C

DEVELOPING A SUCCESSFUL PROGRAM

Lady Vols
1
13

10
Program Planning

SPECIALIZATION: THE KEY TO SUCCESS
by
Val Keller

As an outgrowth of the level IV clinic and as a disturbing backlash in my summer travels throughout Canada, specialization in volleyball seems to be taboo for many coaches. This attitude, created out of either lack of experience or out of an honest desire to serve the individual player, I believe is erroneous.

First, let us examine the primary role of a coach — as opposed to a teacher. The coach has the responsibility of creating an entity called a *team*. This magical, undefinable unit is and must be a "something" which is greater than the sum of its parts. Like a fine watch keeps time when all the parts are put together correctly, a group of athletes produces success when harmoniously grouped. Each component of a watch, specially designed and manufactured, performs a specific function which carries out a signficant and irreplaceable function in the success of the watch keeping time. Although a player cannot be specifically designed or manufactured, he can be trained according to his physical capacities and technical strengths to perform specific functions. Therefore, by taking advantage of his specialties the player makes an even greater contribution to the team's success. No watch maker would expect the balance wheel to be the second hand and no coach would expect a 4'10" setter to be the primary blocker.

Secondly, it is difficult to understand why volleyball coaches seem to seek ways to be unique. In all other team sports specialization is a must. A

5'10" man does not play center on a basketball team when there is a 6'8" player available. A slow lumbering, 250 pound athlete on a football team plays in the line, not as a halfback. The list is endless.

It is true that volleyball rules force us to have players with good, all-round skills as each player must "START" in each of the positions. However, once the play starts the only limitations are on back court players attacking and blocking.

In volleyball we normally identify only two types of specialists — setters and attackers. With most teams who are playing 4-2 this identification covers only one of the formulations, that is, offensive front court assignments. This identification is simply inadequate in the total concept of a team.

As a coach it is our responsibility to:

1. Create a system of play, both offense and defense;
2. Identify skill traits for each position;
3. Identify skill traits for each player;
4. Put players in the position to maximize their effectiveness.

At no time should we have a team in its *offensive* specialty positions when we are playing *defense*.

Therefore, as opposed to the simple setter/attacker designations, players could have multi-titles as determined by their specialization. For example, in a 6-0 (three attacker offensive system) a player could be:

position
front court offense - middle quick attacker
back court offense - setter
front court defense - left blocker
back court defense - right back

Complicated? **Yes!** Important? **Definitely!**

The application of specialization should at any level of play be in defensive tactics. This is where a team has time to switch into their defensive positions.

I feel coaches underestimate both the importance of specialization and the ability of players to understand the maneuvers. At a one-week camp this summer, a group of young high school players learned:

1. A 6-0 offensive;
2. Total defensive specialization;
3. Two types of team defense;
4. Three multiple offense plays.

In this group were two 14 year olds, three 15 year olds, three 16 year olds and four 17 year olds. Specialization can be taught, learned and applied at a very young level.

The final reason for player specialization is to increase the training for each player at his particular position. Every coach now trains setters and attackers, but why not train defensive left backs? When an athlete specializes, he spends more training and competitive time in the position of his specialty. He looks upon that position with familiarity and pride. He knows the requirements of the position and works hard to meet the objectives. Lastly, he knows he is a significant part of a team in which his contribution is mandatory for success.

PLANNING A VOLLEYBALL PRACTICE SESSION

by

Richard G. Layman

Murray State University

In many sports such as basketball, football, soccer or volleyball, a player's achievement will be related to his improved understanding of the game, the perfection of his technique, and the development of his physical and emotional fitness. In planning practice sessions, a coach should keep these three factors in mind. On this basis, he should plan his volleyball practice sessions using three areas of player preparation: 1) teamwork 2) individual technique, and 3) physical fitness.

To develop a team into a highly coordinated unit is the most difficult objective facing the volleyball coach, thus, the correct proportion of time must be allotted to it. The next objective is the improvement of the individual skill and technique of each player. The development of physical fitness poses the least difficulty of the three.

The development of teamwork takes the form of: 1) full team scrimmage, 2) two-man games (doubles), 3) functional training — phase practice, and 4) practical practice.

Fullteam scrimmage is necessary to develop offensive and defensive systems of play and to give each player a general understanding of tactics and actual game-type situations. Nevertheless, the full team scrimmage has a distinct disadvantage in that a player may go for indefinitely long periods of time without even touching the ball.

To offset this weakness of a full team scrimmage, small-sided games, especially, two-man games or doubles are invaluable in any volleyball practice session. First, the two players must learn to work with each other. This involves the three basic principles of offensive play which are the pass, the set, and the spike. Second, each player is responsible for covering more space, thus, he must be even more defense conscious and strive to make the great save. Third, the setter will get more opportunities to act under difficult passes, and the spiker will get fewer perfect sets, thus giving him an oppor-

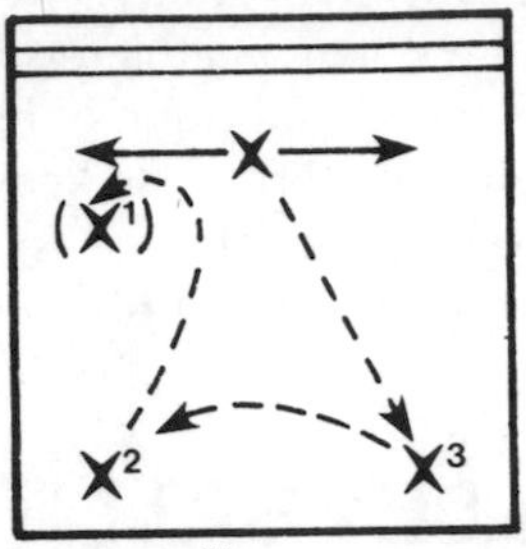

Diagram #1

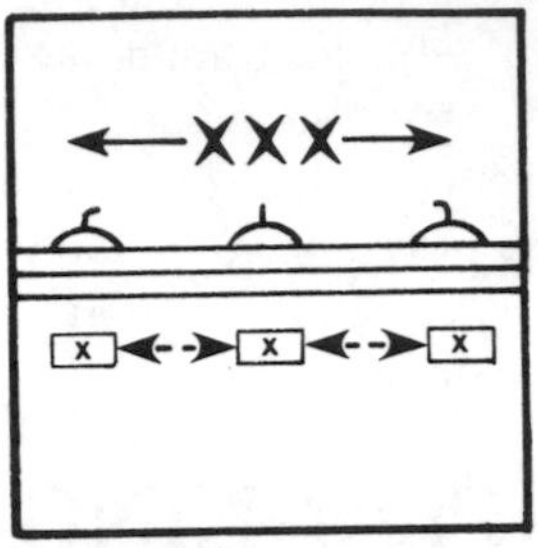

Diagram #2

tunity to practice the dink or soft spikes for placement to the uncovered spaces of the opponent's court.

In functional training or phase practice, we would like to recommend drill one for offense and drill two for defense.

Drill one (Diagram 1) is used for coaching the offensive phase of passing, setting, and spiking. It consists of three players designated as X1, X2, and X3. X1 with a ball stands in the middle of the court with his back near the net. X2 and X3 stand facing X1 in the far back court about 6 feet from each sideline or in a normal receiving position for the left and right back in returning a serve. X1 serves the ball to either X2 or X3. If X3 receives the ball, he must pass it using only a bump pass to X2 who will set to X1. X1 runs to either the left or right forward position and spikes or dinks the set by X2 into the opposite court. The setter must watch where X1 goes for the spike and makes his set accordingly.

Diagram 2 shows drill two which is used for coaching the defensive phase of blocking using two or three blockers. It consists of three forwards (the blockers) and three players standing on stools across the net as spikers in the three blocking zones. The spikers have one ball which they pass back and forth to one another. The blockers shift laterally following the movement of the ball and anticipate the instantaneous spike by one of the spikers. After applying their block, they must recover and be ready for additional shifting and blocking of balls that are being given continuously to one of the three spikers.

The last form of teamwork is tactical practice in which set plays are called for various offensive sets. Since there are as many as six different sets used in high caliber competition, this type of teamwork requires a high degree of understanding, quick thinking, and skill between the setters and spikers. The tactical form of volleyball teamwork may be the most difficult single phase of coaching.

The second phase of player preparation by the coach is in developing individual technique. Technique may be the decisive factor in any athletic performance, so coaches should always be looking for new and better techniques and at the same time give attention to individual strengths and weaknesses.

For individual drills, there should be a ball for every two players and certainly not more than three players to a ball. Proper ball-handling cannot be stressed too much since an improperly hit ball can be a foul and lead to a direct score for the opponents or a side out. Various drills by two players using bumping, setting, and spiking techniques should compose a major portion of each practice session. A certain time set aside for serving should also compose a part of each individual technique session.

Another group drill which we feel will develop individual techniques is a circle drill involving pressure training. This type of training involves submitting a player to a controlled repetition of ball service where he is required to produce several volleyball techniques on receiving the ball. As the player under pressure becomes accustomed to the practice, the rate of ball service is increased. Pressure training's greatest function may be in developing the endurance of a player.

In the circle pressure drill (Diagram 3), player X6 stands in the center of a circle of five other players. Each of the five players has a ball. Beginning with X1, and proceeding clockwise, a ball is served to X6 who might set it or bump it back to X1. According to the proficiency of X6, the next service is delivered earlier or later by X2. Pressure is exerted on X6 by virtue of the fact that he can never take much time dealing with any service; the next server will determine how much time X6 has. When technique begins to show signs of deteriorating, X6 leaves the center and changes places with one of the players in the circle. The types of services to X6 should vary from low and high, to soft and hard, and left and right so that he will be called upon to apply various returns.

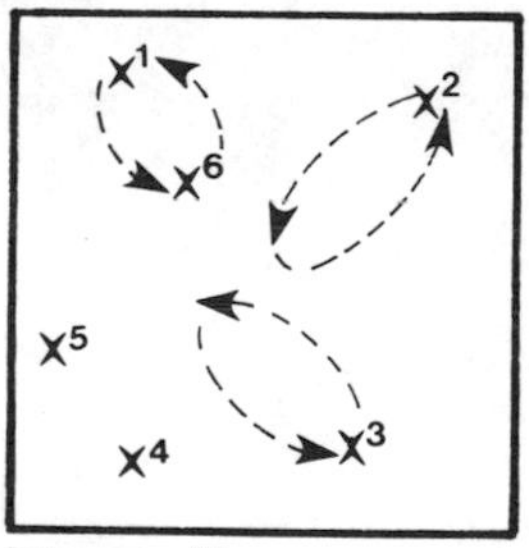

Diagram #3

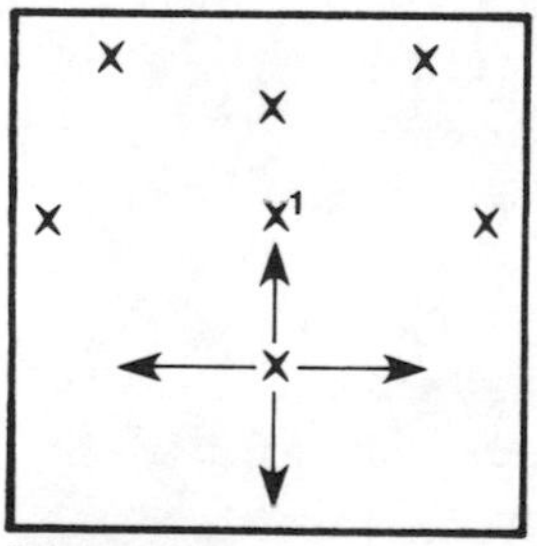

Diagram #4

The third major phase of player preparation by the coach is developing physical fitness. Those qualities of fitness include endurance, power, and mobility. One drill for developing quickness, reaction, mobility, and to a certain degree endurance is what we call the mirror drill.

Diagram 4 shows the mirror drill. A leader is used for every six players although this can vary. X1, the leader begins from a volleyball readiness position with his hands in front of his face as in setting and his legs flexed with one foot in front of the other. Quickly, he may shift right or left while the other players try to stay with him. He may go into a deep squat, jump forward, backward or upward while the others do the same thing. He may reach for a dig with one or both arms, and he may even go into a backward volleyball roll while the other players imitate everything he does. The coach should emphasize reaching, stretching, quickness, and anticipation on the part of all players.

One of the best drills to use in developing endurance and vertical jumping power is to have two players on each side of the net slide, step, jump above the net and touch hands, recover, and slide, jump and touch all along the line of the net. On reaching the end they turn and sprint back and begin again. They should never touch the net and should be encouraged to jump for maximum height at all times. A cross-over step can be added to the slide step for variation.

To build courage and aggressiveness in getting players to try for difficult balls, the coach should use mats and encourage the players to dive and make those seemingly impossible saves. Courage, aggressiveness, and determination in not letting any ball touch the floor and diving to get it should carry over in all forms of drills and scrimmages.

In the final analysis, the coach should vary the periods of each practice session as to when he uses teamwork, individual technique drills, and conditioning. Variety will keep the players interested and not make practice sessions the same monotonous daily routine.

11

Evaluating the Physical Capabilities of Your Players

PHYSICAL TESTING PROCEDURES AND STANDARDS FOR VOLLEYBALL

by

Tsutomu Koyama
Head Volleyball Coach
Japanese Olympic Team
(Montreal)

Yoshiaki Kazio
Japanese National Coaching Staff
Chief of Development and Techniques

To further enhance the skills of volleyball and the enjoyment of the game, one must strive for physical excellence. We postulate that our physical excellence is materialized by such elements as listed below.

1. Agility
2. Strength
3. Endurance
4. Flexibility
5. Coordination

Especially in the case of Olympic style volleyball, long periods of coordinated team play are required; thus, the intensity of the sport is comparable to that of soccer. Therefore, the above listed elements must be developed collectively and our efforts must be focused to such a goal.

As I have mentioned earlier the basis of the skills of volleyball are the complex combination of elements of physical excellence. Thus, to develop the skills, a rational training program developing this basic physical excellence is important.

I THE RATIONAL (PROGRAM PLANNING)

1. First conduct a survey of the physical excellence of each individual (data analysis).

2. As soon as the level of physical excellence is determined, plan a training schedule.

3. Carry out the training schedule.

4. After completing the training schedule, conduct another survey. By comparing the previous data, determine the development of physical excellence and the validity of each component part of the training. Plan a subsequent training schedule to be carried out. There is also a necessity to examine not only the development of the physical excellence, but of correlation to skill.

II THE PHYSICAL SURVEY

Graph I.

	The Elements		Item of Survey
	Physique	Mandatory	Height, Weight, Chest, Reach
		Optional	Thigh, Upperarm, Leg, Arm Length
FUNCTIONAL	Muscle	M	Grip, Back, Situp, Pushup
		O	B Ball Throw, Stretch
	Speed	M	9.3m shuttle, 20m dash
		O	Reaction time, Rolling Test
	Power	M	Sergeant jump
		O	Running Jump, Block Jump
	Endurance	M	Harvard Step Test
		O	Max oxygen usage store
	Flexibility	O	Stretching (forward and back)
	Coordination	M	Hand Stand
		O	Mat work, horse, bars

M = Indicated no need of special equipment
O = Requires special equipment

The Japan Volleyball Association, under the Scientific Research Department, is creating professional tests designed to survey the physical excellence basic to volleyball players and skills required in volleyball.

III THE ADMINISTRATIVE PROCEDURES AND HINTS ON THE PHYSICAL APTITUDE SURVEY

A. Physique

1. Height

Use a wooden scale or metallic Martin scale with bare feet, stand with the toes 30-40 cm apart, the heels, the back, and the buttocks should touch the vertical scale. Hang the arms naturally. Head should be held firmly. The measurer should read the scale with eyes parallel to the measuree's head. Usually the height is bigger in the morning, smaller in the evening. The difference is 1-2 cm. The eyes and the ears of the measuree should stand parallel to the ground. Measure to the nearest 0.1 cm.

2. Weight

Use small automatic scale. Tolerance may be ± 100 g. Stand still in the center of the scale. Use kg. units. There is an increase after meal, therefore, it is advised to measure before breakfast. Record to the nearest 0.1kg.

3. Chest (Bust)

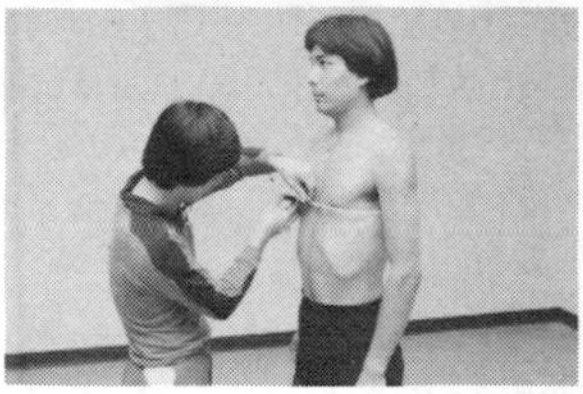

Better to use metallic measure rather than the cloth measure. The measuree stands with arms extended to the side. The measure extends through the shoulder blades and the nipple. Drop arms slowly. Relax the shoulder and arm muscles. Read the measure at the end of the normal breathing cycle. Use the cm units. In case of the mammary gland enlargement period, this will shift the measure slightly up. Read to the nearest 0.1 cm.

4. Reach

Use the same starting position as that of the height scale. Stretch the arm upward. Measure the perpendicular line from the floor to the middle finger. Record to the nearest cm. Use steel measure.

5. Thigh

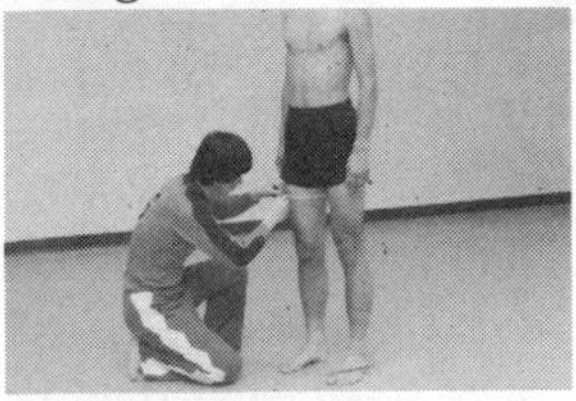

Open the legs approximately 10 cm. Put weight equally on both legs. Stand tall. Take the largest circumference perpendicular to the axis of the limb. Record to the nearest 0.1 cm. Use small steel measure.

6. Upper Arm Circumference

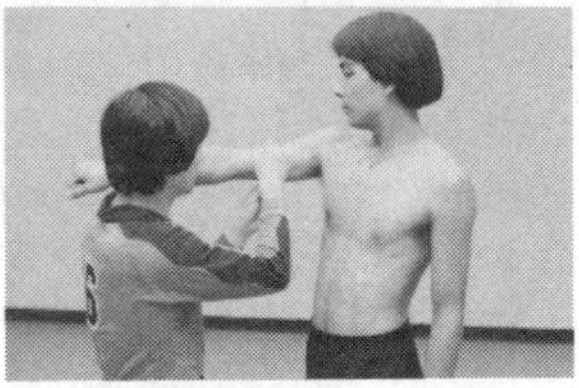

Use steel measure. Extend the arm to the front parallel to the shoulder. Measure the circumference of the middle of the upper arm, perpendicular to the axis. Read to the nearest 0.1 cm.

7. Arm Length

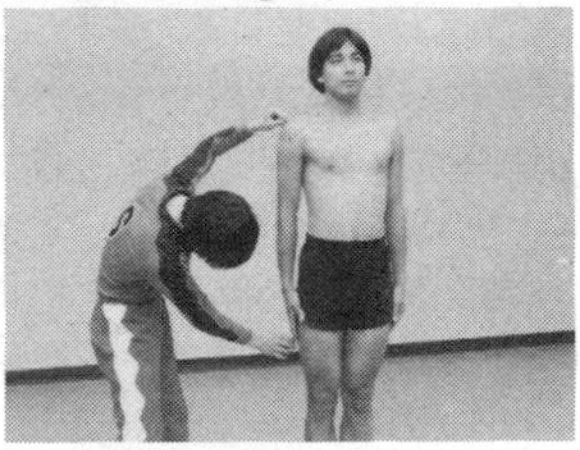

Lower the arm naturally and extend the fingers. Measure from the shoulder joint to the middle finger. Record to the nearest 0.1 cm. Use steel measure.

8. Leg Length

Though methods exist for a direct measure of the leg, since the error factor is great, subtractive interpretation method is used. Record to the nearest 0.1 cm. (Height-sitting height).

9. Sitting Height

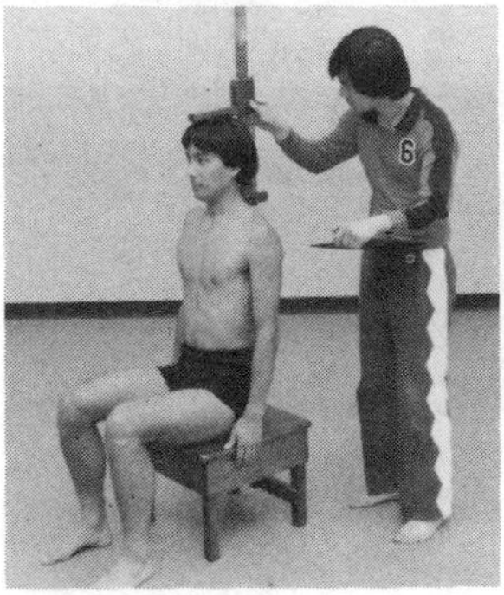

Use scale designed to measure sitting height.

B. Performance Survey

1. Grip Strength

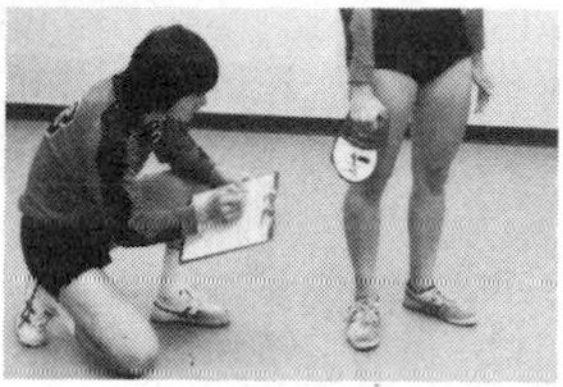

Using the hand dynamometer, place the thumb on the outer frame and squeeze with the other fingers at the 2nd joint. The subject stands with legs slightly opened, arms slightly away from the body, elbows locked and with the measuring window facing away from body. Conduct 3 repetitions of the survey on both hands alternately. Take the largest reading for each hand. Record to the nearest 1 kg.

2. Back Muscle

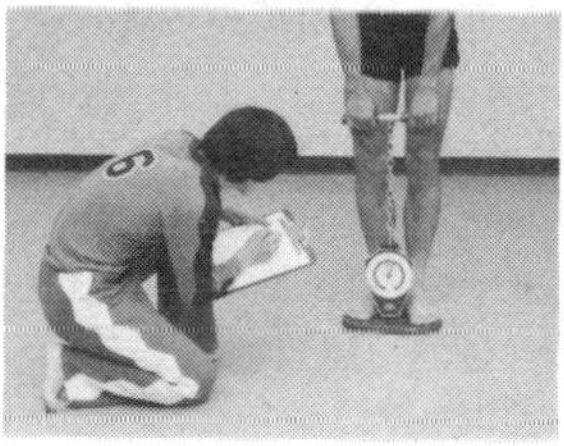

Use back muscle measuring device. The subject's feet should be about 60°. Standing on top of a stand, grip the handle and place upper body at 30°. Locking the elbows and knees, pull the chain as hard as possible. Do this 3 times. Record the highest reading. Record to the nearest 1 kg.

3. Situp

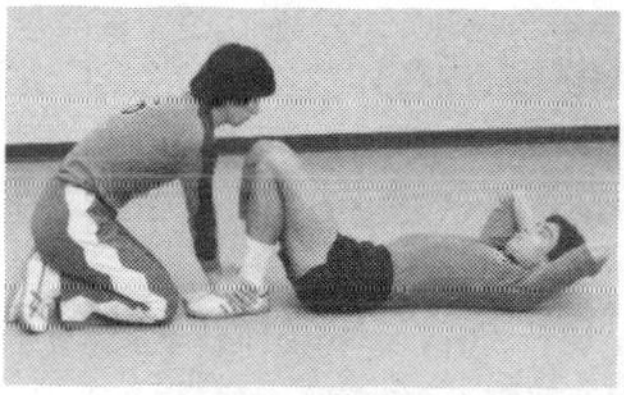

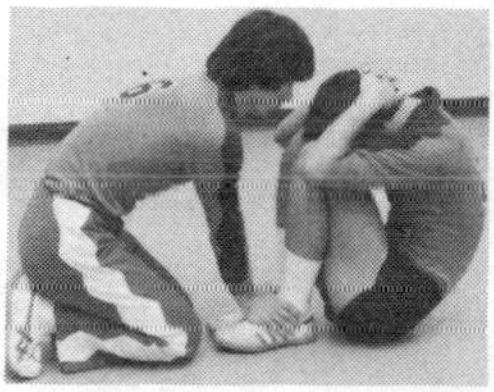

Use a stopwatch. Interlace fingers behind the back of the head, lie down face up. A partner holds down the ankles. Lift upper body and bend until one touches the elbow to the knee. Recover to the starting position. Touch elbow to the ground. Repeat. The interval for males should be 30 seconds. For females it should be 20 seconds.

Count the number of times the elbow touches the knee. Do this survey once.

4. Pushups

On command, assume the front leaning rest position. (or if preferred, proper knee pushing) On command, bend the elbow until the chest touches the ground. Assure that a correct posture is maintained. Do this at the rate of once in 3 seconds Assure that the elbows are locked when at the starting position. As soon as the subject is unable to keep with the rhythm or is unable to maintain proper posture, stop the exercise. Count the number of correctly performed exercises.

5. 20 m Dash

The distance between start line and goal line should be 20 m. The subject runs from the line as fast as possible. It is good practice to run 2 or 3 people with the subject. With rest period in between, run 3 times. Record the best time. The subject starts with his feet abreast stance. Use flags instead of sound. The number of watches should be the same with the number of subjects. Record to the nearest 0.1 seconds.

6. 9.3 m Shuttle (3 reps x 3 m = 9m)

Place 3 balls on the sidelines. At the signal, the subject starts from the other line using feet abreast stance and runs toward the balls. Carry back the balls to the start line. Do this 3 times. Measure the time required to place the last ball on the start line. Do not throw the ball. With rest periods in between, do the event 3 times. Record the best time. Run 3 people at once if possible. Do not use sound, but use flag signals. Use one stopwatch per subject. Record to the nearest 0.1 seconds.

7. Rolling Test

Starting from upright position do 5 forward rolls, then without recovery to the starting position, do another 5 rolls. As soon as this is done, recover immediately to the position of attention. Measure the time interval from the start to recovery to the position of attention. With a rest period in between do 2 repetitions. Record the best time.

8. Sidestep

Standing with a straddle stance over the center line, sidestep to the right line and return to the center line, and sidestep to the left line and again to the center line. Do not jump. Do the above exercise for 2.0 seconds. Each time one sidesteps over a line, give one point (right, center, left, center equals 4 points). Do this event 2 times. Record the best score. Employ stopwatch for timepiece.

9. Backward Stretch

Lie face down, lock arms behind the hips or behind the head. A partner holds the leg down. Stretch as far as possible to the rear. Measure the distance from the floor to the chin. Do this 3 times. Record the best stretch. Do not use bouncing movement. Employ a slow stretching technique. Stop momentarily if the maximum stretch is reached. Record to the nearest 1 cm.

10. Forward Stretch

Both feet on the stand, the toes 5 cm. apart, knees locked, stretch forward while touching the ruler. Do this 3 times. Do not jump or bounce but do this slowly. One may use cloth measure instead of a ruler. Measure from the tips of the finger. The eyes of the tester should be parallel to the finger tips. Record to the nearest 1 cm.

11. Hand Stand

Start with legs and arms on the ground, do a hand stand on the signal "GO". Measure the time required to recover a foot to the floor. Do this 5 times. Record the longest time. Record from the time both feet depart ground to the time one of the feet reaches the floor. Record to the nearest 1 second.

12. Harvard Step Test

For the men, step up and down 50 cm. For the women, step up and down 40 cm. at 30 steps per min. (1 step per 2 seconds) Step up and down correctly. Do not jump up or down. Do this for 5 minutes. Sit down as soon as you are done. Measure the pulse after 1-1.5 min., 2-2.5 min., 3-3.5 min. Record the pulse for 30 seconds. Use the following equations to obtain the index number:

$$X = \frac{\text{work seconds} \times 100}{2 \times (\text{the sum of 3 pulses})}$$

SAMPLE DATA SHEET

Name: ______________________ Sex: ☐ M ☐ F
Date: ______________________ Hand Dominance: ☐ R ☐L
Tester: ______________________

A. PHYSIQUE

1. Height	______.___	cm
2. Weight	______.___	Kg
3. Chest	______.___	cm
4. Reach	______.___	cm
5. Thigh	______.___	cm
6. Upper Arm Circumference	______.___	cm
7. Arm Length	______.___	cm
8. Sitting Height	______.___	cm

B. PERFORMANCE SURVEY

	Trial 1	Trial 2	Trial 3	Trial 4	Trial 5
1. Grip Strength	___.__	___.__	___.__		
2. Back Muscle	___.__	___.__	___.__		
3. Sit-ups/ sec.	_____				
4. Push-ups	_____				
5. 20 m. Dash	___.__	___.__	___.__		
6. 9.3 m Shuttle	___.__	___.__	___.__		
7. Rolling Test	___.__	___.__			
8. Sidestep/20 sec.	_____	_____			
9. Backward Stretch	_____	_____	_____		
10. Forward Stretch	_____	_____	_____		
11. Handstand	_____	_____	_____	_____	_____
12. Harvard Step Test	_____				

$$X = \frac{\text{work sec} \times 100}{2\ (\text{sum of pulses})} \qquad X = \frac{\text{work sec} \times 100}{2(\_\_ + \_\_ + \_\_)}$$

	Trial 1	Trial 2	Trial 3
13. Standing 3 Jump	_____	_____	_____
14. Sargeant Jump	_____	_____	_____
15. Block Jump	_____	_____	_____
16. Running Jump	_____	_____	_____

Table 1

THE IDEAL PHYSICAL EXCELLENCE STANDARDS
FOR VOLLEYBALL PLAYERS

The Japan Volleyball Association Scientific Research Department set the following ideal standards for all Japan, Collegiate, General Public, High School, Jr. High, Elementary School volleyball players. The standards should be strived for constantly.

Physical Excellence Goals for Volleyball Players

Male

Event	**All Japan**	**College Public**	**High School**	**Jr. High**	**Elem.**
Grip	60kg	59-56	55-50	49-45	44
Back Muscle	210kg	209-181	180-150	149-130	129
Vert. Jump	90cm	89-81	80-70	69-60	59
3 Jump	950cm	949-900	899-830	829-760	759
Situp 20 sec.	18	17-16	15-14	13-12	11
20 M Dash	2.8 sec.	2.9-3.1	3.2-3.3	3.4-3.5	3.6
9.3 Shuttle	12.5 sec.	12.6 13.0	13.1-14.0	14.1-14.5	14.6
Rolling Test	9.9 sec.	10.0-12.0	12.1-13.0	13.1-13.5	13.6
Harvard Test	130	129-110	109-100	99-90	89
Front Lean	25cm	24-21	20-17	16-14	13
Back Lean	70cm	69-64	63-60	59-55	54
Hand Stand	90 sec.	89-80	79-60	59-31	30

Female

Event	**All Japan**	**College Public**	**High School**	**Jr. High**	**Elem.**
Grip	45kg	44-40	39-35	34-30	29
Back Muscle	150kg	149-130	129-110	109-95	95
Vert. Jump	65cm	64-59	58-50	49-45	44
3 Jump	750cm	749-700	699-650	649-600	599
Situp 20 sec.	18	17-16	15-13	12-11	10
9.3 Shuttle	13.5 sec.	13.6-14.0	14.1-14.5	14.6-15.0	15.1
Rolling Test	11.0 sec.	11.1-13.0	11.1-13.0	15.1-15.9	16.0
Harvard Test	120	119-110	109-100	99-90	89
Front Lean	25cm	24-21	20-17	16-15	14
Back Lean	65cm	64-60	59-55	54-50	50
Hand Stand	30 sec.	29-20	19-15	14-10	9
20 M Dash	3.1 sec.	3.2-3.5	3.6-4.0	3.9-3.6	3.5

13. Standing Triple Jump

Stand on the sideline of the courts with feet together. Jump 3 times toward the other line. Measure from the heel to the line. Install the device perpendicular to the wall. Without preliminary jump or running, jump as high as possible. Mark the highest point by touching the device with the finger. Do this 3 times standing directly below the highest mark, mark the longest reach of the arm. From the point measure to the highest point. Record to the nearest 1 cm.

14. Sargeant Jump

Use sargeant measuring machine. First apply chalk to the finger tips. Mark the highest point touched by the fingers. Do this three times. Measure from the mark to the floor. Record to the nearest 1 cm.

15. Block Jump

Facing the basketball backboard or some sort of measuring device jump as though blocking. Measure 3 times. Pick the best jump; do not stop between jumps. To prevent injury do some warm ups before this event. Record to the nearest 1 cm.

16. Running Jump

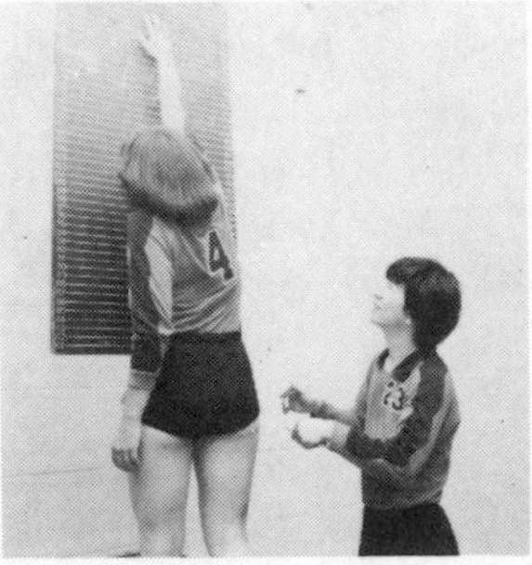

Jump as though spiking. The rest is same as that of block jump.

WORLD MEN AND WOMEN VOLLEYBALL PLAYER'S VOLLEYBALL JUMP INDEX (VJI)

by

Daisen Shimazu

Japan Women's University

To judge the ability of a volleyball player, a volleyball jump index (VJI) system was devised to evaluate a volleyball player by taking out passing power, spiking power, blocking power, serving power, mental power, etc. and putting each of these factors in proper relationship. With the need for an easier evaluation system with about 70-80% accuracy, this volleyball jump index system was improvised. The VJI system gives players with higher jump measurements higher scores. Higher scores indicate their higher value as volleyball players. However, since shorter setters like Nekota (Japan) are not given high scores, the coaches should view this with some caution.

Calculation procedures:

Male Volleyball Jump Index = $\frac{\text{Height}}{243}$ [(Block jump-243)+(Running jump-243)

(Men's net height is 243 cm)

Female Volleyball Jump Index = $\frac{\text{Height}}{224}$ [(Block jump-224)+(Running jump-224)

(Women's net height is 224 cm)

20Measurement Procedures:

Block Jump: Take 2 or 3 steps, jump, touch the board with the fingertips of both hands approximately the same height and more or less together.

Running Jump: Take 2 or 3 steps, jump, touch the board with just one hand.

The Men Players

The team with the highest VJI was East Germany with 131, followed by Poland with 126, USSR and China with 122, All Japan A level with 119, and Mexico with 118. In the future teams, we must strive for an average of 130-135. The top level averages for Japan collegiate, high school, and junior high were 112, 95, 51 respectively. I am curious about the averages of the collegiate and other levels in the USSR, Europe, and the USA.

The Women Players

The Cuban team is the highest with 115. It is followed by China with 96, Canada with 92, All Japan A level with 90, Brazil with 80, All Japan B level with 79, and Peru with 78. The Cuban team is said to train in jumping extensively. This is certainly true. The difference between China and Cuba is 20. Between Japan and Cuba, it is 25. The Japanese women collegiates, high school, and junior high averages were 76, 74, 39 respectively.

When judging the National Team level players by the V.J.I. system, the following table can be used:

	Men	Women
A	150-	120-
B	140-	110-
C	130-	100-
D	120-	99-

The spiker for the men's team should ideally have a running jump of 350 ± cm and blocking jump of 330 ± cm. In the same way, the spiker for the women's team should ideally have a running jump of 210 ± cm and blocking jump of 300 ± cm. The Cuban men's team is said to have 360-370 ± cm.

Table 1 Team Averages Jump Table (Men)

YR. Team	Height (cm)	Weight (kg)	Block Jump (cm)	Running Jump (cm)	V.J.I. (Men)
'73 U.S.S.R.	191	88	312 (302-321)	329 (316-344)	122 (100.3-143.4)
'73 E. Germany	191	84	320 (312-330)	333 (322-348)	131 (112.4-151.5)
'73 China	188	81	313 (303-323)	331)321-338)	122 (102.1-138.3)
'74 Poland	188	87	316 (307-322)	322 (320-337)	126 (106.5-140.1)
'74 Mexico	185	77	314 (308-320)	328 (314-334)	188 (102.1-144.3)
'74 Jpn. A All "A" level	189	85	312 (304-335)	326 (308-351)	199 (82.9-162.0)
'74 Jpn. B All "B" level	188	83	305 (297-317)	319 (310-329)	108 (90.5-128.0)
'74 Jpn. Collegiate	187	78	309 (300-320)	322 (310-332)	122 (91.8-128.8)
'74 Jpn. High School	187	77	300 (284-311)	310 (295-335)	95 (68.1-120.9)
'74 Jpn. Jr. High	169	57	275 (252-299)	284 (258-301)	51.2 (45.8- 80.3)

Table 2 Team Averages Jump Table (Women)

Yr. Team	**Height (cm)**	**Weight (kg)**	**Block Jump (cm)**	**Running Jump (cm)**	**V.J.I. (Women)**
'76 Cuba	174		294 (276-303)	302 (283-315)	115.0 (81.3-137.4)
'76 Canada	176		277 (268-290)	287 (282-293)	91.9 (78.9-112.8)
'73 China	175	65	281 (271-290)	290 (282-298)	96.0 (84.0-107.0)
'73 Jpn. A All "A" level	174	69	274 (266-276)	289 (282-296)	89.6 (75.8-100.4)
'74 Brazil	174	64	270 (256-284)	280 (262-298)	80.2 (50.8-109.5)
'74 Jpn. B All "B" level	171	65	269 (262-276)	281 (258-287)	78.6 (39.3- 89.2)
'74 Peru	168	64	271 (243-284)	281 (261-294)	77.9 (39.8-101.4)
'75 Jpn. Collegiate	170	64	269 (255-278)	279 (274-289)	76.4 (70.5- 88.5)
'74 Jpn. High School	171	65	268 (257'287)	278 (266-294)	74.3 (56.3-105.1)
'75 Jpn. Jr. High	160	50	245 (235-260)	255 (262-271)	38.7 (20.4- 61.5)

12
FIT TO WIN: Conditioning Programs and Principles

STRENGTH TRAINING FOR VOLLEYBALL

by
Daniel Riley
Strength Coach, Washington Redskins

Justification

Volleyball is an activity demanding many physical variables to include power, explosive power, speed of movement, and muscular endurance. All of these physical attributes are primarily dependent upon the strength of the muscles used to perform the skills involved. An increase in strength should improve each of these attributes.

For example, if we were to select a skill such as jumping, and determine what allows an athlete to jump, we would find that there are, primarily, two factors involved: 1) the ability of the athlete to recruit as many muscle fibers as possible, precisely at the right time (neuromuscular efficiency); 2) the strength of those muscle fibers that are being recruited to jump.

If we wish to increase the athlete's ability to jump, we must improve those items that allow the athlete to jump (neuromuscular efficiency and the muscular strength of those particular muscles used to jump).

To improve neuromuscular efficiency, the athlete must practice the specific skill involved. Therefore, to improve the athlete's ability to jump, he/she must practice jumping. Eventually, the athlete's improvement will gradually level off and reach a peak.

The only other means which an athlete has to improve his/her vertical jump is to engage in a strength training program designed to increase the strength of those muscles involved in jumping.

This information cannot be refuted yet, unfortunately, many volleyball coaches fail to recognize the value of strength training as an integral part of the athlete's overall conditioning program.

A significant increase in strength will also stimulate an increase in muscular endurance; that is, the ability to sustain an activity at a high level of intensity, delaying the onset of fatigue. Therefore, an increase in strength will not only improve the athlete's vertical jumping ability, it will also allow him/her to sustain his/her jumping ability for a longer period of time. This should prevent or minimize any decrease in performance potential that might occur during a match or tournament (due to fatigue). This same information can be applied to the muscles of the upper body that are used in skills such as blocking and spiking.

In addition to improving the performance level of an athlete, an increase in strength will help prevent injury.

The female volleyball player should also be encouraged to initiate and continue a properly organized program. The female athlete has just as much, and due to society's suppression of the female athlete, probably more,to gain from a strength training program.

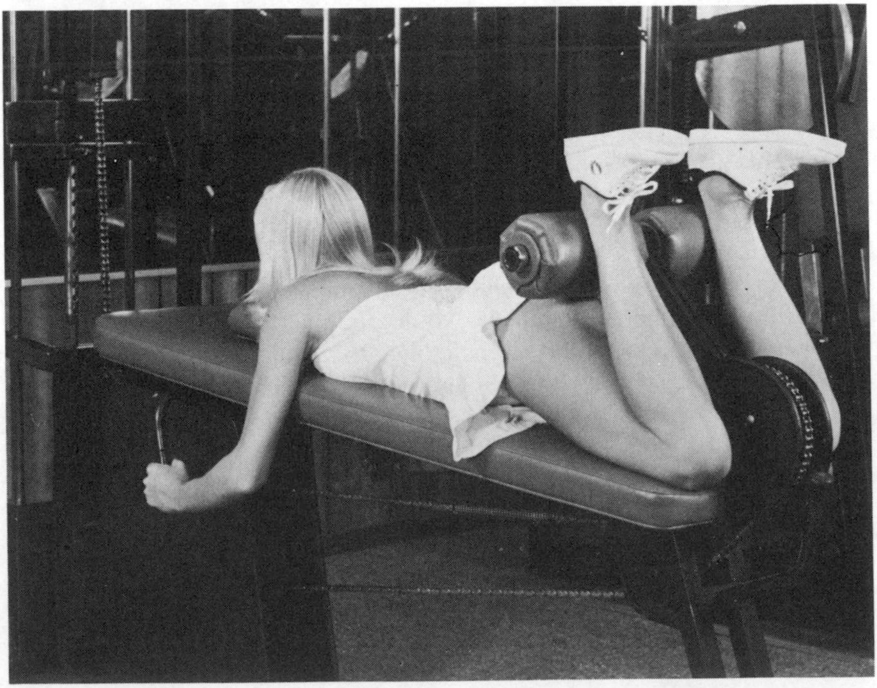

Program Organization

The highly skilled and successful athlete must spend numerous hours practicing and developing those skills needed to excel. Therefore, when conditioning the body, it should be the goal of the athlete to seek and utilize those techniques that are designed to stimuate maximum gains in the least amount of time.

The methods mentioned herein are the most effective and efficient techniques available to date. Any deviation from these prescribed methods will produce less than maximum gains in muscular development. Identical programs should be used for the male and female volleyball players.

The actual organization of a program involves the manipulation of seven training variables. Based upon the existing literature and the most current research, proper manipulation of the following seven training variables will produce the most efficient and effective program available.

1. How many repetitions should be performed?
2. How much weight should be used?
3. How many sets should be used?
4. How much recovery time between exercises?
5. How often should the athlete work out?
6. In what order should the exercises be performed?
7. What exercises should be performed?

Repetitions

A repetition (rep) is the number of times a lift is executed. For maximum muscle fiber recruitment and development, betwen eight and 12 repetitions of each exercise should be performed. If at least eight repetitions of an exercise cannot be done, then the weight is too heavy. If more than 12 repetitions of an exercise can be done, then the weight is too light.

Workload

The workload is the amount of weight to be used when performing an exercise. The athlete should use as much weight as possible (once the proper lifting techniques have been learned) so that the athlete reaches the point of momentary muscular failure somewhere between eight and 12 repetitions. The point of failure has been reached when the athlete can no longer properly perform a repetition. Selecting a starting weight is a trial-and-error proposition, so it is important to be cautious in the process. Once 12 properly executed repetitions can be performed, the athlete should increase the weight. *Do not sacrifice* form or technique to increase the amount of weight used or the number of repetitions performed.

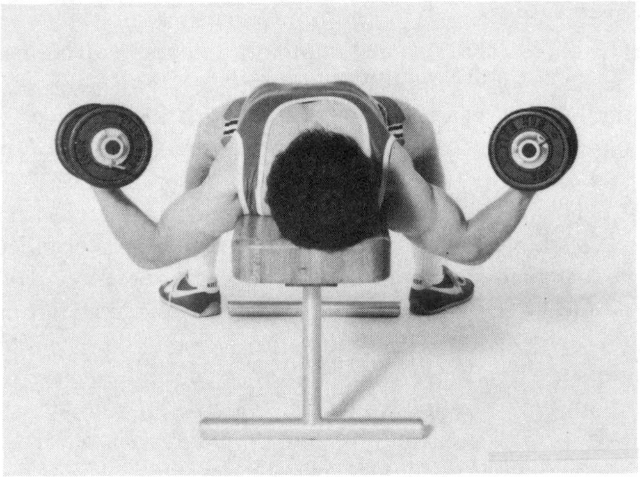

Sets

A set consists of the total number of repetitions executed each time an exercise is performed. We advocate that the athlete perform one "properly performed" set. It should be the goal of the athlete to perform as little exercise as possible to stimulate the greatest increase in strength. If one set is performed properly the athlete should not want to perform a second set, and if a second set was performed properly the athlete would probably not *fully* recover before the next workout. Unfortunately, most athletes do not know how to properly perform an exercise. Consequently, when told that one set of an exercise will stimulate maximum gains in strength, many find this concept hard to believe. Remember, it is not how many sets (or how much exercise) you perform that will stimulate an increase in strength, but how you perform each exercise. Information about how to "properly perform" and exercise is discussed elsewhere.

Recovery Time

Recovery time indicates the amount of time taken to rest between exercises. We would advocate that upon completion of one exercise the athlete should *immediately* move to the next exercise, allowing no time to recover. The advantages of allowing little or no time between exercises are the following:

- Total workout time will be increased significantly.
- Cardiorespiratory efficiency will be improved.
- The increase in strength will be just as significant as when more time is taken to rest between exercises.

Frequency of Workout

The frequency of workout is defined as the number of training sessions per week. During the off-season it is recommended that the athlete train three times per week, alternating days (example: Monday-Wednesday-Friday).

During the season, the athlete should train at least once (the day after a match) and preferably twice during a week's period. If a second workout is performed it should be complete 48-96 hours before the next scheduled match.

In-Season Training

Unfortunately, the emphasis placed on an *in-season* program is usually *non-existent* and often *de-emphasized.* It should be the goal of the athlete to increase strength in the off-season and at least *maintain* strength during the season. It is the misinformed coach who does not incorporate an in-season strength training program to supplement the overall conditioning program.

Most of the attributes contributing to the success of an athlete are primarily dependent upon the strength of the muscles used to play volleyball. Therefore, if an athlete hopes to maintain his pre-season performance level throughout the season, he must maintain his strength level during the season. If strength is not maintained during the season, the athlete's performance potential will probably decrease as the season progresses. A weaker athlete is also more susceptible to injury

Order of Exercise

The order of exercise will determine which exercises should be performed, and in what order. Some degree of flexibility does exist when determining the order of exercise. For maximum efficiency we would recommend that the body be divided into four major segments (excluding the neck which would make five segments). The four segments are the 1) legs; 2) torso; 3) arms; and 4) abdominal. Exercises for these body segments should be grouped accordingly and performed in the following order.

Legs

The muscles of the legs are the largest and strongest muscle groups of the body. Therefore, they should be exercised first. The muscles of the legs include the following: buttocks, quadriceps, hamstrings, calves.

Torso

Upon completion of those exercises for the muscles of the legs the athlete should then proceed to the next body segment, the torso. The muscles of the torso include the following: pectorals (chest), deltoids (shoulders), latissimus dorsi (upper back), lower back muscles, trapezius.

When exercising the muscles of the torso the athlete should alternate, whenever possible, pushing and pulling movements. This will allow opposing muscle groups the opportunity to recover momentarily.

Arms

Upon completion of those exercises for the torso muscles the athlete would then progress to the muscles of the arms. The muscles of the arms include the following: biceps, triceps, forearms.

The muscles of the forearms should be exercised after the biceps and triceps to prevent the pre-exhaustion of the muscles used to grip.

Abdominals

Upon completion of those exercises for the muscles of the arms, the athlete would then proceed to those exercises for the abdominals.

When establishing the order of exercise for your program, remember there are two rules to remember:

- Exercise largest muscles to smallest.
- When exercising the muscles of the torso and arms, alternate pushing and pulling movements.

Exercises to be Performed

The exercises performed will depend upon the equipment available. The exercises performed are not the "key" to strength gains; it is "how you perform the exercise" that will stimulate the maximum gains. Exercises should be selected to develop general overall strength. An exercise should be selected to place the emphasis on each of the major muscle groups within the body. We would advocate that not more than 11-13 exercises be performed in any one workout.

Included in the following are some suggested workouts with the barbell, Universal gym, and Nautilus equipment.

BARBELL WORKOUT

Exercise	Primary Muscles Developed
1. Leg Extension	Quadriceps
2. Squat	Buttocks, Quadriceps
3. Leg Curl	Hamstrings
4. Heel Raises	Calves
5. Bench Press	Pectorals, Deltoids, Triceps
6. Bent Arm Pullover	Shoulder Girdle, Rib Cage, Lats
7. Seated Press	Deltoids, Triceps
8. Upright Rowing	Deltoids, Biceps
9. Good Morning	Lower Back
10. Dips	Pectorals, Deltoids, Triceps
11. Chinups	Latissimus Dorsi, Biceps
12. Wrist Curl	Forearm Flexors
13. Situps	Abdominals

NAUTILUS WORKOUT

Exercise	Primary Muscles Developed
1. Hip and Back	Buttocks, Lower Back
2. Leg Extension	Quadriceps
3. Leg Press	Buttocks, Quadriceps
4. Leg Curl	Hamstrings
5. Heel Raise	Calves
6. Double Chest	
Bent Arms Flies	Pectorals
Decline Press	Pectorals, Deltoids, Triceps
7. Pullover	Latissimus Dorsi
8. Double Shoulder	
Lateral Raise	Deltoids
Seated Press	Deltoids, Triceps
9. Chinups	Latissimus Dorsi
10. Wrist Curls	Forearm Flexors
11. Situps	Abdominals

UNIVERSAL GYM WORKOUT

Exercise	Primary Muscles Developed
1. Leg Press	Buttocks, Quadriceps
2. Leg Extension	Quadriceps
3. Leg Curl	Hamstrings
4. Heel Raise	Calves
5. Bench Press	Pectorals, Deltoids, Triceps
6. Chinups	Latissimus Dorsi, Biceps
7. Seated Press	Deltoids, Triceps
8. Upright Rows	Deltoids, Biceps
9. Dips	Pectorals, Deltoids, Triceps
10. Lat Pulldowns	Latissimus Dorsi, Biceps
11. Wrist Curls	Forearm Flexors, Extensors, Pronators & Supinators
12. Situps	Abdominals

Properly Performed Exercise

As previously mentioned, the key to any exercise program is the quality of the exercise. The actual execution of the exercise will determine how significant the gains in muscular strength will be.

Unfortunately, too few coaches or athletes know how to properly perform an exercise. Consequently, the quality or intensity of the exercise is usually well below what it could or should be to stimulate maximum gains in strength.

Included in the following are those items which we demand of our athletes when performing any exercise designed to increase strength. Any deviation from the techniques mentioned herein will produce less than maximum gains.

A properly performed exercise must include the following checkpoints:

1. Full range exercise
2. Allow the muscles to raise the weight
3. Emphasize the lowering of the weight
4. Reach the point of momentary muscular failure between eight and 12 repetitions
5. Supervision

1) *Full range exercise* indicates that while performing an exercise the athlete must raise and lower the weight through the muscle's full range of movement.

2) *Allow the muscles to raise the weight* while performing an exercise, thereby eliminating all bouncing, throwing, or jerky movements. If an athlete can "throw or explode" with a weight the workload is obviously too light, or the muscles are not doing all of the work. If there are any bouncy or jerky movements involved the weight is being raised by some muscle and some *momentum.* Our guideline is to take approximately *two seconds* to raise the weight.

3) *The lowering of the weight must be emphasized* for two reasons. One half of an exercise is the raising of the weight and the other half is the lowering of the weight. The same muscle that is used to raise the weight is also the same muscle used to lower the weight. The lowering of the weight is just as important as the raising of the weight.

An athlete can lower approximately 40% more weight than he/she can raise. Because the athlete can lower so much more than he/she can raise he/she must take longer to lower the weight to stimulate significant gains. We advocate that the athlete allow four seconds (during normal exercise) to lower the weight. If negative-only exercise (only lower the weight) is performed the athlete should allow eight seconds.

4) *The athlete must reach the point of failure* somewhere between eight and 12 repetitions. For maximum gains the athlete must continue the exercise until he/she can no longer properly perform another repetition. This

should occur between eight and 12 repetitions if the athlete has selected the proper amount of resistance. Keep in mind that a sub-maximal effort will produce less than maximum gains. If an athlete is performing a barbell squat, he/she has reached the point of failure when he can no longer stand up (recover to the starting position).

A coach cannot measure anything less than 100%. The athlete has exerted a 100% effort when he/she fails and can no longer properly perform the exercise.

5) *Supervision.* Without supervision we can assure you that the results will be significantly less than the results that could have been obtained. When left to their own devices (unsupervised), an athlete will make an exercise easier whether it be knowingly or unknowingly. A coach can attempt to stimulate maximum gains by pairing off his/her athletes and allowing them to supervise each other during the execution of each repetition of each exercise. The responsibilities of the spotter include the following:

1. Insure that the lifter adheres to each of the four checkpoints previously mentioned.
2. Prevent injury to the lifter.
3. Verbally encourage the athlete to continue the exercise to the true point of momentary muscular failure.
4. Assist the lifter from start to finish (non-stop) through the entire workout, and then switch roles and allow the lifter to become the spotter.
5. The spotter must record all pertinent workout information to prevent the duplication of a previous workout. Pertinent information would include the date of each workout, the exercises being performed, the amount of weight used and the number of repetitions executed for each exercise. This workout card is the coach's tool for evaluation. The coach and athlete can constantly monitor the progress from one workout to the next.

Summary

Most coaches and athletes are constantly seeking the "added edge" over their opponents. Because most volleyball players neglect their muscular development, a strength training program could prove to be the only edge one highly skilled team may have over another.

Remember, in every instance, **"a stronger athlete is a better athlete."** A stronger athlete will jump higher, and move faster, for a longer period of time

INTERVAL TRAINING THROUGH USE OF THE SET SYSTEM

by
George Colfer
Dean Junior College, Franklin, Mass.

Interval training became a popular training method in the early 50's. It actually originated in Europe in 1920 and in 1930 was adapted to Swedish conditions at which time it became known as the Fartlek or speed play method. After World War II, Emil Zatopek, using intense training known as the Zatopek method, inspired through his success the advent of what we now know as interval training. Since this time there has been an unending controversy about the pros and cons of this method. Perhaps there is not a type of training that has been the target for more use and abuse than interval training. Regardless of one's opinion, most coaches in training use some form of interval workouts in their program.

A general definition of interval training is a period of work or exercise followed by a prescribed recovery interval. This definition implies a measured run with a measured recovery. There are several ways or techniques that may be used in planning interval training workouts. These are generally organized according to the following basic variables.

1. Distance or duration of the run.
2. Speed or intensity of the run.
3. Number of repetitions of the run.
4. The length or duration of the recovery interval.
5. Nature or type of the recovery interval.
6. The frequency of the interval training sessions.

It is no secret that the success of the athlete will depend on the coach's ability to combine these variables in planning the interval workout.

BENEFITS OF INTERVAL TRAINING

When employed wisely, interval training offers many diverse benefits. These are aimed mainly at bettering performances, but also enable the athlete to accelerate more rapidly towards his potential.

1. Interval training provides more work with less awareness of fatigue.
2. More of a challenge is emphasized.
3. Quality over quantity work is emphasized.
4. Competitive conditions are stimulated.
5. Interval training permits rapid progress. Goals are more accurately

planned and measured.

6. A personal approach to training is followed.
7. This method of training requires less time and space. While running at faster rates, more work can be accomplished in shorter periods of time.
8. Flexibility in training is allowed. Workouts can be changed quickly if needed. A well-planned program will prevent overfatigue as a result of training.
9. It is more beneficial to speed and anaerobic development.
10. Aerobic benefits and heart stroke volume may be gained in a shorter period of time.
11. The recovery interval avoids excessive accumulation of fatigue products in the circulatory and cardiovascular systems.
12. A great deal of the research supports the theory that a proper work-recovery ratio is important to successful training.

ABUSE OF INTERVAL TRAINING

Most of the abuse in interval training is caused by human error and the lack of knowledge about the use of this method. It is not a total program, but one of the various methods to be incorporated into a training program at selected times. Poor training, the lack of suitability for the individuals being trained, and poor understanding of interval training principles have developed many of the following disadvantages or weaknesses of the method.

1. Recovery intervals are frequently prolonged by the athlete or coach. This destroys the work-recovery ratio principle.
2. There are limits of work and tolerance. Interval training may try to surpass them too soon.
3. There is a tendency to use distances not pertinent to the sport.
4. Interval training should not be used until a firm foundation of aerobic training is completed.
5. There is a possibility of causing overfatigue by attempting too strenuous a program too soon. This can cause extreme setbacks in training goals. Over-work or excess fatigue will make the athlete more susceptible to physical injury such as strains, pulls, etc.
6. There is a danger of mental fatigue or stress. Interval training involves competition versus the clock. Sometimes the results or analysis can be defeating to the athlete.
7. Through prolonged or excessive use, boredom or monotony can develop. The athlete may lose motivation in his training.

Most of the disadvantages stated can be overcome or need not occur if the program is well planned and the proper combination of interval training techniques and variables is used. The system is a technique which can provide the athlete with the benefits of interval training while offering control over the disadvantages.

THE SET SYSTEM

The use of sets for interval training has several advantages over other techniques. There is greater consistency in the work performed and the measurement or analysis of the work is quite simple. Sets shorten the training time as well as make the workouts seem faster and easier to the athlete. Since consistency of the times of the runs is most important, there is less pressure or stress to record great times in practice. The challenge of the set to the athlete is to be able to repeat the designated workout pace for each interval run of the set. In other words, can he post consistent times? Proper results require serious planning by the coach as well as knowledge of the individual abilities of his athletes. Athletes can work the set together even if their workout paces are different. Competition should not be emphasized except to maintain consistency of the workout pace.

Another objective of the set system is to allow the athlete to work towards his goal pace as quickly as possible. Improvement will only occur when the quality or intensity of the work is increased or the recovery interval is decreased.

To plan a specific workout using sets, the components of the sets must be analyzed. Each set should consist of the following:

1. A designated number of runs.
2. A designated distance for each run within the set.
3. A timed recovery interval, which should be adhered to strictly.
4. A designated workout pace for each run within the set.
5. A rest period following the completion of the set.

Types of Sets

The most efficient type of set is that of repetition of the same running distance within the set. An example would be 8 × 40. The advantage of repetition running is in establishing consistency in the pace. The ladder set would mix different distances in the same set. An example could be 2 × 330, 2 × 440, and 2 × 660. The ladder offers variation in training and in some cases will allow a more flexible approach to interval training. It should be mentioned that in a ladder each distance run should be repeated at least once to offer some consistency in the analysis of the work.

Due to different stages of training and individual differences in ability, it is not possible to say exactly how many sets should be included in a workout. This must be the coach's decision in planning the workout. Sets may be combined using those of the same distance, of different distances or the ladder type to fit the needs of the training program.

Rest Periods Following Completion of a Set

After completion of the last run of a set, there should be a rest period of two to five minutes before moving on to another set or a different phase of the workout. Runners should walk during the rest period. Its length will depend upon the intensity of the workout. The target heart rate between set, should be 120 beats/minute.

A set should consist of no less than three runs and a maximum of eight. Since this training is intense and over-fatigue should be avoided, it would be more beneficial to increase the number of sets rather than surpass the maximum number of runs for a set. Runs of shorter duration would tend to be used in greater numbers. Using this concept, the quality of the training would not be affected. The distance of the event for which the training is being used should also be considered.

DISTANCES FOR THE SET SYSTEM

While almost any distance can technically be put into a set, the quality of the work desired can best be obtained if the runs are kept to a maximum of 660 yards. The distances selected should depend largely on the sport for which the training is planned. The total duration of the run for set intervals should not exceed 120 seconds at longer distances and preferably 90 seconds as the athlete's condition improves.

Recovery Intervals

It is important to emphasize again that the designated recovery interval should not be extended. If an athlete is not able to post consistent times, the workout pace should be lessened, not the recovery interval increased. The maximum recovery for any run should not exceed 90 seconds, while the minimum should be no less than 30 seconds. Deciding upon starting recovery lengths will depend on the condition and ability of the runner. As a rule, it would be better to start at maximums or 3 × workout pace = recovery interval and decrease as the athlete's status changes. The maximum recovery intervals are recommended for the following distances.

LENGTH OF RUN	MAXIMUM RECOVERY LENGTH
220 yards	90 seconds
150 yards	75 seconds
110 yards	60 seconds
60 yards	45 seconds
30 yards	30 seconds

While some recovery intervals do not allow much time, it is best if the runner keeps himself mildly active during the pause. The target heart rate between repetitions should be 150 beats/minute.

WORKOUT PACE (Speed of the Run)

The pace should be established depending upon the ability and condition of the athlete. It should be realistic and attainable. As the status of the runner changes, the pace should be adjusted. In most instances, the pace for a set interval run should be faster than that of the same distance during a continuous run. A more specific method of setting one's pace per repetitionis as follows.

- Establish your fastest time for the specific training distance, off of a running start.
- Using the following formula insert your time.

$$\frac{\text{YOUR TIME} \times 100}{80} = \text{Workout Pace}$$

A good method for checking the physiological effects of the run is to check the pulse rate of the runner at the end of the recovery interval. If the pulse rate exceeds 150, the workout pace should be lessened. This adjustment is effective in the case of the untrained athletes during early season training. However, in highly trained athletes an allowance should be made for individual differences; therefore, this should not be an absolute rule.

PLANNING THE SET

Through the use of the basic variables in interval training, the accompanying chart shows the different methods of planning a set workout. These methods can apply to a single set or a combination of sets. Proper planning of each set will allow for individual differences in ability as well as adding variety and flexibility to the training. The athlete should be able to work toward his goal at a faster rate of progress and with less chance of mental fatigue.

There is no definite order of progression. Combinations other than those given can be used; however, it is not advisable to change too many variables at any one time. Best results are usually obtained by a single change. Crash programs should be avoided. Example #1 is a chart which a coach could keep to easily identify which variable he is going to change. Example #2 is a seven step method of adjusting an interval training program.

#1 Example of Chart for Variables in an Interval Training Program

Methods	Distance	Speed	Number of Runs Per Set	Recovery Length	Number of Sets
Starting Method	Same	Same	Same	Same	Same
1.	Same	Same	Same	Same	Same
2.	Same	Same	Increase	Same	Same
3.	Increase	Same	Same	Same	Same
4.	Same	Increase	Same	Same	Same
5.	Same	Same	Same	Decrease	Same
6.	Decrease	Increase	Same	Same	Same
7.	Same	Increase	Same	Decrease	Same

#2 Example of Adjusting an Interval Training Program

Starting Method. An athlete begins with two sets of 4×440 with a workout pace of 65 seconds and a recovery length of 90 seconds.

When planning a change in this workout as progress demands, the coach may use one of the following:

Method 1. The distance, speed, number of runs, and the recovery length remain the same. The number of sets would be increased.

Method 2. The distance, speed, recovery length, and number of sets remain the same. The number of runs would be increased for each set.

Method 3. The distance of each run would be increased for each set. The speed, number of runs, recovery length and number of sets remain the same.

Method 4. The distance, number of runs, recovery length, and number of sets would remain the same. The speed of each run would be increased.

Method 5. The distance, speed, number of runs, and number of sets remain the same. The time of the recovery length would be decreased.

Method 6. The distance would be decreased, while the speed of each run is increased. The number of runs, recovery length, and number of sets remain the same.

Method 7. The distance, number of runs, and number of sets remain the same. The speed of the runs would be increased and the recovery length is decreased. This method would produce the greatest change in the intensity of the workout.

In conclusion, it is apparent that the success of the set system depends upon the ability of the coach in organizing the training program. A review of the important factors that must be taken into consideration are:

- An adequate knowledge of interval training.
- A preliminary period of aerobic training.
- The integration of interval training into the total program.
- Planning of the set workout; a) emphasizing quality over quantity

work; b) suiting the training to the ability level of the athlete; c) use of the analysis of the training; d) patience in reaching goals and training levels; and e) making the workouts pertinent to the events for which the training is used.

JUMP TRAINING
by
C. E. Lefroy

Jump training can be offered as any training activity in which the emphasis is on improving one's jumping ability. Such a definition is too vague and offers little guidance as to how to improve this all important skill.

A definition such as this would permit a coach to build a jump training program on weight training alone. Any such program would be inadequate as weight training can only increase the athlete's jump indirectly by developing strength and power in the anti-gravity muscles. The principle of specificity of training tells us to duplicate the movements under the conditions which the athlete will have to perform. In short, one must jump to improve one's jump. Further, it is important that each jump be a maximum effort and duplicate as many other relevant game conditions as possible.

Jump training should be defined as any training activity which aims at improving the jumping ability of the player and has the following characteristics. First, it is usually done without a volleyball. Second, each jump is a maximum effort rather than submaximal as is the case when doing endurance training. Thus, quality is more important than quantity and jump training is done to fatigue rather than to exhaustion. Third, every set of jumps is done quickly with no hesitation between jumps. Fourth,at least some training activities should be done while the athlete is either off balance or in transition between skill performances.

The energy requirements for maximal jumping are enormous and can quickly exhaust the athlete if he/she must jump repeatedly. Therefore, several short jump training periods should be interspersed throughout the practice. As a general rule, each jump training period should consist of approximately five work periods of 5-15 seconds'duration separated by up to one minute of rest. Given the brevity of the work periods, it is essential that the players work at absolutely maximal intensity. For some activities it may be necessary to increase the workload by increasing the length of each work period or by adding additional work periods.

Athletes will be encouraged to make a maximum effort rather than pace themselves if they know the number of work periods and length before hand. Therefore, it is important that the coach give this information to the players in one manner or another. The players' motivation will be increased if a record is kept of the number of jumps done each day and the vertical jump is tested regularly. It is a good idea to post these figures on a bulletin board.

The list of jump training ideas is limited only by the coach's imagination. Virtually anything which can be jumped over, on, or off safely, can be used for this crucial aspect of training. Following are a number of ideas which have been successfully used by coaches:

1. *Rebound Jumping:* The Soviets have developed a simple training technique to assist their triple jumpers develop explosive power and lift called rebound or "depth" jumping.
   The technique simply consists of jumping off and on a box or high bench. The idea is to jump to the floor and immediately bounce up again in *one action.* It is essential there be no hesitation between the landing and the rebound jump.
   The athlete continues until tired. Gradually increase the height of the box.
2. *High Skipping:* High rope jumping may be used as a form of rebound training which aims at developing explosive power in the calves. If this type of training is to be successful, it is essential that upper leg involvement be limited to that required to protect the knees. Therefore, while some knee flexion is required on each landing, it should be minimal. Use the following procedures to maximize calf development:
   a) Use single time rhythm, i.e., one jump per turn of the rope.
   b) Each rebound is a maximum effort involving the fullest and most explosive ankle extension possible. A large number of half efforts will not produce as much benefit as fewer high quality jumps.
   c) Do not allow a hesitation between the landing and rebound.
   d) Continue until tired. Do not continue to exhaustion. The objective is to develop a high quality explosive effort rather than endurance which will be the major result of large quantities of sub-maximal muscular contractions.
3. *Jump Touch:* Suspend a rope or similar object so that the bottom end can just be touched when you do a maximum jump. Jump continuously and rapidly to touch the rope. Keep track of the number of touches.
4. *Hop-Step-Hop:* Hop straight up as high as possible on the left foot, step forward with the right foot and hop on it as high as possible. Continue alternating feet for fifteen seconds then jog one lap of the

court. Repeat 5 times. Increase the workload by lengthening each work period or adding additional work periods.

5. *Jump Sideways Over Rope:* Stretch an elastic or rubber rope between two posts. Adjust the rope height to vertical jumping ability (about 4-6 inches below maximum vertical jump Start with your side to the rope. Hop sideways from one side of the rope to the other continuously and rapidly.
6. *Jump Slap:* Assume a blocking stance with a partner on the other side of the net jump and slap each other's hands above the net. If maximum jump training effect is desired, the jumps should be rapid with no hesitation between the landing and next jump.
7. *Medicine Ball Jump:* While working in pairs, jump and throw a medicine ball over a net with two hands.
8. Jump on the bleacher seats; or benches with dumb-bells in the hands. Add weight or raise the height of the bench as progress is made. Depending on your purpose, you may wish to precede each jump with a pre-jump.
9. *Chair Jumping:* Jump over three chairs arranged in a row. Place the chairs approximately 1½ meters apart. Do not pause between jumps. Make sure the chairs are placed so the players will jump over from front to back. Start with four sets of three jumps. Add one set each week until the player is doing ten sets.
10. *Leap Frog:* Arrange the players in a file of not more than twelve people. Each person assumes a crouch position about 1½ meters from the other person in the file. When he reaches the head of the file, he assumes the crouch position. The drill is continuous in that the "last" person in the file comes to his feet and jumps over those who are in front of him and the file works its way forward until it runs out of space.
11. *Jumping over an elastic rope:* Stretch an elastic rope in a zig-zag pattern between six anchor points, chairs will do. Place the rope 4 to 6 inches below maximum vertical jump. Jump over the rope forward (5), backward (5), sideward (5), and forward with weight (5).
12. *Cossack Jumps:* Stand erect, jump high swinging the legs into a straddle pike position with the knees as straight as possible. Try to touch the toes with the hands. Because this is particularly exhausting exercise, it may be wise to keep the work periods brief (5-10 seconds).
13. *Knee Grasp Jumps:* Stand erect, jump high drawing the knees to the chest. Repeat without pause for 5-15 seconds.

"DOYA JUMP TRAINING PROCEDURE"

by
Victor E. Lindal
British Columbia Volleyball Association

This program is a combination of skipping and maximum jumping. The skipping is to be done as a warm-up, but as you progress you will find that it also becomes an endurance builder.

The theory behind this jump program is:

(a) Maximum effort jumping leads to rapid improvement;

(b) Goals that can be seen are more easily attainable (you cut 2 cm's off your card each month)

(c) Your jump improvement will be greatest if you personally direct your own program.

Mr. Hidoe Doya of Japan developed this program from his observations of the ancient samurai warriors' training. In their training they would jump the grass in the field and as the grass grew, they continued to jump. In our case the grass is growing at 2 cm. per month.

ROPE SKIPPING CLARIFICATION

You stay at each level of skipping for the prescribed number of months.

(Example): when you get to regular 2 leg jumping with weights you will have been on the program for 6 months.

ROPE SKIPPING

2 Months

Use one leg and do two sets. Start at 50 with each leg and move gradually to 60.

4 Months

Two leg jumps, but each jump is done with a double turn of the rope.

Start with 20 and progress to 60. Do two sets with a three to five minute rest in between.

1 Month

Regular two leg jumping, but use a weight belt or jacket equal to one-tenth of your body weight.

Start at 30 and progress to 60. Do two sets with a three to five minute rest in between.

2 Months

One leg skipping as in the first month, but now use the same weight as last month. Start at 30 and move to 50 doing two sets with a rest following each set.

3 Months

Two leg jumps with a double turn of the rope as described earlier, use the weight previously mentioned. The rope skipping should be done five to seven days per week as a warm-up to the spike and block jump training that will now be described.

Have your coach test you on your spike reach and your block jump reach. The spike reach test should be done with a 2 or 3 step approach, but the block jump should be done stationary. Do each test 3 times and then take the average of your three jumps. This height becomes your beginning height for the start of your training.

Start your training by making a card as follows:

0		0	Sample and not to scale.
	.5 cm		12th month
	.5 cm		11th month
	.5 cm		10th month
	.5 cm		9th month
	1 cm		8th month
	1 cm		7th month
	1 cm		6th month
	1 cm		5th month
	2 cm		4th month
	2 cm		3rd month
	2 cm		2nd month
	2 cm		1st month

This height is equal to your average after three jumps.

This card, as you can see, is marked off in centimeters.
Note: You will have two cards; one for spike jump and one for block jump.

How Do You Use the Card?

(1) Find a place to hang the card, so that the bottom of the card is equal to the height recorded in your earlier tests.

(2) Do the rope skipping and then follow with your jump training at the card. Three days a week will be devoted to spike jumping and three days to block jumping.

PROCEDURE FIRST MONTH

First 2 Weeks

With the card set at your height do 15 spike jump approaches, touching the card each time (3 days). Alternate with block jumps on the other 3 days.

Second 2 Weeks

As above only do one approach to equal two jumps and complete ten approaches. Do the two jumps in rapid succession.

Next Month and each succeeding month

Repeat the above but cut the card at each of the levels so that your height is increasing at a rate of 2 cm per month. Please cut more off if you feel you are progressing more rapidly.

JUMP TRAINING
by
Hiroshi Toyoda

1. *SKIPPING* - rope goes twice around with each jump.
   - 50 times (first month) then, 100, 150, etc.
2. *HALF SQUAT* - 10 times quickly with a person on your back.
   1st month - 10 times X 3 sets
   2nd month - 10 times X 5 sets
   etc. - 10 times X 7 sets
3. *BACK RAISES* - 10 X 3 - 10 lbs. - weight held in hands behind head
   10 X 5 - 15 lbs. - (2nd month)
   10 X 7 - 20 lbs.
4. *ZIG-ZAG JUMP OVER ELASTIC* - 10 times at knee height continuously, then
   10 times at waist height non-continuously.
5. *JUMPING UP AND DOWN* - with boxes or benches.

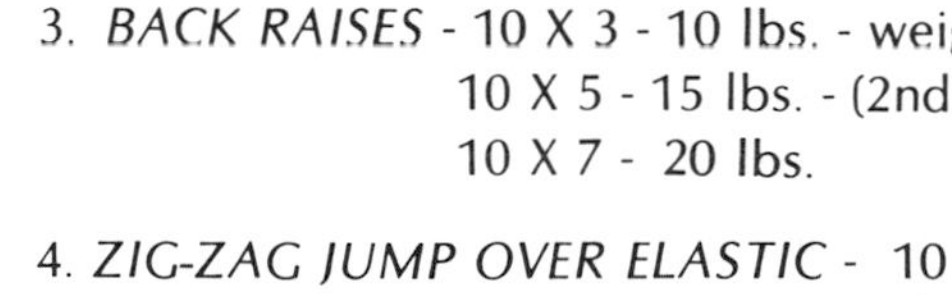

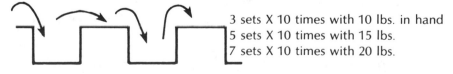

3 sets X 10 times with 10 lbs. in hand
5 sets X 10 times with 15 lbs.
7 sets X 10 times with 20 lbs.

6. *ARM ACTION FOR JUMP* - hyperextension with weights.

1st month - 10 × 3 - 10 lbs.
2nd month - 10 × 5 - 15 lbs.
3rd month - 10 × 7 - 20 lbs. *then spike 1-2 hundred times.

7. *SPLIT JUMPS*
Routine: Jumping and landing with one foot in front of the other.
Repetitions 4 X 12

8. *BENCH JUMPS*
Off and on to another with a weight. The weight should not be more than 50 to 60 lbs.

Routines:

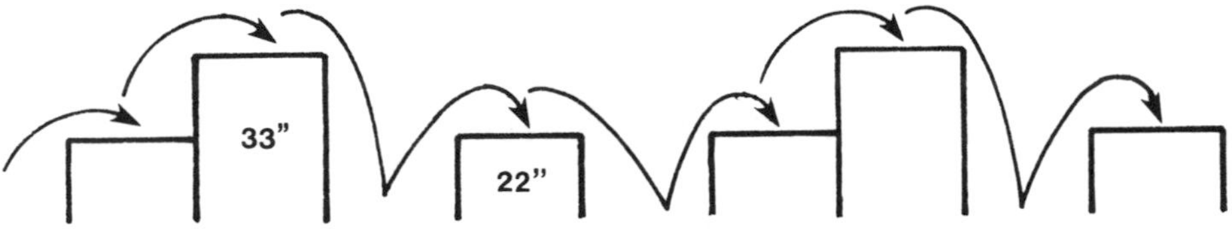

Jump as in the diagram and then walk back and repeat. *Note:* When you come down from the high one you should rebound right up to the next one which is low.

Repetitions: 3 X 6

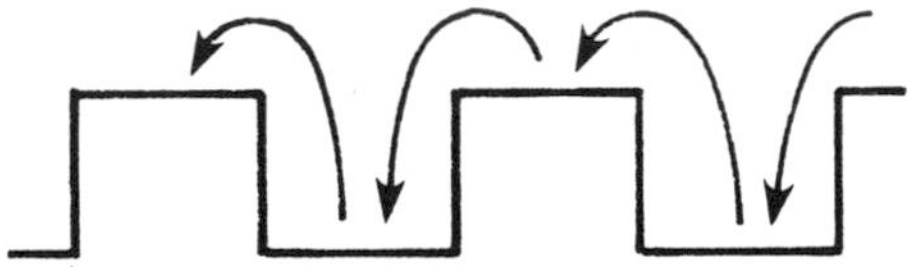

9. *VERTICAL JUMP* (jump reach)
Routine:
Hold a dumbbell in one hand while you jump and reach with the other one.
Repetitions: 3 X 10

10. *SKIPPING* Use ankle weights, or weight jacket.
Routine:
Go for a set distance (a lap of the gym). Use a weight that you can handle easily. Move fast and pick up your knees.

11. *HOPPING ON THE SPOT*
Use a weight that you can handle. Do it very fast and for 30 seconds, you will have to vary the time and sets depending on your conditions. Set a time and stick with it—FAST ! FAST ! FAST !

12. *BUNNY HOPS* (with dumbbell)—Go for 15 meters (50 feet)
Walk back and repeat. *Repetitions* 3 to 8

A TOTAL JAPANESE WARM-UP AND COOL-DOWN PROGRAM

by

Tsutomu Koyama
Head Volleyball Coach
Japanese Olympic Team
(Montreal)

Yoshiaki Kazio
Japanese National Coaching Staff
Chief of Development and Techniques

The warm-up and cool-down program presented in this article is a total physical program used by the Japanese team in training. The concept presented is one of progressively increasing physical exercise. This system gradually prepares the athlete physically and mentally for volleyball training.

It is important that the coach does not totally eliminate a particular area of the warm-up. This would delete a necessary aspect of a player's development. If the coach is limited by the amount of time he can devote to warm-up he should shorten the duration of the exercises but avoid elimination.

This warm-up program also prepares the athlete mentally. It gradually puts him in the frame of mind necessary to maximize his volleyball training time.

The cool-down is also a critical part of training. Many times this is the first area of training which a coach will cut if time becomes a factor. Again we emphasize the importance of not eliminating. The cool-down is crucial to the athlete physically as well as mentally.

I. WARM-UP PROGRAM

The contents and order of a Warm-up Program:

1. Warming-up exercise (includes jogging and footwork)
2. Limbering-up
3. Flexibility exercise
4. Supplementary exercise (divided into groups and include vigorous physical exercise)
5. Coordination exercise

A Series of Warming-up Exercises

Warming-up (Line Formation)

a. Jogging (3 laps)
b. Twist walk (forward)
c. Jogging (1)
d. Toe Touch Walk
e. Jogging (1)
f. One arm up forward lunge walk
g. Jogging (1)
h. Monkey walk (backward)
i. Jogging (1)
j. Bear walk (forward)
k. Jogging (1)
l. Alternating arm circles
m. Jogging (1)
n. High skipping
o. Jogging (3)

Bear Walk

Toe Touch Walk

Monkey Walk

One Arm Up Forward Lunge Walk

Twist Walk

Alternating
Arm Circles

High Skipping

A Series of Limbering-up Exercises

Limbering-up (circle formation)

a. arms front and up, knees bend and stretch
b. chest stretch
c. arm circles
d. trunk twist
e. straddle floor touch
f. trunk rotations
g. side bender
h. wrist shake
i. knee rotations
j. ankle rotations

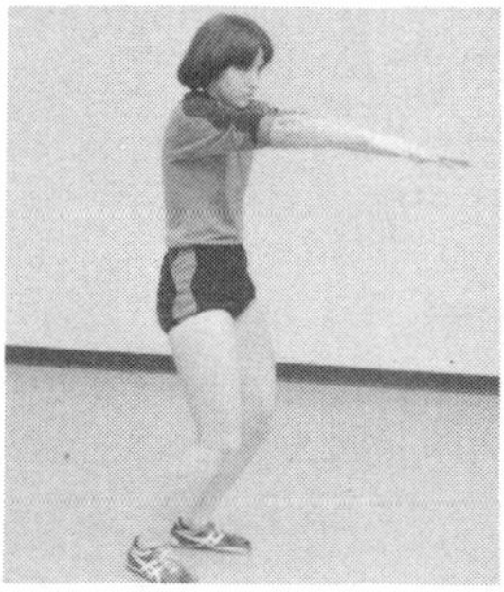

Arms front and up, knees bend and stretch

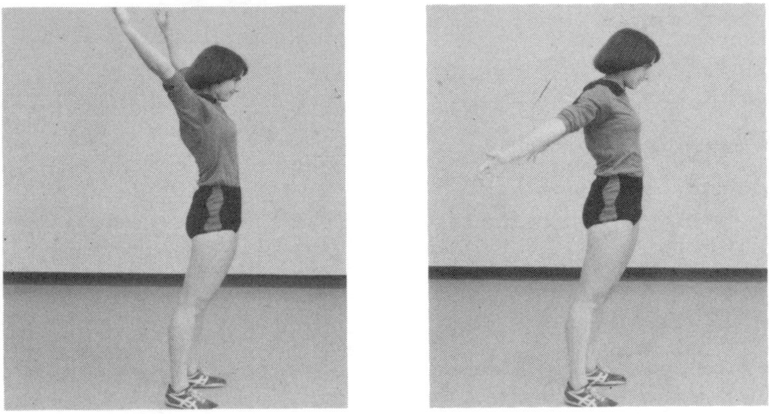

Arm Circles

Straddle Floor Touch

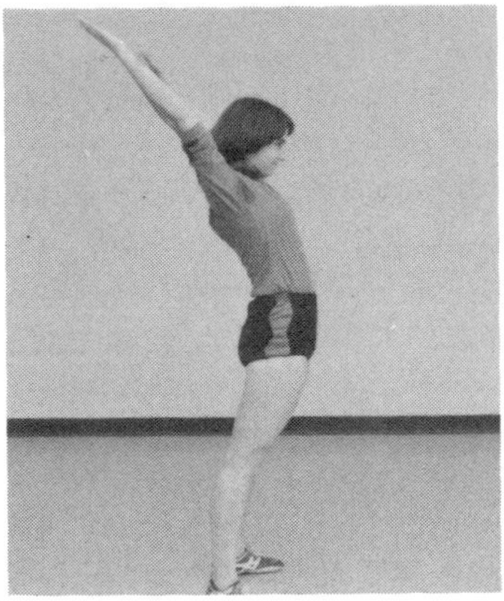

Chest Stretch

Trunk Twist

Trunk Rotations

80 - 89% = B
70 - 79% = C
60 - 69% = D
59 & Below = F

<u>EXTRA CREDIT:</u> A student may receive up to 25 points Extra Credit. See the instructor for assignments available.

VOLLEYBALL 1923

QUIZES & TEST SCHEDULE

T/TH	MWF		
1/23	1/24	Quiz #1	Chapter 1: History of Volleyball Chapter 2: Overhead Pass/Underhand Pass
1/28	1/27	Quiz #2	"Power Volleyball" - Film Quiz immediately following film
2/4	2/3	Quiz #3	Chapter 3: Serve/Spike Chapter 4: Blocking/Digging/Emergency Techniques
2/18	2/17	Quiz #4	Chapter 5: Offense Chapter 7: Spike Coverage
2/25	2/24	Quiz #5	Chapter 8: Defense Chapter 9: Transition, Chapter 12: Conditioning
3/6	3/7	MID-TERM EXAM:	Chapter 20 - Rules
See Schedule of Classes		FINAL EXAM	Chapters 2,3,4,5,7,8,9

GRADING SCALE: 90 - 100% = A

Knee Rotations

Ankle Rotations

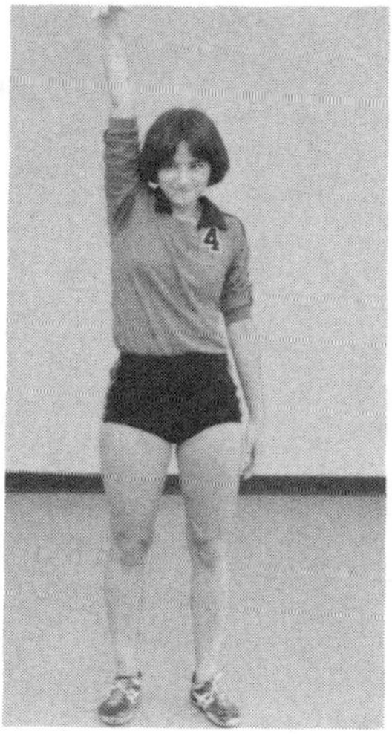

Wrist Shake

Side Bender

A Series of Combination Stretching Exercises

Flexibility Exercise

a. combination chest stretch
b. combination side stretch
c. double shoulder push
d. back carry
e. handstand carry
f. combination side lunge
g. straight legged seesaw
h. straddle seesaw
i. straddle trunk rotation seesaw
j. back to back seasaw

Combination Chest Stretch

Combination Side Stretch

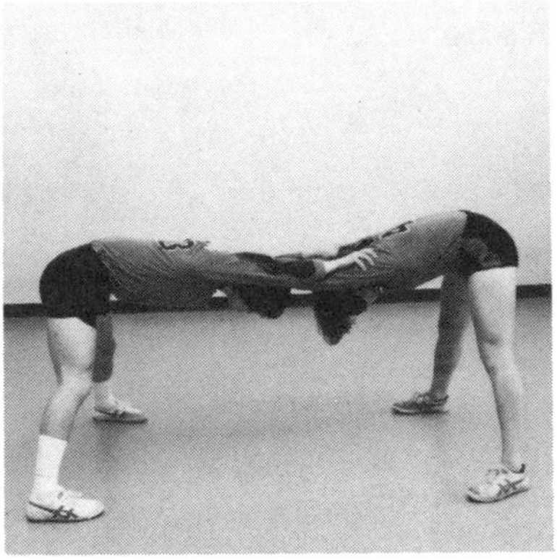

Double Shoulder Push

Handstand Carry

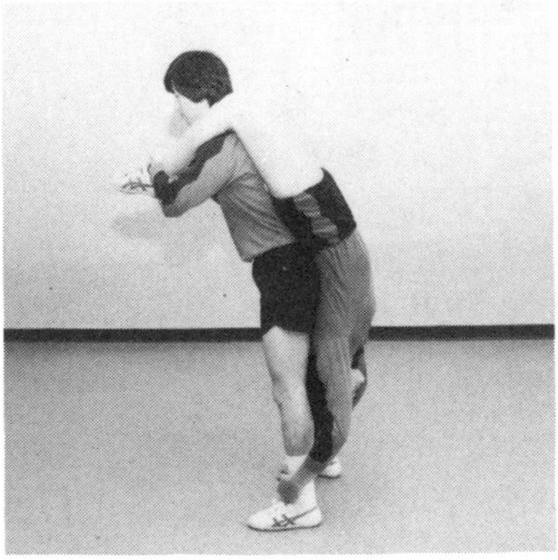

Handstand Carry

Back Carry

Combination Side Lunge

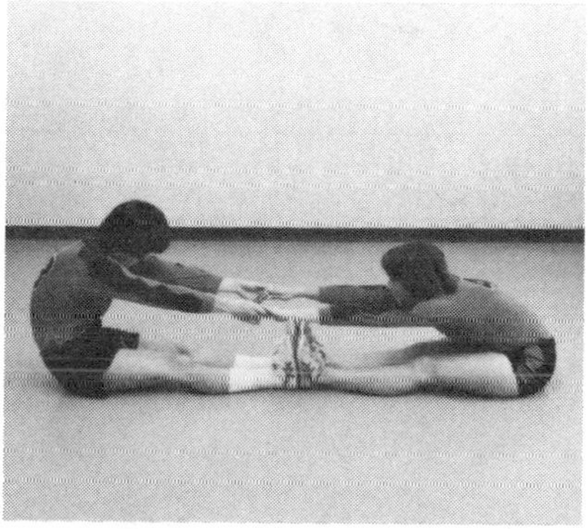

Straight Legged Seesaw

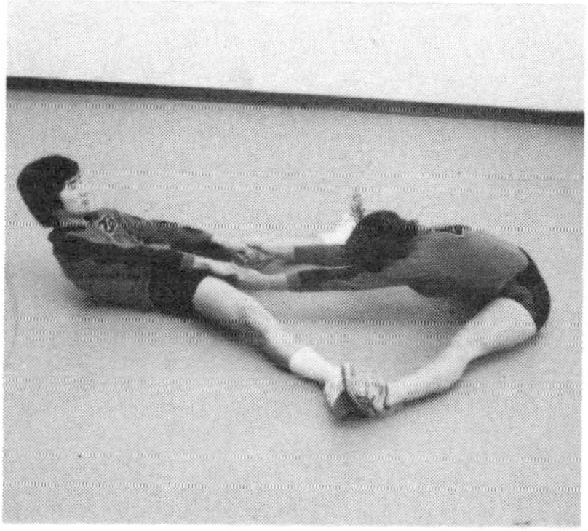

Straddle Seesaw

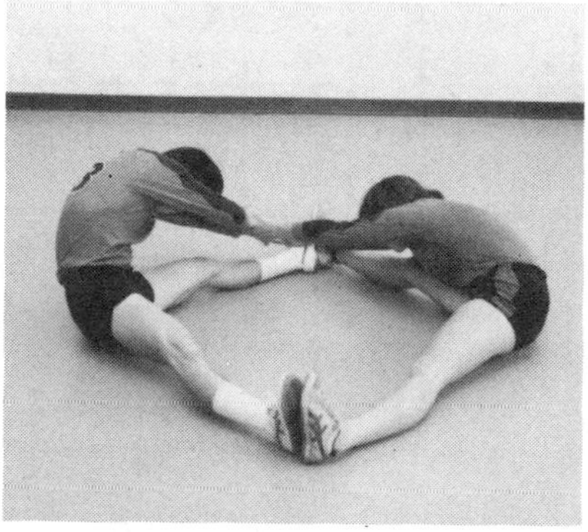

Straddle Trunk Rotation Seesaw

Back to Back Seesaw

An alternating program of supplementary exercises

Supplementary Exercises

Select one of the following groups on an alternating basis

Group A (especially to develop speed)

a. Pattern #1 - sprint to center line, backpeddle to 3m line, sprint under net to opposite 3m line, backpeddle to center line, sprint to finish.

b. Pattern #2 - sprint to 3m line, shuffle facing net to sideline, sprint to center line, shuffle 3m facing net, sprint to 3m line, shuffle to sideline, sprint to finish.

c. Pattern #3 - sprint to center line, turn and sprint on angle to 3m line, turn and sprint under net to opposite 3m line, turn and sprint on angle to center line, turn and sprint straight to finish.

d. Pattern #4 - crossover step along baseline to sideline, sprint to 3m line, crossover step along 3m line to sideline, backpeddle to finish.

e. Pattern #5 - sprint diagonally to center line, shuffle facing net to opposite sideline, backpeddle diagonally to baseline, shuffle to finish.

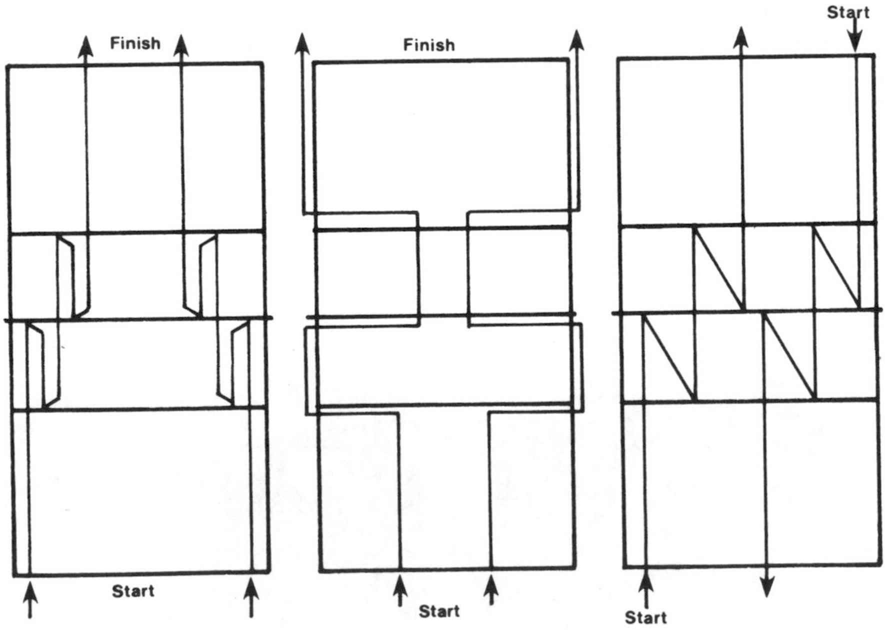

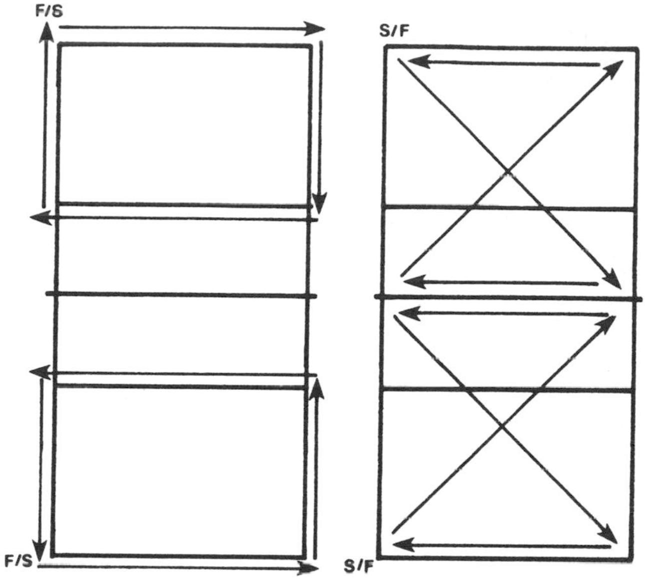

Group B (especially to develop jumping ability)

a. Knee Grasp Jumps
b. Jump Overs
c. Block Jumps
d. Rim Touch
e. Team Leap Frog

Knee Grasp Jumps

Jump Overs

Block Jump

Rim Touch

Team Leap Frog

Group C (actual circuit used by Yashica Volleyball Team)

a. Station #1 - Back Arch Jumps
b. Station #2 - Jack Knife Jumps
c. Station #3 - Horse Jumps
d. Station #4 - Prone Back Arches
e. Station #5 - Push-ups
f. Station #6 - Russian Jumps
g. Station #7 - One Legged Straddle Squat Kicks
h. Station #8 - Supine Leg Lift Pushes

Back Arch Jumps

Jack Knife Jumps

One Legged Straddle Squat Kicks

Russian Jumps

Supine Leg Lift Pushes

Prone Back Arches

Push-ups

Horse Jumps

A Rotational System of Coordination Exercises

Coordination Exercises

Select one group of coordination exercises to be performed daily on a rotational basis

a. Handstand Walk

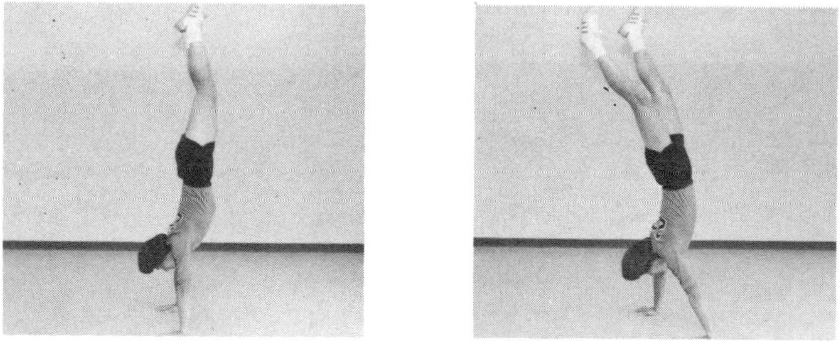

b. Tether ball drills (1-6)

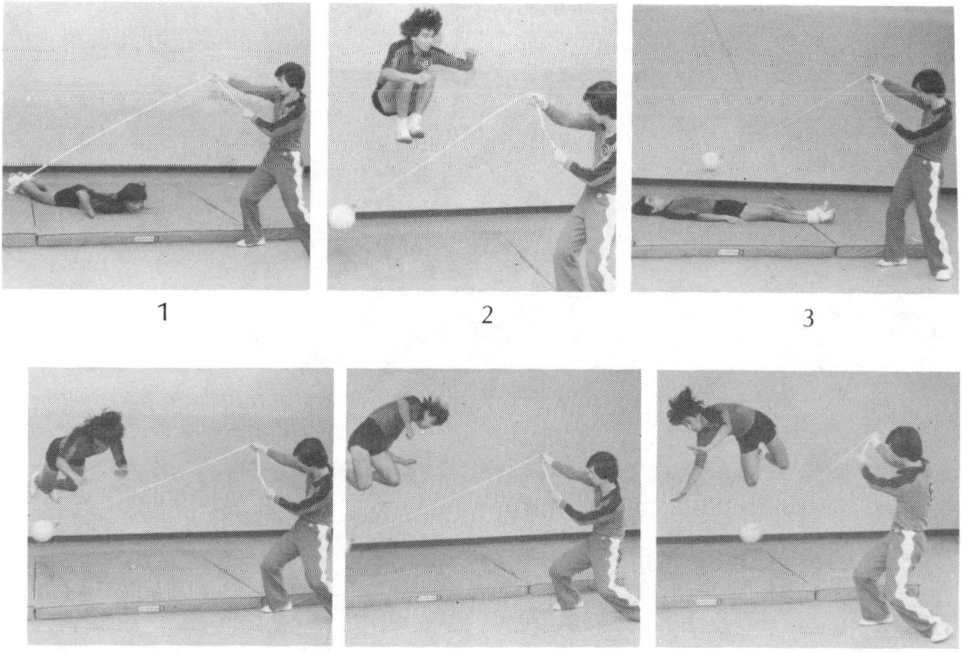

1 2 3

4 5 6

c. Rolling Sequence

Forward Roll

Backward Roll

Straddle Backward Roll

Straddle Forward Roll

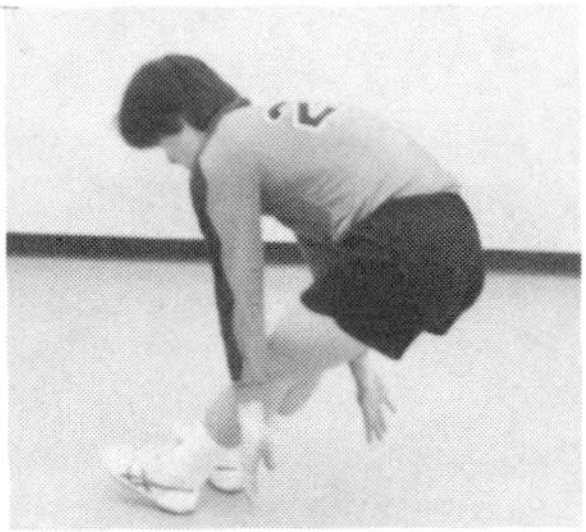
Straight Legged Backward Roll

Straight Legged Forward Roll

d. Vaulting

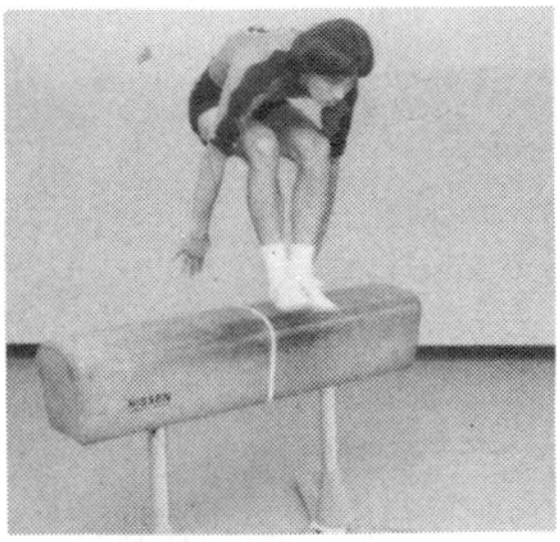
Squat Vault

Straddle Vault

Front Vault

Feet First Vault

Dive Forward Roll Vault

Straddle Vault/ Long Horse

II. MAIN PRACTICE
III. COOLING DOWN
A. The Order and Contents of Cooling Down Exercises

- jogging (5 laps slow and relaxed)
- limbering down exercises (same as in warm-up)
- flexibility exercises
  - a. Crab Stretch
  - b. Cobra Stretch
  - c. Split Series
  - d. Hurdlers Series
  - e. Calf Stretcher

Crab Stretch

Split Series

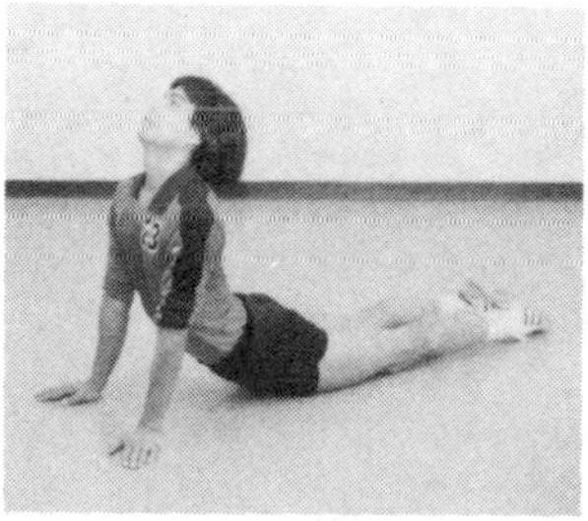

Cobra Stretch

Calf Stretcher

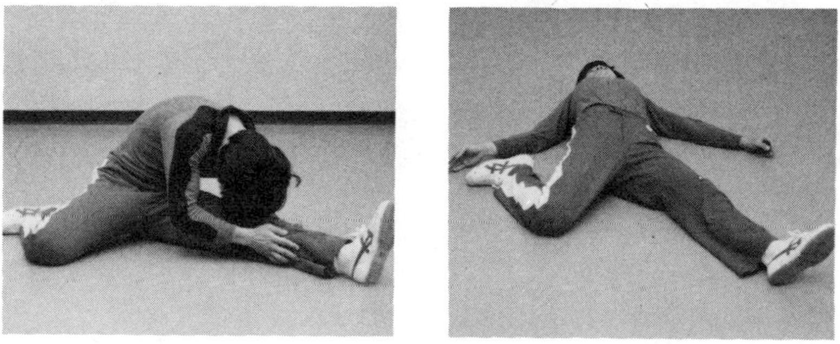

Hurdlers Series

- relaxation exercises
  a. leg relaxation
  b. prone leg shake
  c. prone knee bend shake
  d. long sitting arm shake
  e. prone knee/ankle bend
  f. full body relaxation

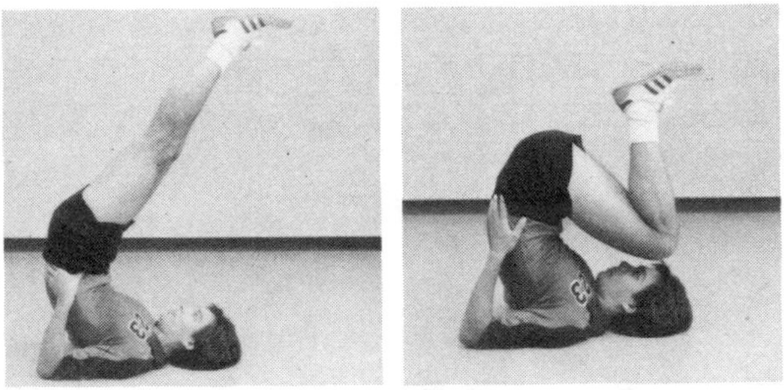

Leg Relaxation

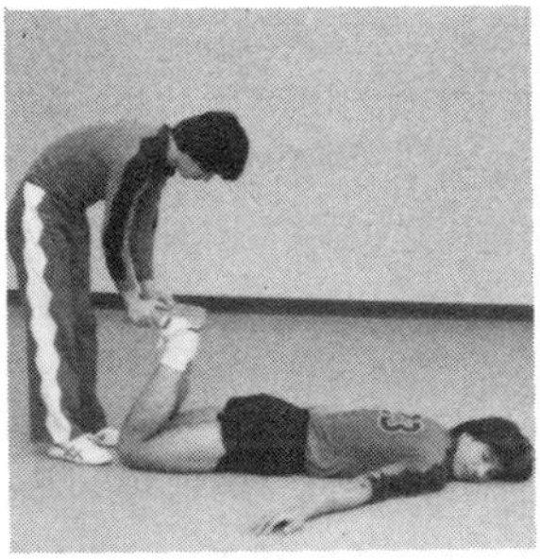

Prone Knee Bend Shake

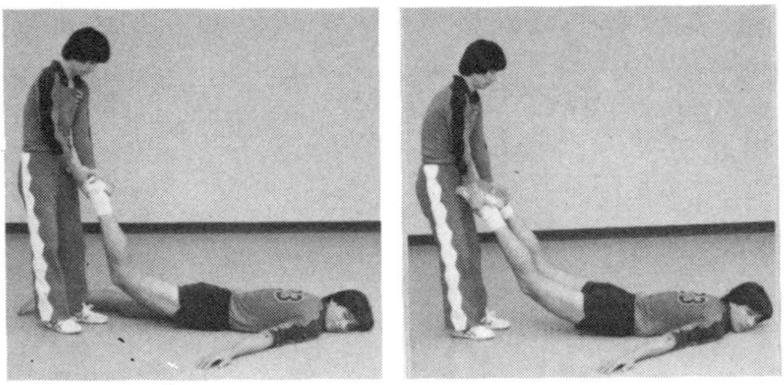

Prone Leg Shake

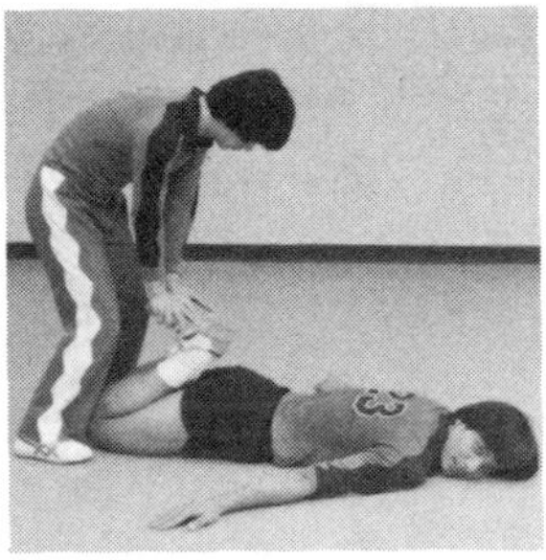

Prone Knee and Ankle Bend

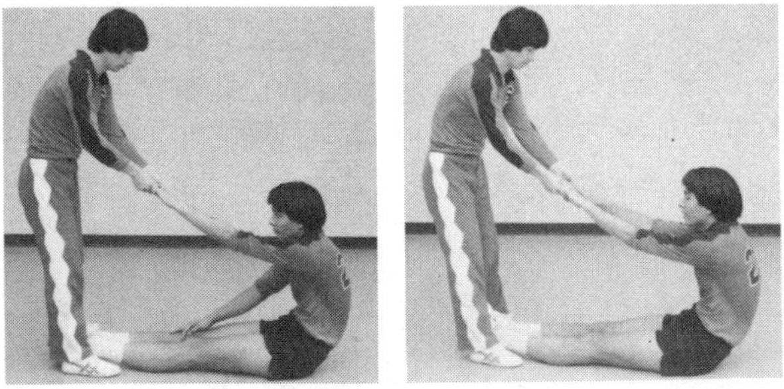

Long Sitting Arm Shake

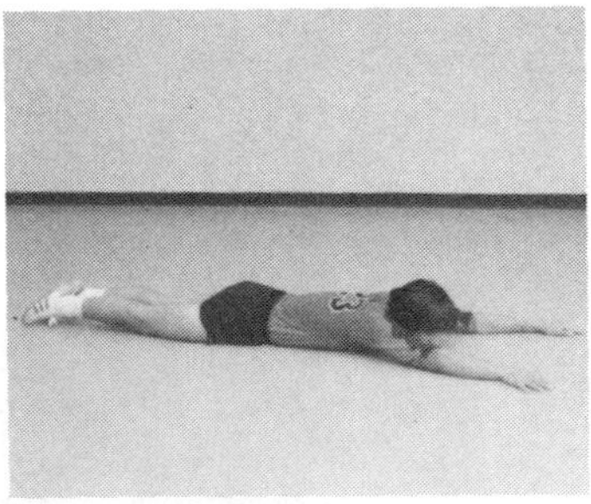

Full Body Relaxation

- massage
  a. simple massage
  b. ball massage

A. Simple Massage

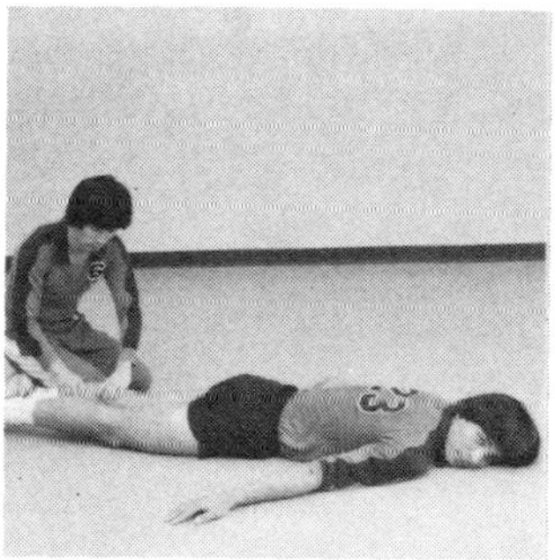

Legs

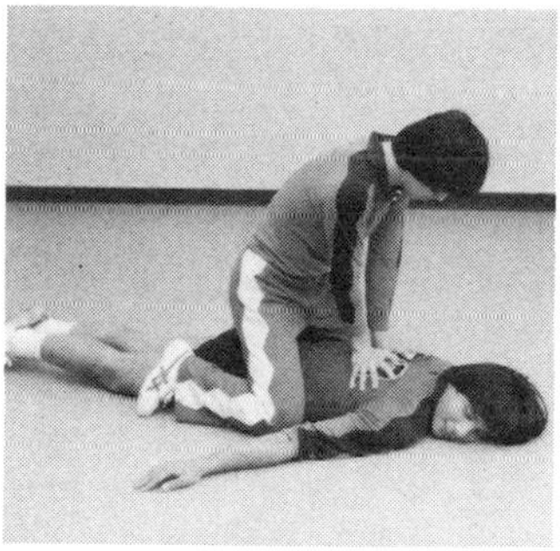

Back

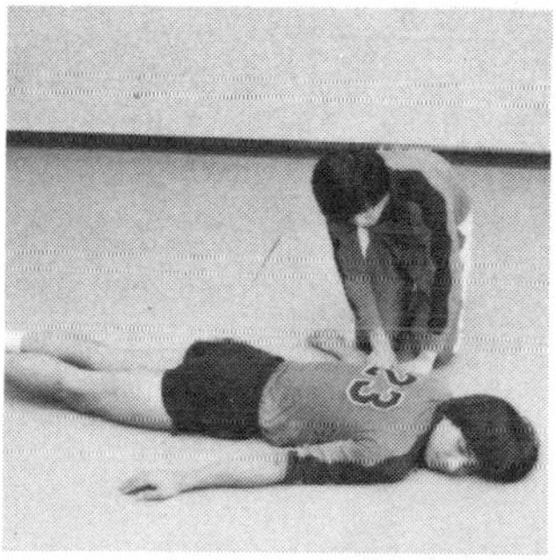

Arms

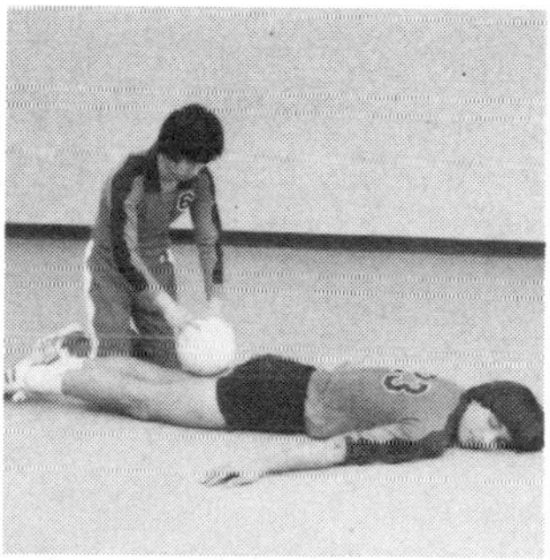

Legs

B. Ball Massage

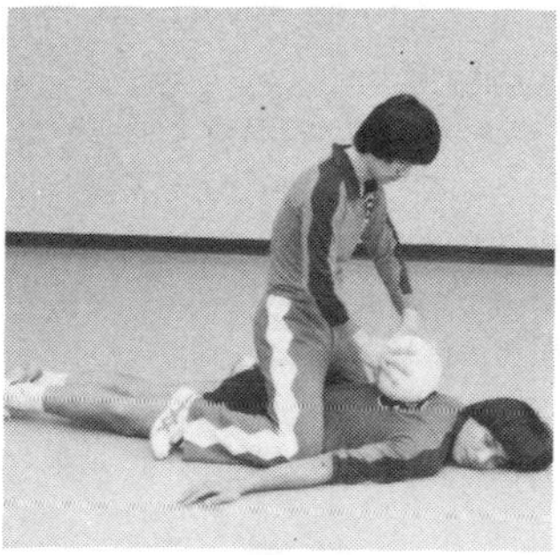

Back

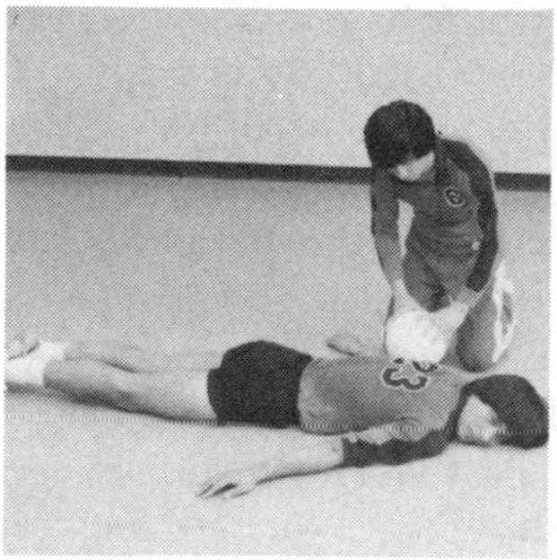

Arms

13 Nutrition

THE PRE-GAME MEAL

by
Fred DeLaceria
Oklahoma State University

In spite of the attention that has been directed to the long-term dietary needs of the athlete, no clear-cut results have been found. Less attention has been given to the short-term needs, and, as a result, these needs are no less certain. Thus, what an athlete eats for a pre-game meal depends primarily on what he believes is good for him.[6] This belief is developed through experience, environmental factors, coaches, fellow athletes, and trainers, all influenced by tradition. If competition is in the afternoon, the pre-game meal resembles breakfast, and if it is in the evening, the traditional meal consists of red meat, potatoes, dry toast, and peas.[8]

The primary purpose of the pre-game meal has been to eliminate hunger and the various problems associated with the *nervous* stomach so common among athletes before competition. Of particular concern has been the problem of the time allowed between the meal and competition. The emotional stress of competition has a significant effect on the length of time required for food digestion. X-ray study has shown that solid food may take up to six hours to digest when the individual is subjected to the emotional stress of competition.[9]

The relationship between the time of meal consumption and subsequent performance has been the subject of experimental study. A meal of cereal and milk consumed at three different time intervals (one-half hour, one hour, and two hours before performance) had no effect on subsequent performance in swimming the 100-yard freestyle. There were no adverse effects in the form of nausea, vomiting or stomach cramps, either during or following the swim.[1] Using the same time intervals and a comparable meal, no adverse effects were noted in running performance for the 440-yard dash, the 880-yard run, the mile run, and the two mile run.[1 2 3] The use of a liquid meal (instant breakfast and milk) at the same time intervals before performance also had no adverse effect on the one mile run.[11]

In a discussion of pre-game meals, it is necessary to understand two basic physiological processes: 1) the digestion of food for absorption into the blood; and 2) the passage of food through the gastrointestinal tract.[7]

With the exception of small amounts of vitamins and minerals, the food for body function can be classified as carbohydrates, fats, and proteins. There are three major sources of carbohydrates usually found in human diet: lactose, found in milk; sucrose, from cane sugar; and the starches which are found in grain products and form the bulk of dietary carbohydrates. Food of both plant and animal origin provides fat in the diet in the form of triglycerides. The dietary proteins are various combinations of amino acids bound together, the source being primarily meats and dairy products. Since few of these foods can be absorbed in their natural form, it is necessary for them to undergo hydrolysis during the digestive process. Hydrolysis is basic for the three food types, the purpose being to break them into particles for absorption from the intestinal tract into the blood. The difference lies in the enzymes required for the hydrolysis of each food type.

The digestion of carbohydrates begins in the mouth through the action of the enzyme ptyalin which hydrolyzes starch to maltose. Although the food does not remain in the mouth long enough to complete the breakdown of starch this enzyme continues to act for as long as 50 minutes after the food enters the stomach. As much as 40 per cent of the starch will be changed into maltose when the food leaves the stomach. The remaining starch is converted to maltose in the duodenum by an enzyme, amylase, found in pancreatic secretion. When entering the small intestine, all the carbohydrate ingested is in the form of maltose, lactose, and sucrose. These will be absorbed into the blood as glucose, galactose, and fructose through the action of specific enzymes located in the cells lining the small intestine. Glucose represents around 80 per cent of the final carbohydrate digestion, the percentage depending upon the amount of starch ingested.

The hydrolysis of protein begins in the stomach through the action of peptic enzymes (two types) which require an acid media for activation. When the protein leaves the stomach and enters the duodenum, about 15 per cent has been reduced to amino acids. In the duodenum the pancreatic secretions contain three enzymes which hydrolyze the remaining protein to amino acids and dipeptides, a two amino acid linkage. The final hydrolysis involves the action of enzymes located in the epithelial cells lining the small intestine. Approximately 2 percent of the protein ingested is not absorbed.

Essentially all fat digestion occurs in the duodenum. In order to digest fat, the fat globules must be broken into smaller particles by the process of emulsification. Emulsification is aided by bile, a secretion of the liver via the gall bladder. Hydrolitic activity is the function of enzyme activity of pancreatic lipase and an enzyme released by the epithelial cells of the duodenum. The end result of fat hydrolysis is fatty acids and glycerol which are absorbed by the small intestine.

A vital function of the gastrointestinal tract is to provide for the passage of food at a pace slow enough for digestion and absorption yet fast enough for nutritional supply of body function. The stomach plays a key role in the passage of food by having the following function: 1) storage of food; 2) mixing of food to form a semi-fluid mixture called chyme; and 3) regulate emptying of chyme into the small intestine.

The duodenum, the first segment of the small intestine, controls the rate at which the stomach releases chyme. This rate of emptying is determined by: 1) the amount of chyme already in the duodenum; 2) the acid content of the chyme; and 3) the type of food substance being released by the stomach. Thus, the release of chyme from the stomach is regulated in accordance with the digestive capability of the duodenum.

Of the three food types, carbohydrates have the most rapid movement through the gastrointestinal tract. Fats have the longest period of movement. Proteins have an intermediate effect on the rate of stomach emptying. The location of enzymes for the breakdown of the three food types determines the rate of passage through the gastrointestinal tract.

For example, the enzymes for fat digestion are located solely in the duodenum. For this reason the release of chyme containing fat must be done slowly by the stomach in order that enzyme activity will have sufficient time to hydrolysize the fat. A fatty meal delays stomach emptying for as long as three to six hours. Carbohydrates can be as much as 40 per cent digested upon leaving the stomach due to activity of ptyalin; therefore, chyme containing carbohydrate can be released rapidly into the duodenum. Since protein is about 15 per cent digested on entering the duodenum the rate of release from the stomach lies between that of carbohydrates and fat.

Once it is in the blood stream, glucose can either be used immediately for energy or it can be stored in the form of glycogen. The glycogen storage is primarily in the liver and muscle cells. Since protein is the building block of the body, the amino acids from protein digestion are carried by the blood stream to the body cells where new proteins needed by the cells are formed. Excess protein is utilized as an energy source or stored as fat. Digested fat can also be used as an energy source; however, it is primarily stored in the form of adipose tissue. Although all three food types can be used as an energy source, there is a definite sequence of utilization. Blood glucose is the first to be used as an energy source followed by the breakdown of glycogen. The glycogen storage is sufficient for a few hours of body energy needs. Fat utilization as an energy source occurs next, being a long term energy source. Use of protein for energy does not occur until the fat stores are virtually depleted.

Consideration of a pre-game meal involves both the time that the meal stays in the gastrointestinal tract and the energy value of the meal. The review of the digestive process shows that carbohydrate stays in the gastrointestinal tract the shortest length of time and is also the food type to be used first as an energy source. While fat is an energy source the time required for digestion is the longest of the three food types. Protein is intermediate in digestive time, but is the last of the basic foods to be utilized as energy. Thus, with regard to the pre-game meal carbohydrate should be the food that is given major emphasis.

Use of a high carbohydrate pre-game meal (cereal, milk, instant breakfast) was supported by studies mentioned previously in this article.[1 2 3 4 11] Rose[10] conducted a study on a liquid pre-game meal which supports the high carbohydrate meal. Toast, honey, and peaches were given to college football players four hours before competition. One and one-half hours later a liquid meal (68 per cent carbohydrate, 24 per cent protein, and 0.8 per cent fat) was ingested. This meal had passed through the stomach in less than two hours, and in many cases was in the large intestine. There were no adverse effects such as hunger, cramps or vomiting.

Bergstrom and Haltman[5] in studying the role of nutrition in maximal sport performance, found that the type of food utilized during the initial phase of an exercise bout was from muscle glycogen. For exercise bouts of less than 2 minutes the muscle glycogen store was adequate. After 10 to 15 minutes of exercise, glucose was released from the liver glycogen, the supply of liver glycogen being adequate for approximately 30 minutes of exercise.

It was also found that the glycogen stores could be increased in those muscle groups performing the heavier work. Six days prior to performance the major muscle groups to be used were utilized in heavy exercise bouts accompanied by a diet low in carbohydrates. The purpose was to deplete the glycogen supply in the muscle. After three days of this procedure, the exercise bouts decreased in severity with the diet being high in carbohydrate for the three remaining days before performance. The day of performance a high carbohydrate meal was ingested.

It seems that a meal high in carbohydrates and low in fat and protein should be ingested by an athlete prior to competition. This type of meal will pass through the gastrointestinal tract and be absorbed into the blood stream at a more rapid rate than the other food types. Also, the glucose from the digested carbohdyrates can be utilized for energy with the excess being stored as glycogen. The high carbohydrate meal can be cereal, pancakes, spaghetti or a liquid meal, the choice depending on the taste preference of the athlete.

BIBLIOGRAPHY

[1]Asprey, G. M., Alley, L. E., Tuttle, W. W.: "Effects of Eating at Various Times on Subsequent Performance in the 440-Yard Dash and the Half-Mile Run." *Research Quarterly.* 34:267-70, 1963.

[2]"Effects of Eating at Various Times Upon Subsequent Performance in the One Mile Run." *Research Quarterly,* 35:227-31, 1964.

[3]"Effect of Eating at Various Times on Subsequent Performance in the Two Mile Run." *Research Quarterly,* 36:3. 1965.

[4]Ball, J. R.: "Effect of Eating at Various Times Upon Subsequent Performance in Swimming." *Research Quarterly.* 33:163-67, 1962.

[5]Bergstrom, J., Haltman, E.: "Nutrition for Maximal Sports Performance." *Journal of the American Medical Association.* 221:999-1006, 1972.

[6]Bobb, A., et al: "A Brief Study of the Diet of Athletes." *Journal of Sports Medicine and Physical Fitness.* 9:355-261, 1969.

[7]Guyton, A. C.P *Textbook of Medical Physiology, Ed*. Philadelphia: W.B. Saunders, 1971, Chap. 63-65.

[8]Hirata, I.: "Pre-Game Meals," *Journal of School Health.* 40:409-413, 1970.

[9]Rose, K. D., Fuenning, S. L.: "Pre-Game Emotional Tension, Gastrointestinal Mobility, and the Feeding of Athletes" *Nebraska Medical Journal.* 45:575-579. 19??.

[10]"A Liquid Pre-Game Meal for Athletes." *Journal of the American Medical Association.* 178:30-33, 1961.

[11]White, J. R.: "Effects of Eating a Liquid Meal at Sports Times Upon Subsequent Performance in the One Mile Run." *Research Quarterly.* 39:206-210, 1968.

As a collegian at Louisiana Tech, Fred DeLaceria competed in weight-lifting. He then coached football and track at the high school level, also serving as athletic trainer. Dr. DeLaceria holds two bachelor's degrees (mathematics and physical therapy) a master's in physical education, and a doctorate in exercise physiology. He is active in both the American College of Sports Medicine and the American Physical Therapy Association.

14

Psychological Aspects

ACHIEVING A PERFORMANCE PEAK THROUGH PSYCHOLOGICAL AND PHYSIOLOGICAL READINESS

by
Dr. Raymond Welsh
Hunter College

Having an athlete peak (achieve his best performance) for the season ending championships is a much pursued objective for both the athlete and the coach. For it is in achieving this objective that one measures the success of the entire season. It is the purpose of this article, therefore, to review present practice with respect to achieving a peak in athletic competition and to formulate some generalizations with regard to this important aspect of coaching.

Empirical observations we made as well as information gleaned from numerous articles concerning athletic training, indicate that a peak performance involves a multitude of interrelated factors chief among which is a psychological and physiological readiness to achieve a top performance at some point in time. Implied in this psychological and physiological readiness is a preparatory phase of weeks and months, wherein, the athlete prepares himself for that eventful day when he will synthesize all his past training into a record-breaking performance.

Diagram 1 attempts to show both the psychological and physiological preparation that gradually progresses as a result of stress adaptation over the weeks and months of training to permit the athlete to achieve his peak.

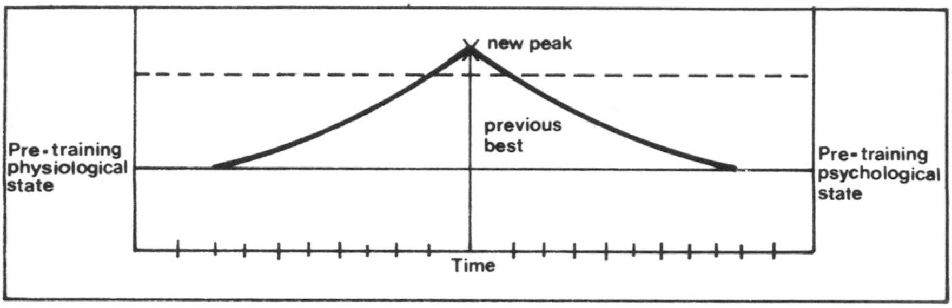

Diagram #1

While this is theoretical, nevertheless, enough is known about the intricacies of preparing athletes to realize that it is close to the mark. The great Bob Kiphuth of Yale, thoroughly versed in the importance of physiological readiness thought it was vital. The late Vince Lombardi was also a strong believer in the importance of both psychological and physiological readiness. Numerous other prestigious coaches view the preparation of their athletes for peak performances as a job involving both psychological and physiological factors. While the necessity of preparing athletes on both the psychological and physiological levels has been known for years, very little with respect to the specific interrelationships of this type of dual preparation has been reported. Actually each athlete, depending on the sport, will approach the task of a peak in a slightly different manner, nevertheless, there appears to be certain common approaches which, if followed, might help an athlete realize a top performance at some point in time no matter what his sport may be.

Psychological Readiness

On the psychological front, evidence suggests that an athlete can best insure a peak if he sets realistic short term and long term goals for himself. The long term goal would represent the hopes for peak. The coach, of course, must assist the athlete in plotting these goals by translating, etc., to be achieved along the road to the peak. According to psychological theory, a realizable goal sustains motivation with respect to the necessary behavior required to achieve the goal, if the goals are, in fact, realistic as a stimulus to the athlete to go on to the next and so on until the final goal or peak is reached. One very successful coach suggests, achieving a goal, even though a short term goal, tends to make a believer out of the athlete. Thus through a continuous sequence of goal sets — motivation— achievement, the athlete enhances the psychological preparation needed to bring himself to the threshold of a performance peak. Diagram 2 shows a sequence of achievable short term goals which, at least theoretically, brings the athlete along psychologically step by step to his final goal or peak.

Of course, the short term goals must relate to the final goal and be of sufficient difficulty to require a serious effort on the part of the athlete. On the other hand, if the short term goals are too difficult, resulting in failure to achieve the goals set, then a negative effect results which might delay or prevent the final peak that is sought.

Beyond the psychological preparation supplied by setting and achieving short term goals, is the important supplementary motivational efforts that are for the most part initiated by the coach. It is the coach who attempts to smooth out any lags in the gradual psychological juggling of reward, punishment, and manipulating the training environment to insure a gradually increasing level of arousal on the part of the athlete that reaches a climax immediately prior to the peak. This latter form of motivation, whereas, the goal set — motivation achievement sequence would more closely resemble intrinsic motivation.

A cautionary note expressed by experienced coaches and reported in the literature suggests that a high level of arousal sustained too long or called for too often leaves an athlete flat and can prevent his achieving a peak at the appropriate time. While some coaches believe in the possibility of several mini peaks during the course of a season, the mini peak concept of the major or final peak. In fact, some evidence suggests that too many minor peaks leave the athlete flat emotionally and incapable of achieving an appropiate arousal level for the championships. The system used to select our Olympic track and field swimming teams with respect to the short time span between the team selection and the Olympic Games themselves (usually 2 or 3 weeks) has often been cited as an example of forcing a premature psychological peak which results in poorer performances in the actual Games themselves. Some time comparisions between team trials and the Olympics made by Forbes Carlile seem to support this contention.

Physiological Readiness

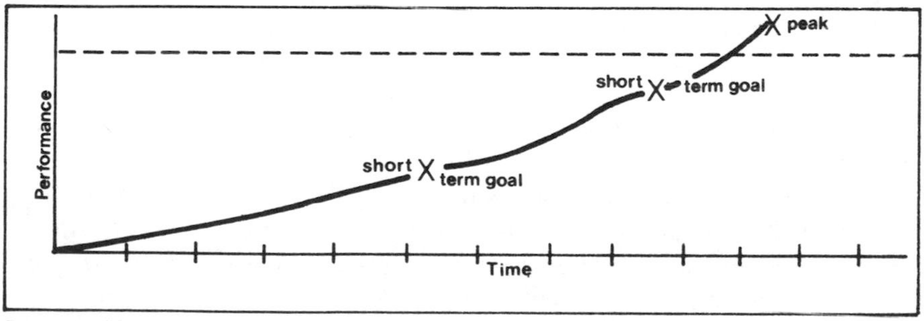

Diagram #2

Corresponding to the long process of gradual psychological readiness is the equally long process of preparing the athlete physiologically for his peak. Physiological preparation in athletics has been compared to the tearing down of the athlete physically and then over time building him up to a point well beyond his initial physical state. In more scientific terms,

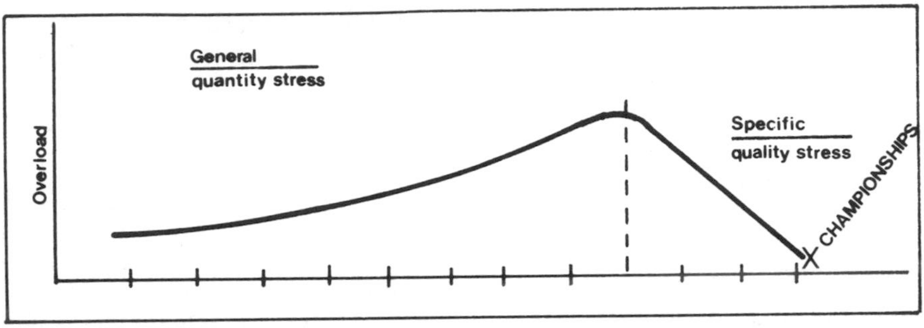

Diagram #3

overload stress in units of weight, distance, time, etc., is imposed on the athlete over long periods of time with the knowledge that his body will adapt to the imposed stress leaving the individual stronger than he was at his initial pre-training state. Hopefully, this final physiological state, along with the previously mentioned psychological state, will converge at some point in time (the day of the championships — diagram 1) and thus enable the athletes to achieve a performance peak.

While the principle of physiological adaptation to overload stress is well known to coaches and can explain general improvement in athletic performance, its application in training is not sufficient to insure a performance peak in championship competition. Evidence clearly suggests, however, that a physiological peak relates more directly to the specificity or quality of stress imposed on the athlete in the weeks (2, 3 or 4 weeks) immediately prior to the championships. In general, most successful coaches lay the groundwork for the physiological peak in the early training sessions by imposing large amounts of general stress on their athletes, and as the championships approach, there is a marked shift to specific stress which approximates as close as possible the stress that will be demanded of the athlete on the day he plans to achieve his peak. Volleyball coaches in particular have had good success in preparing their athletes for a peak by imposing a highly specific type stress in the weeks immediately prior to the championships. These training periods are highly specific with respect to levels needed to achieve the long term goal or projected peak. Thus, the achievement of a physiological peak seems to require an athlete to progress along a training curve marked initially by large quantities of general stress imposed over months followed by a shorter time interval of 2, 3, or 4 weeks (also referred to as the taper period), where there is a decrease in the total amount of work done, but the work done (stress imposed) becomes highly specific to the competitive event being trained for. Diagram 3 shows the shift from quantity to quality stress that seems to foster the physiological readiness needed to achieve a peak.

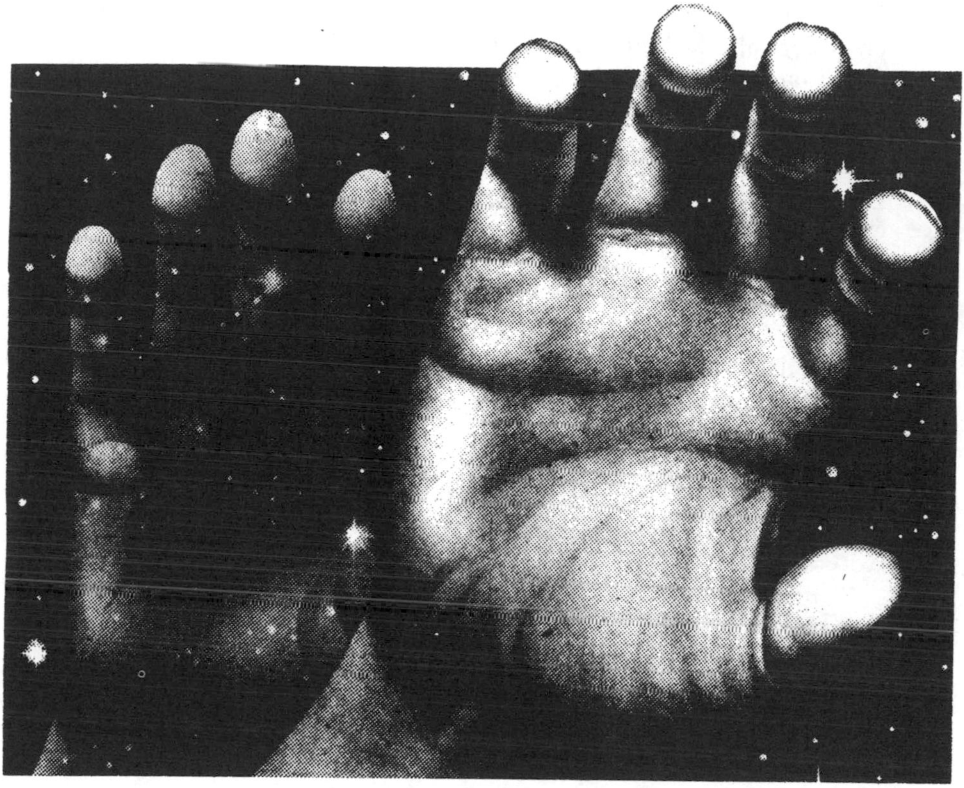

Conclusions

In the final analysis the actual training techniques used in preparing an athlete for a season ending peak will depend on the sport or event being trained for as well as the individual differences of the athlete involved. Nevertheless, there exists enough evidence to support the idea that despite the specifics involved, certain common approaches in training might prove applicable to all training situations in bringing the athlete along to a season ending peak performance. These would include:

1. Planning a season's training both of the psychological and physiological levels around the idea of the season ending peak.

2. Communicate clearly to all concerned that the prime focus of all the training efforts is to prepare oneself gradually psychologically and physiologically so that both dimensions of preparation converge on the day of the championships.

3. Set up a series of achievable short term goals that relate to the final goal or peak and serve to insure a gradual preparation on both the psychological and physiological levels.

4. Limit, to the extent possible, the number of mini or premature peaks demanded of the athlete or in any event, do not permit the mini peaks to be confused with the prime focus of the training, namely, the final peak.

5. Be on guard against the natural tendency of some athletes either to fall behind or race ahead in their psychological or physiological preparation for the peak.

6. Switch to quality stress work at the appropriate time (2, 3 or 4 weeks) before the championships and at the same time reduce the total amount of work done.

7. In the days immediately prior to the peak, increase the tempo of psychological preparation keeping in mind individual differences in response to these efforts.

8. Attempt to be positive in all communications with the athletes particularly as they begin the taper for the peak.

MOTIVATING THE ATHLETE

by

Steven C. Tuttle

Oak Hill High School, Converse, Indiana

Numerous books and articles have been written on motivation and the term has had many connotations. In this article the term refers to all of the factors that affect the human while he performs, and influence the intensity with which he engages in an activity.

John Lawther said, *Man acts as he feels, not as he thinks.* This statement expresses the importance of motivation since it affects all of our everyday actions. Man's learning is intimately related to his motivation because he will learn what he wants to learn, and will do what he wants to do. It is often left to a teacher or coach to inspire the student or athlete to peak learning efforts through various motivational devices. How important is motivation? Tutko and Ogilvie have stated that from 50 to 90 per cent of the coach's responsibility is involved with motivating his athletes and much of the literature has indicated that motivation is the main factor in successful coaching.

Motivating athletes to strive for success in athletics depends, first of all, on different things at different times, and it is up to the coach to recognize these differences. This is a key point in effective motivation. Athletes strive to do their best to gain success or to avoid failure and they react to the stress or tension that is often developed by the coach through some aspect of motivation. Often the coach will exploit sociological factors in an attempt to motivate the athlete and among those most commonly used are: • Prestige among peers. • The opposite sex. • Personal pride. • Parental desire.

Superior athletic performance can occur under conditions of optimal motivation. Some of the important factors in regard to this phenomenon are:

1. Personal pride in peak performance (this is, perhaps, the most common factor involved in this phenomenon).

2. Self-image, or the way one sees himself or the way he thinks others see him.

3. Humiliation or defeat (motivation to do well after a defeat or unfavorable publicity is extremely crucial).

4. Level of aspiration (the setting of goals to be obtained).

5. Challenge (the level to which one aspires to be better than something or someone).

6. Confidence (when one is both mentally and physically ready, he can often do great things).

7. Desire to win (having a winning attitude and an unwillingness to lose).

Motivation is specific in that in an individual sport it comes, basically, from within the individual, while in a team sport the coach must arrange the motivational setting for several individuals.

In what manner can the coach utilize motivation to get athletes to react? First of all, he must convey a feeling to the players that he actually cares for them not just as players, but as individuals. Well-placed praise is effective in getting maximum performance from a player, if it is not done often enough to lessen the reinforcing value. Fear is a negative approach to motivation and places too much stress on the player which often results in a poor reaction. Negative reinforcement tells a player what is wrong not what is correct.

A coach can often get maximum effort from his team by selecting an appropriate challenge to which it can react. Here the coach must possess the quality of being able to raise and lower motivational levels through verbal communications. It is usually easier to raise tension levels than to lower them, and this is facilitated by verbal activity.

A coach can use defeat to his advantage in motivation, providing it does not occur too often. Variety in practice is an important factor in keeping the motivational state high. If every practice is the same the players soon become bored and lose their enthusiasm.

Some coaches use a bulletin board containing clippings of the next opponent in an attempt to motivate teams. The use of game awards such as *lineman of the week, hatchet man, and 110 percent* award have proven to be strong motivators in many programs. Some coaches send pictures so the winners of these awards appear even more coveted, because of the public exposure. This practice can also develop community enthusiasm which will inspire players because they know that the community is behind them due to the publicity. Thus, the coach must also be a public relations man, attempting to get all of the recognition that he can for the athlete because of the powerful motivation influences such recognition possesses.

A related factor to motivation is that of team morale which contains four main factors:

1. The team must have a common goal.
2. Leadership must be provided by both the coach and the players.
3. Interaction between players and between players and coach must approach a family concept.
4. Motivation incentives are provided by the coach.

Occasionally, a coach may seek help in reaching particular players. He may have trouble motivating, or getting to a player and may ask the student's favorite teacher, a parent or another student for assistance in reaching the athlete.

Probably nothing makes a team strive for success more than success itself. This relates to the team as a whole, but is also effective in the case of the individual athlete. Success raises the level of aspiration and failure lowers it; hence, it is the coach's responsibility to see that each player experiences success as often as possible.

One of the most noted motivators in the coaching profession today is the present football coach at Indiana University, Lee Corso. Coach Corso believes that he coaches from the eyebrows up. As much as 50 per cent of his practice sessions are set up to work on the player's mind. Of course, in order for any coach to have a successful program or technique, he must first of all believe in it himself and convey this belief to his players. Lee Corso lists seven factors in successful motivation.

1. A coach must have the respect of his players. This is not his due, but must be earned.
2. The player must be taught to be a better man.

3. The magic of believing must be emphasized. The players must believe in themselves and the coach.

4. A man must never be downgraded; he must be given dignity.

5. The coach must recognize the basic right of every player to be different.

6. Discipline is a must, both as a team aspect and on an individual basis.

7. No one but his family is more important to the coach than the team.

Coach Corso feels that the best combination of the previously mentioned factors is a well-disciplined team that believes in itself.

Motivation then is an individual thing that is specific to the situation. It is an important factor in every coach's success or failure. The faster a coach can determine how to better motivate an athlete, the sooner the athlete can begin to reach whatever potential he possesses. The coach must examine his own philosophy about what is important and his methods of putting these into effect in order to determine what motivational techniques to use. We believe every coach has an obligation to his players to inspire them to their peak performance; they look to him for leadership. Basically, motivation is good interaction and communication between player and coach.

SELF-HYPNOSIS AS A METHOD OF INCREASING PERFORMANCE IN VOLLEYBALL

by

Richard D. Montgomery Ph.D.

Ivan Pavlov has demonstrated through his considerable research efforts that human beings can be conditioned or can condition themselves by the use of mental images, thoughts, feelings or actions. Fortunately, these "conditioning" behavioral changes can be made to, in most instances, either replace or dominate undesirable individual actions. With the aforementioned as the basic premise, and with self-hypnosis as the basic tool, it is theoretically possible for most, if not all athletes, to learn a conditioned-response technique that can improve their overall level of performance in volleyball.

Subject Responsibilities

Subjects should make up their minds that they will be successful at utilizing self-hypnosis as a tool for self-improvement. They must be able to become totally involved. Their efforts should reflect both confidence and concentration. If they have reservations or feelings that may interfere with their ability to fully develop this technique, they should get them "straightened out" before further involvement with the technique. This may require more research into the discipline of self-hypnosis until the connotations associated with the word "hypnosis" are more fully understood.

Subjects should not expect to "feel" anything, except approach relaxation, as they "enter" a hypnotic state. The proper approach toward a hypnotic experience will not allow them the opportunity to assess their progress until they have developed a high degree of ability with the technique so that they can experience the effect of their own suggestions on themselves.

Whatever their reasons for developing this skill, the subjects should first develop self-hypnosis as a tool and then attempt to apply it to improving their volleyball skills. Self-hypnosis, like any skill, must be practiced. Initially, it should be developed and perfected, and then used properly.

The Technique

• Physical Relaxation. The subjects get themselves into a comfortable position where there is little chance of being disturbed. If they are lying down, they should not cross their arms or legs, since their circulation will be partially impaired and this may interfere with their concentration.They should make certain that they have warm clothing, since their body temperature will drop causing them to be distracted. Dim lighting is best. In addition, no subject should be disturbed by tight or binding clothing such as ties, belts or shoes. Once in that position described, the subjects are ready to begin to relax their bodies physically.

The relaxation process consists of tightening a group of muscles, concentrating on the feeling of tension and then relaxation. As a learned response, this becomes easier with practice.

Subjects should start with their toes and point them away from their bodies. Each subject should tighten the muscles...concentrate on the feeling of tension...now relax...no tension...let the muscles go completely. Next, subjects should bend their ankles toward their bodies and go through the same procedure, tighten and then relax. Now the subjects should press their calves and the back of their knees against the floor, tighten their thighs, tighten the muscles in their buttocks and press the small of their backs against the floor. At this point stop, and with their imagination, each subject should visualize each muscle and explore the lower part of his body. Each participant should stop anytime that he/she "sees" a muscle that still has tension, and tighten and then relax that muscle. He/she should continue this process until every muscle from his/her waist to his/her toes is completely relaxed. Next, the subject should concentrate on his/her chest. Five deep breaths should be taken and the breath held for a few seconds. The individual should concentrate on the tension and exhale. As he/she exhales, each subject should imagine that the air is taking any remaining tension in his/her chest out with it. Each breath will take the subject into a deeper more relaxed state of mind. Next, attention is directed to the hands and arms. This area is particularly important since the hands appear to be one of the last strongholds of tension. The muscles in both arms should be tightened. A fist should be made. Next all of the muscles in the face and neck should be tightened, including the tongue. The tongue should be pressed against the roof of the subject's mouth.

Similar to the actions with the lower half of your body, each subject should let his/her mind wander through the body, in an attempt to isolate any residual tension. This exercise in "mental gymnastics" should begin at the left hand and travel up the arm, across the chest and down into the right hand. When the subject is finished, no tension should remain. The feeling of relaxation should be a pleasant sensation with the body almost dissociated, due to lack of sensory imput that the individual is normally accustomed to.

The first time this whole process may take as long as forty-five minutes to complete. However, practice will decrease the time it takes to physically relax. The experienced practitioner can normally complete this process in a matter of seconds.

- Mental Relaxation. Now that the subject is physically relaxed he/she is halfway towards the primary goal. In order to maximize suggestion, the individual must also be *mentally* relaxed. This technique involves a great deal of mental imagery. As the subject creates these mental pictures, he/she should try to utilize all of his/her available senses to make them as real and vivid as possible. For example, a subject could imagine that he/she is walking in a forest on a beautiful sunny day. He/she should be able to see the green color of the trees, to smell the particular odor of the pine, hear the wind as it moves the branches, and feel the sun as it beats down on his/her body. The more of the senses that can be involved in the imagery, the better the degree of mental relaxation that can be achieved.

Once the subject understands what is required, he/she should create his/her own imaginary "place". This "place" should be one that has the type of environment that the individual is most comfortable in. As this "place" is developed in the mind of the subject, the individual should be aware of the euphoric sense of freedom which is associated with the "place". Colors and shapes should be noticed. The individual should feel the warmth, smell the air and let its purity fill his/her lungs. As he/she exhales, the subject should allow himself/herself to become even more relaxed. Some of the objects in the immediate vicinity should be touched and their texture and shape noticed. The subject should remember this "place" that has been created is for him/her alone, and is ideally suited to his/her needs. It is "designed" to create emotional tranquility by the use of images that tend to dissociate the individual from his/her environment.

- Deepening. The individual is in complete control of the depth of relaxation that he/she will experience. The individual can almost always become more relaxed than he/she is at this point of the technique. To go deeper, the subject should COUNT from one to five. When he/she gets to five, he/she should allow his/her eyes to open. The subject should then count backward from five to one and when he/she gets to one, allow his/her eyes to close. When the eyes are closed this is the subjects signal to go even deeper and become even more relaxed. Every individual should remember that he/she can become twice as relaxed, or ten times as relaxed, or one hundred times as relaxed. It all depends on the individual.
- The suggestions. Up to this point the whole process is relatively simple and straightforward. With practice and patience nearly everyone can become good at self-hypnotic induction. However, without the use of suggestion the whole process provides little more value than that of relieving tension.

Suggestion is the key and its proper use is the "Catch 22". It is the process by which sensory impressions are conveyed in a meaningful manner to invoke altered psychophysiologic responses.

Behavior is not changed *by* hypnosis but rather *in* hypnosis. The greater relaxation, concentration, receptivity, and self-objectivity provide an atmosphere where sensorial data or information can be directed to higher centers in the central nervous system. This can result in an effective change in faulty conditioning and the subsequent reinforcement of good behavior patterns.

Since suggestion is the critical factor in the whole process, the athlete is better off using hypnosis under the direction of a competent hypnotherapist who has the experience to maximize and control the whole process. However, several areas exist where the volleyball player can involve himself without extensive experience in suggestion. It is somewhat difficult to list specific suggestions since each one is different and is tailor made to the individual.

There are four areas that seem important to maximizing performance. The first is confidence. Individuals should visualize situations where they are as confident as they have ever been. They should see themselves in a match playing the best that they have ever played. An attempt should be made to isolate the feelings associated with this contest. Subjects should visualize themselves playing in an upcoming contest and bring back these feelings of confidence. These images should be made as vivid and as real as possible.

Second, the subjects should visualize how relaxed they are. Remember that tension interferes with effective movement. Relaxation should not be misinterpreted as laziness. Subjects should notice how hard they are working, how they are sweating, but how smooth their performance is. Everything is going right. Each subject is both confident and relaxed, while working very hard. Subjects should transfer this feeling to their next contest and visualize it happening.

Third, the individual should concentrate. Concentration goes hand in hand with relaxation. Each subject should notice how his/her entire being is involved in the task at hand. Nothing can distract the individual from his/her performance. As they visualize themselves playing, subjects should notice how each aspect builds upon the other to give them more concentration, relaxation and confidence.

Lastly, subjects should visualize themselves going through each of the skills in the game of volleyball. They should see themselves performing well against top players in their league, or even against top players in the Olympic Games. Films or video tapes of the best athletes in the world should be viewed. Each subject should imagine that he/she is performing at that level of skill. Subjects should focus on the hard work and sacrifice it takes to achieve their goals.

Each individual should remember to be creative in his/her suggestions and imagery, but should not be unrealistic. For example, instead of suggesting that he/she is going to jump 50 inches, the subject should visualize himself/herself jumping higher and performing the physical exercises necessary to achieve that goal. Subjects should keep practicing and they will notice a marked improvement in their ability to perform, as well as developing a tool that can be successfully used throughout their lives.

15
Injury Prevention and Treatment

INJURY PREVENTION AND TREATMENT

by
Louis Tomasi
United States Military Academy

Injuries are common in sports such as volleyball that involve jumping. Because of the nature of the sport, volleyball produces numerous injuries to the legs. Most chronic volleyball injuries are a by-product of numerous hours of both leaping and landing in controlled and uncontrolled patterns. Chronic injuries typically involve treatment and attention. Acute injuries, on the other hand, are those which require *immediate* attention. Swelling and pain frequently accompany acute injuries. Some acute injuries also involve capillary damage and possible neurological impairments.

When an acute injury occurs, it is imperative to act immediately to control local swelling. The word "ICE" may be used as a reminder of the immediate steps to be taken. The "I" stands for ice to be applied immediately to constrict the local blood vessels. The "C" means compression that is used to further restrict bleeding by applying pressure to the local capillary bed. The "E" is elevation to further slow local blood flow by making the blood move against gravity. Adherence to the "ICE"' treatment will accelerate the rehabilitation program. Having controlled the swelling, the trainer or coach can now deal with the injury.

It is recommended that ice, compression and elevation be used exclusively only during the acute phase, i.e., 48-72 hours. During this phase, ice should be applied at one-half hour intervals. To extend the ice application time would be counter-productive as vasodiatation will result. Once the acute phase has passed, the application of contrast baths is indicated. The athlete submerges the body extremity into hot water (105^{0}) for one minute. The procedure results in five hot water emersions and four cold water emersions. While the body part is submerged in the whirlpool, a range of motion exercises are encouraged. Following a hydrotherapy treatment, it is recommended that the affected body part be elevated for ten (10) minutes. This allows the dilated blood vessels to return to their normal size and precludes local swelling.

INJURY	CAUSE	SIGNS & SYMPTOMS	TREATMENT & REHABILITATION
I. INJURIES TO LOWER BODY			
1. INJURIES TO THE FOOT			
a. Arch Sprains	Arch sprains may be divided into two causes, traumatic and static. A traumatic sprain is usually the result of a violent acute disruption of the plantar ligaments in the longitudinal arch of the foot. This type of injury occurs when an athlete lands incorrectly and absorbs the landing force within the internal arrangement of the foot. A static arch sprain may also be caused by constant stress, repetitive vigorous exercise in competitive shoes or playing surface or training techniques.	Pain and discomfort along the arch, inability to walk normally, point tenderness, discoloration, arch drop and a history of a traumatic incident or change in activity.	Ice, compression and elevation for the initial forty-eight to seventy-two hours are used. Thereafter, hot whirlpools, deep heat in the form of ultra-sound energy, arch strapping, proper fitting shoes, and/or an arch support to alleviate pain and discomfort. Rehabilitation exercise to strengthen the toe flexor muscles should accompany the therapy. Curling a towel with added weight for resistance is an excellent method of strengthening the muscles on the bottom of the foot. The picking up of pencils and/or marbles with the toes, and other exercises to develop hypertrophy of these muscles are also recommended.
b. Blisters	Local friction between the skin and the new shoe or sock. Ill fitting shoes, wrinkles in socks, a new pair of shoes, poorly applied adhesive tape are all prime causes of blisters.	Fluid accumulation, (water or blood) between layer of skin, a bubbly appearance, or red areas called "hot spots." Blisters may also appear beneath calluses causing pain and discomfort.	When little or no fluid has accumulated, the closed blister can be protected from further irritation by a sponge rubber friction dissipating doughnut. The center of the circular sponge must be large enough to surround the blister and dissipate the friction away from the irritated area. The application of either a petroleum jelly or a skin lubrication may also alleviate the friction element.

			When the radical treatment is used, the blister should be lanced. Lance the blister at the bottom edge of the bubble, allowing the accumulated fluid to drain. Apply an antiseptic and a sterile bandage to avoid infection.
c. Stress Fractures	The actual cause is uncertain, but the fracture is associated with long continuous activity often on a hard or non resiliant surface. An intense vigorous training program often produces a stress fracture.	Chronic foot discomfort upon engagement in even the slightest activity. Often, the pain is mistaken for an arch problem, but it may be recognized by local point tenderness and moderate discomfort.	An X-ray must be taken, although stress fractures appear as X-ray shadows three to four weeks after the acute phase. Early and proper treatment includes adequate supportive measures, rest through the symptomatic phase and restricted physical activity. These procedures must be adhered to when suspicious chronic pain is associated with vigorous training.
d. Traumatic Foot Fractures	The traumatic foot fracture is usually caused by a crushing force delivered to a relatively small area, e.g. being stepped on by an athlete landing on another athlete's foot. These fractures also occur to leaping-jumping athletes when they land and invert the foot. If the weight continues to turn the foot under (inversion), extreme stress is placed on the fifth metatarsal resulting in a fracture.	The initial symptoms of a fracture are extreme discomfort, rapid swelling, point tenderness, grinding sensation and the inability and lack of desire to bear weight.	The foot must be immediately placed in ice to avoid excessive swelling. Immobilize the fractured area, elevate the leg, keep the athlete warm and refer him/her to a physician for X-rays and casting.
2. INJURIES TO THE ANKLE			
a. Ankle Sprains	The inversion sprain is usually caused by a sharp inversional force. The ligaments on the lateral aspect are stretched, torn or completely ruptured depending on the severity of the force. A twisting sprain is a force inversion of the ankle while running or walking on an uneven surface, or when landing incorrectly following a jump.	Moderate to severe pain on the outside and front of the ankle. It will gradually spread throughout the entire ankle and the athlete will demonstrate the inability to bear weight in a normal manner. Point tenderness and the degree of disability depend on the severity of the ligament disruption.	Apply ice for the initial forty-eight to seventy-two hours. Following the acute treatment, a gradual transition to hot whirlpool, range of motion exercises and strength development exercises to increase local muscle strength in area involved. Progressive resistance exercises are recommended during rehabilitation. By

			working in the four planes of movement, local muscle strength is increased. Walking, running and rope skipping utilizing both legs and each leg are excellent reconditioners.
b. Inversion Ankle Fracture	The cause of an inversion ankle fracture is a forced inward twisting of the foot and ankle. The cause is similar to the mechanics involved in an inversion ankle sprain, i.e., the placement of weight on the outside of the foot upon an uneven surface and twisting the foot and ankle inward.	Pain on the outside of the ankle, disability, point tenderness, possible grinding sensations, and severe swelling. The athletes may also show signs of shock, i.e., paleness, nausea, and dizziness.	It is important to maintain muscular strength and cardiovascular fitness during rehabilitation to preclude new injuries upon resumption of competition. When a suspected fracture exists, it must be treated with immobilization, ice, elevation and early referral to the physician for X-rays. It may be necessary to treat for shock by having the athlete lie quiet, elevate the leg and make him comfortably warm.

3. INJURIES TO THE LOWER LEG.

a. Shin Splints The term "shin splints" is an all encompassing term that groups many lower leg phenomenons. Some injuries classified as shin splints are tendonitis, sore, tender leg muscles, stress fractures, ischemic conditions, and minor circulation impairments.	The syndrome is usually initiated by excessive repeated use in an unaccustomed activity or a change in an on-going activity. The change may be in the jumping surface, shoes, style, or any other changes that require adaptation. Other possiblities that may cause shin splints are: inflammation of lower leg muscles, faulty standing, walking or running habits, muscle fatigue, arch disruptions, improper muscle co-ordination between the muscles in front and behind the lower leg, abnormal stress caused by the second toe being longer than the great toe, or any combination of these factors.	Chronic pain along the front inside or outside of the lower leg, discomfort in negotiating stairs, disability during training, needle point sensations along the shin, intermittent numbness in the leg, elevated skin temperature, swelling, discomfort and point tenderness are some of the signs and symptoms of shin splints. Pain along the outside bone of the lower leg, approximately three to four inches above the ankle bone may be the early signs of a stress fracture. When it occurs, refer the athlete to the team physician or orthopaedic surgeon.	Upon the initial signs, ice should be applied to the painful area for the first forty-eight hours. A gradual transition to heat therapy will facilitate healing. Heat therapy in the form of hotpacks, or whirlpool baths (105° - 108°) before activity will alleviate much discomfort. Ice massagae and/or cold whirlpools (50° - 60° F) following activity will prevent unnecessary swelling and discomfort. Strapping the shin, and taping the arch are two techniques that may alleviate the pain associated with shin splints.

4. INJURIES TO THE KNEE.

a. Contusions	A sharp blow which damages protective soft tissue and subsequently produces swelling, disability, plus discomfort. If a blow is delivered to the outside of the knee, and the sensation of pain and swelling is felt on the inside of the knee, the immediate concern should be for ligament injury. If the pain is felt on the same side that received the blow, a contusion is present.	Local swelling, tenderness at the point of contact, a black-and-blue appearance, early disappearance of the signs, and no disruption of the integrity of the ligaments that surround the knee.	Ice, compression and elevation until the swelling has ceased. It is imperative that the contusion be protected from further injury. A sponge rubber doughnut large enough to cover and protect the injury may be fabricated to reduce the chance of additional blows to the area when participating in athletics. The rehabilitation time is usually relatively brief if no further complications occur.
b. Patellar Tendonitis Jumper's Knee	It is usually caused by long arduous training-playing sessions. The patella tendon becomes inflamed and a temporary disability appears.	Chronic pain on the lower pole of the patella, some point tenderness, a history of steadily increased pain, and slowness of heel are the usual signs of Jumper's Knee.	Early recognition is possibly the best treatment. Ice and rest has proved successful. Long term treatment should include hot whirlpools and anti-flamatory prescription items from your team physician.
c. Medial Knee Ligament Injury	Sprains to the knee are common in all athletics. The injury producing force may be delivered in a variety of ways. The athlete may land with a twisting or torsion force. The thigh is rotated outward, and a possible force delivered to the outside of the knee. The severity of the injury depends on the amount of force delivered, the muscular strength, the laxity of the ligaments, and the reaction time of the athlete. Although this is the classic knee sprain, it is by no means limited to these mechanics. For instance, severe rotational sheering actions will cause cartilage to tear, although the cartilage tear is not as serious as ligament disruptions.	Initial signs are immediate pain, disability, instability, weakness, swelling, point tenderness at the point of disruption, laxity in the ligament, and increased mobility of the joint (wobbly knee). Because some ligaments are attached to cartilage, it is not unusual to have a cartilage tear as well as a ligament sprain.	The immediate treatment is ice, compression and elevation. If marked instability and weakness are noted, the athlete must be examined by an orthopaedic surgeon. Depending on the severity of the sprain, the physician's action may be surgery, plaster immobilization, use of crutches, and restricted activity.

d. Lateral Knee Ligament	A sprain to the outside (lateral colateral) ligament of the knee is also not uncommon in athletics. Although the incidence of lateral sprains, is not as high as medial sprains, their occurrence is significant. The foot and lower leg is turned inward, the upper leg turned outward and the injury-producing force delivered to the inside of the knee, or a violent twisting is experienced.	Pain, swelling, weakness, instability, and laxity are noted on the outside of the knee. Point tenderness may also be present at the location of the disruption. The severity of the injury varies from a stretching of fibers, to a complete rupture of the ligament.	Ice, compression, elevation, and orthopaedic surgeon consultation in the more severe cases are the treatment procedures.
e. Medial Cartilage Injury	Knee cartilage injuries are associated with torsion or twisting of the upper and lower leg in opposite directions. A forced internal rotation of the thigh bone upon a stationary lower leg may result in a knee cartilage tear. This type of tear is commonly referred to as a "bucket handle" tear.	There is swelling, functional pain; an audible clicking or snapping sensation in the knee, insecurity (a "give-way" feeling), disability, local pain at the inside joint line, limited range of motion, and pain elicited on forced extension.	The immediate treatment is ice, compression and elevation. When there is uncertainty concerning the extent of the injury, the athlete should consult a physician or an orthopaedic surgeon.
f. Lateral Cartilage Injury	Forced bending of the knee with the lower leg externally rotated, as in squatting or duck waddle-type exercise, inflicts abnormal stress on the lateral cartilage and may result in a tear. When the foot is firmly planted and the thigh is rotated outward upon the lower leg, a cartilage tear is also highly probable.	Similar to above, but on lateral side.	Same as above.
g. Patellar (Knee Cap) Injury	Patellar dislocations or partial dislocations occur in all sports. The cause of a patellar disruption is a violent force delivered against the inside edge of the patella when the thigh is rotated on a planted foot. A violent contraction of the thigh muscle may also cause a patella to dislocate. Picture the patella as a paper clip attatched at a mid-point of a rubber-band that is attached at the hip and just below the knee. The angle formed by phenomenon accounts for the higher rate of patella dislocations in the female population.	Severe pain and point tenderness along the inside border of the knee cap. There may also be an indentation, swelling, muscle spasm, and disability. In many incidents, the patella spontaneously relocates itself, but there will still be the aforementioned symptoms.	In the dislocations where the patella reduces itself, the leg should be immoblized, packed in ice, and referred to a physician. Immobilization is recommended for four weeks and in some cases longer. Physical therapy is required to rebuild the strength in the affected leg. Rehabilitation consists of straight leg raises in four directions, with gradual progression to resistive and range of motion exercise, i.e. isokinetic or isotonic exercise.

5. INJURIES TO THE THIGH

a. Contusions

The quadricep muscle group (thigh muscles) is particularly prone to contusions in many sports. Thigh contusions are usually a result of a direct force applied locally to the thigh muscle. The force is delivered when contact is made with the knee, elbow, or any other instrument that applies force to compress the muscle tissue against the femur. (This type injury is commonly called a Charlie Horse.)

The symptoms and signs are point tenderness, limited range of motion, presence of a **hematoma** caused by internal bleeding, pain, and difficulty in movement of the hematoma.

Treatment of a contusion must be immediate. The "shaking off" of a thigh contusion (continue to play) increases internal bleeding and delays the healing process. With the injured muscle stretched, ice is applied directly to the injury site for forty-five minutes. A compression wrap using a foam rubber pad slightly larger than the injured area may also be utilized to reduce the size of the hematoma. Elevation of the injured leg retards local swelling. The cold compression wrap must be continuously applied with a thirty minute on and **thirty** minute off rotation for the remainder of the day. Nightly elevation, continuous ice applications, and the use of crutches for four to seven days reduces the possibility of reoccuring internal bleeding. Heat therapy should be used only after the hematoma starts to reduce. Whirlpool treatment should precede a running or weight training program. Do not hesitate to regress to ice and compression at the first incidence of re-swelling. Ice will retard the swelling, and the rehabilitation process may proceed.

II. INJURIES TO THE UPPER BODY

1. HAND INJURIES

a. Fractures	The cause is a force delivered to either the long bones of the hand, or the individual bones in the fingers.	Disability, point tenderness, grinding and referred pain on stress are usually the signs of a fracture.	When the fracture is suspected, the affected bone is immobilized by splinting the joints on either side of the fracture. Splinting the hand in a partially flexed position will render the hand immobilized and relatively free from acute pain. Ice is applied to constrict the local blood vessels and decrease swelling.
b. Mallet Finger	"Mallet Finger" fractures occur commonly in sports such as volleyball. The fracture occurs when a player attempts to strike and/or receive the ball, and it makes contact with the tip of the finger. This forces the finger to flex while the extensor tendons are attempting to straighten the finger.	The initial signs of a mallet finger are point tenderness, swelling, crepitus, first joint displacement and the inability to fully extend the tip of the finger. The athlete's finger resembles a mallet.	When a mallet finger is recognized, it must be splinted in a hyperextended position and referred to a physician for X-rays. Expect four to six weeks for recovery.
c. Finger and Thumb Sprains	The joints of the fingers and thumbs are particularly prone to sprains. The injury producing force usually causes the thumb to hyperextend resulting in stretching and/or tearing of the ligaments. Injury to the finger also occurs in volleyball. These injuries must be attended to prevent chronic problems.	Symptoms are joint pain, swelling, limited range of motion and the inability to touch the finger with the thumb without pain. In chronic occurrences there is a recurrent weakness of the ligaments and muscles of the thumb.	Immediate application of ice, compression, elevation and follow-up care is important in the treatment of digit injuries.
d. Finger and Thumb Dislocations	Dislocations are usually the result of a force delivered to the end of the digit causing the distal digit to dislocate. The injury producing force usually causes a disruption of the second joint resulting in the dislocation.	Deformity, limited range of motion, swelling and tenderness are the signs of a partial (subluxation) or complete dislocation of the joint.	Reduction of the dislocation is accomplished by exerting a force along the bone ends pushing the heads of the affected bones away from the joint. The connective tissue of the joint will be less damaged when the reduction is accomplished using this techni-

			que. Pack the finger in ice and seek medical attention to eliminate the possibility of a fracture.
e. Thumb Fractures	The force is delivered either directly on the bone or along the shaft. The fracture may be caused by colliding with another player, a twisting action, or a hyperextension suffered in blocking or setting. The thumb is forced back toward the wrist resulting in a fracture.	Pain associated with movement of the thumb, weakness, point tenderness, disability, swelling and limited range of motion are the initial symptoms. The thumb must be immobilized, packed in ice and a physician consulted.	Seek proper medical treatment and assistance. The thumb is the most important digit in the hand. Improper or inadequate healing of a fracture may result in a permanent disability of the thumb.
f. Long Hand Bone Fractures	Metacarpal (hand bone) fractures are usually caused by a direct blow either to the end of the bone, the shaft, or the neck. The force is a crushing one and may be caused when diving, rolling or a collision with another player.	It is recognized by point tenderness, local pain, swelling, and referred pain at the fracture site when tapping pressure is applied along the axis of the metacarpal. Additional signs of a fracture are a shortening of the metacarpal, a grinding sensation, and an obvious deformity in the hand.	Treated carefully to avoid soft tissue, neurological or blood vessel damage. The fracture should be splinted and wrapped to immobilize the joint above and below the fracture sites. The athlete should see an orthopaedic surgeon for proper alignment and plaster immobilization as soon as possible after the injury.
2. INJURIES TO THE WRIST AND FOREARM			
a. Sprains and Fractures	Hypertension and hyperflexion sprains, strains and fractures are probably the most common athletic injuries to the wrist. These injuries usually occur by falling on the outstretched hand, or excessive force applied to the palm of the hand. Although the athlete may be schooled to avoid landing on the outstretched hand, it is an uncontrolled response by the body to protect the vital area by absorbing the shock with the wrists. In a hyperextension sprain the hand is usually forced past normal extension resulting in pain, swelling and possible numb-	The area of point tenderness for the navicular bone, is at the outside base of the thumb. Swelling and limited range of motion will accompany point tenderness. The lunate bone in the mid-wrist may also dislocate resulting in pain, discomfort, pressure in the carpal tunnel and numbness in the finger. There may also be a palpable depression on the posterior side of the wrist and a	Many wrist fractures are frequently diagnosed as bad sprains. It is recommended that X-rays be taken of all severe wrist injuries. Even if X-rays are negative, the possibility of navicular fracture still exists if the symptoms persist. Incomplete healing caused by a poor blood supply will delay bone healing for as long as one year. Cases of plaster immobilization for as long as one year do

	ness of the wrist. When the fall is very severe, the carpal bones may transfer the force to the navicular bone in the wrist resulting in a fracture to its narrowest point.	bulge on the anterior side of the wrist.	occur. Sprained wrists that fail to heal within 6 to 8 weeks should be suspicious and once again referred for X-ray.
b. Forearm Splints	Forearm splints are like shin splints and are caused by minute disruptions in the membrane between the forearm bones (ulna and radius) brought about by an occluded blood supply. The problem occurs as a result of continually landing on the hand, i.e., a dive or roll for a dig.	It is believed that forearm splints are minute tears caused by continuous stress placed on the forearm muscles. The splints are usually presented as dull aching pains in the forearm, weakness and/or chronic pain.	If these symptoms appear early in the season, moist heat, deep heat in the form of ultra sound, and rest are all the proper forms of therapy. If the symptoms appear late in the season, strapping with tape and therapy may help the athlete survive the final events.
c. Contusions	A contusion may result from the force of the ball striking the arm.	Immediate swelling, restrictive active movement, and a hematoma will appear.	Ice compression, elevation and restrictive motion retards the swelling. Padding and strapping precludes a re-injury to the athlete's arm during recovery. If a contusion is treated correctly, and the athlete resumes competition too soon, calcification of the damaged tissue mass may result, rendering the athlete inactive until the mass reabsorbs.
d. Fractures	A radial or ulnar fracture occurs when a direct force is delivered to the forearm. Falling on an outstretched arm may also fracture one or both of the forearm bones. In this type of fracture, forearm bones may be jammed resulting in a telescopic fracture of the radius.	Although rare, this is one of the many injuries that may occur when athletes are unaccustomed to falling or fall incorrectly. The athlete reaches out with the arm to cushion his impact to the ground or mat, and the force is dissipated at the end of the forearm bone causing injury.	The forearm is always splinted when a fracture is suspected. Neurological, circulatory, and bone damage may result when the fracture is mishandled.

3. INJURIES TO THE ELBOWS

a. Hyperextension	Hyperextension injuries to the elbow most frequently occur when digging or diving and the athlete falls on the outstretched arm. The elbow is forced to extend beyond normal.	The signs and symptoms of an elbow hyperextension are pain on the inside of the elbow, swelling, disability, point tenderness along the inside collateral ligaments plus the inability and little desire to fully extend the elbow	Immediate first aid is the application of ice and elevation for forty-eight hours, then a gradual transition to heat therapy. When the athlete continues athletic participation, strapping the arm to prevent hyperextension is recommended to avoid further injury to the elbow.
b. Dislocations	Falling on an outstretched hand with the arm extended is the primary cause. The hand, wrist, and forearm remain stationary, but the upper arm bone (humerus) continues in the downward direction departing the notch it usually articulates with, and comes to rest on the ulna.	There is severe swelling, pain, disability and the elbow fixed in moderate flexion or extension. In the posterior dislocations, more common, the point of the elbow is prominent. In an anterior dislocation, the elbow point is lost The appearance of the elbow indicates it is obviously malaligned. Elbow dislocations involve extensive ligament damage, plus it is accompanied by hemorrhaging, possible circulatory and/or neurological disruptions.	The emergency treatment is ice, compression, elevation, and immobilization. Absence of a radial pulse indicates occluded or impaired blood supply and transportation to a medical facility must be accelerated. The athlete should also be tested for sensory and motor functions of the hand to determine if any neurological damage has occured, e.g., a hand drop. Setting a dislocated elbow is accomplished by a physician, and the time lapse between dislocation and reduction must be minimal to avoid extensive tissue damage. Immobilization and sling suspension is usually prescribed for approximately three weeks. Gradual range of motion, forearm flexion exercises and hydrotherapy are used for rehabilitation. A too strenuous or too early rehabilitation program may result in a calcium build-up in the elbow.

4. SHOULDER INJURIES a. A-C Sprains	The A-C separation injury occurs in one of two ways: the athlete falls on the point of the shoulder driving the acromion process of the scapula down; or, falling on an outstretched arm with the arm close to, and slightly in front of the body.	Depending on the severity, pain, disability, point tenderness, elevated clavicle or depressed scapula, ligamentous laxity, and relief with sling suspension will appear. In an A-C sprain, the coracoclavicular (CC) ligament may also be involved which accounts for the elevated clavicle.	Ice, sling and swatch, and early referral to an orthopaedic surgeon in moderate to severe cases. Rehabilitation of an AC separation is dependent on the severity of the injury. Ice and pressure are used for forty-eight to seventy-two hours with a gradual transition to heat and deep therapy, if no surgery is required. Range of motion exercises may begin as soon as the sub-acute phase has passed. Similar to all the previous rehabilitation programs, constant orthopaedic surgeon-therapist-trainer rapport is needed.
b. Dislocations	Falling on the outstretched arm or a force applied to an abducted and/or external rotated arm is severe enough to tear the capsular ligaments resulting in the relocation of the head of the humerus. Blocking a spike or receiving the driving force on a hyperextended shoulder may result in injury to the joint.	Obvious deformity, pain and disability are the symptoms of a shoulder dislocation. The arm fixed in abduction and external rotation, loss of the round shoulder appearance, prominent acromion, and the inability to touch the opposite shoulder with the affected arm's hand are other signs.	Reduction by the orthopaedic surgeon is required and should be accomplished as quickly as possible. In many instances, the surgeon is not immediately available; therefore, rapid transportation to the physician is necessary. It is wise to telephone ahead to the hospital to inform the emergency room of the situation. Complications that may arise with a dislocated shoulder are loss of blood flow, nerve severance, or a fractured humerus or scapula. Rehabilitation may begin when range of motion exercises are pain free. The internal rotators of the humerus are the most important muscles during rehabilitative strength training.

That is not to say the other motions are not important. Horizontal and anterior shoulder flexion, abduction, plus the other motions, must be strengthened. Physical therapy includes hydroccolator packs, diathermy and/or ultra sound. It is safe for the athlete to resume normal activity when his strength is back to normal (about three to five weeks). Strapping or taping is recommended in severe or chronic cases of shoulder dislocations.

5. Head Injuries

Head injuries present special problems in athletics. A blow to the head is the usual cause of the injury. Because of the close proximity of the brain, head injuries are serious injuries and must be regarded as potentially life threatening.

The presence of fluid dripping from the nose or ear are symptoms of serious head injuries. Unilateral pupil dilation, lack of reaction to light, non-coordinated eye movement, impaired vision, decreasing blood pressure, and nausea are additional symptoms of a serious head injury. Although mild concussions seldom present any side effects, a moderate concussion poses a more serious medical problem. In a moderate concussion, the athlete is usually temporarily unconscious, has a headache, impaired vision or balance, tinnitus (ringing in ears), possible personality changes, and impaired neurological signs. The moderate concussion may have many compli-

The first step in the treatment of head injuries is to establish an airway to maintain proper ventilation. Make sure the tongue or dental fixtures are free of the airway. Prevent excessive head movement. When an athlete sustains a moderate or severe concussion, the individual should be removed from contact sports for at least three weeks or longer depending on the severity of the injury. In moderate cases, the athlete may begin participating in sports again within two to three weeks by light running. If the recovery progresses well, the intensity and duration of athletic participation may be increased. If an athlete sustains three significant concussions, he is susceptible,

		cations, and for this reason when unconsciousness occurs, a medical examination and hospitalization are strongly recommended. A severe concussion represents a medical emergency. Extended unconsciousness and severe indications of any of the aforementioned symptoms indicate that the athlete needs medical assistance immediately.	and future participation in contact sports is questionable. Head injuries are a significant problem in athletics. Unfortunately, such injuries occur all too frequently. Proper coaching techniques, use of protective equipment, and prudent participation in athletics go a long way in guarding against these unfortunate injuries.
6. Spleen	Internal injuries to vital organs of the body may be serious and tragic in nature. The injury that is of utmost concern is a spleenic injury. Spleenic injuries are caused by a blow to the left thoracic area. Contact sports produce the greatest amount of these injuries in athletics. Athletes with suspected or confirmed infectious mononucleosis are particularly susceptible to injury because while they have this disease the spleen is enlarged and very fragile. A blow delivered to the area of the spleen may rupture it.	Pain in the spleenic area, nausea, abdominal pain, white skin color, rigid or tight abdominal muscles, slowing heart rate, falling blood pressure, unconsciousness, shock and possibly cardiac arrest are all symptoms of spleenic injury.	This is a medical emergency, and the actions must be undertaken immediately. If no ambulance is around, the athlete should be made comfortable, treated for shock, and transported to the hospital as soon as possible. To forewarn the hospital of the incident, someone should telephone ahead to the emergency room. This action will save precious minutes and possibly save the life of the injured athlete.
7. Heat Injuries	Fall sports participants seem to incur the majority of heat injuries. The athletes return to the campus in mid-August to participate in preseason practice. The prime candidate is the overweight, poorly physically conditioned, athlete that spent the entire summer working in an air conditioned environment. When this athlete is exposed to the hot-humid days of late summer, with temperatures of greater than 90°F and relative humidity of greater than 40%, a	The symptoms and signs of heat injury are the keys to early recognition and emergency care. These signs are not absolute. Several combinations of symptoms may be exhibited. Heat casualties may progress from one level of severity to another in a very short period of time. The course of heat injury does not always follow a	Emergency Care and Treatment: The immediate first aid of a heat problem may be the most important step in recovery. At the first sign do not discuss what should be done. DO IT. 1. Remove clothing without delay. 2. Cool body either with hose, shower, ice, anything.

Charles Perry
///

heat injury will most likely occur. Ironically, heat injuries also occur at relatively low temperatures, such as 60°F, when the relative humidity is high (90% to 100%). When the athlete initiates physical activity, various metabolic processes are increased. This increase in activity results in an increase in the body core temperature. When the core temperature increases, heat transfers from the vital organ to the blood. The blood transports the core heat to the skin blood vessels. The skin, cooled by evaporation of perspiration, facilitates heat transfer because of the increased thermal gradient between the skin and blood. The cooled blood returns to the core to further relieve the body of heat. If the relative humidity and temperature is high, and the air is saturated and unable to accept additional moisture, problems can and often do arise. When the sweat is not evaporated the skin surface is not cooled and blood, carrying core heat to the skin surface, is not cooled. Consequently, heat is returned to the body core and the thermal regulatory system is hindered. If the body cannot dissipate heat because of restrictive clothing, the problems are compounded. The internal body temperature continues to rise with no outlet and severe heat injury can easily occur.

set pattern. Heat injury is a death situation and must be treated appropriately. Excess water loss and heat cramps f quently precede the heat pro blem. The symptoms and sign heat illness are:

Heat Exhaustion

Symptoms—Fatigue, listlessnes faintness, heart palpitations, nausea, vomiting, headache, dizziness, vertigo, shortness of breath, obstructed vision, hyper ventilation, and cramps;

Signs—Shock, profuse sweating, weak and rapid pulse, low blood pressure, ashen in color, wet skin;

Heat Stroke

Symptoms—Sensation of extreme heat, mental confusion, headache, vertigo, intolerance to light, collapse;

Signs—Cessation of sweating, hot-dry skin, high fever, low blood pressure, rapid and weak pulse, slow tendon response, dilation of pupils, deliria, comatose, and labored breathing.

...hen referring to ...eat illnesses. This potential danger should be a major concern to athletes when activity occurs on hot-humid days. It is also an excellent idea for athletes to use a weight chart to monitor their weight. If an athlete loses 5% to 10% of his body weight during practice, and he has not replenished that weight by the next practice session, then he is a prime candidate for heat injury. The weight loss is from fluids, which should be replaced before the individual participates again.

Chuck's
2
STEAK HOUSE

16 Scouting

SCOUTING

by
Bob Bertucci
University of Tennessee

The time has come in the sport of volleyball where it is critical for a coach to scout his opponents at every opportunity. The influx of offensive variations, hidden spikers, switches and attack combinations can render a team unprepared and bewildered. In the coming pages, a sample scouting report similar to the one used by the United States coaching staff in the 1976 Olympics is presented. These materials have been reviewed with the intent of constructing one scouting form which will satisfy the needs of any coach. The form attempts to take an objective look at an opponent and to chart vital information to guide a coach in establishing a successful game plan.

It must be noted that this form is multi-faceted and almost impossible for one person to complete alone. It is suggested that a team or coaching staff work together to compile a detailed scouting report. When possible, scout a team more than once, adding any new information to the original form. By competition time, you will have at your disposal an extensive analysis of the opposition.

TEAM: ________________ vs. ________________ DATE: ________________

SCORES: ____

ROSTER COACH: ____

#	NAME	AGE	HEIGHT (cm.)	POSITION (FRONT & BACK ROW)
1				
2				
3				
4				
5				
6				
7				
8				
9				
10				
11				
12				

(INT. POSITION)

STARTING ROTATION

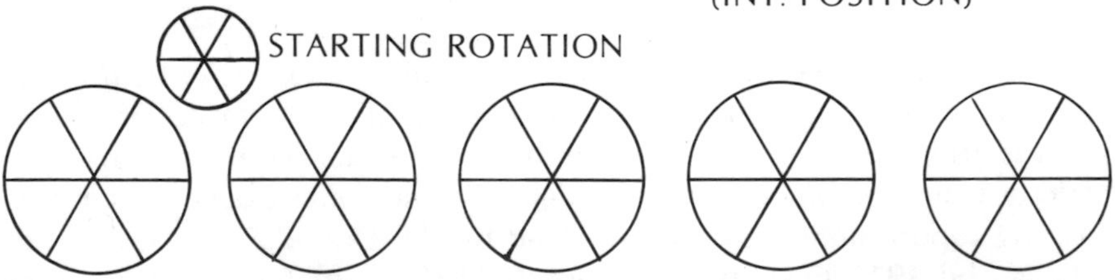

GAME # 1 2 3 4 5

Illustration #1 — Cover Page

This is the cover sheet of the scouting report. This page should be filled in before warm-ups begin. Early arrival to the match will facilitate the gathering of vital information and finding an acceptable vantage point from which to scout.

ANALYSIS OF THE OPPONENT'S SERVICE TECHNIQUE

#	TYPE	PLAYER SERVED	POSITION SERVED	PECULIARITIES/ VARIATIONS

1. WHO IS THE BEST SERVER?
2. WHO IS THE BEST SERVER OF SUBSTITUTES?

Illustration #2—Service

This is an analysis of the opponents' service technique. The numbers of the players can be recorded immediately upon their lining up on the baseline for the start of the game. The type of serve must be recorded followed by the number of the receiver and the court position served. Later this will begin to show serving strategies of the individual players and the teams if any exist. It is also important to note any other information in the section for peculiarities or variations.

SERVICE RECEPTION CHARTING/ATTACK COMBINATION CHARTING

(Keep Rotational Order)

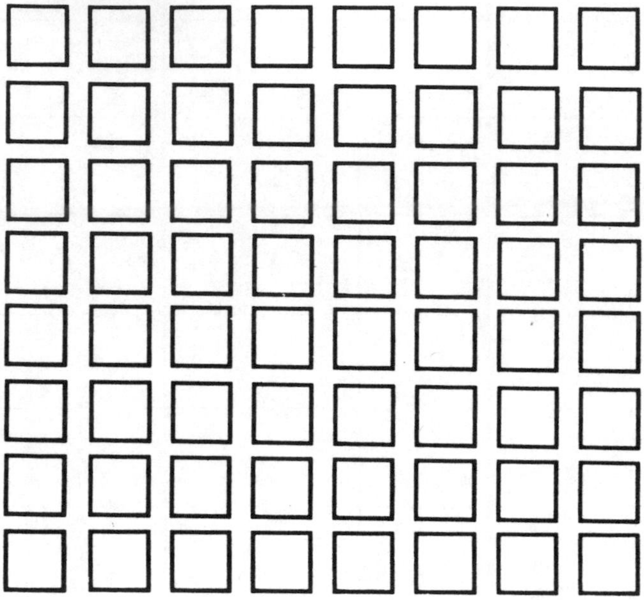

1. WHAT WOULD BE THE MOST EFFECTIVE POSITION TO SERVE?
2. WHO IS THE WEAKEST RECEIVER?
3. WHICH TYPE OF SERVE WILL BE MOST EFFECTIVE?
4. WILL SERVING IN THE PATH OF THE SETTER BE EFFECTIVE?

Illustration #3—Service Reception/Attack Combination

Service reception/attack combination charting is designed to show a team's exact reception formation, its rotational order and what attack combination is used after reception. This charting will eventually begin to show tendencies of a team. A team may run a particular attack combination in a specific reception rotation. When these tendencies can be determined a coach can prepare his team to defend against them. This charting also gives a coach information on how to attack with the serve.

Figure #1 is an example of the procedure to follow in charting a series of plays on illustration #3.

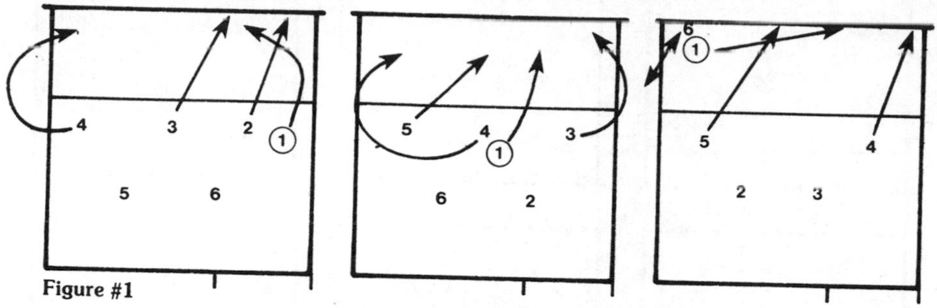

Figure #1

SETTING

1. STABILITY/CONSISTENCY OF THE SETTERS:
2. DO THEY TELEGRAPH THE SET?
3. DOES THE SETTER VARY THE DIRECTION OF THE SET?
4. DOES THE SETTER VARY THE SPEED OF THE SET?
5. DO THE SETTERS HAVE A PATTERN OR TENDENCY (ESPECIALLY IN CERTAIN SITUATIONS)?
6. WHERE DOES THE SETTER PLAY IN THE FRONT ROW?
7. WHERE DOES THE SETTER PLAY IN THE BACK ROW?

Notes

Illustration #4—Setting

Setting questions have been listed and should be answered completely and accurately. Any other pertinent information relating to the setter should also be noted. A coach is looking for information which will aid in his attacking strategy, defensive alignment or understanding of his opponent.

SPIKING SHOT CHART

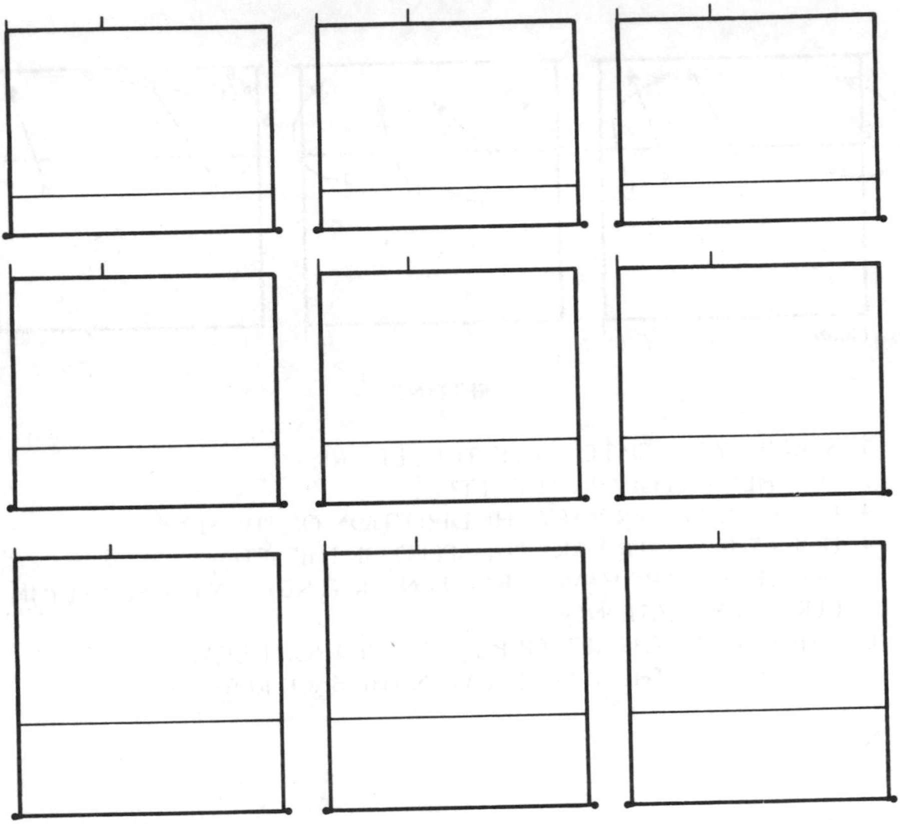

1. WHICH SPIKER IS THE CHIEF ATTACKER?
2. WHO IS ABLE TO MIX UP ATTACK (POWER, DINK, WIPE, ETC.)?
3. HOW DO THEY SPIKE? (QUICK, 2 COUNT, HIGH HIT)

Illustration #5—Spiking

On a spiking shot chart a coach will be able to see the exact effectiveness of an opponent's spiking. Also shown are the tendencies of a particular spiker.

The chart may show he only spikes crosscourt or down the line. Using the following basic code I will chart a spiker as would be done when scouting on illustration #5:

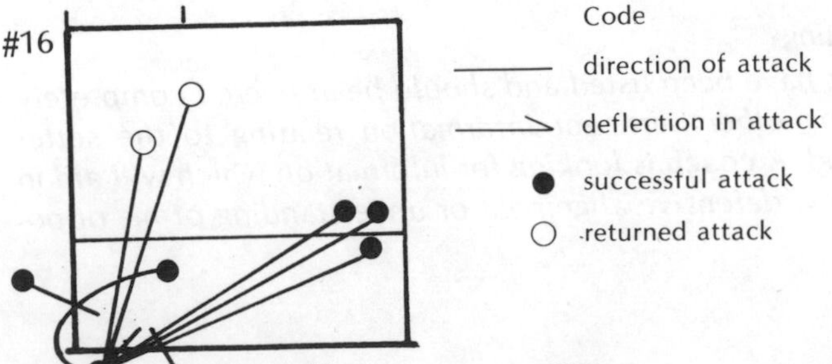

Figure #2

In figure #2 player #16 clearly shows he is effective with a crosscourt spike. He also shows he will try to spike both line and crosscourt. A coach looking at this chart would immediately only concern himself with defending against the crosscourt spike because his line shot is playable. There are three other marks on the shot chart. One shows a blocked ball which landed on the spiker's court. The second shows the spiker successfully dinking over the block. The third shows a successful wipe-off shot.

The shot chart can be a very effective tool for a coach. It must be noted in figure 2 that we only charted the #4 position. You may chart shots from the #3 and #2 positions. This will also tell you what position the spiker plays and also where the spiker is in different combinations.

SPIKER COVERAGE

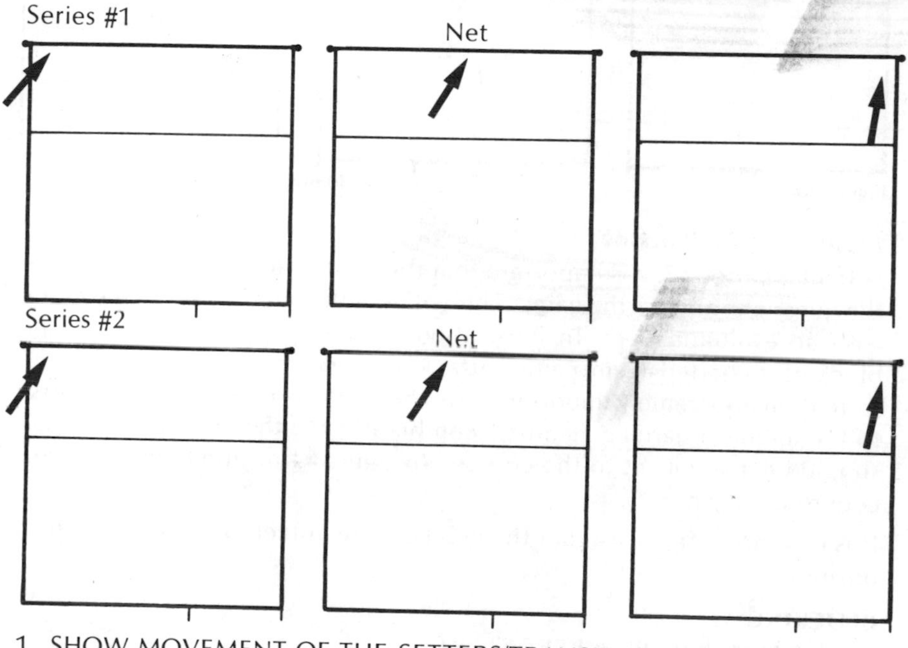

1. SHOW MOVEMENT OF THE SETTERS/TRANSITION TO DEFENSE.
2. SHOW MOVEMENT OF THE OTHER PLAYERS/TRANSITION TO DEFENSE.

Illustration #6—Spiker Coverage

There are a few reasons for charting spiker coverage.If a team does not cover the spiker well, an attack block can become very effective. If they do cover, it is helpful to know if they are using a 2-3 or 3-2 coverage. A good blocking team will be able to adjust and block to an area which is not covered properly. This is not as difficult as it sounds. A coach who has done his work scouting and finds that a team uses 3-2 coverage with the second line of coverage playing too close will be able to train his team to block deep against this particular team.

In figure 3, a 3-2 system of coverage has been observed and charted. It is obvious that the coverage is too close. The coach sees its deficiency and will train his team accordingly.

In illustration #6, you have 2 sets of 3 positional charts. Be sure to chart coverage when the opposition spikes from positions #4, #3 and #2. Also #1 series can be used for a high conventional attack, #2 series for a fast combination attack.

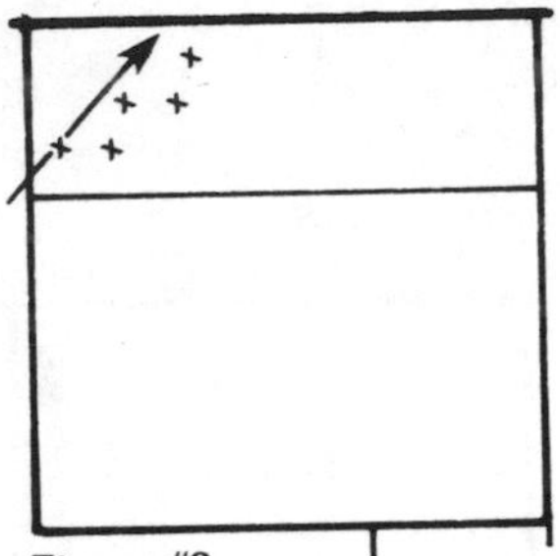

Figure #3

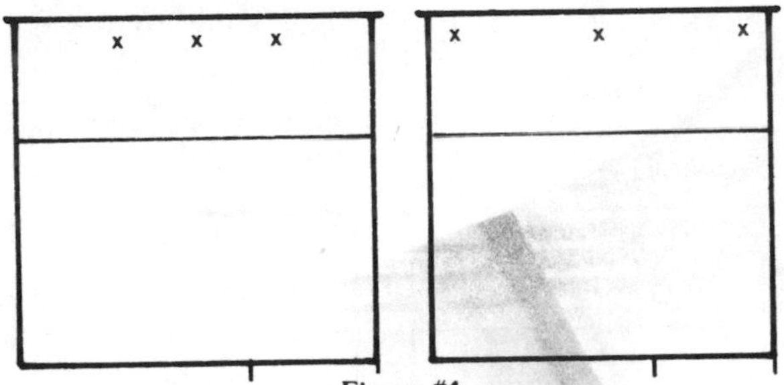

Figure #4

Illustration #7—Blocking

In illustration #7, it is important that the coach familiarize himself with the questions prior to the game. This will enable him to observe the block with an evaluating eye. In illustration #7, the starting position of the blockers is charted against a fast attack and against a high attack. This information is extremely important to a coach. If the blockers are too close to the middle, guarding against a combination to the middle, the attack should be a shoot set to the corners. In figure #4, a simple charting procedure is shown.

It is obvious in figure #4 that the blockers are vulnerable in either starting position.

BLOCKING

1. CHART WHERE BLOCKERS START.

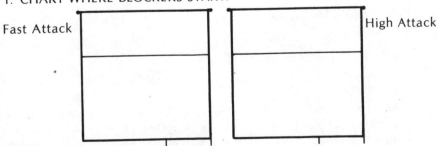

Fast Attack

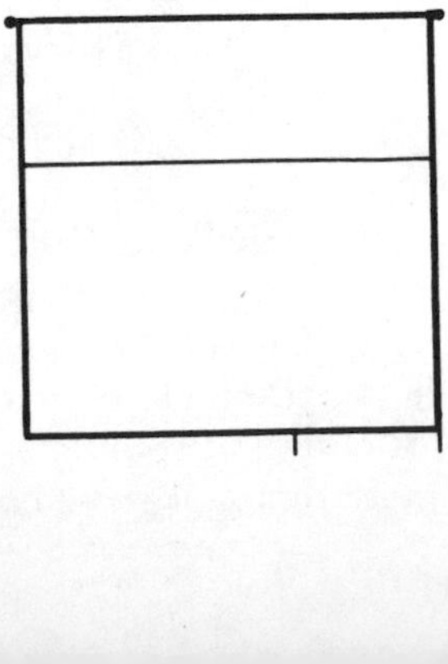

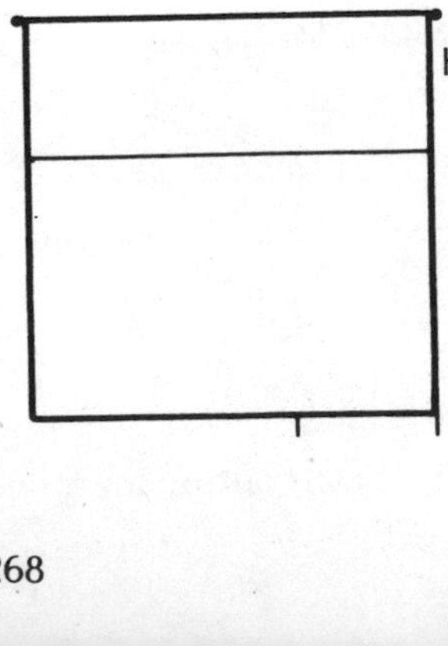

High Attack

2. WHAT IS THE EFFECTIVENESS OF MIDDLE BLOCKERS?
3. HOW MANY PLAYERS ARE BLOCKING AT ONE TIME?
4. WHAT IS THEIR BLOCKING PHILOSOPHY?
5. WHAT TYPE OF BLOCK IS BEING USED?
6. WHO IS THEIR STRONGER BLOCKER?
7. WHO IS THEIR WEAK BLOCKER?
8. WHAT IS THE MOST EFFECTIVE ATTACK TO USE?

DEFENSE

Rotation #'s	Notes	HIGH OFF.	COMBO OFF. (PLAYS)

1. WHO IS THE BEST DIGGER?
2. WHO IS THE WEAKEST?
3. WILL A TOSS TO THE SETTER BE EFFECTIVE?
4. WHAT AREAS ARE VULNERABLE TO OFF-SPEED ATTACK?

Illustration #8 — Defense

In this illustration you must chart the following:

a) The direction of the spike
b) The position of the block
c) The formation of the secondary or backcourt defense
d) The position of the setter, designated by a circle
e) Any special notes in left column next to diagram

In figure #5 is shown charting procedure for illustration #8.

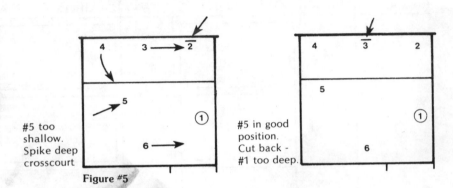

#5 too shallow. Spike deep crosscourt

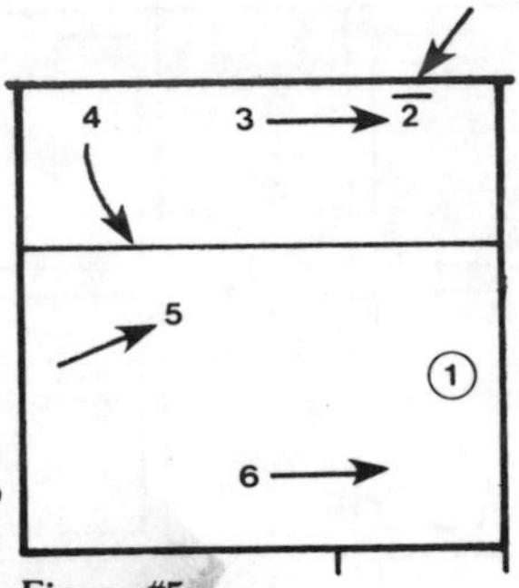

#5 in good position. Cut back - #1 too deep.

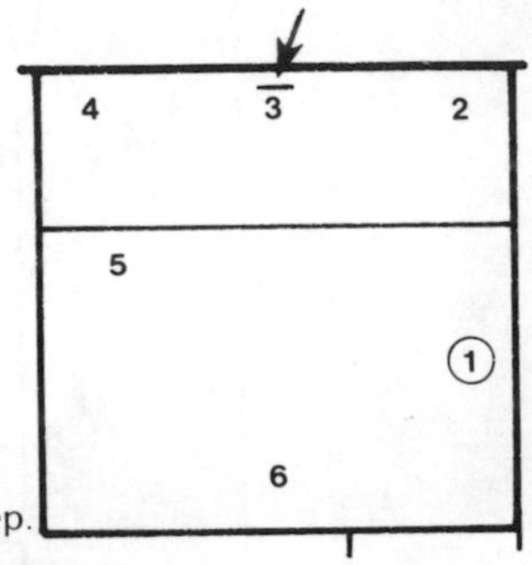

Figure #5

OTHER PERTINENT INFORMATION

Tactics:

1. HOW DO THEY USE TIME-OUTS?
2. HOW DO THEY USE THEIR SUBSTITUTES?
3. DO THEY HAVE ANY SPECIAL FREE BALL PLAYS?
4. WHO CALLS THEIR PLAYS, HOW AND WHEN?
5. WHAT IS THE KEY TO THE OPPOSING TEAM'S SUCCESS?

AN ANALYSIS OF PHYSICAL ABILITIES AND MENTAL ATTITUDE

Physical Abilities:

1. ARE OPPOSING PLAYERS GOOD AT JUMPING?
2. ARE THEY PHYSICALLY BETTER THAN YOURS?
3. WHAT ABOUT THEIR STAMINA?
4. ARE THEY IN GOOD CONDITION?
5. ARE OPPOSING PLAYERS QUICK AND AGILE?

Mental Attitude:

1. DO ALL MEMBERS OF THE OPPOSING TEAM MAKE A GOOD START IN THE GAME?
2. WHAT IS THE CAUSE OF MOST ERRORS WHEN THE TEAM LOSES MANY CONSECUTIVE POINTS?

3. WHAT KIND OF FORMATION ARE THE OPPONENTS USING THEN?
4. WHO IS THE LEADER OF THE OPPOSING TEAM? DOES THE CHIEF ATTACKER HAVE THE EXCELLENT MENTAL ATTITUDE FOR THE GAME?
5. WHICH PLAYER SHOULD BE SUBSTITUTED? WHAT IS THE SUBSTITUTE'S PLAYING ABILITY/MENTAL ABILITY?

FACTORS INFLUENCING A COACH'S ABILITY TO ANALYZE

by
Andrew Grieve
SUNY—Cortland

Suppose a basketball team is facing a defense which is constantly thwarting their offense and the regular offensive patterns are proving to be completely ineffective. The ground game of a football team is gaining very little yardage, even though in previous games certain plays worked successfully. A soccer team finds itself completely inept at penetrating an opponent's defense using their normal strategic attacks. In these situations, the coaches must analyze the situations and make the correct adjustments, or at least those which they think are correct. This is what we infer in reference to a coach's ability to analyze.

As the situation now exists in most team and some individual sports, the coach has assumed this responsibility. There are many who feel these solutions should be left strictly to the players, but in actual practice this is not the case, at least not at present. The team members often do make decisions but overall plan and the necessary adjustments are most often made by the coach.

Our purpose is to determine what factors influence a coach's ability to make adjustments. Some are quite obvious, while others may not be. In some instances, it would be possible to correct negative influences, while in others it is doubtful if such changes can be made. For some individuals this could be a problem without an answer, but a realization of the factors which influence such decisions might assist coaches in improving this ability.

From our personal experience these situations have arisen on numerous occasions. They have involved our coaching staff, coaches with whom we have worked, and opposing coaches. The latter proved to be the most satisfactory situation. From such observations it would seem this ability varies among coaches. There are coaches who can recognize changes immediately and make the proper adjustments. On the other hand, there are numerous coaches who cannot make on the spot adjustments and this could be due to any number of factors. The recognition of such factors is the purpose of this article.

The time element has a great deal to do with an understanding of this problem. There are four periods of time when a coach must utilize his ability to analyze the opponent. The first is in his preliminary planning, where he utilizes information available on the opponents, usually gained from scouting reports, to prepare his overall plan for the particular contest. Some coaches have the ability to make the most of such information where others do not recognize certain important aspects.

The second phase would be in formulating the practice plan which would be an outgrowth of preliminary planning. A comprehensive plan would depend upon the coach's ability to include in his practices factors related to the overall plan. Once again, there is a variation in ability among coaches in this area.

The third time period, and probably the most critical, would be the ability to analyze during the game itself. A coach who is able to analyze during all the other time periods may not be able to do it during the actual contest. This ability is the one with which we should be most concerned, and where most of the problems exist.

The fourth time period where ability to analyze is necessary is following the contest. Many coaches make post-game notes immediately following the competition while the information is still uppermost in their minds. While this procedure has no effect upon the outcome of the recently completed contest, the coach will be able to note where the team was successful or unsuccessful and why. The coach should be able to use a great deal of this information in future contests. This is one of the many values of filming athletic contests. However, the coach must remember that hindsight is always more correct than foresight. Many coaches always say, *If we had done this we would have been more successful.* The question is why did they not do so during the game rather than stating the correct adjustments following the contest?

There are numerous factors which influence the coach's ability to make the proper decisions. We feel the major influence is the emotional involvement, which would be considered as an intrinsic factor. Emotional involvement will be discussed later, but we would like to begin with the effects of what we refer to as outside influences. Although we may refer to them as outside influences, some could have a definite effect upon the intrinsic or emotional involvement. In certain areas, it would be quite obvious to the coach that there is no possibility of his changing such factors and he will accept them with little emotional response. On the other hand, there are other areas which will develop an emotional reaction even though there is little the coach can do about them at that particular time.

The nature of a sport will have a great deal to do with the coach's ability to analyze, or at least the rapidity with which he can do so. In activities such as wrestling, tennis, fencing, etc., a coach may be able to analyze the strategy of the opponent rather easily due to concentration. With only two competitors as the focal point, a capable coach can readily point out proper adjustments to the athlete. On the other hand, team sports may be somewhat more difficult to analyze. Football, because of the close action and the number of players involved, demands tremendous concentration and a rather effective ability to analyze. Basketball, because of the rapidity of movement and constant action, also develops a difficult situation.

There is always the question of player influence. Being closer to the action, often they are able to analyze more effectively and are better able to judge the situation. Is it more appropriate for the coach to indicate adjustments since he has a better overall view of the action? In this situation, there have been numerous occasions when players have influenced the decision of the coach. In many instances, these influences have had negative effects. During their careers many coaches undoubtedly have had some second thoughts on following the suggestions of their players as the ultimate results proved such suggestions to be incorrect.

The time of the season will have a great deal to do with the coach's ability to analyze. This is particularly true in preliminary planning. Early in the season a coach may not have sufficient information on an opponent due to a lack of scouting reports and it will be difficult to determine the overall strategy. Previous experience with these opponents in other seasons might be of value but often opposing coaches will make radical changes which make previous information of little value.

The location of a contest might very well affect the analyzing procedure. In certain sports, the home court is a definite advantage due to the home team's familiarity with the facilities. However, crowd reaction is more important. A coach, as well as the players, can be tremendously influenced by the crowd reaction. There would be, without a doubt, some emotional reaction on the part of the coach and all the players in an obviously hostile atmosphere, and this could influence the coach's ability to analyze the situation properly. It would be valuable if a coach were slightly deaf at away contests so he might not hear the crowd reaction.During the past several years there has been an increase in afternoon games. In this situation the spectators are almost always a home crowd and this develops an unusual condition as all positive reaction is limited to the performance of the home team.

Weather conditions at outdoor contests will often demand a change in strategy on the spot. The coach can do little about the situation but he must be ready for such eventualities. Thus many coaches schedule practice sessions during inclement weather in order to familiarize the player with making adjustments which the weather conditions may demand.

The coach has little control of the factors related to the trip if the contest happens to be away from home. A short trip in comfortable circumstances will have little effect on a coach's ability to concentrate. On the other hand, a rather lengthy, uncomfortable trip may develop an atmosphere which acts as a deterrent. Arriving at the site of the game rather late will not only affect the players but also the coach. Arriving too early results in a long waiting period and can also have negative effects.

The matter of concentration and its effects upon the coach's ability to analyze is also influenced by his individual personal problems. If certain problems are pressing such as family difficulties, finances, and health, these could very well influence his capacity for analyzing.

Officials have a considerable effect upon a coach's ability to concentrate and avoid emotional reactions which detract from his ability. The coach often feels that officials tend to favor the home team. This is another area which could well be the basis of a psychological study. Are there factors which definitely influence officials, without their knowledge, to favor the home team? Disregarding the factor of the possibility of *homers*, a coach is influenced by his judgment as to the competence of game officials. Officials who, in the coach's opinion, are not performing in a competent manner, will cause emotional reactions which will hinder him in the task of analyzing the necessary facets of the contest.

One of the major dangers of excessive concern over officials and their calls is that a coach may spend a major part of his time being critical of officials. His energies and concentration are directed almost completely to this critcism and he is usually not capable of analyzing the game situation. When a coach is busy criticizing officials, he is not coaching.

There are several other factors which might well influence the coach and his ability to analyze. Assistant coaches can do a great deal to enhance this ability. However, this depends upon their individual ability, and the method they use to inform the head coach of their observations. A team's season record might also influence the degrees to which the coach feels extensive analysis is necessary. Injuries will also have a similar effect, because a coach may be limited by the capabilities of the athletes in the contest.

We believe it is possible to develop this particular ability, at least to some degree. The first method would be through training or educational background. During this period of education there are courses which should help a future coach develop this ability. Such information should be one of the major units of any coaching course but, unfortunately, we have rarely observed this problem discussed extensively, even though it has tremendous ramifications in the area of coaching.

Experience is probably the greatest teacher but this does not mean that all coaches have analytical ability as a result of their experience. The beginning coach is often limited in this characteristic, simple lack of experience in recognizing the need for adjustment is typical of younger coaches. Some who do recognize the need for such adjustments may have the background necessary to provide the players with the needed changes.

Another notable characteristic of young coaches, and some experienced coaches, is an attempt to introduce a new strategy or technique in the midst of a game. Obviously, a team which has not practiced such a variation will definitely experience difficulties. A knowledgeable coach will usually have provided his team with a variety of adjustments for particular situations during practice sessions. If the strategy is not effective his team is prepared to attempt another, but not without some experience in its intricacies. If it would be possible to eliminate or regulate the negative influences, and provide the ideal conditions for every athletic contest, the factor of emotional involvement would still be the determining factor in the coach's ability to analyze and provide the necessary information for the team. The major problem for many coaches is not being capable of providing possible solutions due to the emotional involvement. Extremely strong emotions, which the coach is unable to control, will interrupt or deter logical thinking. Although it may be somewhat difficult to describe the problem, one might say the coach is looking at the wrong things. He becomes strictly concerned with the performance of his athletes at a focal point. This focal point would be the point a spectator directs his attention. In football it is usually at the ball-carrier, in basketball it is the man who has the ball, and in baseball it would be the pitcher and the batter. Although there are 22 players on a football field, 99 percent of those in attendance are watching the man with the ball. Naturally this is the focal point of the game, but the coach who is concerned with analyzing the game must direct his attention to numerous other areas. Is the blocking in the line effective? Is the quarterback carrying out his fake when he does not have the ball? Is a decoying receiver holding the defensive secondary?

Basketball also provides numerous observation points. Did the screener do an effective job in freeing the man with the ball? If the team is using a pattern are the players away from the ball following the proper movement, or are they standing around watching the ball? In playing against a zone defense, rather than watching the ball, is the coach watching the defensive shift to determine where there might be a weak spot?

There are numerous other examples but these should suffice. Actually, the coach who recognizes that there is more than just one focal point will be concerned with an overall view of the situation. It is this overall view which will provide him with the information necessary to analyze and provide the needed information to the team. Telling the team they are not gaining yardage, or are not putting the ball into the basket is not news to them. They recognize these factors; they want to know how to overcome these shortcomings. By recognizing the overall situation on the field or on the court, the coach should be capable of indicating to them what adjustments should be made and will probably result in more success.

Another danger of lack of emotional control is exemplified by the coach who uses the times-outs or the half-time period to berate the players. As in the situation of constantly badgering officials, a coach who is guilty of this action is not coaching. There are reasons why players may be performing poorly and one reason may be that the opponents are superior. Coaches must learn to accept this in certain situations. However, in many cases the athlete's performance, or lack of the same, is due to poor strategy by the coach. Even slight adjustments will often provide the players with opportunities that were not previously available to them.

There are factors which influence the emotional impact of the contest. The more important the game, the greater is the emotional effect. A game for the state championship will most certainly develop a greater emotional reaction on the part of the coach than possibly the opening game of the season. A contest with an arch rival is another example of a situation which will arouse strong emotions. There are degrees of emotional response.

The closer the outcome of a game, the greater is the emotional involvement. Many coaches will indicate they would rather win by 20 or lose by 20 points than have to go through the stresses of a tight contest. Some coaches virtually freeze when it comes down to the last few seconds of a close game and they must decide what has to be done. Many make the wrong decisions because their emotions interfere with the logical thinking processes.

The pressures of having winning seasons will depend upon circumstances. Many coaches are under constant pressure to have winners, either by students or the alumni. This is the type of coach who must be under extreme emotional strain because his future in the profession is at stake. Most coaches, however, develop such pressure on themselves, and even though the outside pressure may be at a minimum, they are still under an emotional strain which is often self-developed.

Finally, in this area of emotional involvement, a great deal depends upon the emotional characteristics of the coach. This is a part of his personality, and according to many psychologists, is determined at a very early period in his life. The emotional reaction of the coach may not only be characterized during his coaching responsibilities, but the same would be reflected as he faces other situations which develop tension. The individual who is emotionally mature in his day-to-day experiences will normally reflect a similar maturity when he is coaching.

What is the solution or solutions in controlling the emotions as a coach so one might better develop the ability to analyze? As mentioned previously, experience can do much to improve this ability. Self-discipline is probably the term most appropriate as one attempts to improve. If the individual takes a self-inventory, he must recognize instances in his coaching responsibilities where he did not analyze properly due to his lack of emotional control. The coach who can recognize such instances will be well on his way to improving this ability.

The coach must consciously work to develop this ability. He might observe other teams in competition, and concern himself with a strict analysis of the strategies used by these teams. He should consciously recognize the numerous variations and practice such recognition. Oddly enough most coaches do this in the scouting process because it is imperative for them to provide all the pertinent information on an upcoming opponent. However, too many coaches lose this ability when their own teams are involved due to the emotional concern. We think practice and the observation of other teams in action constitute a good starting point.

When the team is playing, the coach must be as objective as possible. If the players are not capable of performing as the situation demands then they should be replaced. If the replacements are not capable then the coach may be in for a long, lean season.

This reminds us of the coach whose team was playing up to their potential but were behind 48 to 0 at half-time to the best team in the state. What was he to say? Being a rather emotionally mature individual he did not berate his players, but rather corrected some of their minor errors and the team went back out for a 64 to 60 defeat.

A coach cannot be involved without emotions, but these must be kept in check in order not to interfere with his objective approach in observing an overview of the situation. He must analyze the situation as calmly as possible, making notes on a pad if he considers this necessary, but when the team surrounds the coach during a time-out or at half-time, he should have something constructive to tell them. A team that has confidence in the coach knows he will provide them with information which should improve performance.

51
Cal

PART D

TOURNAMENTS, OFFICIATING, AND RULES

17
Tournament Administration

GUIDELINES FOR CONDUCTING SANCTIONED VOLLEYBALL TOURNAMENTS

To assure maximum efficiency and consistency in conducting tournaments and equitable treatment of teams and players, the following principles and guidelines have been established by the United States Volleyball Association.

Where indicated as mandatory, these guidelines shall not be abrogated and shall be an integral part of the sanction agreement. Failure to conform to these standards may lead to penalties by the Regional Commissioner assessed against the host organization. Such penalties may be cancellation of the tournament, refusal of future sanctions, or such deemed advisable by the Commissioner.

Any tournament sponsor wishing to deviate from these guidelines **must receive permission, in writing from the Commissioner.** Furthermore, said release must be included in the written materials released to participating teams prior to the tournament. In no instance where there is inter-region competition shall the mandatory provisions be waived.

*Mandatory items

1. All tournament directors should receive a copy of "Information for Sponsors" from the Regional Commissioner. This covers the rules on sanctions, eligibility, publicity, officials, and uniforms. These rules must be strictly observed.

*2. There must be
   a. A non-playing tournament director with the sole responsibility of getting matches and officials on and off the courts on time;
   b. or, a court manager for each court who is charged with the above responsibility (It is preferable for each court to have a non-playing manager,); and

c. a non-playing certified head official responsible for the assignment of officials throughout the tournament.

3. Realizing that each tournament director has many problems peculiar to his own situation no standard entry fee has been established. It should be commensurate with the expenses incurred and in keeping with the practices in planning tournaments and setting entry fees:
   a. Free food
   * b. Paid officials
   c. Contributions to Olympic Fund and for USVBA
   d. Payment of expenses of a distant visiting team
4. Scheduling during a tournament must be realistic: A basic rule of thumb would be to allow a minimum of 60 minutes for two 15 point games. Because of various scheduling problems, some directors may change to 11 point games during preliminary rounds. This is not allowable for playoff situations. These are minimum time allowances: (this includes warmup time of 5 minutes maximum before each match).
   a. Two 15 pt. games .... 60 min.
   b. Two 11 pt. games .... 45 min.
   c. Match—2 of 3, 15 pts. .... 90 min.
   d. Match—2 of 3, 11 pts. .... 60 min.
5. At least 5 minutes and preferably 10 minutes EXTRA time shall be allotted for the first competition of the day for each team.
6. The final match should be scheduled to start by 8:30 P.M. at the latest. These schedules should have built-in, at least, a half-hour cushion for playoffs if round robin play eliminates teams from play-off competition.
7. Types of tournaments:
   a. Double Elimination has the advantage of requiring fewer matches to complete a tournament. It also protects the second best team from early elimination at the hands of the best team. It is more difficult to schedule because of the uncertainty of length of matches. Also, it may tend to discourage weaker teams from making a long trip to a tournament.
   b. Round Robin Tournaments are the most unanimously accepted because all teams are assured of the same number of games (except play-offs). In a round-robin, it is also easier to assign teams for officiating duties. A round-robin may be played with or without play-offs.
   c. The Power Bracket, used in Round-Robin Tournaments, is established by placing all the better teams in one bracket while the weaker teams are in one or more other brackets. A greater proportion of the stronger teams then qualify for the play-offs.

*8. NO TEAM SHALL BE ELIMINATED FROM CHAMPIONSHIP COMPETITION ON A POINT SYSTEM.
   a. Teams qualifying for the playoff, but tied for position, shall not compete in a play-off game for position assignment. Rather assignment shall be made as determined by a point system according to the listed priority:
   1st Between the tied teams as a result of their scheduled match in the round robin, if still tied, then
   2nd A comparison of the total round-robin results in competition with all teams. The team with the greatest "points won minus points lost" total will be judged the superior team. (The international system of point ratios may be used if so specified.)
   b. If a team(s) is to be eliminated from the play-offs, then 15 point game competition will decide the team to be eliminated. There are many possible variations of this tie situation. Generally, the point spread will decide all but the final position in the play-offs. Then the last number of 15 point games will decide the remainder.

For example:

a. Two teams tie for last position—one 15 pt. game.

b. Three teams tie for last two positions—top position—point spread, last position—one 15 pt. game.

c. Three teams tie for last position—point spread decides superior team for position in play-off.

9. In tournaments where preliminary play classifies teams for play-offs, teams one and four would be in the same bracket and teams two and three should be in the same bracket. Not more than 50% of the preliminary pool entries shall qualify for a play-off round. Total round-robin should avoid play-offs.

10. Every effort should be made to pre-assign referees, inasmuch as possible to assist in expediating tourney play.

SANCTIONED USVBA TOURNAMENTS

Court Protocol

These are the recommended standard procedures to be used in all official competition.

1. The officials should be certified officials of the USVBA.
2. Players' uniforms must be uniform in color and design and have players' numbers on front and back (4.04).
3. **Start of Match:**
   a. The referee calls the captains together well ahead of the start of the match and has the toss of the coin.
   b. As the time for the start of the match approaches, the umpire or referee walks to the center of net sounding the whistle requesting all players to cease their warm-up and leave the court.
   c. Referee and other officials take up their positions.
   d. Referee signals, with the whistle and motion of hand, the teams (six starting players on each team) to line up at the end of their respective playing area.
   e. When the teams are ready, facing each other, a signal with whistle and hand motion is given to both teams to take their positions on the playing area. (Line-ups may not be changed after whistle has blown for team to take court positions.)
   f. As soon as players of both teams are ready the whistle is blown and a visual signal given to commence play. Previous to the serve the offensive players should halt their movements because continual running about makes it impossible for official to determine position and such movement may be misconstrued as screening.
4. **Substitution:**
   a. Substitutions after reporting to scorer should approach the umpire. The substitute entering court should raise his hand and the player being substituted should raise his hand also, so there is no doubt who the replacement is.
5. **Sportsmanship:**
   a. When a foul is called on a player for hitting net, double foul, foot fault, etc., the official shall point at the individual responsible, and the player shall raise his hand indicating acknowledgement of the call.
6. **End of Game and Start of Next Game:**
   a. Following the blowing of the whistle indicating end of game, players should line up at the end line.
   b. As soon as both teams are ready, the referee will signal with whistle and hand motion to the teams to change sides. The captain of each team leads his players in a single line, counter clockwise around the court (running) to the opposite side and they line up at the end line, facing the net.

c. When all players are in their position, the referee will signal with whistle and motion of the hand a dismissal between games. Players may now meet at the sideline and speak with their coach for the duration of the intermission.

CEREMONIAL PRESENTATION FOR MAJOR COMPETITIONS

by

Brasil — 77

Organizing Committee

Volleyball World Championships (Juniors)

Development

1. The referee calls the captains together well ahead of the start of the match and has the toss of the coin. As the time for the start of the match approaches, the referee walks to the center of the net sounding the whistle requesting all players to cease their warm-up and leave the court. The players and officials will form-up outside the main entrance and await signal to enter.
2. Music for entrance of referees and teams.
3. Entrance, referees and teams in single line, according to the following order:
   a) Referees - First Referee
   Second Referee (Umpire)
   Scorekeeper
   Linesmen
   b) Teams - The team that will defend the south side of the court, captain at its head.
   - the team that will defend the north side of the court, captain at its head.
4. The referees line up near the net, parallel to the side lateral line, at the west side of the court, while the teams line-up at the backline of their respective courts.
5. First coaches, second coaches, etc., do not participate and must be seated on their respective benches before referees and teams enter the court.
6. When everybody is placed, music stops and the announcer begins introductions. The visiting gets introduced, then the home and finally the officials. At the end of introductions the referee whistles authorizing greetings in the center of the court. Captains exchange greeting first then return to position. Then the entire 2 teams meet at the net to exchange greetings.

7. After greetings, the teams come back to their positions.
8. Referees' presentation.
9. The first referee whistle again. The teams have 10 minutes for warming up, 5 minutes each or 10 minutes together. In case of separate warm-up, the team that won the coin toss must start its warm-up first.

After the Match

10. When the match has finished the teams line up in the back of the court and after the referee has authorized they meet in the center for greetings, returning to their back line.
    Simultaneously, substitute players gather together their material (warm clothes, balls, etc.) and meet the others outside the court.

Music for Referees and Teams Exit

11. Referees and teams exit in line, observing the following chronological order:
    a) First referee at the head of other referees walking parallel to west lines.
    b) the south team approaches the referees, walking parallel to the west line and leaves the court following the referees.
    c) the north team observes the same procedure and follows the south team.

Ceremonial for the 5th Game

When the 4th set ends the teams line up in the back of their own courts and await the first referee to authorize exit, there is not an existing ceremonial for it.

When the 5th set will start the first referee reunites the other officiating members and the 12 starting players.

- Music for referees and teams' entrance.
- Referees and teams (6 initial players from each) in line according to the following order.
    a) Referees - First Referee
       Second Referee
       Linesmen
    b) Teams (6 players each)—the team that will defend the south court, captain at its head.
       The team that will defend the north court, captain at its head.

"LET'S MAKE OUR TOURNAMENTS MATCH PLAY ALL THE WAY"

by

Barbara L. Viera

Volleyball schedules for collegiate teams are including more tournament play and fewer dual and tri-matches. This type of play can be the answer to some teams who find themselves working within a very limited budget. With as few as eight teams at a tournament, an entering team can be guaranteed at least five matches. This means that for the same transportation cost, which seems to be the biggest expense of any away match, teams can play five matches instead of the normal one or two.

Tournament format in USVBA sanctioned events usually consists of pool play competition where small numbers of teams compete in round robin format within pools. The upper teams in each pool then advance to the semi's and finals. Pool play competition is often not match play. It consists of two games against every team in a pool, with no third game in case of a split in the first two. The games are often only eleven points in length. The split situation is what causes the most dissatisfaction among players. Match play often results in just two games also, but in case of a tie the third game is played. This would happen more often in matches between teams which are close to each other in ability. The advantages of best-of-three matches are:

1. There is always a winner.—Team records are more meaningful. Statistics are easier to keep.
2. Less emphasis is put on the results of any single game. Coaches are more likely to substitute, giving more players game experience.
3. If tournaments are set up properly teams can be ranked in order, so that each team knows how it stands in relation to every other team.
4. Point spread has to be used less frequently as a means of determining which team will go into the bracket play. Game results can be used before point spread is checked.
5. Teams get the most competition against other teams which are closest to them in ability.

In addition to the match play format, more has to be done to allow losing teams to stay in the competition longer. Every team usually pays the same entry fee. If the purpose of tournament scheduling is to play as many opponents as possible in a one or two day period, then teams should not be eliminated at the end of pool play or even after one or two rounds of bracket competition. In order to keep these teams in competition the following things should be done!

First, in addition to an elimination bracket for the teams with the best records following pool play, a consolation bracket for the lower teams should also be run. In the initial rounds of bracket play a team should compete against a team from another pool.

Second, each bracket should have a winner's side and a consolation side. In this way every team will continue to play and not be eliminated.

Third, teams should play off for every position in the line up. For instance, teams should play off for ninth place as well as third spot in the ranking.

Lastly, each team will be guaranteed a given number of matches during the tournament.

In the following pages, complete instructions are given for eight, twelve and sixteen team tournaments. In the eight team tournament each team is guaranteed five matches. In the twelve team tournament four teams will be guaranteed five matches while eight teams will be guaranteed six matches. In the sixteen team tournament all teams will be guaranteed six matches. If a tournament format guarantees five or six matches to *all* participating schools, the tournament director will have no difficulty in finding teams who want to participate.

Each of the following tournaments is set up based on the availability of at least four playing courts. If less than four are available the set up would have to be modified accordingly. It might be difficult under those circumstances to run such a tournament, especially one with a twelve or sixteen team format. It is most important that you have a facility which will house all the needed matches and still allow teams to leave early enough on the second day so that they will get home safely. The time schedules reported here have been used successfully with both men's and women's competitions. The running of a highly organized tournament can be a beautiful experience for players, coaches and officials.

TOURNAMENT FORMATS

I. Eight Team Format
  a. There will be two pools of four teams each.
  b. Pool play will be match play, best of three, 15 point games. Match play will also be used during the bracket competition.
  c. After pool play, the top two teams in each pool will advance to the quarter finals of the elimination bracket, the lower two teams in each pool will continue competing in a consolation bracket.
  d. Ties in match standings which result at the end of pool play will be resolved as follows:
    1. The team that won in the match between the two teams which are tied will be selected to proceed to the elimination bracket.
    2. Game record will be checked next.
    3. Point spread will be used last.

e. The following schedule* will be followed:

POOL A	POOL B
Teams	Teams
1 strongest	5 strongest team
2	6
3	7
4 next strongest team	8 next strongest team

Morning

Pool Play		Court 1	Court 2	Corut 3	Court 4
Round I	8:30 a.m.	1-2	5-7	3-4	6-8
Round II	10:00 a.m.	5-8	1-3	6-7	2-4
Round III	11:30 a.m.	2-4	5-6	7-8	2-3

ELIMINATION BRACKET

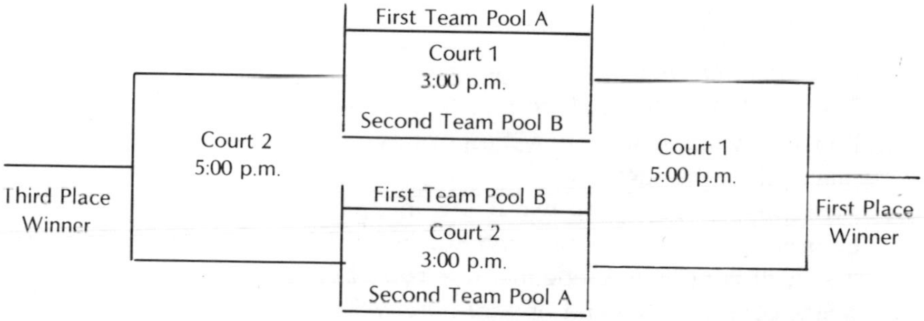

CONSOLATION BRACKET

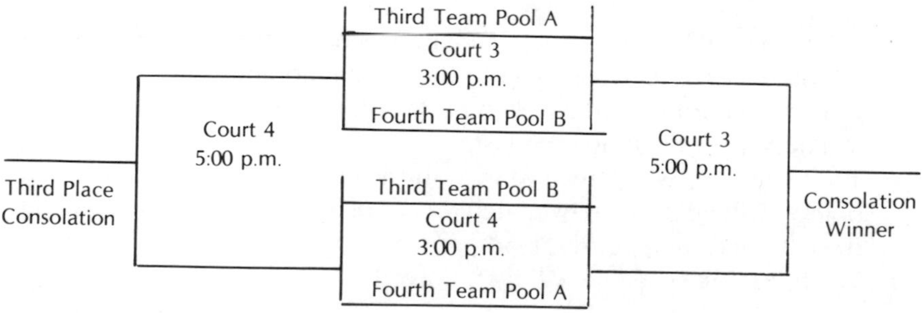

*All scheduling is based on the availability of four courts. If only three courts are available the schedule should be adjusted accordingly. The time schedule is only a suggested schedule. It may be changed according to the host school's scheduling requirements. Scheduling is based on a one-day tournament format. The times given here have been tested and are quite reasonable.

Afternoon

Semi-finals Elimination, 3:00 p.m.
Court 1—First Team A vs. Second Team B
Court 2—First Team B vs. Second Team A

Semi-finals Consolation, 3:00 p.m.
Court 3—Third Team A vs. Fourth Team B
Court 4—Third Team B vs. Fourth Team A

Finals—5:00 p.m.
Court 1—Winners of elimination semis play for first place trophy.
Court 2—Losers of elimination semis play for third place.
Court 3—Winners of the consolation play for consolation trophy. (fifth place)
Court 4—Losers of the consolation semis play for seventh place.

II. Twelve Team Format
a. There will be three pools of four teams each.
b. Pool play will be match play, best of three, 15 point games. All bracket play will be the same.
c. After pool play, the top two teams in each pool will advance to the quarter finals of the elimination bracket, the lower two teams in each pool will continue competing in a consolation bracket. The top two teams overall at the end of pool play will receive byes in the quarter finals in each bracket.
d. Ties in match standings which result at the end of pool play will be resolved in order as follows:
   1. the team that won in the match between two teams which are tied will be selected to proceed to the elimination bracket.
   2. game record will be checked next.
   3. Point spread will be used last.
e. The two teams which receive byes in the elimination and consolation bracket will be decided by match record first, game record second and then, if necessary, point spread.
f. The following schedule will be followed:

Pool I	Pool II	Pool III
1 strongest team	5 strongest team	9 strongest team
2	6	10
3	7	11
4 next strongest team	8 next strongest team	12 next strongest team

First Day—Evening

Pool Play		Court 1	Court 2	Court 3	Court 4
Round I	6:30 p.m.	1-2	5-6	9-10	3-4
Round II	7:45 p.m.	7-8	11-12	2-3	1-4
Round III	8-9:15	9-12	6-7	10-11	

Second Day—Morning

Pool Play		Court 1	Court 2	Court 3	Court 4
Round IV	8:45 a.m.	1-3		4-2	
Round V	10:00	9-11	5-7	12-10	8-6

Bracket Play

11:15 a.m. Quarter final matches-elimination and consolation

Court 1	Court 2	Court 3	Court 4
Match B	Match C	Match L	Match M

Second Day-Afternoon

2:00 p.m. Semi final matches-elimination and consolation

	Court 1	Court 2	Court 3	Court 4
Matches	E	F	O	P

3:30 p.m. Losers play for placing in third place elimination and consolation.

Court 1	Court 2	Court 3	Court 4
G	H	Q	R

Matches

6:30 p.m. Finals and third place playoffs-elimination and consolation.

Court 1	Court 2	Court 3	Court 4
I-1st	J-3rd		

5:00 p.m.

Court 1	Court 2	Court 3	Court 4
U-5th	S-Consolation winner	T-9th place	V-11th place

Trophies will be awarded to the First, Second and Third place teams at the conclusion of play. This will take place on Court 1.

*All scheduling is based on the availability of four courts. If only three courts are available, the schedule should be adjusted accordingly. The time schedule is only a suggested schedule. It may be changed accordingly to the host school's scheduling requirements. Scheduling is based on a two-day tournament format.

III. Sixteen Team Format

a. There will be four pools of four teams each.
b. Pool play will be match play, best of three, 15 point games. Match play will also be used during the bracket competition.
c. After pool play, the top two teams in each pool will advance to the quarter finals of the elimination bracket, the lower two teams in each pool will continue competing in the consolation bracket.
d. Ties in match standings which result at the end of pool play will be resolved as follows:
   1. the team that won in the match between the two teams which are tied will be selected to proceed to the elimination bracket.
   2. game record will be checked next.
   3. Point spread against all opponents will be used last.
e. The following schedule will be followed:*

Pool I	Pool II	Pool III	Pool IV
1	5	9	13
2	6	10	14
3	7	11	15
4	8	12	16

First Day-Evening

Pool Play		Court 1	Court 2	Court 3	Court 4
Round I	6:30 p.m.	1-2	5-6	9-10	13-14
Round II	7:45 p.m.	3-4	7-8	11-12	15-16
Round III	9:00 p.m.	1-4	5-8	9-12	13-16
Round IV	10:15 p.m.	2-3	6-7	10-11	14-15

Second Day-Morning

Pool Play					
Round V	8:30 a.m.	1-3	5-7	9-11	13-15
Round VI	9:45 a.m.	4-2	8-6	12-10	16-14

Bracket Play

11:00 a.m. Quarter finals of the consolation bracket

Court 1	Court 2	Court 3	Court 4
Match A	B	C	D
3rd team pool I	3rd team pool II	3rd team pool III	3rd team pool IV
vs.	vs.	vs.	vs.
4th team pool III	4th team pool IV	4th team pool I	4th team pool II

12:15 p.m. Quarter finals of the elimination bracket

Court 1	Court 2	Court 3	Court 4
Match E	F	G	H
2nd team pool III	2nd team pool IV	2nd team pool I	2nd team pool II

TWELVE TEAM TOURNAMENT

Elimination Bracket

All times are for the second day of a two day event.

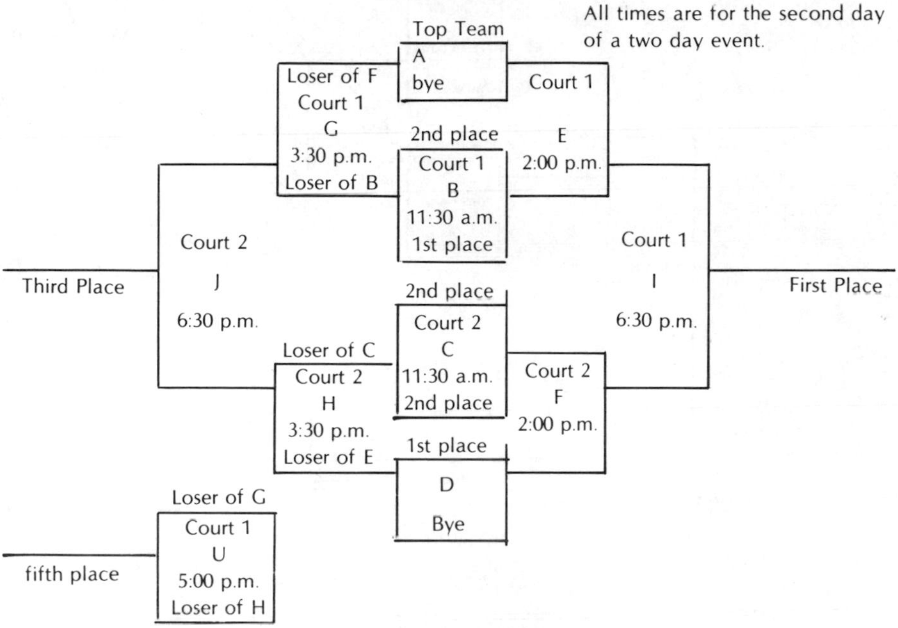

CONSOLATION BRACKET

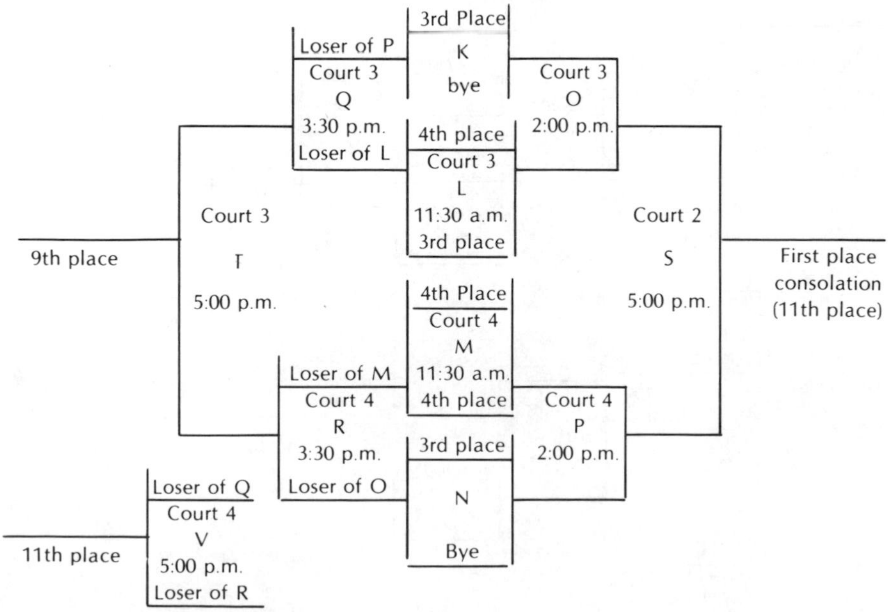

Sixteen Team Tournament
ELIMINATION BRACKET

All times are for the second of a two day event

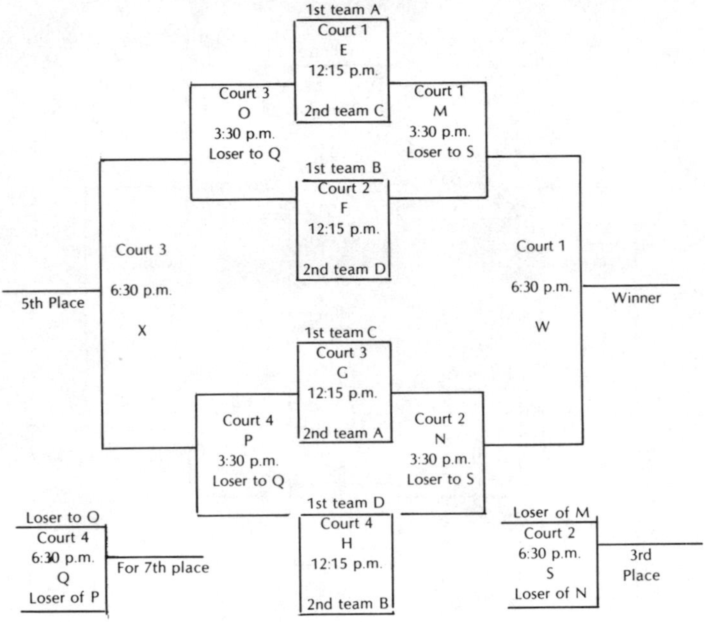

CONSOLATION BRACKET

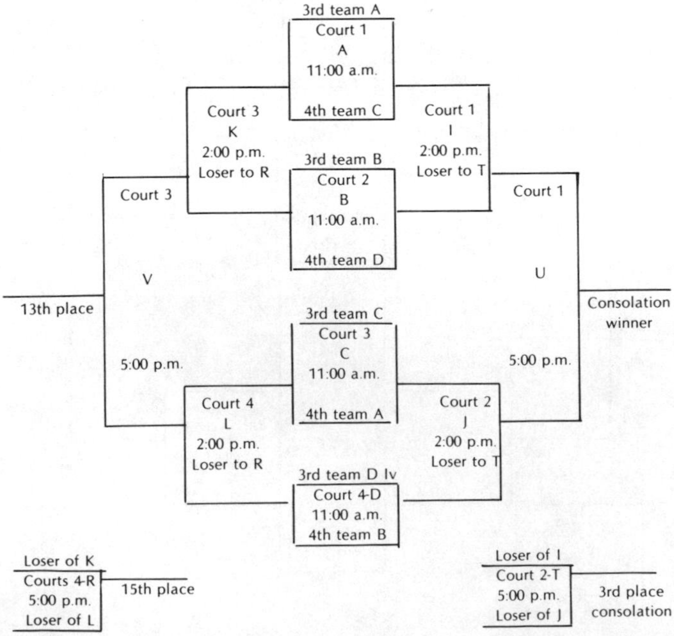

Second Day-Afternoon

2:00 p.m. Semi finals-consolation (Winners and losers bracket)

Court 1	Court 2	Court 3	Court 4
Match I	J	K	L
Winners of A	Winners of C	Losers of A	Losers of C
vs.	vs.	vs.	vs.
Winners of B	Winners of D	Losers of B	Losers of D

3:30 p.m. Semi finals-elimination (Winners and losers brackets)

Court 1	Court 2	Court 3	Court 4
Match M	N	O	P
Winners of E	Winners of G	Losers of E	Losers of G
vs.	vs.	vs.	vs.
Winners of F	Winners of H	Losers of F	Losers of H

5:00 p.m. Finals & third place play offs-consolation

Court 1	Court 2	Court 3	Court 4
Match U	T	V	R
Winners of I	Losers of I	Winners of K	Losers of K
vs.	vs.	vs.	vs.
Winners of J	Losers of J	Winners of L	Losers of L
for	for	for	for
9th place	10th place	13th place	15th place

6:30 p.m. Finals and Third Place playoffs-elimination

Court 1	Court 2	Court 3	Court 4
Match W	S	X	Q
Winners of M	Losers of M	Winners of O	Losers of O
vs.	vs.	vs.	vs.
Winners of N	Losers of N	Winners of P	Losers of P
for	for	for	for
First Place	Third Place	Fifth Place	Seventh Place

Trophies will be awarded at the conclusion of play. The awards ceremony will take place on Court 1.

Place the strongest two teams in each pool at the top and at the bottom. EX. 1 and 4, 5 and 8.
*All scheduling is based on the availability of four courts. If only three courts are available the schedule should be adjusted accordingly. The timing is only a suggested model to follow. It may be changed according to the host schools scheduling requirements. Scheduling is based on a two day tournament format.

David Perry

20

1.

-3

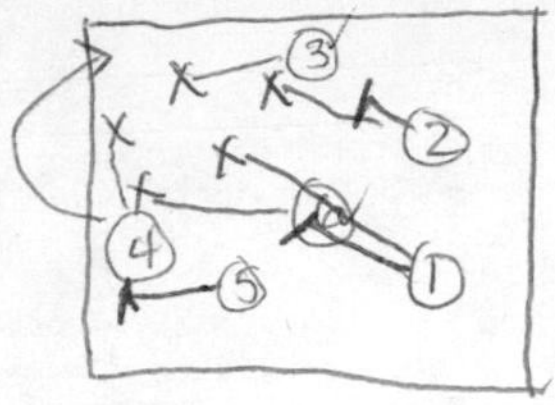

2. Spike coverage is protecting against a blocked attack.

3. When the opposing team has ~~strong~~ weak
-1 blockers they usually block to the deep court.

4. ① Follow the ball to the attacker
② Fill holes between players

5. opposite

6.

7. In the 4-2 off. the setter is in the middle front while in the 4-2 International the setter is on the outside front.

1986 JR. OLYMPIC TRY-OUTS

Session I

Station 1) a. Verticle Jump test (measure reach and verticle jump- 3 tries)
b. Number of rolls in 30 seconds (alternate directions right-left-forward)

Station 2) Serving accuracy

12 serves-2 per zone
(serve in order of zones)

Station 3) Forearm pass

Pass 6 balls then off
Repeat
Count number of passes to target out of 12 passes

18
Becoming an USVBA Official

BECOMING AN USVBA SCORER
by
The United States Volleyball Association
Officials and Certification Committee

Becoming A Volleyball Referee

Certification of Volleyball Referees is under the Jurisdiction of the United States Volleyball Association. The USVBA has established three classifications of referees: Provisional, Regional and National.

Provisional and Regional Referees will be certified within their respective Regions under the supervision of the Regional Officials Chairman in cooperation with the Regional Commissioner.

National Referees will be certified or recertified by the National Chairman of Officials *only*.

Provisional Referees

To become certified as a Provisional Referee the Candidate must:

1. File the Official USVBA application form with his/her Regional Officials Chairman
   A. These forms are available from your Regional Officials Chairman
2. Attend a minimum of one (1) Regional Officials Clinic per season
3. Score "100" on the approved USVBA Officials written test
4. Pass the Regional Scorers test, that will be given during the Regional Officials Clinic, in order to attain his/her Provisional Referee Certification
5. Show aptitude to officiate (referee) during this clinic
   A. The Regional Officials Chairman, or his/her designated represen-

tative, will observe all Provisional Referee Candidates, prior to rating, either before, during, or after the Regional Officials Clinic

B. Each Provisional Referee Candidate must receive two (2) or more ratings by the Regional Officials Chairman, or his/her designated representative, in three (3) games. All Provisional Referee Candidates must receive a minimum grade of "65" on the combined rating sheets to receive consideration to be certified as a Provisional Referee

6. After completion of the clinic, if approved by the Regional Officials Chairman, the candidate for Provisional Referee shall:
   A. Accept tournament assignments from Regional Officials Chairman at which time(s) candidates will be rated in a minimum of five (5) matches. These five (5) matches may be "spread over" several tournaments
   B. Candidates must be rated by a panel of three or more Regional or National Referees in all 5 matches
   C. Candidates must receive an average rating of "65" (in the 5 matches) on the USVBA approved rating sheet to qualify as a Provisional Referee
7. If the Candidate for Provisional Referee successfully meets the requirements for Provisional Referee rating, the Regional Officials Chairman shall authorize the purchase of the official USVBA uniform emblem
8. Provisional Referees may elect to become a candidate for Regional Referees rating only after one year as a Provisional Referee, or they may remain as a Provisional Referee for an indefinite period of time.
9. On approval of the Regional Commissioners, an application fee may be assessed, and shall be made payable to the Region for applicable costs of materials, pertinent services and clinician expenses

Regional Referees

To become certified/recertified as a Regional Referee the Candidate must:

1. File the Official USVBA application form with his/her Regional Officials Chairman
   A. These forms are available from your Regional Officials Chairman
2. Attend a minimum of one (1) Regional Officials Clinic per season. Said clinic(s) shall be approved by the Regional Commissioner and shall be scheduled by the Regional Officials Chairman and conducted by the Regional Officials Chairman and Regional Scorers Chairman or their duly authorized designates. The Regional Scorers test shall be a part of all Regional Officials Clinics
3. Score "100" on approved USVBA Officials written test

4. Candidates applying for Regional Officials Certification (for the first time) must have served as a Provisional Referee for a minimum of one (1) season
5. Regional Referee Candidates must be rated in a minimum of two (2) matches or four (4) games during sanctioned USVBA Tournaments, during the current season, by a minimum of 3 raters. These raters will be assigned by the Regional Officials Chairman
6. Regional Referee Candidates must be prepared to accept tournament assignments, from the Regional Officials Chairman, at the time of the Regional Officials Clinic
7. Regional Officials Candidates must receive an average rating of "75" (in the 2 matches or 4 games) on the approved USVBA rating sheet to be eligible for certification/re-certification as a Regional Referee
8. Successful Regional Referee Candidates will receive their Regional Referees' card and certificates from the Regional Officials Chairman and will be authorized by the Regional Officials Chairman to purchase the Regional Referees' emblem
9. Regional Referees must be re-certified annually
10. On approval by the Regional Commissioner, an application fee may be assessed, and shall be made payable to the Region for applicable costs of materials, pertinent services and clinician expenses

National Referees

To become certified/recertified as a National Referee the Candidate must:

1. File the Official USVBA application form with the National Chairman of Officials
   A. These forms are available from the Regional Officials Chairman or the National Chairman of Officials
2. All candidates for National Referee certification/re-certification must be approved by his/her Regional Officials Chairman
3. A candidate for certification as a National Referee (for the first time) must be certified by the National Chairman of Officials or his duly authorized representative *ONLY*. This National Certification may be obtained by:
   A. Attending the National Officials Clinic at time and site of the USVBA National Tournament. Candidate must officiate at National USVBA Tournament and pass all requirements and tests of the Officials and Certification Committee
4. A National Referee must be recertified every year through the following process
   A. Attend the National Referees Clinic and successfully complete all current requirements approved by the Referees and Certification Committee, including satisfactory performance as a referee and or

umpire at the National Tournament, or:

B. Petition the Chairman of the Referees Committee, in writing, for an extension of his/her National Certification for the year that he/she was unable to attend the National Referees clinic and National tournament.

Note: Re-certification of a National Referee may be done only by the Chairman of Referees and Certification Committee. The written petition to extend certification for a non-attending official must be submitted prior to the national clinic and tournament, and must show "just cause" why he/she cannot be in attendance.

5. Any USVBA Referee, officiating at the USVBA National Tournaments, must have officiated at his/her Regional Championship Tournament that season
6. The Regional Scorers test will be a part of the National Officials Clinic. Candidates (those referees that are applying for their National Certification for the first time) will be required to pass the Regional Scorers test
7. Successful National Referee candidates will receive their National Referee Cards/Certificate from the National Chairman of Officials and will be authorized by the National Chairman of Officials to purchase the National Referees* official uniform shirt.

Referees' Uniforms

All USVBA Referees, Provisional, Regional or National are required to wear the official Referee's uniform when officiating. The official USVBA uniform for both men and women is:

Shirt—Official USVBA Referee's shirt, can be purchased from USVBA National Referees Certification Committee
Slacks—Blue dacron or polyester.
Shoes—Blue shoes, low cut.
Sox—White, sweat.
Belt—Black.
Jacket—Optional

International Arbiter

The procedure for obtaining the candidate for International Arbiter (Referee) is controlled by the Arbiters Commission of FIVB. The Arbiters Commission places special emphasis upon the following:

1. Must have at least 3 years experience as a National Referee of the member country of FIVB.
2. Must be recommended by National Referees Chairman of member country of FIVB.

3. Must not be over the age of 39 years when attending first International Referees Clinic.
4. Must attend 1 2 week Referees Candidates' Course conducted by or under the supervision of the FIVB Arbiters Commission.

NOTE: In the continuing effort to standardize rules, protocol and other items pertaining to volleyball nationwide, the following list of play situations has been developed and the signals for each situation ruled on by the National Rules Interpreter:

		SIGNAL
1.	Server steps on end line during service	8
2.	Server has foot contacting floor outside service area at time of service	22
3.	Server fails to serve within 5 seconds after referee whistles for service	18
4.	Server hits teammate with the served ball	25
5.	Server catches or is contacted by ball after tossing it for service	18
6.	Served ball hits net	19
7.	Served ball hits overhead obstruction	25
8.	Serving team is screening at time of service	21
9.	Player out of position (overlap) at time of service	22
10.	Referee signals for service to begin; (no official signal)	
11.	Ball illegally held, thrown, pushed	11
12.	Ball not clearly released at time of service	17
13.	Ball makes multiple contact with player not in a block	12
14.	Ball contacts a player below the player's waist	13
15.	Ball hits net and falls to the floor inbound on attacker's side of the net	2
16.	Ball hits net and falls to the floor inbounds on defender's side of the net	19-2-1
17	Ball hits blocker and falls to the floor inbounds on attacker's side of the net	2
18.	Ball hits blocker and fall to the floor inbounds on defender's side of the net	2
19.	Ball hits blocker and falls out of bounds on attacker's side of the net	4
20.	Ball hits blocker and falls out of bound on defender's side of the net	4–6
21.	Ball not touched by player lands out of bounds	4
22.	Ball touched by player lands out of bounds	4–6
23.	Ball hit by attackers contacts out of bounds area on attacker's side of the net	4
24.	Ball hits net on 3rd team hit and then contacts player on the attacking team	9
25.	Ball hits overhead obstruction and continues across net into opponent's court	25
26.	Player attacks ball over opponent's court	23
27.	Ball not directed into opponent's court contacted over the net by defensive player	23
28.	Ball touches antenna	4 - point at antenna
29.	Ball crosses net outside antenna	4
30.	Ball touches net on or outside antenna	4
31.	Ball touches cables, net support, referee's stand or other object outside the court	4
32.	Ball touched by player blocking outside antenna over opponent's court	4–6
33.	Ball trapped against the net by a player	11 or 12
34.	Ball under net contacted after passing the vertical plane of the net	4–10–20
35.	Simultaneous contact by opponents suspends ball momentarily over the net	20
36.	Player reaches under net and interferes with ball over the opponent's court	10–22
37.	Player contacts net on or between the antennas	19
38.	Opponents simultaneously contact the net on or between the antennas	19–20
39.	Spiker's follow through causes contact with net	19

40. Back court player blocks the ball 21
41. Ball contacts player in multiple block containing a back court player 21
42. Back court player in front of attack line spikes the ball 24
43. Back court player in front of attack line directs ball across net after contacting the ball while it was fully above the height of the net 24
44. Player's foot contacts opponent's court fully beyond vertical plane of center line 10
45. Player lands on center line and causes interference with opponents 10–20
46. Offensive player outside the court on opponent's side of center line plays ball which had not crossed plane of the net 1022
47. Referee declares a sideout 1
48. Referee awards a point 27
49. Referee or Umpire acknowledges a request for team timeout for rest 15
50. Referee or Umpire acknowledges a request for substitution 16
51. Referee grants injury timeout . . . . Touch chest with both hands-follow with 15
52. Referee warns a player or team . . . . 26 (yellow card only)
53. Referee penalizes a player or team . . . . 26 (red card only)
54. Referee ejects a player for misconduct . . . .
Red & yellow card together—display number of fingers corresponding to number of games player(s) are ejected for 26
55. Referee signals end of game or match 14

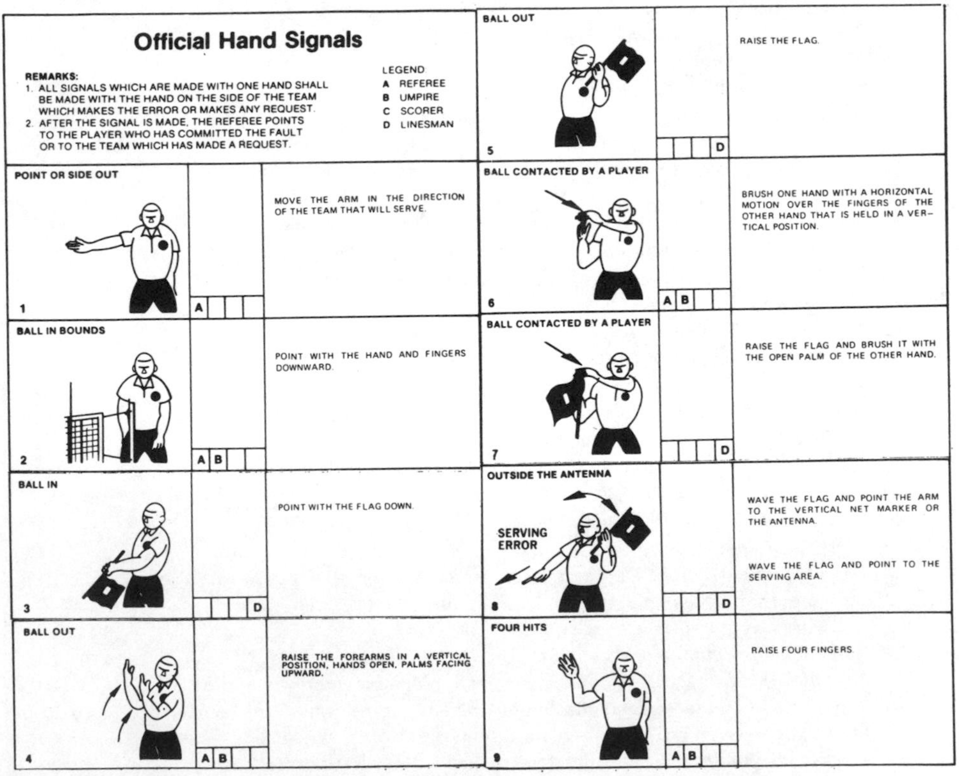

No.	Signal	Illustration		Description
10	CROSSING CENTER LINE		A B	POINT TO THE CENTER LINE AND AT THE SAME TIME INDICATE WITH THE "SERVICE" SIGNAL TO THE OPPONENTS' SIDE. POINT TO THE PLAYER WHO COMMITTED THE FAULT.
11	HELD BALL		A	SLOWLY LIFT ONE HAND WITH THE PALM FACING UPWARD.
12	DOUBLE HIT		A B	LIFT TWO FINGERS IN VERTICAL POSITION.
13	BALL CONTACTED BELOW THE WAIST		A	POINT TO THE PLAYER WHO COMMITTED THE FAULT WITH ONE HAND AND MOTION WITH THE OTHER HAND FROM WAIST DOWNWARD.
14	END OF GAME OR MATCH		A	CROSS THE FOREARMS IN FRONT OF THE CHEST.
15	TIME OUT		A B C	PLACE THE PALM OF ONE HAND HORIZONTALLY OVER THE OTHER HAND, HELD IN VERTICAL POSITION, FORMING THE LETTER "T". FOLLOW BY POINTING TO THE TEAM REQUESTING THE TIME OUT.
16	SUBSTITUTION		A B	MAKE A CIRCULAR MOTION OF THE HANDS AROUND EACH OTHER.
17	BALL NOT RELEASED AT TIME OF SERVICE		A	LIFT THE EXTENDED ARM, THE PALM OF THE HAND FACING UPWARD.
18	DELAY OF SERVICE		A	RAISE FIVE FINGERS IN A VERTICAL POSITION.
19	BALL IN THE NET AT TIME OF SERVICE PLAYER TOUCHING NET		A	TOUCH THE NET WITH THE HAND. TOUCH THE NET WITH THE HAND AND POINT TO THE PLAYER WHO COMMITTED THE FAULT.
20	DOUBLE FOUL OR PLAY OVER		A	RAISE THE THUMBS OF BOTH HANDS.
21	BACK LINE BLOCK		A B	RAISE BOTH ARMS AND POINT TO THE PLAYER COMMITTING THE FAULT.
22	OUT OF POSITION		A B C	MAKE A CIRCULAR MOTION WITH THE HAND AND INDICATE THE PLAYER OR PLAYERS WHO HAVE COMMITTED THE FAULT.
23	OVER THE NET		A	PASS THE HAND OVER THE NET AND POINT TO THE PLAYER WHO COMMITTED THE FAULT.
24	BACK LINE SPIKER		A B	MAKE A DOWNWARD MOTION WITH THE FOREARM AND POINT TO THE PLAYER WHO COMMITTED THE FAULT.
25	BALL TOUCHING OBJECT		A B	POINT TO THE PLAYER OR TO THE OBJECT TOUCHED BY THE BALL.
26	WARNING-PENALTY-EXCLUSION		A	SHOW A YELLOW-COLORED CARD. SHOW A RED-COLORED CARD. SHOW BOTH THE YELLOW AND RED CARDS. CALL THE CAPTAIN OF THE OFFENDING TEAM AND ADVISE THE CAPTAIN WHETHER THE EXCLUSION IS FOR ONE OR MORE GAMES OR FOR THE ENTIRE MATCH.
27	POINT		A	RAISE THE INDEX FINGER AND ARM ON THE SIDE OF THE TEAM THAT SCORES THE POINT.

***Signals used by permission of Alex Valow.**

19

Becoming an USVBA Scorer

by

The United States Volleyball Association Officials and Certification Committee

How to Become a Certified USVBA Scorer

Interest and time available are the basic essentials required to become a certified U.S. Volleyball Scorer. There are two levels of rank for certification, Regional and National. The entry level of "Regional Scorer" can be most easily obtained by attending a local scoring clinic, successfully pâssing both a written and practical test, and demonstrating the necessary interest to continue scoring. Clinic participation is helpful to become better acquainted with the scoresheet and with the rules as they apply to scoring procedures. Interested candidates should contact their Regional Scorers' Chairman for additional and specific information regarding their local program.

In order to become certified as a "National Scorer," it is required that you have first gained proficiency as a Regional Scorer and be recommended as a candidate for national rank by the local Regional Chairman. Each candidate must attend the National Scorers' Clinic at the National USVBA Championships and successfully pass the written and practical examination. For further information regarding the National Scoring Certification Program, please contact either your Regional Scoring Chairman or the National Chairman of Scoring and Certification.

This season will mark the beginning of instruction and testing for use of the approved FIVB scoresheet. Each National Scorer will be authorized to score at USVBA sponsored international matches within the geographic boundaries of the United States following their certification/recertification at the National Championships. Scorers for these exhibitions are to be assigned through the Regional Scoring Chairman and/or National Scoring Chairman from the approved list of National Scorers, as listed in the current Guide.

Becoming An USVBA Scorer

Familiarization of the scoring procedure is highly recommended for each referee. USVBA referees/candidates are required to take the written scorers' test prior to certification. Since there is a major change in the USVBA scoring system this season, it is strongly recommended that each currently certified scorer attend one of their regional clinics.

INSTRUCTIONS FOR USE OF OFFICIAL VOLLEYBALL SCORE SHEET

by

Nancy S. Sharpless

The scorer shall first prepare 2 scoresheets by printing the information required for upper and lower parts of scoresheet. Scorer shall then get the roster and line up sheet from each team. The team representative shall write the players' numbers on the line-up sheet before the start of each game. The scorer shall verify the players' numbers by checking with roster.

After the toss for serve and playing area, the scorer shall point, on left side of scoresheet, the name of team that will play in left area and, on right side, the team in right area and mark a cross in "first serve" square of team serving first. He shall then write the players' numbers in serving order from line-up sheet and write "c" after captain's number.

Scoring for first round of serves should be in blue (or black), second round of serves in red, third round of serves in blue (or black) etc.

When line-ups are initially recorded on the scoresheet, pencil or light pen is permissible, since line-ups may be changed up to the first service. After the first service, line-ups are to be recorded permanently, and erasers are not to be used.

Scorer shall draw a circle for the server at the time the ball is contacted for the service (circle should touch both upper & lower lines). This gives the scorer required control of the scoring process. When the referee signals point, the scorer shall write the point number in that circle- when the referee signals playover, the scorer shall write the letter "P" in that circle; when the referee signals sideout (rotate), the scorer shall write the letter "R" in that circle.

When a point is awarded without service, put point number in a square in the scoring column. In the running score column, put a square around the point number. (The term "scoring column" refers to the column where the serves are recorded. The term "running score column" refers to the vertical score column in the center of the scoresheet.) When a playover or sideout is indicated by the referee when no serve is involved, the scorer shall draw a square denoting the action awarded.

The code letter "M" is used to indicate a referee's mind change. When the referee changes his decision, the letter "M" is recorded in the scoring column after the circle, a slash cancels referee's first decision, and the second decision is recorded in a square. If a point was made as the referee's first decision, the letter "M" is also placed in the running score column. This letter "M" will be circled (or squared) when the point is remade.

Points cancelled because of scorer's error will be slashed both in the scoring column and in the running score column. When the points are remade, the point numbers are repeated in the scoring column, and the remade number is circled (squared) in the running score column. Always slash through cancelled points.

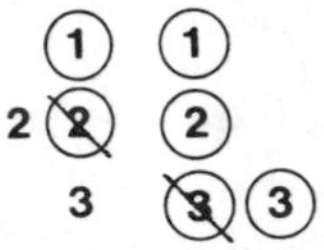

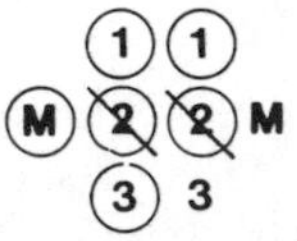

If the scorer makes an inadvertent error in the scoring column, cross out mistake with an "X" and replace with correct symbol.

The "Comments" section is to be used any time a noteworthy situation occurs during the game:

1. Referee shows a Red Card, indicating penalty point or penalty sideout, but never when a referee holds up a yellow card, indicating warning.
2. Referee shows a Red/Yellow Card, indicating player is disqualified (ejected).
3. Points removed because of scorer error and acted upon by the referee (i.e., wrong server, wrong position entry, entry of player not on roster, entry of player exceeding player or team substitution, entry of disqualified player).
4. Abnormal substitution allowed because of injury.
5. Protested game (follow same procedures as in past: i.e., score, time remaining to play, team areas, player serving, relative positions of both teams at time of protested play; referee writes or dictates protest claims and signs; both captains and scorer sign).
6. Pertinent information relating to unusual circumstances in the conduct of the game.

NOTE: Back of scoresheet should be used if necessary. When another scoresheet is printed on the reverse side, use space available for comments. Only one game should be recorded on any one scoresheet for this reason.

When game is finished, final recording of necessary information should be written in blue (black): Winning team and score on top, losing team and score next; time game finished; names of referee, umpire and scorer are written; all heading information is complete; "Score of Game" number is circled. The scorer puts a large circle in the scoring column of each team, and then signs the sheet. (Eliminate the use of the double slash after the last point of the game.) At the end of the match, the umpire signs the scoresheets. The referee enters the final scores of each game in the larger circles made by the scorer, verifying that the score is correct. The referee then signs the scoresheets.

Explanation of Scoring in Example

In this sample game, most of the anticipated errors/violations are illustrated to give the reader an opportunity to become better acquainted with proper scoring procedures. These examples are not to be construed as "delay of game" situations.

In this 3rd and deciding game of the match, the coin is tossed, and Blue team serves first. White team chooses court to the left of the scorer.

The scoresheet for a deciding game is used (different from the sheet used for other game of a match). This sheet provides for the placement of information on the scoresheet consistent with the court for each team. This requires that information for the team on the left (White team) needs to be transposed to the right of the scoresheet when the teams change courts at either 8 points or 4 minutes. Since minimum time is available between serves, it is imperative that the scorer try to record information on both sides of the scoresheet as the game progresses to point 8 or 4 minutes, particularly as it relates to the starting line-up, substitutions, and time-outs. The score at the time of the court change should also be circled in the running score columns to the right of the scoresheet, taking particular note that the team references are now reversed (i.e., Blue team is now to the scorer's left, and White team is to the scorer's right). Procedurally, the last action recorded by the team moving from left to right prior to the court change shall be repeated the right side. It is imperative, however, that the scorer stay with the game on the left side of the scoresheet until teams change courts. If necessary, enough time should be given during court change for scorer to "catch up" before the game will continue, without causing undue delay.

Ⓟ Ⓡ Blue #2 serves twice, volleys resulting in a playover and a sideout.

(1) (2) (R) White #17 serves two fast points; his third serve is a sideout.

(1) (R) Blue #8 serves their first point; his coach substitutes #14 for #10. Scorer records player #14 in the square under player #10, and records the score at the time of substitution in the square to the right of player #14. Score of team requesting substitution is listed first, so 1-2 is written in "Score at Time of Substitution" column. Team substitution #1, under the scoring column, is circled. Player #8's second serve results in a sideout.

(3) (4) (5) (R) Scorer notices that #7 is holding the ball to serve, but #1 is supposed to be the next server. Before the ball is served incorrectly by player #7, scorer sounds horn (or whistle). Position of White team is corrected before the illegal service, and no penalty is given. (Scorer should be alert to note which player is going into the serving corner while teams are beginning to get into position, thus avoiding possibility of an incorrect server hitting the ball). White #1, the correct server, then serves points 3 and 4. Opponents call timeout. Scorer records in Blue's time-out square under scoring column, first listing score of team requesting time-out, followed by score of opponent (recorded 1-4). Blue's coach calls for a substitution during the time-out, player #5 for #20. Scorer records #5 under #20 in "players' numbers" column, followed by the score 1-4, then circles team substitution #2. White #1 serves 1 more point, then serves a sideout.

(2) (3) (R) Blue #14 serves three times, scoring 2 points before losing his serve.

(R) White #7, the captain, is due to serve. Before he does, his coach substitutes player #15 for #7. Coach designates player #9 as the new floor captain. Scorer puts small "c" next to player #9 in "players' numbers" column, as well as puts player #15 under the 7c, with the score 5-3 next to player #15. Team substitution #1 is circled. Blue's captain requests a substitution, player #16 for #14. Scorer informs captain this is a wrong position entry and refuses the substitution. Nothing is written on the scoresheet since no penalty is involved. White #15 serves a sideout.

(~~4~~) (P) (4) (R) Blue #5 serves, and scorer records point 4 in the scoring column as well as in the running score column in error. The referee's signal was a playover, not a point. Scorer puts a large "X" through point 4 in the scoring column and records "P" in a circle immediately after. Since the referee's only signal was a playover, and the scorer erred in observing the hand signal, the "P" is recorded in a circle, not a square. In the running score column, scorer puts an "X" through point 4 that was circled, rewrites number 4 on the outside of the running score column. White captain questions the decision in playover. Referee holds up a yellow card and points to Blue #2, warning him to stop the derogatory remarks toward his opponents. Nothing is recorded on the scoresheet for a warning. Blue #5 serves for the second time, making point 4. Scorer circles the remade number 4 in the running score column. White captain #9 calls for their second team substitution,

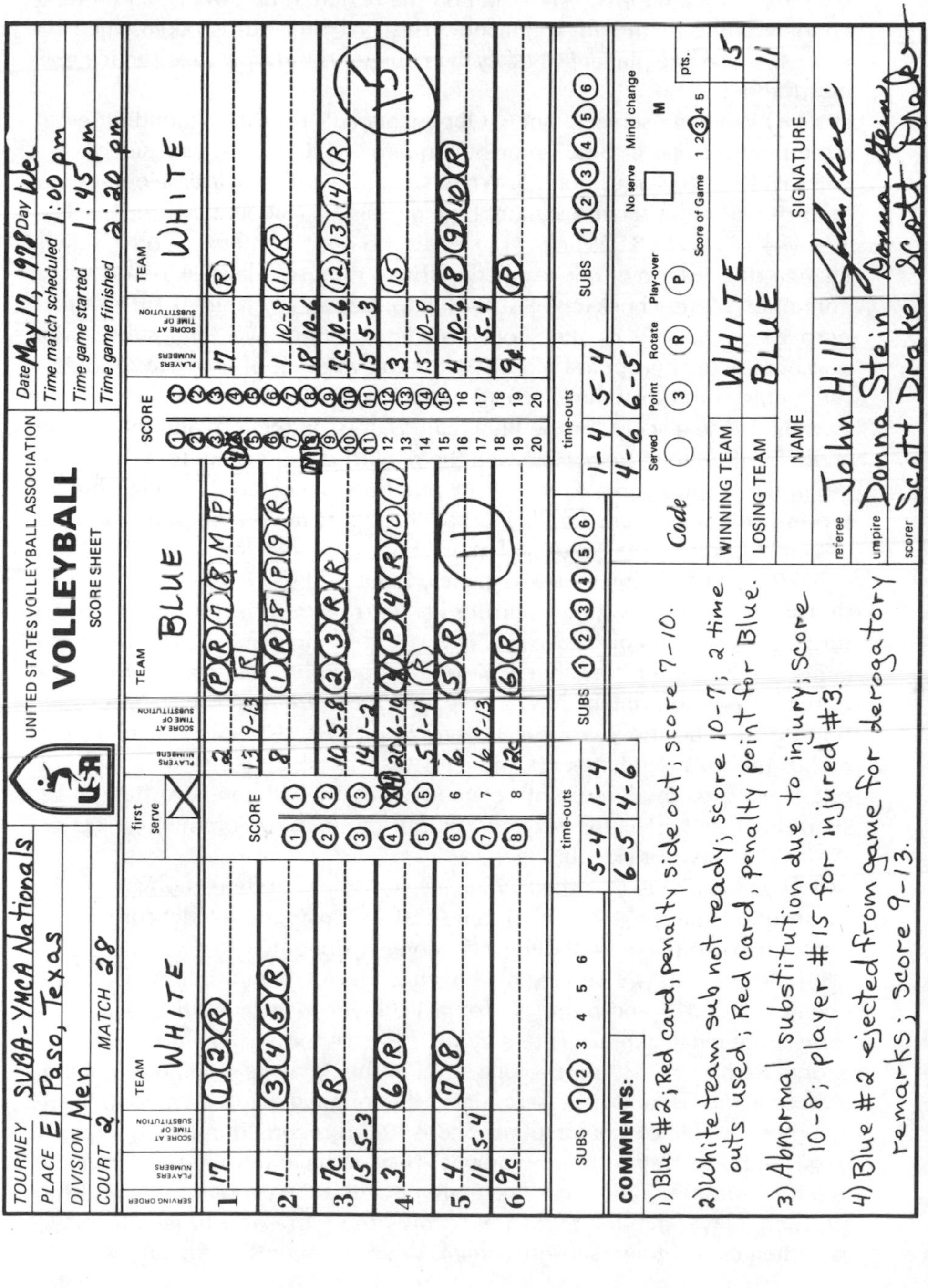
TOURNEY SVBA-YMCA Nationals
PLACE El Paso, Texas
DIVISION Men
COURT 2 MATCH 28
UNITED STATES VOLLEYBALL ASSOCIATION
VOLLEYBALL
SCORE SHEET
USA
Date May 17, 1978 Day Wed
Time match scheduled 1:00 pm
Time game started 1:45 pm
Time game finished 2:20 pm
SERVING ORDER
PLAYERS NUMBERS
SCORE AT TIME OF SUBSTITUTION
TEAM
WHITE
first serve
BLUE
SCORE
SUBS
time-outs
5-4 1-4
6-5 4-6
1-4 5-4
4-6 6-5
COMMENTS:
1) Blue #2; Red card, penalty side out; score 7-10.
2) White team sub not ready; score 10-7; 2 time outs used; Red card, penalty point for Blue.
3) Abnormal substitution due to injury; Score 10-8; player #15 for injured #3.
4) Blue #2 ejected from game for derogatory remarks; Score 9-13.
No serve
Mind change
Code
Served
Point
Rotate
Play-over
M
Score of Game 1 2 3 4 5
pts.
WINNING TEAM WHITE 15
LOSING TEAM BLUE 11
NAME
SIGNATURE
referee John Hill
umpire Donna Stein
scorer Scott Drake

player #11 for #4. Player #11 is still on the bench in his sweats, and referee charges White team with a time-out. This first time-out is taken when the score is 5-4. White player #11 takes the court, and Blue #5's next service goes into the net.

(6) (R) White #3 serves point 6. Opponents call for their second time-out. Scorer records 4-6 in Blue's time-out square. White #3 serves a sideout.

(5) (R) Blue #6 serves point 5. White's captain calls for a time-out. Scorer records 6-5 in the second square. Blue #6 serves a sideout.

(7) (8) (9) (10) (R) White #11 serves points 7 and 8. Scorer signals change of sides (point 8 is reached before 4 minutes elapses). Before game continues, scorer checks to be sure all information for White team is copied onto the right side of the scoresheet (including player and substitution numbers, with appropriate scores, and scores at point of time-outs; scores in the running score columns are recorded for both teams). Scorer must be sure that the running score for the Blue team is now on the left, and the running score for the White team is now on the right (this is opposite to what is written in the running score for the first 8 points of the game). Nothing from the scoring column is transferred, except for the last action made by the team originally on the left. White's 8th point is copied onto the right side. Scorer checks line-ups on the floor, and game continues. Before referee blows whistle for service, Blue captain calls for his third team substitution, player #10 for #14, with the score 5-8. Since #10 is the original starting player in the game, he may enter the game in his original position. Score is recorded next to player #10, showing he has entered, and there are no more legal substitutions for that position. White #11 serves points 9 and 10. Blue coach forgets he has used his two time-outs and calls for a third. Scorer refuses the time-out, if not already done so by referee or umpire. Nothing is written on the scoresheet, either in the scoring column or in the "Comments" section. White #11 serves a sideout.

(6) (R) Blue player #12, the captain, serves point 6. White captain calls for substitution, player #18 for #1. Team substitution #3 is circled. Score of 10-6 written next to player #18. Blue #12 serves a sideout.

(R) Before White #9 serves, his coach calls for a multiple substitution, player #7 for #15 and player #4 for #11. Player #7 is again the captain (as soon as original captain enters game, he is automatically floor captain). Scorer slashes the "c" next to player #9 in the "players' numbers" column, although this is not necessary since the original captain automatically assumes the role of floor captain. Score 10-6 is recorded in the square next to #7 and next to #4, showing original players have returned to the game. Team substitution numbers 4 and 5 are circled. Blue captain calls for a substitution, player #20 for #5. Scorer records the score of 6-10 next to player #20, then circles team substitution #4. White #9 serves a sideout.

This completes the first round of serves for all players.

Scorer reaches for red pen, ready for the second round.

(7) (~~8~~) M [P] [R] Blue player #2 serves points 7 and 8. White captain questions the referee about the ball being inside or outside the line? Referee confers with linesman, then changes point 8 to a playover. Scorer puts slash through referee's first decision, writes code letter "M", and puts referee's second decision in a square because no serve is involved in his second decision. Next to point 8 in running score column, scorer writes the code letter "M". Blue player #2 shouts a derogatory remark to his opponents (#2's second outburst). Referee holds up a red card, points to offender, and talks to captain. He then signals sideout, which scorer records in a square. Scorer notes red card penalty in "Comments" section.

(R) White #17 serves a rotate.

[8] (P) (9) (R) Before Blue #8 serves, White captain #7 calls for a substitution to remove a player on his team affected by opponent's poor sportsmanship, #1 for #18. Player #1 is not ready to play. White team has already taken their 2 allowable time-outs. Since a time-out cannot be awarded, the delay requires a red card penalty. Scorer notes penalty in "Comments" section given when score was 10-7. Scorer then records point 8 in a square. In running score column, scorer indicates the 8th point is remade by putting the "M" in a square. White player #1 then enters the game. Scorer notes the score of 10-8 next to White #1 and circles team substitution #6 for Whites. Blue #8 serves again. During the volley, referee notices that White #3 is injured and immediately blows his whistle to stop play, indicating a playover on the service. White #3 is not able to remain in the game. Since White team has no additional players on their roster, a substitute who has already played in another position may replace an injured player, regardless of position. This does not count as a team substitution, either, since they have used all 6 allowable substitutions. White captain puts player #15 for #3, with score 10-8, and scorer notes abnormal substitution in "Comments" section. Blue #8 serves point 9, then a sideout.

(11) (R) Before White #1 serves, Blue captain requests a substitution, player #14 for #10. Since player #14 has already been in the game once, this substitution requested is denied. No penalty for request; nothing written on the scoresheet. White #1 serves twice, making point 11 and a sideout.

(R) Blue #10 serves into the net.

(12) (13) (14) (R) White captain #7 serves points 12 and 13. Blue coach calls for a substitution, player #16 for #6. Scorer records substitution, noting score 9-13, and circles team substitution #5. While the substitution is taking place, Blue #2 verbally abuses the opposing team and an official. Referee signals that player #2 has been ejected by holding up both the red and yellow card. He indicates the number of games the player is ejected by holding up the appropriate number of fingers. (Since this is the deciding game of the match,

the referee holds up one finger.) Blue captain is called to the stand to be advised of the situation. Scorer records information in "Comments" section. Blue captain substitutes player #13 for #2, with the score 9-13. This uses Blue's final allowable substitution. White #7 serves point 14, then a sideout.
(10) (11) (R) Blue #20 serves point 10, point 11, then a sideout.
(15) Before White #15 serves, Blue captain calls for substitution, player #6 for #16. Since this would be a seventh team substitution for Blue team, the substitution is denied—no penalty, nothing written on the scoresheet. White #15 serves game point, point number 15.

The scorer puts a large circle in the scoring column of each team; fills out the rest of the scoresheet in blue (black); records winning team, White with 15 points, on top—then Blue, with 11 points; notes the time the game ended at top of sheet; makes sure scoresheet is checked carefully to insure its completeness (game number must be circled). Scorer signs and makes sure umpire signs name to all three scoresheets. The referee enters the final scores of all 3 games in the circles provided by the scorer, verifying that the scores are correct, then the referee signs all three sheets.

Masters' Matches—Games with Twelve-Team Substitutions

The USVBA scoresheet can be used for 12-team substitution play. The scorer enters player numbers in "players numbers" column as well as in "time of substitution" column and uses an S or SX to denote exactly where substitution has taken place. This is the same as the old USVBA scoresheet (code letters S-Substitution; code letter X-opponents). Slash through player number, as in sample score sheet (page 309).

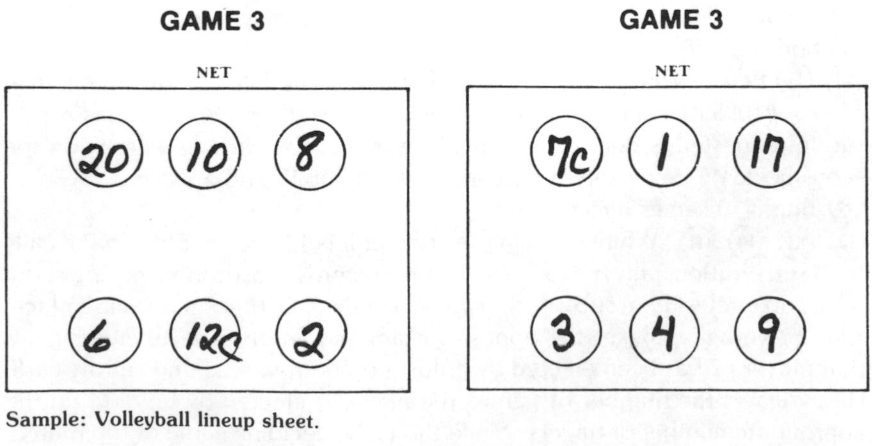

Sample: Volleyball lineup sheet.

20

OFFICIAL 1982–1984 UNITED STATES VOLLEYBALL RULES

as approved by The United States Volleyball Association

The United States Volleyball Rules are those of the International Volleyball Federation as adopted by the United States Volleyball Association, the National Governing Body for Volleyball in the United States. The IVBF rules are used world wide. It is difficult to translate and interpret precisely these rules from one language to another. The United States rules shall be in effect through the conclusion of the 1984 Olympiad.

CHAPTER I
FACILITIES, PLAYING AREA AND EQUIPMENT

RULE 1. PLAYING AREA AND MARKINGS

Article 1. COURT—The playing court shall be 18 m. long by 9 m. wide (59′ x 29′6″). A clear area of 2 m. (6′6″) should surround an indoor court. A clear area of 3 m. (9′10″) should surround an outdoor court.

Article 2. COURT MARKINGS—The court shall be marked by lines 5 cm. (2″) wide. Areas being defined by court markings shall be measured from the outside edge of the lines defining such areas.

Article 3. CENTER LINE—A line 5 cm. (2″) wide shall be drawn across the court beneath the net from side line to side line dividing the court into two equal team areas.

Article 4. ATTACK LINE—In each team area a line 5 cm. (2″) wide shall be drawn between the side lines parallel to the center line and 3 m. (9′10″) from the middle of the

center line to the rearmost edge of the attack line. The attack area, limited by the center line and the attack line, extends indefinitely beyond the side lines.
Article 5. SERVICE AREA—At a point 20 cm. (8") behind and perpendicular to each end line, two lines, each 15 cm. (6") in length and 5 cm. (2") in width, shall be drawn to mark the service area for each team. One line is an extension of the right side line and the other is drawn so that its farther edge is 3 m. (9'10") from the extension of the outside edge of the right side line. The service area shall have a minimum depth of 2 m. (6'6").
Article 6. OVERHEAD CLEARANCE—For the Olympic Games there must be a clear space of 12 m. 50 cm. (41') above the court. For the final rounds of the World Championships, or similar competitions, the same clearance is required unless the Executive Committee of the International Volleyball Federation makes a special concession. For all other competition, there should be an overhead clearance free from obstructions to a height of 7 m. (23') measured from the playing surface.
Article 7. SUBSTITUTION ZONE—The substitution zone is an area extending from the imaginary extension of the attack line to the imaginary extension of the center line between the court boundary and the scorer's table.
Article 8. MINIMUM TEMPERATURE—The minimum temperature shall not be below 10 degrees centigrade (50 degrees farenheit).

COMMENTARY ON RULE 1
PLAYING FACILITIES

1) *COURT CLEARANCE—In order to provide adequate room for playing of the game, a clear space of 3 m. (9'10") should surround an outdoor court and a clear space of 2 m. (6'6") should surround an indoor court. For the Olympic Games, there should be a clearance behind the end lines of 8 m. (26') and beyond the side lines of 5 m. (16'6"). For the final rounds of the World Championships, and similar competitions, the same clearances are required unless the Executive Committee of the IVBF makes a special concession. The referees' stand must present the least possible obstacle. If the stand should present an unfair hindrance to play, or if low hanging objects protrude into the clear space specified above, the referee may direct a play-over if they interfere with play.*
2) *OTHER FACTORS—The court must be flat and horizontal. For outdoor courts a slope of 5 mm. per m. is allowable for drainage. The game may be played indoors or outdoors.*
3) *ASSUMED EXTENSION OF LINES—All lines on the court are considered to have an assumed indefinite extension.*
4) *CEILING CLEARANCE—For other than Olympic Games or World Championships, a ball contacting a ceiling or object connected to the ceiling shall remain in play if the ceiling is less than 7 m. above the playing surface. The ball may not legally strike above the opponent's area nor may it legally fall to the opponent's area after striking the ceiling or objects connected to the ceiling. Walls, or objects connected to walls, shall not be in play. Low objects protruding into the 2 m. free zone around the court may be ruled a play-over if they interfere with a play that could normally be made if the objects were not within the free zone.*
5) *UNSUITABLE COURTS—The court must be approved by the Special Referees Commission to be acceptable for competition in International matches. The court,*

in all cases, must be under the control of the first referee before a match. The first referee alone is responsible for deciding whether or not the court is suitable for play. The first referee will declare the court unfit for play in the following cases:

a) If snow or rain has made the court soft or slippery.

b) When play can be dangerous due to any hazardous condition of the court surface or equipment.

c) When fog or darkness makes it impossible to officiate properly.

6) *BAD WEATHER—In case of bad weather (thunderstorms, showers, high winds, etc.) the first referee can postpone the match or interrupt it.*

7) *BOUNDARY MARKERS—Wood, metal, or other solid material may not be used for outdoor courts since the ground can erode, thus causing lines to protrude above ground level and present a hazard to players. This applies to brick or other hard material. Hollowed out lines are not recommended. The court lines should be marked before the beginning of a match. On an outdoor court, the lines must be clearly marked with whitewash, chalk, or other substance which is not injurious to eyes or skin. No lime nor caustic material of any kind may be used. Lines must be marked in such a manner as to not make the ground uneven. Indoors the lines must be of a color contrasting to that of the floor. Light colors (white or yellow) are the most visible and are recommended.*

8) *LIGHTING—Lighting in a playing facility should be 500 to 1500 luxes measured at a point 1 m. above the playing surface.*

9) *SCOREBOARD—No special recommendations are made as to the size of the scoreboard. It should be divided into two parts with large numbers to provide a running score for each team. The name or initials of the two teams should be shown at the top of each side. Information displayed on the scoreboard is not official and may not be used as a basis of protest.*

10) *ADJOINING COURTS—Where competition (including warmups preceding a match) is being conducted on adjoining courts, no player may penetrate into an adjoining court before, during or after playing the ball.*

11) *DIVIDING NETS OR OTHER PARTITIONS—Where dividing nets or other hanging partitions of a movable nature separate adjoining courts, only the player actually making the attempt to play the ball may go into the net or move it. It should be ruled a dead ball and a fault if a teammate, substitute, coach or other person deliberately moves the net to assist play.*

12) *BLEACHERS AND WALLS—Players may not enter bleachers for the purpose of playing the ball. Players making a play on the ball over bleachers must have a foot in contact with the floor if the remaining foot is contacting a bleacher at the time of contact with the ball. After contact with the ball, players may enter the bleachers without penalty. When playing the ball near a wall, players may not use the wall to gain a height advantage. If the wall is contacted by the foot of a player prior to making contact of the ball, at least one foot must be on the floor at the time the ball is contacted.*

RULE 2. THE NET

Article 1. SIZE AND CONSTRUCTION—The net shall be not less than 9.50 m. (32′) in length and 1 m. (39″) in width throughout the full length when stretched. A double thickness of white canvas 5 cm. (2″) wide shall be sewn along the full length of the top of the net. A flexible wire rope shall be stretched through the upper canvas and the lower edge of the net. The end of the net shall be capable of receiving a wooden dowel to keep the ends of the net in straight lines when tight. For detailed specifications, see the section on specifications approved by the USVBA Equipment Committee.

Article 2. NET HEIGHT—The height of the net measured from the center of the court shall be 2.43 m. (7′11 5/8″) for men and 2.24 m. (7′4 1/8″) for women. The two ends of the net must be at the same height from the playing surface and cannot exceed the regulation height by more than 2 cm. (3/4″).

Article 3. VERTICAL TAPE MARKERS—Two tapes of white material 5 cm. (2″) wide and 1 m. (39″) in length shall be fastened to the net, one at each end, over and perpendicular to each side line and the center line. The vertical tape side markers are considered to be a part of the net.

Article 4. NET ANTENNAS—Coinciding with the outside edge of each vertical tape marker, an antenna shall be fastened to the net at a distance of 9 m. (29′6″) from each other. The net antennas shall be 1.80 m. (6′) in length and made of safe and moderately flexible material with a uniform diameter of 10 mm. (3/8″). The upper half of each antenna shall be marked with alternating white and red or orange bands not less than 10 cm. (4″) and not more than 15 cm. (6″) in width. The antennas will be affixed to the net with fasteners that provide for quick and easy adjustment of the antenna. The fasteners shall be smooth surfaced and free of any sharp edges that might be considered hazardous to players.

Article 5. NET SUPPORTS—Where possible, the posts, uprights, or stands, including their bases, which support the net should be at least 50 cm. (19 1/2″) from the side lines and placed in such a manner as to not interfere with the officials in the performance of their duties.

COMMENTARY ON RULE 2
THE NET

1) *NET SUPPORTS—Round net support posts are preferable since they are convenient for the referees and are less hazardous to the players. They must be of a length that allows the net to be fixed at the correct height above the playing surface. Fixing the posts to the floor by means of wire supports should be avoided if possible. If wire supports are necessary, they should be covered with a soft material to provide protection for the players. It is recommended that strips of material be hung from the wire to alert players of their presence.*
2) *NET ADJUSTMENTS—The height and tension of the net must be measured before the start of the match and at any other time the first referee deems advisable. Height measurements should be made in the center of the court and at each end of the net perpendicular to the side boundary lines to assure that each end of the net is within the prescribed variation. The net must be tight throughout its length. After being tightened, the net should be checked to assure that a ball striking the net will rebound properly.*

3) *ANTENNAS AND VERTICAL MARKERS—Antennas and vertical tape markers on the net should be checked by the first referee before a match to assure that they are properly located on the net, are properly secured and properly aligned. Special attention should be given to any exposed ends at the bottom of the antennas to assure that they are smooth and round or are covered with tape so as not to present a safety hazard to players.*
4) *NET TORN DURING PLAY—If a net becomes torn during play, other than a served ball contacting the net, play shall be stopped and a play-over directed after the net is repaired or replaced.*

CURRENT PRACTICES FOR RULE 2

1) NET HEIGHTS FOR AGE GROUPS—The following net heights are currently in practice for the below indicated age groups:

	HEIGHT OF NET	
AGE GROUPS	GIRLS	BOYS
11 years and under	1.85 m. (6'1")	1.85 m. (6'1")
13 years and under	2.12 m. (7'2 1/16")	2.24 m. (7'4 1/8")
16 years and under	2.24 m. (7'4 1/8")	2.43 m. (7'11 5/8")
19 years and under	2.24 m. (7'4 1/8")	2.43 m. (7'11 5/8")

RULE 3. THE BALL

Article 1. SIZE AND CONSTRUCTION—The ball shall be spherical with a laceless leather or leatherlike cover of 12 or more pieces of uniform light color with or without a separate bladder; it shall not be less than 62 cm. nor more than 68 cm. (25" to 27") in circumference; and it shall weigh not less than 260 grams nor more than 280 grams (9 to 10 oz.) See detailed specification approved by the USVBA Committee on Equipment.

COMMENTARY ON RULE 3
THE BALL

1) *APPROVAL OF BALLS—Balls used for any international match must be those approved by IVBF. Balls used for sanctioned USVBA competitions must be those approved by the USVBA Committee on Equipment.*
2) *RESPONSIBILITY FOR EXAMINING BALL PRIOR TO PLAY—It is the responsibility of the first referee to examine the balls prior to the start of a match to determine that they are official and in proper condition. A ball that becomes wet or slippery during competition must be changed.*
3) *PRESSURE OF THE BALL—The pressure of the ball, measured with a special pressure gauge, must be between 0.40 and 0.45 kg/cm² (5.5 to 6.5 lbs/sq. in.). However, the structure of the ball may affect the maximum variation of the pressure allowed; for this reason, jurys of international competition may reduce this margin of difference within the above range.*
4) *MARKINGS ON THE BALLS—A maximum of 25% of the total exterior surface area of the ball may be covered with logo, name, identification and other markings*

and coloring, which is to say that a minimum of 75% of the exterior surface of an approved ball shall be of uniform light color.

5) *THREE BALL SYSTEM DURING A MATCH—The following procedures will be followed when using the three ball systems during a match:*
   a) *Six (6) ball retrievers will be used and shall be stationed as follows: (1) One at each corner of the court about 8 m. from the end lines and 4 m. to 5 m. from the side lines; (2) One behind the scorer; (3) One behind the referee. (NOTE: Ball retrievers may use chairs)*
   b) *At the start of a match, a ball will be placed on the scorer's table and one given to each of the ball retrievers nearest the serving areas. These are the only ones authorized to give the ball to the server.*
   c) *When the ball is outside the playing areas, it should be recovered by one of the ball retrievers and given to the one who has already given the ball to the player who will make the next service; (2) If the ball is on the court, the player nearest the ball should immediately place it outside the court.*
   d) *At the instant the ball is ruled dead, the ball retriever nearest the service area will quickly give the ball to the player who will be executing the next service. Players may not give the ball to the server.*
   e) *During a time-out, the first referee may authorize the second referee to give the ball to the retriever nearest the area where the next service will occur.*
   f) *A ball being returned from one ball retriever to another will be rolled, not thrown, along the floor outside the court. A ball being returned should be delivered to the ball retriever who has just given a ball to the server.*

CHAPTER II
PARTICIPANTS IN COMPETITION

RULE 4. RIGHTS AND DUTIES OF PLAYERS AND TEAM PERSONNEL

Article 1. RULES OF THE GAME—All coaches and players are required to know the rules of the game and abide by them.

Article 2. DISCIPLINE OF TEAM—The coaches, managers and captains are responsible for discipline and proper conduct of their team personnel.

Article 3. SPOKESMAN OF THE TEAM—The playing captain is the only player who may address the first referee and shall be the spokesman of the team. The captains may also address the second referee, but only on matters concerning the captain's duties. The designated head coach may address the referees only for the purpose of requesting a time-out or substitution.

Article 4. TIME-OUT REQUESTS—Requests for time-out may be made by the designated head coach and/or the playing captain when the ball is dead.

a) Each team is allowed two time-outs in each game. Consecutive time-outs may be requested by either team without the resumption of play between time-outs. The length of a time-out is limited to 30 seconds.

b) If a team captain or head coach inadvertantly requests a third time-out, it shall be refused and the team warned. If, in the judgement of the first referee, a team requests a third time-out as a means of attempting to gain an advantage, the offending team will be penalized with loss of service, or if not serving, the opponents shall be awarded a point.
c) During a time-out, the players are not allowed to leave the court and may not speak to anyone except to receive advice from one coach who may stand near, but not on the court.
d) A team attendant may approach the players on the court for the purpose of providing water, towels, medical assistance, etc., but must move back from the side of the court when not engaged in administering such duties.

NOTE: NAGWS rules provide that either the head coach or the assistant coach may request a time-out. During a time-out, two persons may approach the side of the court and both may speak to the players on the court.

Article 5. TEAM BENCHES—Benches are to be placed on the right and left of the scorer's table. Team members shall occupy the bench located on the side of the net adjacent to their playing area. Only the coaches, a trainer, a doctor or masseur and the reserve players can be seated on such benches. Coaches shall be seated on end of the bench nearest the scorer's table.

Article 6. ACTS SUBJECT TO SANCTION—The following acts of coaches, players, substitutes and other team members are subject to sanction:

a) Addressing of officials concerning their decisions.
b) Making profane or vulgar remarks or acts to officials, opponents or spectators.
c) Committing actions tending to influence decisions of officials.
d) Coaching during the game by any team member from outside the court.
e) Crossing the vertical plane of the net with any part of the body with the purpose of distracting an opponent while the ball is in play.
f) Shouting or yelling in such a manner as to distract an opponent who is playing, or attempting to play, a ball.
g) Leaving the court during an interruption of play in the game without the permission of the first referee.
h) It is forbidden for teammates to clap hands at the instant of contact with the ball by a player, particularly during the reception of a service.
i) Shouting or taking any action conducive to distracting the first referee's judgement concerning handling of the ball.

Article 7. SANCTIONS—Offenses committed by coaches, players and/or other team members may result in the following warning, penalty, expulsion from the game or disqualification from the match:

a) WARNING: For minor unsportsmanlike offenses, such as talking to opponents, spectators or officials, shouting or unintentional acts that cause a delay in the game, a warning (yellow card) is issued and is recorded on the scoresheet. A second minor offense must result in a penalty.
b) PENALTY: For rude behavior or a second minor offense, a penalty (red card) is issued by the first referee and is recorded on the scoresheet. A penalty automatically entails the loss of service by the offending team if serving, or if not serving, the awarding of a point to the opponents. A second act warranting the issue of a

penalty by the first referee results in the expulsion of a player.

c) EXPULSION: Offensive conduct (such as obscene or insulting words or gestures) towards officials, spectators or opponents, results in expulsion of a player from the game (red and yellow cards together). A second expulsion during a match must result in the disqualification of a player or team member.

d) DISQUALIFICATION: A second expulsion during a match or any attempted or actual physical aggression towards an official, spectator or opponent results in the disqualification of a player or team member for the remainder of a match (red and yellow cards apart). Disqualified persons must leave the area (including spectator area) of the match.

COMMENTARY ON RULE 4
RIGHTS AND DUTIES OF PLAYERS AND TEAM PERSONNEL

1) REFEREE RESPONSIBILITY—The first referee is responsible for the conduct of the coaches, players and other team personnel. Under no circumstances will the first referee allow incorrect or unsportsmanlike behavior or rude remarks.

a) Only the first referee is empowered to warn, penalize or disqualify a member of a team.

b) If the captain asks in a proper manner, the first referee must give the reason for a penalty or disqualification and must not allow any further discussion.

(1) Should there be a disagreement pertaining to a sanction assessed by the referee, team captains may state their case in writing on the scoresheet after completion of the match.

2) HEAD COACH—One person on the team roster must be designated as the head coach. That person may request time-outs or substitutions when not in the game as a player, or when in the game as a player if designated as the playing captain on the lineup sheet. The head coach is responsible for the actions of team members on the bench.

3) PLAYING CAPTAIN—One of the six players on the court shall be designated as the playing captain. The captain designated on the lineup sheet submitted at the start of a game shall remain the playing captain at all times when in the game. When replaced, the captain shall designate another player to assume the duties of captain until replaced or the designated captain returns to the game.

4) REPORTING OF RUDE REMARKS—Other officials (second referee, scorer and linesmen) must immediately report to the first referee any rude remark that is made by a player or team member about an official or opponent.

5) RECORDING WARNINGS AND PENALTIES—All warnings and actions penalized by loss of service, by a point for the opposite team or the disqualification of a player or team member for a game or match, must be recorded on the scoresheet.

6) CONDUCT BETWEEN GAMES—Minor unsportsmanlike behavior between games of a match is ignored. If the behavior is of sufficient nature (such as a derogatory remark or act), the first referee may expel a player or team member from the next game or may disqualify them from the remainder of a match. No penalty, other than expulsion or disqualification, will be assessed between games of a match.

7)· *DISQUALIFICATION—If the first referee feels that a player or team member has committed a serious unsportsmanlike act that warrants disqualification from more than the match in which the act was discovered, a report must be made to the authority in charge of the tournament for final action. First referees are authorized to disqualify players for one match only. Disqualification does not carry any further penalty (i.e., point, side-out, time-out). Disqualified personnel must immediately leave the area of the match, including any spectator areas.*

8) *TEAM BENCHES—Coaches, substitutes and any other team members not playing in the game shall remain seated on the team bench unless requesting a time-out, requesting a substitution, warming up preparatory to entering a game, a substitute reporting to the scorer, trainers or doctors assisting a player on the bench, coaching duties requiring discussion with a player on the bench, periods between games of a match or other such times as authorized by the first referee. Team members shall occupy the bench located on the side of the net adjacent to their playing area and shall immediately change benches when the teams change in the middle of a deciding game of a match. The designated head coach, or person in charge of the conduct of players on the bench if the head coach is playing or has been disqualified, shall occupy the seat nearest the scorer's table.*

9) *COACHING—A coach during sanctioned USVBA competition, except Junior teams in Junior competition, may not give instructions to players during the match and may not argue or protest to the referees. Coaches, substitutes and other team members shall be seated on the team bench during play. Coaches may rise and stand in front of the team bench for the purpose of*

   a) *Requesting a time-out or substitution.*
   b) *Reacting spontaneously to an outstanding play by a member of the team.*
   c) *Attending an injured player when beckoned onto the court by a referee.*
   d) *Conferring with substitutes or other personnel on the team bench.*
   e) *Conferring with players at the side of the court during a charged time-out.*

The same applies, throughout the match, to all persons located on the team bench.

On the first occasion, if such a fault occurs in any one game, the first referee must warn the team concerned. On the second occasion, a penalty is given and noted on the scoresheet and the team at fault penalized by loss of service or the opponent gains a point. NOTE: Non-disruptive coaching will be permitted in NAGWS and Inter-Collegiate competition.

10) *TIME-OUT PERIODS—If a captain or coach of either team asks the second referee for a time-out after the first referee has blown the whistle for service, the second referee must refuse the request. If, however, the second referee blows the whistle and play is stopped, the team making the request shall not be penalized, but the request will be denied and the first referee shall direct a playover.*

   a) *Teams granted a legal time-out may terminate the time-out period at any time they indicate that they are ready to resume play. If the opponents wish to extend the time-out period, that team shall be charged with a team time-out.*
   b) *If a team fails to return to play immediately upon the signal indicating the end of a time-out period, that team shall be charged a time-out. If such time-out is the first or second time-out charged the team, the team may use the 30 seconds. If such delay is after a team has used its two time-outs, the team shall be*

penalized (point or side out) and may not use the 30 seconds.

c) *If a team makes a third request for time-out, the request shall be refused and the team warned by the first referee. If the request is inadvertantly granted, the time-out shall be terminated immediately upon discovery and the team warned. Any additional requests shall result in a penalty (point or side out). If, in the first referee's opinion, a third request for time-out is made as a means of gaining an advantage, it shall be charged as a serious offense and the team penalized (point or side out).*

d) *If a player or team member, other than the designated coach or playing captain, requests a time-out, the request will be denied and the team warned. If the request results in the granting of a time-out, it shall be terminated immediately upon discovery of the illegal request and the team warned.*

11) *CONDUCT DURING GAME—During play, if a player shouts or yells at an opponent or crosses the vertical plane of the net for the purpose of distracting an opponent, the first referee shall:*

a) *If the distraction does not cause a fault or hinder play, wait until the conclusion of the play and then warn the player, or;*

b) *If the distraction causes a fault or hinders play of an opponent, immediately stop play and penalize the player for serious unsportsmanlike conduct.*

RULE 5. THE TEAMS

Article 1. PLAYERS' UNIFORMS—The playing uniform shall consist of jersey, shorts and light and pliable shoes (rubber or leather soles without heels).

a) It is forbidden to wear a head gear or any article (jewelry, pins,. bracelets, etc.) which could cause injuries during the game. If requested by a team captain before the match commences, the first referee may grant permission for one or more players to play without shoes.

b) Players' jerseys must be marked with numbers 8 to 15 cm. (3" to 6") in height on the chest and 15 to 24 cm. (6" to 9") in height on the back. The width of the strip forming the number shall be 2 cm. (3/4") in international matches. The captain in international competition shall wear a badge on the left side of the chest 8 cm. by 1.5 cm. (3" by 1/2") in a color different to that of the jersey.

c) Members of a team must appear on the court dressed in clean presentable uniforms (jerseys and shorts) of the same color, style, cut and trim. For the purpose of identical uniforms, shoes and socks are not considered a part of the uniform and are not required to be identical for team members. During cold weather, it is permissable for teams to wear identical training suits provided they are numbered in accordance with the specifications of paragraph b) above and are of the same color, style, cut and trim.

Article 2. COMPOSITION OF TEAMS AND SUBSTITUTIONS—A team shall consist of six players regardless of circumstances. The composition of a complete team, including substitutes, may not exceed twelve players.

a) Before the start of a match, teams shall give the scorer a roster listing all players, including substitutes, and the uniform number each player will wear. Rosters shall also indicate the designated head coach. Once the roster has been received by the scorer, no changes may be made.

b) Prior to the start of each game of a match, the head coach or captain shall submit to the scorer a lineup of players who will be starting the game and the position in the service order each will play. Lineups will be submitted on the official lineup sheets provided by the scorer. After the lineup sheets have been received by the scorer, no changes may be made unless necessitated due to a scorer error or omission. Players listed on the lineup sheets may be replaced prior to the start of play through a substitution request by the team coach or captain under the provisions of paragraph e) below. One of the players on the lineup sheet must be designated as the playing captain. Opponents will not be permitted to see the lineup submitted by the opposing team prior to the start of play.

c) Substitutes and coaches must be on the side of the court opposite the first referee and shall remain seated during play. Substitutes may warm up outside the playing area providing they do not use a ball and that they return to their designated places afterwards if not immediately entering the game.

d) Substitution of players may be made when the ball is dead, on the request of either the playing captain on the court or the designated head coach off the court and when recognized by either referee. A team is allowed a maximum of six (6) team substitutions in any one game. Before entering the game, a substitute must report to the second referee in proper playing uniform and be ready to enter upon the floor when authorization is given. If the requested substitution is not completed immediately, the team will be charged with a time-out and shall be allowed to use such time-out unless it has already used the allowable number of time-outs. In case the team has already exhausted the allowable two time-outs, the team shall be penalized by loss of service or, if not serving, the opponents shall be awarded a point.

e) The captain or coach requesting a substitution(s) shall indicate the number of substitutions desired and shall report to the scorer and second referee the numbers of players involved in the substitution. If the coach or captain fails to indicate that more than one substitution is desired, the first or second referee shall refuse any additional substitute(s) until the next legal opportunity. Following a completed substitution, a team may not request a new substitution until play has resumed and the ball is dead again or until a time-out has been requested and granted to either team. During a legal charged time-out, any number of requests for substitution may be made by either team. Immediately following a time-out, an additional request for substitution may be made.

f) A player starting a game may be replaced only once by a substitute and may subsequently enter the game once, but in the original position in the serving order in relation to other teammates. Only the original starter may replace a substitute during the same game. There may be a maximum of two players participating in any one position in the service order (except in case of accident or injury requiring abnormal substitution under the provisions of paragraph h) below). If an illegal substitution request is made (i.e., excess player entry, excess team substitution, wrong position entry, etc.) the request will be refused and the team charged a time-out. At the expiration of the time-out period, if a substitution is still desired, a new request must be made.

g) If a player becomes injured and cannot continue playing within 10 to 15 seconds, such player must be replaced. After that brief period, if the team desires to have the player remain in the game, and if the player cannot continue to play immediately, the team must use a charged time-out. If the player is replaced, regardless of time required to safely remove the player from the court, no time-out shall be charged.

h) If through accident or injury a player is unable to play and substitution cannot be made under the provisions of paragraph f), or if the team has used its allowable six (6) team substitutions, such player may be replaced in the following priority without penalty:
(1) By any substitute who has not participated in the game.
(2) By the player who played in the position of the injured player.
(3) By any substitute, regardless of position previously played.
Players removed from the game under the abnormal substitution provisions of paragraph h) will not be permitted to participate in the remainder of the game.

i) If through injury or accident a player is unable to play and substitution cannot be made under the provisions of paragraphs f) and h), the referee may grant a special time-out of up to three (3) minutes. Play will be resumed as soon as the injured player is able to continue. In no case shall the special injury time-out exceed three minutes. At the end of the special time-out, a team may request a normal time-out charged to that team provided they have not already used their allowable two (2) time-outs. If, after three minutes, or at the expiration of time outs granted subsequent to the special time-out, the injured player cannot continue to play, the team loses the game by default, keeping the points acquired.

NOTE: Senior Division and NAGWS competition will be governed by the special provisions set forth in Current Practices for Rule 5.

j) If a team becomes incomplete through disqualification of a player, and substitution cannot be made under the provisions of paragraph f) above, the team loses the game by default, keeping the points acquired.

COMMENTARY ON RULE 5
THE TEAMS

1) NUMBER OF PLAYERS—Each player must wear a number on the front and back of the shirt while participating in the game. The shirts may be numbered between 1 and 15 inclusive for international competition. For USVBA competition, shirts may be numbered between 1 and 99 inclusive. No player shall participate without a legal number. No player shall change numbers during a match without permission of the first referee.

2) COLORS—When opponents have jerseys of the same color, it occasionally creates confusion as to the player who has committed a fault and the team for whom the player plays. Therefore, the home team should change colors if possible.

3) JEWELRY AND OTHER ARTICLES—Rings, with the exception of flat bands without projections, bracelets, dangling earrings and necklaces long enough to clear the chin must be removed. Necklaces of multi-piece construction (beads, etc.) must also be removed due to possible breakage that could result in a delay in the game. If an article cannot be removed, it must be taped securely to allow the player to play. Braided hair with beads must be secured so that it will not present a safety hazard to the player, teammates or opponents. Hair barrettes may be used to secure the hair. It is not necessary that the barrettes be taped. If play must be stopped to allow a player to remove illegal jewelry or equipment, that team shall be charged with a time-out. If the team has not used its allowable two time-outs, they may use the time. If they have used their allowable two time-outs, they shall be penalized (point or side out) and may not use the time.

a) The wearing of a hard cast of any nature, hard splint, or other type of potentially dangerous protective device shall be prohibited, regardless of how padded. The wearing of a soft bandage to cover a wound or protect an injury shall be permitted. The wearing of an "air-filled" type cast on the lower extremities may be permitted.

b) "Head-gear" is interpreted to mean no hats or bandanas. A sweat band of soft pliable material or bandana folded and worn as a sweat band is permissible.

4) LOW TEMPERATURE—If the temperature is low (about 10 deg. centigrade; 50 deg. farenheit), the first referee may allow players to wear sweatsuits provided they are all of the same style and color and are legally numbered in accordance with the provision of Rule 5, Article 1.

5) REQUIRED NUMBER OF PLAYERS—Under no circumstances may a team play with less than six (6) players.

6) SUBSTITUTIONS—Only the head coach designated on the roster, or the playing captain on the court, may ask the referees for permission to make a substitution.

a) Substitutes must be already standing so that the replacement can be made immediately when authorized by the second referee.

b) The captain or head coach must first announce the number of substitutions desired and then the numbers of the players exchanging positions. Failure to indicate that multiple substitution is desired shall limit the team to one substitute. In the event that more than one player attempts to enter, such player(s) will be refused entry and the team shall be warned. After making a request and indicating the number of substitutions desired, if the head coach or captain refuses to complete the substitution or reduces the number of substitutions to be made, the team shall be charged with a time-out. If the time-out is the first or second charged to the team, the team may use the 30 seconds. At the expiration of the time-out period, if a substitution is still desired, a new request must be made. If the time-out results in a third charged time-out, the team shall be penalized (point or side out) and may not use the 30 seconds. (EXCEPTION: If the change in request is due to a referee's mind change, the request will be honored and no time-out shall be charged)

c) Substitutes going on the court must raise one hand and wait by the side of the court in the designated substitution zone until permission is given by the second referee for the exchange to be made. Players leaving the court must raise one hand and touch the hand of the substitute entering the court. Such procedure allows the scorer to correctly identify the players who are exchanging positions.

d) *If a player or team member, other than the captain or designated coach, makes a request for substitution, the request shall be refused and the team warned by the first referee. If the same act occurs again during the same game, it shall be deemed a serious offense and the team penalized by the first referee.*

e) *Each time a player is replaced, it shall count as an entry for the entering player.*

(1) *Each player may enter the game a maximum of one time. Starting the game shall not count as an entry.*

f) *Each player entering the game counts against the six substitutions allowed to the team. If the team attempts to make a seventh substitution, the team shall be charged a time-out. Teams may use the 30 seconds unless it results in a third charged time-out. If the time-out results in a third charged time-out, the team shall be penalized and may not use the 30 seconds.*

g) *Players attempting to enter a game an excessive time, in a wrong position or if not listed on the team roster submitted prior to the beginning of a match shall result in the team being charged with a time-out. If the time-out is the first or second charged to the team, the team may use the time. If it is a third charged time-out, the team shall be penalized and may not use the time.*

h) *Players attempting to enter a game after having been expelled, disqualified or replaced under the abnormal substitution rule for injuries shall result in the team being penalized (point or side out) without warning.*

i) *When either referee notices an injured player, play shall be stopped immediately. If the player indicates that play without replacement might be possible, the first referee may allow the player 10 to 15 seconds to make such determination. If play is not possible afer that brief interruption, the player must be replaced or the team must use a charged time-out if the player is to remain in the game.*

1) *If removal of an injured player causes a delay, no time-out will be charged, regardless of length of time required to safely remove the player from the court. Safety of the player(s) is the primary consideration.*

7) *SUBMITTING LINEUPS—If a team fails to submit a lineup to the scorer before the expiration of the rest period between games of a match, that team shall be charged with a time-out. After an additional 30 seconds, if the lineup has not been submitted, an additional time-out will be charged. The team may use the 30 second time-out periods. If, after the expiration of the second charged time-out, the team has not submitted the lineup, the first referee shall declare a default charged to the offending team.*

a) *Opponents will not be permitted to see the lineup submitted to the scorer by the opposing team prior to the start of play.*

b) *After a lineup has been received by the scorer, no changes may be made in listed players or positions on the court unless a recording error or omission is made by the scorer. Between the submitting of a lineup to the scorer and the start of play for a game or match, teams may request a substitution to replace a player listed on the lineup sheet. Such replacement shall count as both a player and a team substitution. There is no requirement for the replaced player to participate in a play before being replaced. Such requests shall be governed by the provisions of Article 2 e).*

CURRENT PRACTICES FOR RULE 5

1) UNIFORM—Where reference is made to identical uniforms, it is construed to mean only the jerseys and shorts. It is recommended that the lower edges of numerals on the jerseys be at least 4 inches above the waist line and that the color of the numerals be in sharp contrast to that of the uniforms to which they are attached. Reference to home team colors may be ignored.
2) SUBSTITUTIONS FOR SENIOR DIVISION AND NAGWS COMPETITION:
   a) A player shall not enter the game for a fourth time (starting shall count as an entry). A team shall be allowed a maximum of twelve (12) substitutions in any one game. Players starting a game may be replaced by a substitute and may subsequently re-enter the game twice. Each substitute may enter the game three times. Players re-entering the game must assume the original position in the serving order in relation to other teammates. No change shall be made in the order of rotation unless required due to injury requiring abnormal substitution under the provisions of paragraph b) below. Any number of players may enter the game in each position in the service order.
   b) If through accident or injury a player is unable to play, and substitution cannot be made under the provisions of paragraph a), or if the team has used its allowable twelve (12) team substitutions, such player may be replaced in the following priority without penalty:
      (1) By the starter or substitute who has played in the position of the injured player, if such starter or substitute has not already been in the game the allowable three times, or by any player who has not already participated in the game.
      (2) By any player on the bench who has not been in the game three times, regardless of position previously played.
      (3) If all players have been in the game the allowable three times, by the substitute who previously played in the position of the injured player.
      (4) By any substitute, even though all substitutes have been in the game the three allowable times.
   c) If through injury or accident a player is unable to play and substitution cannot be made under the provision of paragraphs a) or b), the first referee may grant a special time-out under the provisions of Rule 5, Article 2 e).
   d) If a team becomes incomplete through disqualification or expulsion of a player and substitution cannot be made under the provision of paragraph a) above, the team loses the game by default, keeping the points acquired.

CHAPTER III
RULES OF PLAY

RULE 6. TEAM AREAS, DURATION OF MATCHES AND INTERRUPTIONS OF PLAY

Article 1. NUMBER OF GAMES—All International matches shall consist of the best of three out of five games.

Article 2. CHOICE OF PLAYING AREA AND SERVE—The captains will call the toss of a coin for the choice of team area or the service. The winner of the toss chooses: 1. first serve, or; 2. choice of team area for the first game. The loser of the toss receives the remaining option.

Article 3. CHOICE OF PLAYING AREA FOR DECIDING GAME—Before the beginning of the deciding game of a match, the first referee makes a new toss of the coin with the options described in Article 2. The captain of the team not calling the toss of the coin for the first game shall call the toss of the coin for the deciding game.

Article 4. CHANGE OF PLAYING AREAS BETWEEN GAMES—After each game of a match, except when a deciding game is required, teams and team members will change playing area and benches.

Article 5. CHANGE OF PLAYING AREA IN DECIDING GAME OF A MATCH—When teams are tied in number of games won in a match, and one of the teams reaches eight (8) points in a deciding game, the teams will be directed to change playing areas. After change of areas, the serving will continue by the player whose turn it is to serve. In case the change is not made at the proper time, it will take place as soon as it is brought to the attention of the first referee. The score remains unchanged and is not a grounds for protest.

Article 6. TIME BETWEEN GAMES OF A MATCH—A maximum interval of two (2) minutes is allowed between games of a match. Between the fourth and fifth games of a match, the interval shall be five (5) minutes. The interval between games includes the time required for change of playing areas and submitting of lineups for the next game.

Article 7. INTERRUPTIONS OF PLAY—As soon as the referees notice an injured player, or a foreign object on the court that could create a hazard to a player(s), play will be stopped and the first referee will direct a play-over when play is resumed.

Article 8. INTERRUPTIONS OF THE MATCH—If any circumstances, or series of circumstances, prevent the completion of an International match (such as bad weather, failure of equipment, etc.), the following shall apply:

a) If the game is resumed on the same court after one or several periods, not exceeding four hours, the results of the interrupted game will remain the same and the game resumes under the same conditions as existed before the interruption.
b) If the match is resumed on another court or in another facility, results of the interrupted game will be cancelled. The results of any completed game of the match will be counted. The cancelled game shall be played under the same conditions as existed before the interruption.
c) If the delay exceeds four hours, the match shall be replayed, regardless of where played.

Article 9. DELAYING THE GAME—Any act which, in the judgement of the first referee, unnecessarily delays the game may be penalized (Rule 4, Article 7b).

COMMENTARY ON RULE 6
TEAM AREAS, DURATION OF MATCHES
AND INTERRUPTIONS OF PLAY

1) CHANGING SIDES—Changing sides during the deciding game of a match must be done with a minimum of delay.
a) No instructions can be given players as they change sides.
b) Players must assume the same positions they were in before changing team areas.

2) TIME BETWEEN GAMES OF A MATCH—At the expiration of the allowable rest period between games, teams must report immediately to the end line of their playing areas.
a) If a team fails to report to the end line of their playing area immediately upon the signal indicating the expiration of the period between games, that team shall be charged with a time-out. After an additional 30 seconds, if the team has failed to report to the end line, the team shall be charged with an additional time-out. The team may use the 30 second time-out periods. If, after the expiration of the second charged time-out, the team has not reported to the end line, the first referee shall declare a default charged to the offending team. Score of the defaulted game shall be recorded at 15-0.
b) A two minute period shall begin immediately after a game has been declared defaulted by the first referee. During the two minute period, teams shall change sides and submit lineups for the next scheduled game.
c) If the same team again fails to report to the end line within the provisions of (a) above, the match shall be declared a default by the first referee. A defaulted match shall be recorded as 2-0 or 3-0, depending upon the number of games scheduled.

3) DELAYING THE GAME—In order to clarify the interpretation of Rule 6, Article 9, it is necessary to explain that any attempt to delay the game shall result in a warning from the first referee. If the attempt is repeated, or it is determined that the attempt is deliberate by a player or team, the referee must penalize the team or player by denoting it a serious offense (Rule 4, Article 7b).

CURRENT PRACTICES FOR RULE 6

1) ONE GAME PLAYOFF—A one game playoff shall be considered as a deciding game of a match and the teams shall change sides when one team has scored eight points.

2) MATCHES WITHOUT DECIDING GAMES—In the interest of consistency, a toss of the coin should be held prior to a third or fifth game of a match in which such games will be played regardless of outcome of preceding games of the match.
a) In the final game of a three or five game match where all games are played,

regardless of outcome, teams will change playing areas when one team has scored its eighth point.

3) TIME GAME—In circumstances where the efficient management of a tournament or series of matches requires adherence to a time schedule in order to complete the competitions, the time game may be employed. Such time games may be played on the basis of ball-in-play-game or 15 points, whichever occurs first. Such basis must be established before the first game where round robins, a specific number of games, etc., are indicated as the format.

RULE 7. COMMENCEMENT OF PLAY AND THE SERVICE

Article 1. THE SERVICE—The service is the act of putting the ball into play by the player in the right back position who hits the ball with the hand (open or closed) or any part of the arm in an effort to direct the ball into the opponent's area.

a) The server shall have five seconds after the first referee's readiness to serve whistle in which to release or toss the ball for service.
b) After being clearly released or thrown from the hand(s) of the server, the ball shall be cleanly hit for service. (EXCEPTION: If, after releasing or throwing the ball for service, the server allows the ball to fall to the floor (ground) without being hit or contacted, the service effort shall be cancelled and a replay directed. However, the referee will not allow the game to be delayed in this manner more than one time during any service).
c) At the instant the ball is hit for the service, the server shall not have any portion of the body in contact with the end line, the court or the floor (ground) outside the lines marking the service area. At the instant of service, the server may stand on or between the two lines, or their extensions which mark the service area.
d) The service is considered good if the ball passes over the net between the antennas or their indefinite extensions without touching the net or other objects.
e) If the ball is served before the first referee's whistle, the serve shall be cancelled and a re-serve directed. The first referee will not allow a player to delay the game in this manner more than one time.

Article 2. SERVING FAULTS—The referee will signal side-out and direct a change of service to the other team when one of the following serving faults occurs:

a) The ball touches the net.
b) The ball passes under the net.
c) The ball touches an antenna or does not pass over the net completely between the antennas or their indefinite extensions.
d) The ball touches a player of the serving team or any object before entering the opponent's playing area.
e) The ball lands outside the limits of the opponent's playing area.

Article 3. DURATION OF SERVICE—A player continues to serve until a fault is committed by the serving team.

Article 4. SERVING OUT OF ORDER—If a team has served out of order, the team loses the service and any points gained during such out of order service. The players of the team at fault must immediately resume their correct positions on the court.

Article 5. SERVICE IN SUBSEQUENT GAMES—The team not serving first in the preceding game of a match shall serve first in the next game of the match, except in the deciding game of a match (Rule 6, Article 3).

Article 6. CHANGE OF SERVICE—The team which receives the ball for service shall rotate one position clockwise before serving.

Article 7. SCREENING—The players of the serving team must not, through screening, prevent their opponents from watching the server or the trajectory of the ball.

a) Any player on the serving team who has hands clearly above the height of the head, extends arms sideward, moves the arms to distract the opponents, jumps or moves sideways, etc., while the serve is being effected, is guilty of making an individual screen.

b) A team makes a group screen when the server is hidden behind a group of two or more teammates and the ball is served over them in the direction of the opponents.

Article 8. POSITIONS OF PLAYERS AT SERVICE—At the time the ball is contacted for the serve, the placement of players on the court must conform to the service order recorded on the scoresheet as follows (the server is exempt from this requirement):

a) In the front line, the center forward (3) may not be as near the right sideline as the right forward (2) nor as near the left sideline as the left forward (4). In the back line, the center back (6) may not be as near the right sideline as the right back (1) nor as near the left sideline as the left back (5). No back line player may be as near the net as the corresponding front line player. After the ball is contacted for the serve, players may move from their respective positions.

b) The serving order as recorded on the official scoresheet must remain the same until the game is completed.

c) Before the start of a new game, the serving order may be changed and such changes must be recorded on the scoresheet. It is the responsibility of the head coach or team captain to submit a lineup to the scorer prior to the expiration of the authorized rest period between games of a match.

Article 9. ERROR IN POSITION OR ILLEGAL PLAYER IN GAME—When a player(s) of a team is found to be illegally in the game or has entered in a wrong position in the service order, the play must be stopped and the error corrected. A red card penalty shall be issued to the player(s) at fault by the first referee and the following corrective action taken:

a) If discovered before a service by the opponents, all points scored by the team while any player(s) was illegally in the game or in a wrong position in the service order shall be cancelled. If the team at fault is serving at the time of discovery of the error, a side out will be declared.

b) If the team at fault is not serving at the time of discovery of the error, all points scored by the opponents will be retained. The serving team shall be awarded a point unless discovery of the error is immediately following a play in which the serving team scored a point. In such case, no additional point will be awarded. The wrong position will be corrected and play continued without further penalty.

c) If it is not possible to determine when the error first occurred, the first referee shall issue a red card to the player(s) at fault and the team in error shall resume the correct position(s) and, if serving, shall have a side out declared against it. If the other team is serving, it shall be awarded a point unless the play immediately preceding discovery of the error in position or player illegally in the game resulted in a point.

d) If correction of the error requires a substitution due to an illegal or wrong position entry of a player(s), neither the team or player(s) will be charged with a substitution. In addition, any player or team substitutions charged at the time of the wrong entry shall be removed from the scoresheet as though they had never occurred.

COMMENTARY ON RULE 7
COMMENCEMENT OF PLAY AND THE SERVICE

1) THE SERVICE—If the server releases or tosses the ball for service, but does not hit it and it touches some part of the server's body as it falls, this counts as a fault and the ball shall be given to the other team.

a) If the server releases the ball preparatory to serving, but allows it to fall to the floor (ground) without touching it, the first referee shall cancel the serve and direct a second and last attempt at service (replay) for which an additional five seconds is allowed. If the player does not serve within these time limits, a serious offense is committed which must be penalized by loss of service.

b) The server is not allowed to delay service after the first referee's whistle, even if it appears that players on the serving team are in a wrong position or are not ready.

c) Service cannot be made with two hands or arms.

d) At the moment of service, the server's body may be in the air entirely forward of the end line provided the last contact with the floor (ground) was within the legal service area.

e) If a service fault occurs (Rule 7, Article 2) and the opposing team commits a positional fault at the moment of service (Rule 7, Article 8), the server's team scores a point.

f) If an illegal service occurs and the opposing team commits a positional fault at the moment of service, the ball is given to the opponents. The service is illegal when:

(1) The player serves while in contact with the floor (ground) outside the service area.

(2) The ball is thrown or pushed for service.

(3) The player serves with two hands or arms.

(4) The service is not made following the correct rotational order.

(5) The ball is not thrown or released before it is hit for service.

(6) Service actions not initiated within five seconds after the first referee's readiness-to-serve whistle.

2) SCREENING—In order for members of the serving team to be called for a group screen at the moment of service, the ball must be served in such a manner that it passes over at least two members of the serving team, including players who are in the act of switching positions. The mere grouping of players close together does not constitute a screen unless the ball passes over them. If a single player of the serving team raises the hands clearly above the height of the head, extends arms to the side, jumps or moves sideways at the moment of service, such player shall be charged with a fault for an individual screen, regardless of the path of the ball.

a) If a member of the serving team deliberately takes a position in front of an opponent for the purpose of screening the action of the server, or if the opponent moves and the member of the serving team also moves to a position in front of the opponent, the player shall be penalized (red card) for unsportsmanlike conduct.

b) If, in the opinion of the first referee, a player jumps from the floor for the purpose of distracting an opponent immediately after the ball has been contacted for service, such player shall be guilty of unsporting conduct and a sanction shall be imposed by the first referee.

3) POSITION OF PLAYERS—The position of players is judged according to the position of their feet in contact with the floor (ground) at the time the ball is contacted for service. For the purpose of this rule, the service area is not considered to be a part of the court. All players, except the server, must be fully on the court at the time the ball is contacted for service. Players in contact with the center line are governed by the provisions of Rule 9, Article 6. At the instant the server hits the ball for service, all players must be in their proper positions corresponding with the order noted on the scoresheet. The server is exempt from the rule governing the positions of players on the court at service (Rule 7, Article 8). A positional fault should be signalled by the referee(s) as soon as the ball has been hit by the server.

a) Occasionally there may be doubt as to whether a player is a front or back line player. In such cases, the referee may withhold the whistle and check the lineup sheet after the play has been concluded. If a check of the lineup sheet reveals that a player was out of position, the call may be made, even though late.

4) WRONG SERVER—When it is discovered that a wrong player is about to serve the ball, the scorer shall wait until the service has been completed and then blow the horn/whistle or stop the game in any manner possible and report the fault to one of the referees. Any points scored by a wrong player shall be removed, a side-out declared and players of the team at fault must immediately resume their correct positions on the court.

CURRENT PRACTICES FOR RULE 7

1) PRELIMINARY SERVICE ACTION—Preliminary actions, such as bouncing the ball on the floor or lightly tossing the ball from one hand to the other, shall be allowed, but shall be counted as part of the five seconds allowed for the server to initiate service release or toss the ball preparatory for the service.

2) SERVICE FOR ELEMENTARY GRADE PLAYERS—Where elementary grade age players are in a competition, it can be considered legal service if the ball is hit directly from the hand of the server, not necessarily dropped or tossed. Where this serve is acceptable, it should be established in advance or otherwise agreed upon mutually before competition starts and the officials notified. In such levels of team play, players should be encouraged to develop ability and skills necessary for a serve which does satisfy the requirements of the official rule.

3) REQUESTING LINEUP CHECK—Team captains may request verification of the service order of their team if done on an infrequent basis. Requests for lineup checks for opponents will be limited to determining whether or not the players are legally in the game. No information will be provided to disclose which opposing players are front line or back line players.

RULE 8. PLAYING THE BALL

Article 1. MAXIMUM OF THREE TEAM CONTACTS—Each team is allowed a maximum of three (3) successive contacts of the ball in order to return the ball to the opponent's area. (EXCEPTION: Rule 8, Article 11)

Article 2. CONTACTED BALL—A player who contacts the ball, or is contacted by the ball, shall be considered as having played the ball.

Article 3. CONTACT OF BALL WITH THE BODY—The ball may be hit with any part of the body on or above the waist.

Article 4. SIMULTANEOUS CONTACTS WITH THE BODY—The ball can contact any number of parts of the body down to and including the waist providing such contacts are simultaneous and that the ball rebounds immediately and cleanly after such contact.

Article 5. DOUBLE CONTACT—A player contacting the ball more than once with whatever part of the body, without any other player having touched it between these contacts, will be considered as having committed a double hit. Such contacts are a fault. (EXCEPTION: Rule 8, Article 11)

Article 6. HELD BALL—When the ball visibly comes to rest momentarily in the hands or arms of a player, it is considered as having been held. The ball must be hit in such a manner that it rebounds cleanly after contact with a player. Scooping, lifting, pushing or carrying the ball shall be considered to be a form of holding. A ball clearly hit with one or both hands from a position below the ball is considered a good play.

Article 7. SIMULTANEOUS CONTACTS BY OPPONENTS—If the ball is held simultaneously by two opposing players, it is a double fault and the first referee will direct a play-over.

a) If the ball is contacted simultaneously by opponents and is not held, play shall continue.
b) After simultaneous contact by opponents, the team on whose side the ball falls shall have the right to play the ball three times.
c) If, after simultaneous contact by opponents, the ball falls out of bounds, the team on the opposite side shall be deemed as having provided the impetus necessary to cause the ball to be out of bounds.

Article 8. BALL PLAYED BY TEAMMATES—When two players of the same team contact the ball simultaneously, this is considered as two team contacts and neither of the players may make the next play on the ball. (EXCEPTION: Rule 8, Article 11)

Article 9. ATTACKING OVER OPPONENT'S COURT—A player is not allowed to attack the ball on the opposite side of the net. If the ball is hit above the spiker's side of the net and then the follow-through causes the spiker's hand and arm to cross the net without contacting an opponent, such action does not constitute a fault.

Article 10. ASSISTING A TEAMMATE—No player shall assist a teammate by holding such player while the player is making a play on the ball. It shall be legal for a player to hold a teammate not making a play on the ball in order to prevent a fault.

Article 11. BLOCKING—Blocking is the action close to the net which intercepts the ball coming from the opponent's side by making contact with the ball before it crosses the net, as it crosses the net or immediately after it has crossed the net. An attempt to block does not constitute a block unless the ball is contacted during the effort. A blocked ball is considered to have crossed the net.

a) Blocking may be legally accomplished by only the players who are in the front line at the time of service.
b) Multiple contacts of the ball by a player(s) participating in a block shall be legal provided it is during one attempt to intercept the ball.
   (1) Multiple contacts of the ball during a block shall be counted as a single contact, even though the ball may make multiple contacts with one or more players of the block.
c) Any player participating in a block shall have the right to make the next contact, such contact counting as the first of three hits allowed the team.
d) The team which has effected a block shall have the right to three additional contacts after the block in order to return the ball to the opponent's.
e) Back line players may not block or participate in a block, but may play the ball in any other position near or away from the block.
f) Blocking of the ball across the net above the opponent's court shall be legal provided that such block is:
   (1) After a player of the attacking team has served, spiked the ball, or, in the first referee's judgement, intentionally directed the ball into the opponent's court.
   (2) After the opponents have completed their allowable three hits; or,
   (3) After the opponents have hit the ball in such a manner that the ball would, in the first referee's judgement, clearly cross the net if not touched by a player, provided no member of attacking team is in a position to make a legal play on the ball; or,
   (4) If the ball is falling near the net and no member of the attacking team could reasonably make a play on the ball.

Article 12. BALL CONTACTING TOP OF NET AND BLOCK—If the ball touches the top of the net and a player(s) participating in a block and then returns to the attacker's side of the net, this team shall then have the right of three more contacts to return the ball to the opponent's area.

Article 13. BACK LINE ATTACKER—A back line player returning the ball to the opponent's side while forward of the attack line must contact the ball when at least part of the ball is below the level of the top of the net over the attacking team's area. The restriction does not apply if the back line player jumps from clearly behind the attack line and, after contacting the ball, lands on or in front of that line.

a) A player commits a fault when, as a back line player, he/she is in the front zone or touching the attack line, or its imaginary extension, and hits the ball while it is completely above the height of the net and if the ball crosses directly and completely the vertical plane of the net.

COMMENTARY ON RULE 8
PLAYING THE BALL

1) *RECEPTION OF THE BALL—Contact with the ball must be brief and instantaneous. When the ball has been hit hard, or during setting action, it sometimes stays very briefly in contact with the hands of the player handling the ball. In such cases, contact that results from playing the ball from below, or a high reception where the ball is received from high in the air, should not be penalized. The following actions of playing the ball should not be counted as faults:*
   a) *When the sound is different to that made by a finger tip hit, but the hit is still played simultaneously with both hands and the ball is not held.*
   b) *When the ball is played with two closed fists and the contact with the ball is simultaneous.*
   c) *When the ball contacts the open hand and rolls off the hand backward without being held.*
   d) *When the ball is played correctly and the player's hands move backwards, either during or after the hit.*
   e) *When a poorly hit ball is caused to rotate (such as a defective spike where the ball is spun and not hit squarely or a set ball is caused to rotate due to improper contact).*
2) *HELD BALL ON SERVICE RECEIVE—Receiving a served ball with an overhead pass using open hands is not necessarily a fault. Such service receives must be judged the same as any open handed pass. If the served ball is travelling in a low and relatively flat trajectory, receiving it with open hands and passing without holding the ball is extremely difficult. If the serve is high and soft, the pass can be made legally the same as any similar ball crossing the net after the service.*
3) *SIMULTANEOUS CONTACTS—The ball may contact several parts of the body at the same time legally, provided the ball is not held.*
4) *DOUBLE CONTACT—Double contact faults are to be judged by sight, not sound. Referees must be careful to closely observe contact with the ball and must not let unusual body positions or unusual flight of the ball after contact influence their determination of a "double-contact".*
5) *SIMULTANEOUS CONTACT BETWEEN OPPOSING PLAYERS—The rules are designed to insure the continuity of play. During contact of the ball simultaneously by opposing players, the first referee must not blow the whistle unless the ball is momentarily suspended between the hands of opposing players and clearly comes to rest. In such a case, the ball must be replayed without a point or change of service being awarded.*
6) *SIMULTANEOUS CONTACT BETWEEN TEAMMATES—When two players of a team attempt to play the ball at the same time, resultant action can cause the appearance of simultaneous contact. Referees must be positive that simultaneous contact has been seen before charging that team with two hits. If there is any doubt, only one hit should be called.*
7) *ATTACK HIT—A hit by a player in an intentional effort to direct the ball into the opponent's court. A third hit by a team is considered to be an attack hit, regardless of intention. A served ball is considered to be an attack hit.*

8) *BLOCKING—Any ball directed towards the opponent's area as an attack hit, including a served ball, can be blocked by one or a group of opposing front line players.*

   a) *If members of a composite block are to benefit from the rule allowing multiple contacts of the ball by blockers, they must be close to the net and close to each other at the time the ball is contacted by the block. If a player is attempting to block, but is separated from the block contacted by the ball, such contact will count as the first of three contacts allowed to return the ball to the opponent's area.*

   b) *Players may take a blocking position with the hands and arms over the net before the opponent's attack hit providing there is no contact with the ball until after the opponents have had an opportunity to play the ball a third time or in action (such as a spike or service) which directs the ball across the net. Immediately after such contact by the attacking team, blockers may contact the ball in an effort to prevent it crossing the net.*

   c) *Multiple contacts of the ball may be made by any player or players taking part in a block and shall constitute one contact of the ball. After such contact, the team is allowed three additional contacts to return the ball to the opponent's area. The multiple contact is legal even if it can be seen that during the blocking action the ball has contacted in rapid succession:*

      (1) *The hands or arms of one player; or,*

      (2) *The hands or arms of two or more players; or*

      (3) *The hands, arms or other parts of one or more players on or above their waists.*

   d) *If the ball touches the top of the net and the hands of an opposing blocker(s), the ball shall be considered to have crossed the net and been blocked. After such contact, the attacking team is allowed an additional three contacts of the ball.*

   e) *Blockers may reach across the plane of the net outside the antenna, but may not contact the ball over the opponent's area. If contact of the ball over the opponent's area is made while any part of the blocker or member of a composite block is outside the antenna across the plane of the net, the block is illegal.*

9) *BACK LINE PLAYERS—A back line player who is inside the attack zone, or its assumed extension may play the ball directly into the opposite court if, at the moment of contact, the ball is not completely above the level of the top of the net. If a back line player jumps from the floor (ground) clearly behind the attack line, the ball may be spiked or intentionally directed into the opponent's area, regardless of where the player lands after hitting the ball.*

   a) *A ball contacted from above the height of the net (including a spiked ball) and directed towards the opponent's court by a back line player forward of the attack line does not become an illegal hit unless it is the third team hit, the ball passes fully beyond the vertical plane of the net or is legally blocked by the opponents before passing beyond the vertical plane of the net. If the ball is legally blocked by an opponent(s) before crossing the net, the hit by the back line player becomes illegal and the ball becomes dead. If an illegal blocker blocks the ball, it is assumed that the hit became illegal at the moment of contact by the attacker and only the illegal hit shall be penalized.*

b) If a back line player at the net, along with the blockers, lifts hands or arms towards the ball as it comes across the net and is touched by the ball, or the ball touches any of the players in that block, it is a fault; back line players not having the right to participate in a block. However, if the block containing the back line player does not touch the ball, the attempt to block is not considered to be a fault.

c) Back line players may not participate in a block, but there is no restriction on their being next to a block for the purpose of playing the ball in other than blocking action.

RULE 9. PLAY AT THE NET

Article 1. BALL IN NET BETWEEN ANTENNAS—A ball, other than a served ball, hitting the net between the antennas may be played again. If the ball touches the net after a team's allowable three contacts and does not cross the net, the referee should not stop the play until the ball is contacted for the fourth time or has touched the playing surface. (See Rule 10, Commentary 1)

Article 2. BALL CROSSING THE NET—To be good, the ball must cross the net entirely between the antennas or their assumed indefinite extension.

Article 3. PLAYER CONTACT WITH NET—If a player's action causes the player to contact the net during play, whether accidentally or not, with any part of the player's body or uniform, that player shall be charged with a fault. If the ball is driven into the net with such force that it causes the net to contact a player, such contact shall not be considered a fault.

Article 4. SIMULTANEOUS CONTACT BY OPPONENTS—If opponents contact the net simultaneously, it shall constitute a double fault and the first referee shall direct a replay.

Article 5. CONTACT BY PLAYER OUTSIDE THE NET—If a player accidentally contacts any part of the net supports (e.g. a post, cable), the referee's stand, etc., such contact should not be counted as a fault provided that it has no effect on the sequence of play. Intentional contact or grabbing of such objects shall be penalized as a fault.

Article 6. CROSSING THE CENTER LINE—Contacting the opponent's playing area with any part of the body except the feet is a fault. Touching the opponent's area with a foot or feet is not a fault providing that some part of the encroaching foot or feet remain on or above the center line and does not interfere with the play of an opponent.

a) It is not a fault to enter the opponent's side of the court after the ball has been declared dead by the first referee.

b) It is not a fault to cross the assumed extension of the center line outside the playing area.

   (1) While across the extension of the center line outside the court, a player of the attacking team may play a ball that has not fully passed beyond the plane of the net. Opponents may not interfere with a player making a play on the ball.

   (2) A player who has crossed the extension of the center line and is not making a play on the ball may not interfere with an opponent.

Article 7. BALL PENETRATING OR CROSSING THE VERTICAL PLANE—A ball penetrating the vertical plane of the net over or below the net, whether over or outside the court, may be returned to the attacking team's side by a player of the attacking team provided the ball has not yet completely passed beyond the vertical plane of the net when such contact is made. A ball which has penetrated the vertical plane above the net may be played by either team.

COMMENTARY ON RULE 9
PLAY AT THE NET

1) BALL CROSSING VERTICAL PLANE OF THE NET—If a ball penetrates the vertical plane of the net over the net, under the net, or outside the antennas, the attacking team is allowed to attempt to play the ball back into their team area, providing the ball has not fully passed beyond the vertical plane of the net at the time of contact. The opponents are not allowed to intentionally touch the ball under the net during such play. However, if the ball inadvertently contacts an opponent beyond the plane under the net, the ball becomes dead and is not considered to be a fault by the opponents.

a) Once the ball penetrates the vertical plane above the net, the opponents have equal right to play the ball.

2) CONTACT WITH OPPONENT'S AREA—If a player is legally on or above the center line with a foot or feet in contact with the opponent's area, and such foot or feet should cause interference with an opponent who, in the first referee's judgement, could make an immediate subsequent play, it shall be considered a fault. If such contact does not affect play, it shall be ignored.

3) CONTACT WITH OPPONENT BEYOND THE VERTICAL PLANE—If a player makes contact with an opponent beyond the vertical plane of the net, and if such contact is inadvertent, the contact shall be ignored unless, in the first referee's judgement, such contact prevents an opponent making a play on the ball. If the contact is intentional, it shall be penalized by the referee without warning.

a) Flagrant intentional contact shall result in disqualification of the player responsible for the contact.

4) CROSSING THE CENTER LINE—It is not a fault to cross the center line onto the opponent's side of the net provided that no contact is made with the opponent's playing area. While across the center line extended, a member of the attacking team is permitted to make a play on the ball provided the ball has not passed fully beyond the vertical plane of the net at the time of contact.

5) CONTACT WITH POSTS, CABLES, ETC—If a player accidentally contacts a cable (including the cables supporting the net) or a post, cables supporting a post, referee stand, etc., it should not be counted as a fault unless it directly affects the subsequent sequence of a play. If the stand, posts, etc., are intentionally grasped or used as a means of support, such action constitutes a fault.

RULE 10. DEAD BALL

Article 1. WHEN BALL BECOMES DEAD—A live ball becomes dead when:

a) The ball touches an antenna or the net outside an antenna.

b) The ball does not cross the net completely between the antennas.
c) The ball strikes the floor, wall or any object attached to the wall.
d) The ball contacts the ceiling or object attached to the ceiling at a height of 7 m. or more measured from the playing surface.
e) A player(s) commits a fault.
f) A served ball contacts the net or other object.
g) The first or second referee blows a whistle, even though inadvertently.
h) A player causes the ball to come to rest on a rafter or other overhead object that is less than 7 m. above the height of the playing surface.

COMMENTARY ON RULE 10
DEAD BALL

1) *INADVERTENT WHISTLE—The blowing of an inadvertent whistle causes the ball to become dead immediately. In such cases, the first referee must make a ruling that will not penalize either team. For instance, if the attacking team has hit the ball in such a manner that it is falling in an area where no member of the offensive team could logically make a play on the ball, and if the referee blows the whistle before the ball has touched the playing surface, by rule the ball becomes dead immediately. In this case, the first referee should rule as though the ball had touched the playing surface at the time the whistle blew. Another example should be after a third hit with the ball striking the net near the top and the first referee inadvertently blowing the whistle. After the whistle, if the ball were to roll in such a manner that it crossed the net into the defending team's area, a replay should be called for by the first referee.*
2) *BALL CONTACTING OVERHEAD OBJECT—If the ceiling or other overhead objects attached to the ceiling extend to a height of less than 7 m. above the playing surface, such areas allow the ball to remain in play if struck. However, if the ball strikes such objects and then crosses the vertical plane of the net, the ball becomes dead.*
   a) *Some overhead objects, such as basketball baskets protruding from walls or ceilings so that they are within the 2 m. free zone around the court, may be ruled as unfair hampering of the normal play of the ball and may be declared as a replay by the first referee. Also, where objects such as rolled curtains, etc., are suspended over the net, if the first referee feels that such objects unfairly hamper normal play, a replay may be ruled on any ball, other than a served ball, contacting such objects.*
   b) *Any special ground rules for a match must be specified in the pre-match conference by the first referee.*
3) *BALL CONTACTING ANTENNA—If the ball contacts the antenna above or below the height of the net, the ball becomes dead.*

RULE 11. TEAM AND PLAYER FAULTS

Article 1. DOUBLE FAULT A double fault occurs when players of opposing teams simultaneously commit faults. In such cases, the first referee will direct a play over.

Article 2. FAULTS AT APPROXIMATELY THE SAME TIME—If faults by opponents occur at approximately the same time, the first referee shall determine which fault occurred first and shall penalize only that fault. If it cannot be determined which fault occurred first, a double fault shall be declared.

Article 3. PENALTY FOR COMMITTING FAULTS—If the serving team, or a player of the serving team, commits a fault, a side-out shall be declared. If the receiving team, or a player of the receiving team commits a fault, the serving team shall be awarded a point.

Article 4. TEAM AND PLAYER FAULTS—A fault shall be declared against a team or player when:

a) The ball touches the floor (R. 10 A. 1)
b) The ball is held, thrown or pushed (R. 8 A. 6)
c) A team has played the ball more than three times consecutively (R. 8 A. 1)
d) The ball touches a player below the waist (R. 8 A. 3)
e) A player touches the ball twice consecutively (R. 8 A. 5)
f) A team is out of position at service (R. 7 A. 9)
g) A player touches the net or antenna (R. 9 A. 3)
h) A player completely crosses the center line and contacts the opponent's playing area (R. 8 A. 9)
i) A player attacks the ball above the opponent's playing area (R. 8 A. 9)
j) A back line player while in the attack area hits the ball into the opponent's court from above the height of the net (R. 8 A. 9)
k) A ball does not cross the net entirely between the antennas (R. 9 A. 2)
l) A ball lands outside the court or touches an object outside the court (R. 10 A. 1)
m) The ball is played by a player being assisted by a teammate as a means of support. (R. 8 A. 10)
n) A player receives a personal penalty (R. 4 A. 7)
o) A team, after having been warned, receives instructions from coach, manager or substitutes (R. 4 A. 6) NOTE: Non-disruptive coaching is allowed in NAGWS play.
p) A player reaches under the net and touches the ball or an opponent while the ball is being played by the opposite team (R. 9 C. 1)
q) The game is delayed persistently (R. 6 A. 9)
r) An illegal substitution is made (R. 5 A. 2)
s) A team makes a fourth request for time-out after warning (R. 4 A. 4)
t) Extension of a second time-out beyond 30 seconds (R. 4 C. 10)
u) Delay in completing substitution after having used two time-outs (R. 5 A. 2)
v) Player(s), after warning, leaving court during interruption of play without permission of first referee during game (R. 4 A. 4)
w) Players stamp feet or make distracting sounds or gestures towards opponents (R. 4 A. 6)
x) Blocking is performed in an illegal manner (R. 8 A. 11)
y) Illegally served ball or service fault (R. 7 A. 2; R. 7 C. 1f)

RULE 12. SCORING AND RESULTS OF THE GAME

Article 1. WHEN POINT IS SCORED—When a fault is committed by the receiving team, a point is awarded to the serving team.
Article 2. WINNING SCORE—A game is won when a team scores 15 points and has at least a two point advantage over the opponents. If the score is tied at 14-14, the play continues until one team has a lead of two points. (e.g. 16-14, 17-15, 18-16 etc.)
Article 3. SCORE OF DEFAULTED GAME—If a team does not have sufficient players to start a game or refuses to play after the referee requests play to begin, that team shall lose the game by default. Score of each defaulted game will be 15-0.
Article 4. SCORE OF DEFAULTED GAME DUE TO INJURY—If a game is defaulted due to a team being reduced to less than six players because of an injury, the defaulting team shall retain any points earned. The winning team shall be credited with at least 15 points or will be awarded sufficient points to reflect a two point winning advantage over the opponents.
Article 5. SCORE OF DEFAULTED GAME DUE TO EXPULSION OF A PLAYER—If a game is defaulted due to expulsion or disqualification of a player, the defaulting team shall retain any points earned. The offended team shall be credited with at least 15 points or a sufficient number of points to indicate a two point winning advantage over the opponents.

COMMENTARY ON RULE 12
SCORING AND RESULTS OF THE GAME

1) *DEFAULTED GAME—If a team defaults a game due to failure to have sufficient players to start a game at the scheduled time, the score will be recorded as 15-0. A waiting time of up to 15 minutes shall be allowed for the team to have sufficient players to play the next game. If the team has at least six players present prior to the expiration of the waiting time, play shall begin. If, after the 15 minute waiting period, a team does not have six players present and ready to play, the second game shall be declared a default. If the match consists of the best 3 out of 5 games, an additional 15 minute waiting period shall be allowed before declaring the match a default.*
   a) *If neither team has six players available at match time, each team shall be charged with a loss by default.*
   b) *Score of each defaulted game is 15-0. Score of a defaulted match is 2-0 or 3-0, depending upon the number of games scheduled to be played.*
2) *REFUSAL TO PLAY—If, after receiving a warning from the first referee, a team refuses to play, the game shall be declared a default and recorded as a score of 15-0. A two minute period shall then be granted in order for the teams to change sides of the court and submit lineups for the next game of the match. If the team again refuses to play at the expiration of the two minute period, the match shall be declared a default. A defaulted match shall be recorded as 2-0 or 3-0, depending upon the number of games scheduled to be played.*

RULE 13. DECISIONS AND PROTESTS

Article 1. AUTHORITY OF THE REFEREE—Decisions based on the judgement of the referee or other officials are final and not subject to protest.
Article 2. INTERPRETATION OF THE RULES—Disagreements with interpretations of the rules must be brought to the attention of the first referee prior to the first service following the play in which the disagreement occurred. The captain of the protesting team may be the only one to bring the protest to the attention of the first referee.
Article 3. APPEAL OF DECISION OF THE REFEREE—If the explanation of the first referee following a protest lodged by the team captain is not satisfactory, the captain may appeal to a higher authority. If the protest cannot be resolved, the first referee shall proceed to the scorer's table and shall record, or cause to be recorded, on the scoresheet all pertinent facts of the protest. After the facts of the protest have been recorded, the first referee will continue to direct the game and will forward a report later on the protest in question.
Article 4. DISAGREEMENT WITH REFEREE'S DECISION—If a team captain disagrees with a judgement decision of the referee(s), such decision is not protestable, but the team captain may state such disagreement in writing on the back of the official scoresheet after completion of the match.

COMMENTARY ON RULE 13
DECISIONS AND PROTESTS

1) PROTEST MATTERS NOT TO BE CONSIDERED—Protest involving the judgement of a referee or other officials will not be given consideration. Some of these items are:
   a) Whether or not a player on the court was out of position at service.
   b) Whether or not a ball was held or thrown.
   c) Whether or not a player's conduct should be penalized.
   d) Any other matters involving only the accuracy of an official's judgement.
2) PROTEST MATTERS TO BE CONSIDERED—Matters that shall be received and considered by the first referee concern:
   a) Misinterpretation of a playing rule.
   b) Failure of a first referee to apply the correct rule to a given situation.
   c) Failure to impose the correct penalty for a given violation.
3) RECORDING FACTS—The following facts should be recorded on the scoresheet concerning any protest situation:
   a) Score of the game at the time of the protest.
   b) Players in the game at the time of the protest and their positions on the court.
   c) Player substitutions and team substitutions made prior to the protested situation.
   d) Team time-outs charged prior to the protested situation.
   e) A synopsis of the situation that caused the protest and the rule violated or omitted or the penalty improperly imposed.
   f) Signatures of the scorer, both team captains and the first referee, to indicate that the facts have been correctly recorded.
4) PROTEST COMMITTEE ACTION—During the Olympic Games, World Champion-

ships and similar competitions, the Jury shall rule upon the protested situation before play continues.

5) RULING OF THE JURY AND EFFECT—The Jury, after hearing the facts of the protest, may rule that the protest is valid and will be upheld or that the protest is not valid and will be denied. If the protest is upheld, the game will be replayed from the point immediately preceding the play which prompted the lodging of a protest. If the protest is denied, the score and situation will remain as though the protest had never been lodged.

CURRENT PRACTICES FOR RULE 13

1) PROTEST COMMITTEE—Where possible in tournament play, it is advisable to have a protest committee assigned and available to rule upon a protest situation as soon as possible, preferably pior to the first service following the protest. Such action will preclude having to play the match over from the point of protest if the protest is upheld. The situation can be immediately corrected and only the play in question played over.
   a) During sanctioned USVBA competition, the protest committee will rule upon the protested game immediately upon its completion and before another game of the match is played.

CHAPTER IV
OFFICIALS AND THEIR DUTIES

NOTE: Chapter IV is included as a guideline for officials and shall not be construed to be a part of the official playing rules subject to protest by teams.

RULE 14. THE FIRST REFEREE

Article 1. AUTHORITY OF THE FIRST REFEREE—The first referee is in full control of the match and any judgement decisions rendered by the first referee are final. The first referee has authority over all players and officials from the coin toss prior to the first game of a match until the conclusion of the match, to include any periods during which the match may be temporarily interrupted, for whatever reason.
Article 2. QUESTIONS NOT COVERED BY RULE—The first referee has the power to settle all questions, including those not specifically covered in the rule.
Article 3. POWER TO OVERRULE—The first referee has the power to overrule decisions of other officials when, in the first referee's opinion, they have made errors.
Article 4. POSITION OF FIRST REFEREE DURING MATCH—The first referee shall be located at one end of the net in a position that will allow a clear view of the play. The referee's head should be approximately 50 cm. above the top of the net.
Article 5. PENALIZING VIOLATIONS—In accordance with Rule 4 the first referee penalizes violations made by players, coaches and other team members.
Article 6. USE OF SIGNALS—Immediately after giving a signal to stop play, the first

referee shall indicate with the use of hand signals the nature of the violation, if a player fault, the player committing the fault and the team which shall make the next service.

COMMENTARY ON RULE 14
THE FIRST REFEREE

1) *SIGNALING SERVICE—The first referee will blow a whistle at the beginning of each play to indicate that service shall begin and at any other time judged to be necessary.*
2) *INTERRUPTING PLAY—Each action is considered finished when the first referee blows a whistle, other than that to indicate service. Generally speaking, the first referee should only interrupt the play when certain that a fault has been committed, and should not blow the whistle if there is any doubt.*
3) *REQUESTING ASSISTANCE—Should the first referee need to deal with anything outside the limits of the court, the first referee should request help from the organizer and players.*
4) *OVERRULING OFFICIALS—If the referee is certain that one of the other officials has made an incorrect decision, the first referee has the power to overrule that official and apply the correct decision. If the first referee feels that one of the other officials is not correctly fulfilling the duties as outlined by the Rules, the referee may have the official replaced.*
5) *SUSPENDING THE MATCH—Should an interruption occur, particularly if spectators should invade the court, the referee must suspend the match and ask the organizers and the captain of the home team to re-establish order within a set period of time. If the interruption continues beyond this period of time, or if one of the teams refuses to continue playing, the first referee must instruct the other officials to leave the court along with the first referee. The first referee must record the incident on the scoresheet and forward a report to the proper authority within 24 hours.*
6) *AUTHORITY OF THE REFEREE—Although the referee is in full control of the match and any judgement decisions rendered are considered final, this in no way relieves the right of team captains to protest and record matters allowed under the provisions of Rule 13, Article 6.*

RULE 15. THE SECOND REFEREE

Article 1. POSITION DURING MATCH—The second referee shall take a position on the side of the court opposite and facing the first referee.
Article 2. ASSISTING THE FIRST REFEREE—The second referee shall assist the first referee by making calls such as:
a) Violations of the center line and attack line.
b) Contact with the net by a player.
c) Contact of the ball with an antenna or ball not crossing the net entirely inside the antenna on the second referee's side of the court.

d) Foreign objects entering the court and presenting a hazard to the safety of the players.
e) Performing duties in addition to those outlined when instructed to do so by the first referee.

Article 3. KEEPING OFFICIAL TIME—The second referee shall be responsible for keeping official time of time-outs and rest periods between games of a match.

Article 4. CONDUCT OF PARTICIPANTS—The second referee shall supervise the conduct of coaches and substitutes on the bench and shall call to the attention of first referee any unsportsmanlike actions of players or other team members.

Article 5. SUPERVISION OF SUBSTITUTIONS—The second referee shall authorize substitutions requested by captains or the head coach of the teams.

Article 6. SERVICE ORDER OF TEAMS—The second referee shall verify at the beginning of each game that the positions of the players of both teams correspond with the serving orders listed on the scoresheet and the lineups as given to the scorer. The second referee shall supervise the rotation order and positions of the receiving team at the time of service.

Article 7. GIVING OPINIONS—The second referee shall give opinions on all matters when so requested by the first referee.

Article 8. ENDING PLAY—The play is considered as ended when the second referee blows a whistle.

COMMENTARY ON RULE 15
THE SECOND REFEREE

1) *KEEPING OFFICIAL TIME—It is the responsibility of the second referee to keep the official time during time-outs, and between games of a match. When a time-out is charged, the second referee will signal the first referee the number of time-outs that have been charged to each team. At the expiration of the time-out, the second referee shall notify the coach or captain the number of time-outs they have taken.*
2) *SUBSTITUTIONS—The second referee will authorize a substitution when the substitute is ready to enter the game. Before allowing the substitute to enter the court, the second referee will make certain that the scorer has the necessary information to properly record the substitution.*
3) *CONTROL OF THE BALL—The second referee shall be responsible for the ball during interruptions of play.*
4) *REPLACING FIRST REFEREE—Should the first referee suddenly be indisposed, it shall be the responsibility of the second referee to assume the responsibilities of the duties of the first referee.*
5) *ASSISTING REFEREE—The second referee will make calls and perform duties in addition to those outlined when instructed to do so by the first referee.*
6) *VERIFYING LINEUPS—It is the duty of the second referee to use the official lineup sheets submitted by the teams to verify that the lineups are correct at the start of a game. When the teams change courts during the middle of a deciding game of a match, it is the duty of the second referee to once again verify that the players of both teams are in their correct service order as listed on the scoresheet.*
7) *GIVING INFORMATION TO TEAM CAPTAINS—Upon request of a team captain*

for verification that the opponents are in their correct service order or that players are not in the game illegally, the first referee may direct the second referee to verify that the players are correct or incorrect. No direct identification of opposing players will be given to the team captain. Requests for such information by team captains will be limited to infrequent occasions. If it is found that the players are in an incorrect position or illegally in the game, the first referee will direct the second referee and scorer to correct the error.

RULE 16. THE SCORER

Article 1. POSITION DURING MATCH—The scorer's position is on the side of the court opposite the first referee and behind the second referee.

Article 2. RECORDING INFORMATION—Prior to the start of a match, the scorer obtains the lineup sheets and records the names and numbers of the players and substitutes on the scoresheet. Between games of match the scorer reminds the second referee to obtain new lineups from captains or coaches in order to properly record any changes in the lineups. In addition, the scorer:

a) records the score as the match progresses.
b) makes sure that the serving order and rotation of players is followed correctly.
c) carefully checks the numbers of substitutes to determine that they may legally enter the game before recording the information on the scoresheet.
d) records time-outs and notifies the second referee and the first referee the number of time-outs which have been charged to each team.

Article 3. DURING DECIDING GAME OF MATCH—During the deciding game of a match the scorer signals the referees when one of the teams has scored an eighth point and indicates that the teams should change playing areas.

Article 4. VERIFICATION OF FINAL SCORE—At the conclusion of a match, the scorer secures the signatures of the referees to verify that the winning score has been recorded and the match is official.

COMMENTARY ON RULE 16
THE SCORER

1) *GIVING INFORMATION TO TEAMS—The scorer, when requested to do so by one of the referees, must tell either of the coaches or captains the number of substitutions and time-outs that have been charged to their team. Information pertaining to opponents will not be given to a coach or captain by the scorer.*
2) *LINEUPS—Prior to the start of each game of a match, the coach or team captain must send a lineup to the scorer on the official form provided. Opponents will not be permitted to see the lineup submitted by the opposing team prior to the start of play.*
3) *RECORDING OF REMARKS—The scorer must write all remarks pertaining to penalties, protests, etc., that occur during the progress of the game. Incidents leading to the disqualification of a player must be entered on the scoresheet.*
4) *ORDER OF SERVICE—The scorer must control the order of service. If a wrong*

server is in the service position at the time the referee whistles for service, the scorer shall wait until the ball is contacted during service and then sound a horn/whistle and notify the referees of the fault.

5) *THE SCORE—The scorer must score each point made by a team. The scorer must make sure that the score on the visible scoreboard agrees with the score recorded on the scoresheet. In the event of a discrepancy, the scoresheet shall be official and the discrepancy is not grounds for protest by a team.*

RULE 17. THE LINE JUDGES

Article 1. POSITION DURING MATCH—During the match, the line judges will be stationed:

a) with two line judges, they must be placed diagonally opposite each other, one at each end of the court at the corner away from the serving area, at a minimum distance from the corner of 1 m. indoors and 3 m. outdoors.
b) With four line judges, one line judge shall be placed opposite each service area with the sideline extended approximately 2 m. behind the end line. One line judge shall be placed approximately 2 m. outside the sideline nearest the service area in line with the end line extended. Each line judge watches the line to which assigned.

Article 2. USE OF SIGNAL FLAGS—Each line judge shall be responsible for signaling to the first referee when a ball is "OUT" by raising the flag above the head, and when a ball is "IN" by pointing the flag towards the floor (ground) of the playing area.

Article 3. WHEN FLAGS NOT AVAILABLE—When flags are not available for use by line judges, they shall be instructed to raise the hands over the shoulders with the palms facing down to indicate when a ball is "OUT", and to extend the arms downward towards the playing area to indicate when a ball is "IN".

Article 4. OTHER DUTIES—The line judges shall also signal the first referee when:

a) foot fault errors are made by a player when serving.
b) the ball touches an antenna (above or on the net).
c) the ball does not pass over the net completely between the antennas or their indefinite extension.
d) The ball which is "OUT" was contacted by a player before contacting the floor (ground) or object outside the playing area.

COMMENTARY ON RULE 17
THE LINE JUDGES

1) *POSITION DURING MATCH—During the match, the line judges shall be standing in their assigned areas and shall move from those areas only for the purpose of avoiding interfering with players playing the ball or to better observe a ball crossing the net near an antenna.*
2) *NUMBER OF LINE JUDGES—For important competitions, it is recommended that four line judges be used.*
3) *SIGNALING THE FIRST REFEREE—Whenever a line judge needs to attract the attention of the first referee due to a fault committed by a*

player, or to a rude remark made by a player, the flag shall be raised above the head and waved from side to side.

GAME PROCEDURES

These are the recommended standard procedures to be followed for the conduct of all official USVBA competition:

1. **OFFICIALS**
   a) The officials should be certified referees and scorers of the United States Volleyball Association.
2. **UNIFORMS**
   a) All players must wear uniforms prescribed by USBVA rule 5.
3. **PRE-GAME PROCEDURES**
   a) Well ahead of the starting time for the first game of the match, the first referee will call the captains together to conduct a coin toss.
   b) After the coin toss, the first referee will supervise warm-up periods with the serving team having use of the court for the first three minute warm-up period if the captains have elected to use separate warm-ups. If the team captains elect to warm-up together on the court, the first referee shall allow six minutes.
   c) At the end of the warm-up period, the first or second referee will walk to the center of the court and blow a whistle to indicate that the warm-up period is over and that players are to clear the court.
   d) Referees and other officials take their places.
   e) Teams line up on the end line of their respective areas. When both teams are ready and facing each other, the first referee will blow a whistle and motion for teams to take their positions on the court.
   f) Second referee will verify that players are on the court in positions listed on the official lineup sheets submitted to the scorer by each team. No corrections may be made unless there has been an error or omission made by the scorer or unless a legal substitution has been made prior to the start of play under the provisions of Rule 5, Commentary 7b. No other changes may be made in the lineups to correct an error made by teams in preparing the lineup sheets.
4. **START OF GAME**
   a) As soon as lineups are verified and teams are ready, the whistle is blown and a visual signal is given by the first referee for service to begin.
   b) Prior to the serve, the offensive players will halt their movements to allow officials to determine their positions. Continual movement may be misconstrued as screening.
5. **SUBSTITUTION PROCEDURES**
   a) Substitutes should approach the second referee in the substitution zone and wait to be recognized for entry. Substitutes entering the court and players leaving the court shall touch hands in the substitution zone and wait to be authorized to enter by the second referee.

6. END OF GAME AND START OF NEXT GAME

a) Following the blowing of a whistle indicating the end of a game, players should line up on the end line of their playing areas. When both teams are in position and the second referee has verified that the winning point has been recorded, the first referee will blow a whistle and dismiss the teams for the rest period between games. Players may then leave the court.

b) At the end of the rest period, the second referee will blow a whistle and teams shall immediately report to the end of their playing areas for the next game.

7. CHANGE OF PLAYING AREAS DURING GAME

a) When teams are required to change playing areas during a deciding game of a match, the first referee will blow a whistle and indicate both teams to move to the end line of their respective playing areas.

b) After both teams are in position, the first referee will blow a whistle and motion for both teams to proceed in a counter-clockwise direction to the opposite end without delay.

c) Substitutes and other team personnel will change benches so as to be seated on the side of their playing area.

d) When teams are in position on the end line of the new playing areas, the first referee will blow a whistle and motion for both teams to move onto the court.

e) The second referee will then verify that players are in their correct positions on the court.

8. AT THE END OF THE MATCH

a) Following the blowing of whistle indicating the end of match, players will line up on the end line of their respective playing areas.

b) When both teams are in position and the second referee has verified that the winning point has been recorded by the scorer, the first referee will signal with whistle and motion for the teams to form a single line and proceed to the center of the court to shake hands with the opponents.

c) Referees will then proceed to the score table to verify and sign the scoresheets.

d) The second referee will assure that the game ball is returned to the designated area for safekeeping.

COMMENTARY ON GAME PROCEDURES

(1) Unless a protest has been lodged in accordance with Rule 13, Article 3, referees are not to review the scoresheets at the conclusion of a match to determine if scorer errors have been made during the progress of the match. The first referee will determine that a winning score has been attained in each game and will record the final score in circles in the scoring column of each team. The first referee will then verify that the games are official by signing the bottom of each sheet.

UNITED STATES ONLY

SPECIAL RULES

The following four items have to do with competition other than regular six player team play. They are practically verbatim from previous years and it is acknowledged that there are probably more deviations than compliances in actual usage. The Committee on Rule and Interpretations solicits the experience of those groups and organization which do conduct and sponsor special competitions such as beach play, doubles, triples, co-ed, mixed doubles, etc.

1) Co-Ed Play—The rules in general shall govern play for females and males on the same team with the following exceptions:
   a) The serving order and positions on the court service shall be an alternation of male and female, or vice-versa.
   b) When the ball is played more than once by a team, at least one of the contacts shall be made by a female player. Contact of the ball during blocking shall not constitute playing the ball. There is no requirement for a male player to contact the ball, regardless of the number of contacts by a team.
   c) Uniforms of players shall be identical within the following provisions:
      (1) All female players shall be attired in identical jerseys and shorts.
      (2) All male players shall be attired in identical jerseys and shorts.
      (3) All uniforms shall be numbered in compliance with Rule 5, Article 1b. There shall be no duplicate numbers regardless of color of the jerseys.
   d) When only one male player is in the front line at service, one male back line player may be forward of the attack line for the purpose of blocking.
      (1) Male back line players shall be governed by the provisions of Rule 8, Article 13 when playing the ball in other than blocking action.
      (2) Only one male back line player may be forward of the attack line when a male back line player is participating in a block.
      (3) No female back line player may participate in a block.
   e) The height of the net for Co Ed play shall be 2.43 m.
2) Reverse Co-Ed Play—The rules in general shall govern play for females and males on the same team with the following exceptions:
   a) The serving order and positions on the court at service shall be an alternation of male and female, or vice-versa.
   b) When the ball is played more than once by a team, at least one of the contacts shall be made by a male player. Contact of the ball during blocking shall not constitute playing the ball.
   c) Uniforms of players shall be identical within the following provisions:
      (1) All female players shall be attired in identical jerseys and shorts.
      (2) All male players shall be attired in identical jerseys and shorts.
      (3) All uniforms shall be numbered in compliance with Rule 5, Article 1b. There shall be no duplicate numbers, regardless of color of the jerseys.
   d) When only one female player is in the front line at service, one female back line player may be forward of the attack line for the purpose of blocking.

(1) Female back line players shall be governed by the provisions of Rule 8, Article 13 when playing the ball in other than blocking action.
(2) Only one female back line player may be forward of the attack line when a female back line player is participating in a block.

e) No male player may participate in a block.
f) No male player forward of the attack line may contact the ball and cause it to enter the opponent's playing area.
g) The height of net for Reverse Co-Ed play shall be 2.24 m.

3) BEACH PLAY—The rules in general shall govern play on beaches with the following exceptions:
   a) The net height shall be 2.39 m. on hard packed sand and 2.36 m. on loose packed sand.
   b) Playing areas shall be changed during each game after multiples of 5 points have been scored.
   c) Ropes shall be used as boundary lines and center line.
4) DOUBLES PLAY—The rules in general shall govern for two-player (doubles) teams with the following exceptions:
   a) Each team area shall be 7.62 m. long.
   b) There shall be only two players with no substitutes on each team.
   c) There shall be only 2 positions, left and right half areas.
   d) The service shall be made from any position behind the end line.
   e) A game is won at 11 points, or if time is a factor, after 5 minutes of ball-in-play time has elapsed, whichever occurs first.

COMMENTARY ON SPECIAL RULES

1) *During co-ed play, if a team contacts the ball more than one time during offensive action, one of the contacts must be by a female player, but there is no restriction that prevents all three team hits being made by female players. Contact of the ball during blocking action does not count as one of the three team hits. Therefore, after a block, a male player may play the ball back over the net since such contact would be considered to be the first team hit.*
2) *During co-ed play, if the ball (other than a spiked ball) is contacted more than one time by a team and is directed over the net without being contacted by a female player, the hit does not become an illegal hit unless the ball passes fully beyond the vertical plane of the net (or is legally blocked).*
3) *During co-ed play, when there are two females and one male player in the front line at the time of service, one male backline player may be forward of the attack line for the purpose of participating in blocking action, but is restricted by the provisions of Rule 8 when playing the ball during offensive action.*
4) *During co-ed play, when there is one male back line player participating in a block, the other male back-line player shall remain behind the attack line until the ball has been contacted by the blockers or has been hit in such a manner that no block is possible.*

5) *During reverse co-ed play, if a team contacts the ball more than one time during offensive action, one of the contacts must be by a male player.*
6) *A male player taking off from on or in front of the attack line during reverse co-ed play may not hit the ball in such a manner that it enters the opponent's playing area. If such a hit is legally blocked across the plane of the net by an opponent, the ball is deemed to have crossed the plane of the net and the hit is illegal. If the ball is hit in such a manner that it would cross the net, but is contacted by a female player before crossing the net, the hit is legal.*
7) *There is no restriction on a male player hitting the ball into the opponent's court if the player takes off clearly behind the attack line before contacting the ball.*
8) *During reverse co-ed play, when there are two male and one female player in the front line at the time of service, one female player from the back line may be forward of the attack line for the purpose of participating in blocking action, but is restricted by the provisions of Rule 8 when playing the ball during offensive action.*
9) *During reverse co-ed play, when there is one female backline player participating in a block, the other female backline player shall remain behind the attack line until the ball has been contacted by the blockers or has been hit in such a manner that no block is possible.*

SIGNAL FOR ILLEGAL CONTACT

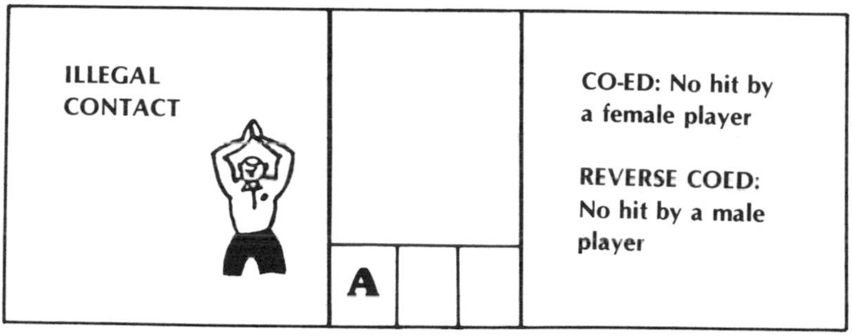

INTERPRETATIONS

Questions regarding interpretations of the present rules and current practices may be addressed to the Chairman of the Committee on Rules and Interpretations or to the Official Interpreter. Enclose a self addressed, stamped envelope with your inquiry for prompt return. All inquiries will receive replies. Because of the transition to international rules, some queries may involve consultations, but answers will be forwarded as promptly as possible.

CHANGES

Suggestions for changes, results of experiences, innovation proposals, and other rules related ideas may be transmitted through committee members, regional officials' chairmen or commissioners during the season. Explanation and rationale of proposed modifications must be in the chairman's hands before April 1, 1983, if they are to be considered at the annual meeting of the USVBA.